Britain's Chief Rabbis and the religious character of Anglo-Jewry, 1880–1970

Manchester University Press

Britain's Chief Rabbis and the religious character of Anglo-Jewry, 1880–1970

BENJAMIN J. ELTON

Manchester University Press

Manchester and New York

distributed in the United States exclusively by Palgrave Macmillan

Published by Manchester University Press
Oxford Road, Manchester M13 9NR, UK
and Room 400, 175 Fifth Avenue, New York, NY 10010, USA
www.manchesteruniversitypress.co.uk

Distributed in the United States exclusively by
Palgrave Macmillan, 175 Fifth Avenue,
New York, NY 10010, USA

Distributed in Canada exclusively by
UBC Press, University of British Columbia, 2029 West Mall,
Vancouver, BC, Canada V6T 1Z2

British Library Cataloguing-in-Publication Data is available

Library of Congress Cataloging-in-Publication Data is available

ISBN 978 0 7190 9547 4 *paperback*

First published by Manchester University Press in hardback 2009

This paperback edition first published 2014

Printed by Lightning Source

Contents

List of illustrations   vii
Acknowledgements   ix

Part I: Religious and historical context

1   Introduction   3
2   Historical context   21
3   Jewish religious responses to modernity: a typology   40
4   Intellectual context: theology and theologians   52

Part II: Theology and policy, 1891–1946

5   The theology of Hermann Adler   71
6   The religious policy of Hermann Adler   108
7   The theology of J.H. Hertz   164
8   The religious policy of J.H. Hertz   199

Part III: Post-War developments

9   From the Second World War to the Jacobs Affair   241
10 The religious character of the Chief Rabbis and of
    Anglo-Jewry   264

Bibliography   274
Index   287

List of illustrations

1   Nathan M. Adler, Chief Rabbi 1845–1890 (*Illustrated London News*, 1 February 1890), author's collection   146

2   Hermann Adler, Chief Rabbi 1891–1911 (*Jews' College centenary volume*, ed I. Harris, London 1906), courtesy of the London School of Jewish Studies   147

3   Joseph Herman Hertz, Chief Rabbi 1913–1946 (*The Graphic*, 19 April 1913), author's collection   148

4   Israel Brodie, Chief Rabbi 1948–1965 (*Essays presented to Israel Brodie*, ed H.J. Zimmels, J. Rabbinowitz and I. Finestein, London 1967), courtesy of the London School of Jewish Studies   149

5   Immanuel Jakobovits, Chief Rabbi 1967–1991 (*Tradition and transition*, ed J. Sacks, London 1986), courtesy of the London School of Jewish Studies   150

Acknowledgements

It is a great pleasure to thank those who have helped me to complete this book. I am grateful to the staff of the London Metropolitan Archives, the Southampton University Library, the Jewish and National University Library, Jerusalem, and the libraries of the Jewish Theological Seminary, New York and the London School of Jewish Studies who cheerfully guided me round their collections. I am indebted to my editors at the Manchester University Press.

I would thank the individuals I interviewed: Chimen Abramsky, Dudley Cohen, the Rev. Alan Greenbat, the Rev. Isaac Levy (of blessed memory) and Graeme Morris. Others gave generously of their time and insight: the Chief Rabbi, Dr Jonathan Sacks, Dayan Ivan Binstock, Rabbi David Kamenetsky, the Rev. Leslie Hardman (of blessed memory), Stefan Reif, Rabbi Dr. Elliot Cosgrove, Marc Shapiro, Michael Meyer, Oliver Harris, Jonathan Joseph and Daniel Elton. The contributions by Professor David Hillel Ruben, Dr. David Feldman and Richard Rosten have been invaluable. All errors and omissions are, of course, entirely my own.

Above all, however, I want to thank my parents, to whom this book is dedicated, for all they have done and continue to do.

Benjamin J. Elton
London

Part I

Religious and historical context

Chapter 1

Introduction

IN AN UNFINISHED autobiography Immanuel Jakobovits, Chief Rabbi 1967–91, described a visit he made to Chief Rabbi J.H. Hertz, when Jakobovits was minister of the Brondesbury Synagogue. Jakobovits was experiencing difficulties and went to Hertz for advice. Hertz responded: 'If you multiply your *tsores* [troubles] by a hundred, you will know what I am going through'.[1] Jakobovits came to know exactly what Hertz meant, when he became Chief Rabbi himself, although whether Hertz's reply was of much help at the time is a different matter. This anecdote highlights one of the paradoxes of the British Chief Rabbinate. Historically, it has carried enormous prestige but it has also brought with it difficulties and worries for the incumbent; in many ways it carries the advantages and disadvantages of any synagogue pulpit, only magnified. A Chief Rabbi needs many attributes if he is to make a success of his office, including tact and diplomacy, persuasive skill, administrative ability and a solid grounding in Jewish learning. He also needs to have a view of what Judaism is and ought to be, what Jews should believe and how Jews should behave – in other words, a theology.

This book is an analysis of Britain's Chief Rabbis over the ninety years between 1880 and 1970, and the impact they made upon Anglo-Jewry's religious character. In attempting this analysis I examine the theologies of the Chief Rabbis and their contemporaries in depth. So much attention will be paid to theology because, I argue, the key to understanding why individuals took certain actions, why they opposed some individuals and movements and supported others, is differing theologies. Two synagogues could hold a near-identical service, two rabbis could each dress in robes and preach in mellifluous English, yet fierce arguments could rage between them because of their differing theologies. Similarly, a highly acculturated Jewish religious leader could appear to have little in common with a traditional rabbi, yet the two could each regard the other as a partner in the same enterprise, defending and upholding what they regarded as traditional Judaism. For example, an analysis based on religious styles would lead a historian to identify the pre-War United Synagogue and Louis Jacobs' New London Synagogue of the 1960s and after, as almost identical institutions. An analysis based on theology shows how different they were, and therefore why Louis Jacobs could not remain in the United Synagogue, and indeed never could have found a place there.

The Jacobs Affair is therefore an important and illuminating episode, which I thoroughly examine, but its significance for this study is in what it allows us to say about the Chief Rabbis as a whole, not as an isolated incident. For my theological analysis also helps explain why such highly traditional figures as Rabbi Isaac Elhanan Spector regarded the Anglicised Chief Rabbi Hermann Adler as an authentic Jewish religious figure, when an examination of religious style would show that they had very little in common. An examination of religious style is essential, but it is insufficient. A much fuller understanding comes from incorporating a serious study of theology, and that is the task of this study.

The theology of Britain's Chief Rabbis has either not been regarded as particularly significant, or has been identified as less traditional than one would expect from a rabbinical leader in the classical mode.[2] Alderman, for example, has referred to Hermann Adler's 'intellectual limitations' whereas Hervey Meirovich argues strongly that Hertz was what would today be described as a 'Conservative Jew'.[3] This study subjects those claims to detailed analysis. I investigate the theology of the Chief Rabbis between 1880 and 1970 by looking at their statements and religious policies. I examine themes of continuity and change in the Chief Rabbis' theology, assess the degree of ideological movement over the period and try to explain what I find. Finally, I place the Chief Rabbis' theology in its intellectual context, to see where their approach fits into the spectrum of Jewish religious responses to modernity, which emerged following the Enlightenment and Jewish Emancipation.[4] To help do that, I suggest an outline of a general typology, and locate the Chief Rabbis and those of similar attitudes within that typology.

My analysis suggests that, as well as being highly consistent, the Chief Rabbis' theology was more interesting than has often been considered and more worthy of consideration than it has been credited for thus far. The changes in religious policy should be attributed, I argue, more to changes in the lay leadership than changes in the Chief Rabbinate itself. I suggest that there were important changes in the religious complexion of the community, but the Chief Rabbis were beneficiaries of that change, rather than part of it – that is, they did not become inclined to greater stringency, but rather it became possible to implement the stringencies they favoured.

I begin my study with Nathan Marcus Adler, Chief Rabbi from 1845, but my intensive analysis starts in 1880 when Hermann Adler became Delegate Chief Rabbi on his father's semi-retirement to Brighton. Hermann Adler became Chief Rabbi after his father's death in 1890 and served until his death in 1911. The second Chief Rabbi I examine closely is Joseph Herman Hertz, appointed in 1913, who held the office until he died in 1946. The insights into Adler and Hertz's theology enable us to place in proper context their successor as Chief Rabbi, Israel Brodie, who assumed the office in 1948 and held it until 1965. Finally, I examine the election of Immanuel Jakobovits, Chief Rabbi 1967–91, and his early years in office.[5]

The British Chief Rabbis have not been a primary focus of historians of Anglo-Jewry. There is no full-length scholarly analysis of any Chief Rabbi, let alone the office as a whole. The pioneering narrative work was undertaken by Cecil Roth who contributed a chapter on Nathan and Hermann Adler and Joseph Hertz to a book edited by Leo Jung on *Jewish leaders*.[6] This remains an invaluable source of basic information, but it is a descriptive rather than an analytical piece. This tradition was continued by Derek Taylor in his *British Chief Rabbis, 1664–2006*, which is a survey of all the Hahamim and Chief Rabbis, including the ones I examine.[7] Taylor is generally sympathetic to the Chief Rabbis, and credits them with the dominance of traditional Judaism in Britain.[8] Most recently, Meir Persoff has published *Faith against reason: religious reform and the British Chief Rabbinate, 1840–1990*, which is in essence an excellent collection of primary sources on the Chief Rabbis and their more radical opponents in the Jewish community, linked with explanatory narrative.[9] There is some analysis, either in the form of quotations from historians or Persoff's own, but as Todd Endelman writes in the introduction, the book tends to leave 'the reader to reach his or her own judgment'.[10]

Otherwise, the historiography does not emphasise the contribution of the Chief Rabbinate to the development of Anglo-Jewry. The major studies on the history of the Jews in England touch only briefly on the contributions of the Chief Rabbis, and argue that the Chief Rabbis were not a major factor in the development of Anglo-Jewry. Geoffrey Alderman's *Modern British Jewry* deals in some (though not great) detail with the history of the British Chief Rabbinate.[11] Todd M. Endelman's *The Jews of Britain, 1656 to 2000* is equally important, and I consider these two works first.[12] As this study questions many aspects of the existing historiography, I quote extensively from their works, so that it is absolutely clear what they have said, in their own words, and therefore what I am contesting.

Alderman is extremely critical of all the Chief Rabbis we examine. He states, for example, that Hermann Adler was 'an object of ridicule and contempt' among the immigrant community.[13] He also argues that Hermann Adler was 'more accommodating' than his father and permitted many modifications which 'could just about be reconciled to orthodoxy in the loosest sense' with the exception of mixed choirs, which were forbidden by Jewish law, but which Hermann Adler permitted anyway.[14] Alderman argues that even those modifications that did not directly break Jewish law would still have been condemned by eastern European rabbis, but were permitted by Adler in order to keep the community together.[15] I examine the reasons, so far as they can be determined, for Hermann Adler's decisions, and how he took into account Jewish Law in order to understand why he acted as he did and whether it was because he held to low halakhic standards or as a result of a more considered strategy. The reasons why Hermann Adler was more accommodating that his father are important to understanding both Adlers' approach to communal leadership.

Alderman depicts Hermann Adler's adherence to classic Jewish beliefs as lukewarm, for example in his remark that the views of Morris Joseph, who became minister of the West London Synagogue, were 'damned *even* in the eyes of Hermann Adler' [emphasis added] implying that even if Adler was not prepared to accept Joseph (for reasons I examine) he was prepared to countenance some untraditional thinking.[16] We will see whether this claim is supported by Adler's theological statements and actions prompted by theological motives. Alderman is extremely critical of Adler's policy of centralising religious authority, which he argues 'contributed much to the erosion of his status and standing', and of what he argues was his negative attitude towards the more traditional and recently immigrant Jews.[17] Alderman asserts that Adler's Beth Din was of a poor standard, refers to his 'religious latitudinarianism' and casts doubt upon Adler's level of Jewish learning.[18] Alderman's verdict is that 'a wiser man, knowing his own intellectual limitations, would have acted with circumspection and diplomacy' particularly with Machzike Hadath.[19] To test this statement I investigate the level of Adler's learning, that of his *dayyanim*, the degree to which he imposed a policy of religious centralisation and why, and his relationship with immigrant Jews, who, Alderman contests, regarded Adler as 'an object of ridicule and contempt'.[20]

Alderman identifies J.H. Hertz as an exponent of 'progressive conservatism', which Alderman holds is not a traditional theological position. He argues that Hertz wished to contain even Reform under the umbrella of the Chief Rabbinate but found his 'middle-of-the-road' ideology under attack from European refugees like Julius Jakobovits, Isidore Grunfeld, Alexander Altmann and Yehezkel Abramsky.[21] Alderman suggests that, after the marriage of his daughter Judith to Rabbi Dr Solomon Schonfeld of the Adath Yisroel, Hertz came under his influence and moved to a more traditionalist position.[22] I examine what Hertz meant by 'progressive conservatism' and assess what Hertz's policies implied about his theology. How far Hertz's tolerance towards Jewish religious movements extended indicates those to whom Hertz felt he could offer shelter under his umbrella. When evaluating the influence of immigrant rabbis I look briefly at their religious views and the reasons why they took a leading role in Anglo-Jewry. Finally, to judge whether Schonfeld was responsible for Hertz's increased traditionalism, I examine whether Hertz did indeed become more traditional.

Alderman argues that Brodie was 'neither a scholar nor an original thinker' and so was in awe of his Beth Din and allowed himself to be dominated by them.[23] This is the basis of Alderman's approach to the Jacobs Affair. He argues that Jacobs' New London Synagogue is, in form at least, essentially identical to the pre-war United Synagogue, but that the United Synagogue underwent a 'relentless move to the right' to a more traditionalist position, which meant that Jacobs' theology was out of place by the 1960s.[24] An investigation of this analysis is bound to form a large part of any examination of the twentieth-century Chief Rabbinate. I look into Brodie's theology, his scholarship, his relationship with his *dayyanim* and the role they took in decision-making. I also examine the central thesis that Jacobs' views would have been at home in the United Synagogue of Hermann Adler and J.H. Hertz, and that a shift towards traditionalism left him in confrontation with a transformed organisation.

There are major areas of broad agreement between Endelman and Alderman. They both argue, for example, that the Chief Rabbinate moved to a more traditionalist position under pressure from bodies such as the Union of Orthodox Hebrew Congregations after the Second World War, when the latitudinarianism of the Adler and Hertz regimes was replaced by a stricter regime.[25] However, Endelman is more nuanced and seeks to uncover more of the wider implications of the activities of the Chief Rabbis. He emphasises how the Chief Rabbis were perceived by the traditionalist immigrants, rather than asserting what they were, as Alderman does. Endelman acknowledges the success of the Chief Rabbis in maintaining communal unity, but highlights the price at which, he argues, it was bought: 'by centralising religious authority and preventing the emergence of an independent, native born rabbinate, Alder . . . helped to guarantee the institutional hegemony of Orthodox Judaism in Britain . . . However, this achievement was not without its downside. The stifling of religious innovation robbed communal life of the intellectual ferment that accompanied the debate about Reform in more open, pluralistic communities . . . [this] reinforced its [Britain's] status as a cultural backwater'.[26]

Ruderman noted this aspect of Endelman's approach to Anglo-Jewish history in the context of the eighteenth century and the *Haskalah*, and traced it to Endelman's appreciation of the new social history of the 1960s and 1970s, which rejected the privileging of intellectual over social history, and held that important historical development need not be the result of consciously thought-through ideology.[27] His *Jewish enlightenment in an English key* takes issue with Endelman's downplaying of the intellectual aspect of Anglo-Jewish history in the eighteenth century and seeks to revise the prevailing understanding. In many ways this study tries to do the same from the mid-nineteenth to the mid-twentieth century, by considering, the extent to which Britain was, in Jewish terms, a cultural backwater.

Endelman comments about Hertz's Beth Din appointments that 'in 1935 they [the highly traditional] gained a foothold on the London Bet Din when Hertz appointed Rabbi Yehezkel Abramsky . . . despite opposition from the United Synagogue, whose leaders recognised that Abramsky's fundamentalism was out of step with mainstream Anglo-Jewish practice. Abramsky . . . moved the bet din in a conservative direction.' Endelman argues that once he was in place Abramsky asserted himself over Hertz, implying that Hertz was less traditional that Abramsky, and perhaps even opposed Abramsky's policies, but was powerless to prevent them.[28] Persoff agrees with this assessment and suggests that from the 1940s onwards the Beth Din moved from a subordinate to a more assertive stance in its relationship with the Chief Rabbinate.[29] I will examine the relationship between Hertz and the *dayyanim*, to assess this statement, and also the relationship between Abramsky's ideology and that of the leaders (religious and lay) and members of the United Synagogue.

Regarding relations between the traditional rabbinate and other Jewish denominations Endelman writes: 'the polarisation of Anglo-Jewish religious life took on both trivial and not so trivial forms. Orthodox rabbis refused to appear on platforms with Reform or Liberal rabbis' and 'Chief Rabbis Brodie [and] Jakobovits . . . attacked liberal forms of Judaism in terms that encouraged polarisation.'[30] We will have to determine whether there was a movement to greater opposition to these 'liberal' sections of Anglo-Jewry or whether we can uncover themes of continuity.

Endelman's verdict, that 'Chief Rabbi Brodie, whose English bearing and speech outweighed his learning and who thus was easily influenced by his dayyanim', is much the same as Alderman's.[31] His suggestion that Brodie's veto over Jacobs' appointment 'was unprecedented: previous chief rabbis never imposed an ideological test in certifying congregational appointments' can be tested very simply.[32] The suggestion that 'the Masorti movement . . . embodied the moderate traditionalism of the prewar United Synagogue' goes further than Alderman.[33] I show that this is a valid judgement, if religious practice is used as the sole or dominant criterion. However, I argue that greater emphasis should be placed on theology than has generally been the case. Once different individuals are analysed in terms of their theological views, rather than solely or predominantly their religious practices, the actions they took and the disputes between them make more sense. This different analytical approach leads to a different conclusion from Endelman's.

More broadly, and elsewhere, Endelman has written of 'the decline of moderate traditionalism in Anglo-Jewish practice, and the ascendancy of right-wing views and standards . . . counter to the easygoing latitudinarianism' of the early 1900s.[34] He attributes much of this movement to a changed and more traditional lay leadership and community, and this part of his analysis is indisputable. William Rubinstein makes a similar point when he writes that the Jacobs Affair showed 'increasing anti-liberal tendencies within the United Synagogue' and that Jacobs' 'position was that of the United Synagogue mainstream a generation before', although even amongst the laity I want to distinguish between the leadership and the rank and file.[35] However, Endelman goes further and argues that 'the outlook of the Chief Rabbinate and the United Synagogue [under Adler and Hertz] was latitudinarian, undemanding, concerned more with unity, respectability and civility than differentiating between "authentic" and "inauthentic" forms of Judaism' but that this was overturned because 'the religious atmosphere shifted rightwards' between those days and the 1950s.[36] Persoff concurs, and has written that 'during the Chief Rabbinate of Israel Brodie conservatism overpowered progressivism in the hearts and minds of the centrist establishment'.[37] These are judgements not just about the community or the lay leaders but about the Chief Rabbis themselves. They ascribe a more liberal theological and halakhic stance to the early Chief Rabbis and a greater strictness to their successors. That is a view that this study will questions.

V.D. Lipman's attitude to the Chief Rabbinate is the most sympathetic. Lipman argues that Hermann Adler came under the heavy influence of lay leaders, but he maintained services in United Synagogues that 'did not deviate from the minimum requirements of orthodoxy' with the exception of mixed choirs.[38] Israel Finestein concurs with this judgement in his study of Hermann Adler, in his *Anglo-Jewry in changing times*.[39] Persoff challenges the widely shared notion that Adler's liturgical reforms were successful in maintaining a high level of allegiance to traditional Judaism. He writes that his modifications of 1892 'appeared to fail in their purpose [as] looks manifest in the foundation of the Jewish Religious Union some ten years later'.[40] I therefore examine the extent of Adler's achievement.

There are a number of other important studies. Bernard Homa's essential history of Machzike Hadath, *A fortress in Anglo-Jewry*, and Julius Jung's *Champions of orthodoxy* are highly polemical, written to celebrate Machzike Hadath and the Federation of Synagogues respectively. Their central thesis is that the Chief Rabbis were weak in learning and suspect in theology, and that they presided over religious laxity which the leaders of the new organisation found unacceptable and rose up to oppose.[41] David Englander's brilliant essay *Anglicized not Anglican: Jews and Judaism in Victorian Britain* looks at Anglo-Jewry too much through the prism of Marxist history, but is often extremely insightful; this study uses a number of ideas found there.[42]

Miri Freud Kandel's pioneering work, *Orthodox Judaism in Britain since 1913: an ideology forsaken* covers Hertz, Brodie and Jakobovits, and reiterates many of the themes of change in the Chief Rabbinate laid out by Alderman and Endelman. She argues that Hertz advocated a synthesis of Jewish and non-Jewish wisdom, although Jewish values always took priority and determined which non-Jewish ideas could be accepted.[43] She suggests that this was the result of Hertz's rejection both of 'right wing' tendencies (espoused by the Adath Yisroel and others), which denied the value of non-Jewish wisdom, and of the approach of lay leaders such as Robert Waley Cohen, whose 'spiritist' attitude emphasised the spirit over the letter of the law.[44] In contrast to these two groups, Hertz strove to develop an ideology that would form a bridge between East End and West End, native and immigrant, and, most importantly, equip young Jews from traditional backgrounds confronted with secular scholarship to retain loyalty to Judaism.[45]

Freud Kandel argues that after Hertz's death in 1946 his successor, Israel Brodie, forsook this ideology. She argues that the right-wing section of the community grew in assertiveness, in particular Dayan Abramsky, who was keen to assert his authority over the community and took from Brodie the halakhic supremacy that Chief Rabbis had previously enjoyed and made the Chief Rabbi subservient to the Beth Din.[46] Brodie, she argues, was essentially non-intellectual and without a positive theology of his own. This made him particularly susceptible to the influence of the right wing.[47] Furthermore, the impact of the Holocaust made Brodie fearful of the non-Jewish world and its values.[48] Thus 'under Brodie the influence of the right wing was being allowed to exert itself on mainstream Anglo-Jewish Orthodoxy in a manner that had never previously been possible'.[49] She highlights in particular the replacement of Hertz's ideology of synthesis with one of 'compart-mentalization', which the Adath largely, if not entirely, espoused.[50] This asserted that engagement in the non-Jewish world might be necessary for the purposes of making a living, but was otherwise illegitimate.[51]

This shift, Freud Kandel argues, had huge implications for Louis Jacobs. Jacobs, like Hertz, argued for a synthesis, although Hertz would not have agreed with Jacobs about the Pentateuch.[52] However, because of Brodie's weakness in the face of the right wing, the ascendancy of the Beth Din and the increased traditionalism of the lay leadership, 'the theological position espoused by Jacobs . . . had come to be officially marginalized'.[53] Jacobs was thus left stranded by changes in the theology of the Chief Rabbinate and United Synagogue. As Freud Kandel concludes, 'by defining the theology of Jacobs as outside the confines of the Orthodoxy advocated within the mainstream institutions of the community, the theological position of the Chief Rabbinate and United Synagogue became more rigid, representative of a far smaller section of the religious spectrum in Anglo-Jewry'.[54]

I undertake a close analysis of Freud Kandel's argument, in particular whether Hertz's ideology was perceived by him to be a bridge between the opposing approaches he found in Britain or a more positive con-struction with deeper roots, whether Brodie was indeed non-intellectual or, in fact, possessed a theology. We will see whether the 'right wing' of the Adath under the Schonfelds or the Golders Green Beth Hamedrash did indeed advocate compartmentalisation and whether Brodie was weak in the face of the pressure they applied, and *vis-à-vis* the Beth Din. The questions of whether the Chief Rabbinate changed its ideology as a result of all this, and whether the placing of Jacobs' theology as beyond the pale was a departure from previous attitudes are particularly impor-tant and form a major focus of this study, because they have become a central piece of evidence used by those who make this argument, and therefore a case to test the whole weight of my argument.

A very important work on Hertz is Harvey Meirovich's study, *Vindication of Judaism: the polemics of the Hertz Pentateuch.*

Meirovich's analysis of the Hertz *Pentateuch* is groundbreaking and perceptive, and this study will make much use of his work on Hertz's attitude towards Hellenism, other religions and Liberal Judaism. Meirovich argues in that work that Hertz was a Conservative Jew, by which he means that he deviated from classical Jewish tradition on issues such as the origin of Jewish texts and the nature of Jewish Law.[55] In doing so, like Freud Kandel, he makes the case for placing the pre-War United Synagogue and Louis Jacobs in the same camp on a theological basis, in parallel, as it were, with Alderman and Endelman who do so more on the basis of practice. Meirovich argues that Hertz belonged to the *Wissenschaft des Judentums* school, what Moshe Davis called the Historical School, which he defines as untraditional because of their application of critical methods to the study of post-Biblical material, particularly the Talmud. Meirovich hints that the major reason why Hertz and his teachers did not apply the same scientific methods to the Pentateuch was that it would undermine the counter-attack against the antisemitic Bible scholars led by Julius Wellhausen, who used their analysis of the Pentateuch to attack Judaism, and would thus lead young Jews to lose faith.[56]

Meirovich's second point is that the Historical School, to which Hertz belonged, understood the evolving nature of Jewish law and therefore denied the final authority of the sixteenth-century code of Jewish Law, the *Shulhan Arukh*.[57] Meirovich quotes Hertz's teacher Morais as saying in 1875 that a new code, taking into account changed conditions, needed to be written. Meirovitch also points out Hertz's belief in the sanctifying power of history and tradition, and therefore identifies him as a follower of Zachariah Frankel, founder of the Jewish Theological Seminary of Breslau, which Meirovich argues was opposed to the traditional theology of Samson Raphael Hirsch and Esriel Hildesheimer. He quotes Hertz's public declarations of allegiance to positive historical Judaism, and his respect for the Breslau Seminary.[58]

Meirovich points out that Hertz crystallised this theological position into 'progressive conservatism', defined as 'religious advance without loss of traditional Jewish values and without estrangement from the collective consciousness of the House of Israel'.[59] Finally Meirovich highlights Hertz's continued association with the Jewish Theological Seminary under Schechter's leadership and that of his successors, Cyrus Adler and Louis Finkelstein, and in particular Hertz's close friendship with and admiration for Solomon Schechter himself.[60] I will seek to carry out an extensive examination of Hertz's theology to test Meirovich's argument.

The views on the Chief Rabbis already mentioned also find expression in less major works. Aubrey Newman delivered a lecture on Hertz, to mark the centenary of his birth, in which he describes Hermann Adler as 'an English gentleman, externally an English clergyman . . . as much at home in the Athenaeum as in the Synagogue, and had almost as much in common with the higher ranks of the Anglican clergy of his day as the Anglican clergy themselves'.[61] Newman emphasises Hertz's traditionalism and insistence on the classic religious principles of Judaism, points I expand upon, but he also suggests that Hertz did come under the influence of his *dayyanim*, Schonfeld and others later in life, which pulled him further from the vision of 'progressive conservatism' which he laid out earlier in his Chief Rabbinate.[62] Pamela Shatzkes' book *Holocaust and rescue* contains a short *en passant* description of Hertz, which is close to that which this study arrives at. She highlights his 'commitment to Jewish values', saying that he was 'deeply committed to the preservation of Judaism and Jewish scholarship and 'an uncompromising representative of the religious cause'.[63] Another work which does not concentrate on the Chief Rabbis, but mentions them and their contribution, is Stefan Reif's *Judaism and Hebrew prayer*. He credits the Chief Rabbis with creating the hegemony they enjoyed, writing that they 'ensured that they retained the loyalty of the majority of the community, withstood significant encroachment from Reform and Eastern European Orthodox and remained the "umbrella" organisations for traditional Judaism that was a unique feature of Anglo-Jewry'. This Reif attributes to 'a shift of the central institutions towards the left'.[64]

The view of a general move towards increased traditionalism is found in other sources. In his 1962 survey of Anglo-Jewish religious life, Norman Cohen drew two portraits. The first was of the Anglo-Jewish minister of the 1920s and 1930s, 'Reverend [i.e. without rabbinic ordination] X' who 'carried his umbrella on the Sabbath [in violation of the laws of the Sabbath] and was very broadminded about the dietary laws'. He compared this character with the contemporary United Synagogue minister, now 'Rabbi Y' who 'comports himself in an orthodox pattern'.[65] Cohen talked also of the 'ascendancy of the right wing' in the United Synagogue.[66] Elsewhere, commenting on the causes of the Jacobs Affair, Cohen wrote 'the old easy going tolerance was being relentlessly edged out. Freedom of opinion was diminishing and, to qualify for respectability, a doctrine had to meet the most stringent requirements of rigidity'.[67] Fifteen years later, the then Chief Rabbi, Immanuel Jakobovits, wrote that 'at several important levels the gulf between [the United Synagogue, and more traditionalist groupings] is gradually narrowing'. Jakobovits meant that the United Synagogue was becoming more traditional.[68] There are a number of important articles that supply a great deal of useful evidence, for example, Stephen Sharot's 'Synagogue service in London, 1870–1914' in the *Jewish Journal of Sociology* and John Shaftesley's 'Religious controversies' in Levin (ed) *A century of Anglo-Jewish life*. I bring evidence from these studies to test the arguments advanced in the survey works I have just reviewed.

If I can show that there was theological continuity in the Chief Rabbinate, that it was consistently traditional and that religious policy was aimed at preserving adherence to tradition, we can amend and revise the judgements in the major works on the Chief Rabbis. If I can suggest that they were able interpreters of Jewish tradition who tried to create a coherent synthesis of traditional and modern scholarship and forge a response to modernity that did not sacrifice what they regarded as indispensable religious principle, then I hope I can deepen the understanding of the Chief Rabbis and of Judaism in the UK because of the central role the Chief Rabbis played.

This may help to answer the major question of why institutional Judaism in England has remained so traditional and has such a high proportion of the Jewish population as (at least nominal) adherents. We may find that in addition to other social, cultural and political factors, which historians have well explored, the policies of the Chief Rabbis, which have not been as emphasised, played an important part. I also reconsider the role of British Jewry in the development of Judaism, particularly traditional Judaism, in the world as a whole in the last hundred and fifty years, for there are intellectual and ideological connections between the Chief Rabbis and Jewish religious leaders trying to confront the same issues and problems. This may reveal that Britain was not a 'cultural backwater' in this period but played a part in developments in Judaism on an international level.

The historiography on the development of traditional Judaism as it encountered modernity is vital for our understanding of the British Chief Rabbis. The challenges involved in upholding religious authority in an age of reason that were faced around the Jewish world were faced too by Britain's Chief Rabbis. The response of some Jewish leaders is well known – for example, the eastern European rabbis who rejected the modern world and its trappings. However, it is more useful to examine such leaders as Esriel Hildeseimer and S.R. Hirsch in Germany, and Sabato Morais and H. Pereira Mendes in America, who did not simply reject modernity but sought to come to an accommodation with it, within their conception of authentic Judaism.

As well as placing the Chief Rabbis within this wider context, this book also argue that the Anglo-Jewish experience as a whole is worthy of examination alongside the German and American experiences and that, despite the diverse contexts, it slots nicely into the established literature on traditional Judaism in Germany, France and the USA, as a different but comparable case. There are many points of reference in the career of Hildesheimer, as analysed in David Ellenson's outstanding studies, *Rabbi Esriel Hildesheimer and the creation of a Modern Jewish Orthodoxy* and *After Emancipation*, which show how traditionalist Jewish leaders can be analysed and understood. Mordechai Breuer's *Modernity within tradition* shows how traditional Judaism developed in Germany in the nineteenth and twentieth centuries, which will illuminate our study of Anglo-Jewry, while Michael Meyer's *Judaism within modernity* looks at all streams, not restricted to Germany, and is equally enlightening. Marc Shapiro's *Between the yeshiva world and modern orthodoxy: the life and times of Rabbi Yehiel Yaakov Weinberg* stands alongside Ellenson's work on Hildesheimer as a model of biographical writing on a traditional Jewish leader. Moshe Davis' *The emergence of Conservative Judaism: the Historical School in 19th-century America* provides many instructive American parallels to developments in Britain, while Jack Wertheimer's *Tradition renewed* and Robert Fierstein's *A new spirit* are vital to any understanding of the early days of the Jewish Theological Seminary and the United Synagogue of America.[69] I look at other European developments, for example in France, which Phyllis Cohen Albert addressed in *The modernization of French Jewry* and Jay Berkovitz in *Rites and passages*, and more widely among the examples in Frankel and Zipperstein's collection *Assimilation and community*.

These works developed the required analytical tools to understand traditional leaders in modern times. Ellenson argues convincingly for the increased importance of persuasion over dictat or coercion as the primary method of upholding tradition; these scholars point out the vital necessity of flexibility within the tradition, allowing change when fundamental principles were not at stake, and they emphasise the distinction between a successful approach for the leader of a small but highly traditional community, in order to maintain his tight knit group at their high level of religious observance, and the approach suitable for the leader of a larger but less committed community who is seeking to maintain certain minimum standards of Jewish life, to keep his followers within the traditional Jewish world, albeit not at the highest level.[70] Before I apply these insights to Britain, I wish to lay out the sources used and the methodologies employed in this study.

This book uses a variety of methods. The accounts in the major works which touch upon Britain's Chief Rabbis and Anglo-Jewish religious history that I have just reviewed will be tested against the evidence to be found in primary sources. These sources come in three forms. First, a great deal of information was extracted from the *Jewish Chronicle*, the leading newspaper of Anglo-Jewry in this period. Archival material was consulted, particularly in the London Metropolitan Archives of the Chief Rabbinate, the United Synagogue and the Court of the Chief Rabbi (London Beth Din) but also in the Anglo-Jewish Archives at Southampton University, where Hertz's and H.M. Lazarus' private papers are kept, the Adler and other papers in the Jewish Theological Seminary, New York, in the collections of the Hebrew University, Jerusalem, which include Samuel Hillman's papers, and the London School of Jewish Studies. Finally, use was made of oral testimonies from individuals with first-hand knowledge. As a source, the *Jewish Chronicle* is as reliable, and as unreliable, as any other newspaper. Historically, it often had axes to grind, but a lot of its reports were very dry. Synagogue meetings were often reported in great detail with little or no comment. Of course, as Carr argues, the selection of details to report is in itself a form of distortion, but that is a caveat about the source rather than a dismissal of its usefulness and reliability.[71] Even more usefully the *Jewish Chronicle* often printed, in full, United Synagogue reports, Chief Rabbis' sermons and lectures and, of course, letters to the editor, which tell us exactly what was proposed, preached and debated in public, and what it was that proponents for a particular case wanted others to believe.

The archives consulted contain letters to and from the religious and lay leaders of the United Synagogue and others, minutes of meetings, rabbinical rulings and so forth. We would not today ascribe the same reliability to these sources as Elton or Namier might have done, but they do give an important insight into the private feelings of the leading participants and the nature of the debates between them.[72] We do not have to believe every word they said or wrote to find the fact that they said or wrote it useful.[73] They have been relatively neglected until now and it has been possible to extract important evidence for the first time to establish a new understanding.

Finally, we come to the last source, oral testimony. An attempt was made to speak to as many people with first-hand knowledge as possible, for example the former United Synagogue ministers Isaac Levy and Leslie Hardman, the son of Yehezkel Abramsky, Chimen, and the former Executive Director of the Chief Rabbi's Office, Alan Greenbat. Although oral history is now recognised as a valid source, it remains difficult to work with. Memory is an individual's imaginative recreation of his or her past, and it can sometimes be very imaginative indeed.

Furthermore, it fades and changes over time. However, initial concern about the 'truthfulness' of oral testimony has been replaced by a realisation that what people believed happened can be as important, in shaping their views and actions, as what actually happened. My interviewees' opinions have helped shape the relationship between the Anglo-Jewish community and its history.

This study tries to avoid the terms 'orthodox', 'conservative', 'reform', 'right' and 'left' to describe religious positions. Instead the terms 'traditional' and 'radical' will be employed, supported by specifying detail. The terms 'orthodox', 'reform' and so forth contain no fixed meaning. They have been used at different times by different people to mean different things. For example, Robert Waley Cohen described Rabbi J.J. Weinberg in 1934 as 'ultra-orthodox' a term that would not be applied to him today.[74] The same Robert Waley Cohen protested that his brand of orthodoxy was being overtaken by ultra-orthodoxy because of pressure to close shops at the time when the Sabbath began on a Friday afternoon, however early, rather than waiting for six o'clock.[75] It is unlikely that anyone today would claim that orthodoxy was compatible with keeping businesses open into the hours of darkness on a Friday.

Morris Joseph described the Principal of Jews' College, Michael Friedlander, in 1902 as 'conservative' whereas Meirovitch himself calls Friedlander 'a strict traditionalist'.[76] 'Positive historical' was used by Frankel to describe his ideology, but Hertz talks of the 'positive historical Judaism of our fathers' in a reference to what we would now call orthodoxy.[77] Hertz elsewhere described S.R. Hirsch as 'the most ardent defender of Traditional Judaism in the nineteenth century' although we would hardly associate Hirsch with the rather tepid implications that the term 'traditional' carries today.[78] Hertz himself used the terms 'orthodox,' 'conservative,' 'traditional,' 'historical' and 'positive historical' interchangeably.[79] We have to recognise what Oswald John Simon in 1915 called the 'folly of religious labels' and avoid using the terms employed in the past to define contemporary theological positions. We will leave them well alone and define what is meant when necessary, rather than relying on fundamentally unreliable shorthand. One function of the typology we will now introduce will be to provide alternative shorthand, which will be used in preference to the more conventional labels.

Notes

1 M. Persoff, *Immanuel Jakobovits: a prophet in Israel* (London 2002), 13.

2 'Tradition' is, of course, something that is constantly changing and

developing, as I discuss later. In this context 'less traditional' means estranged from the consensus among those who consider themselves, at the time, to be traditional.

3 G. Alderman, *Modern British Jewry* (Oxford 1992), 147; H. Meirovich, *A vindication of Judaism* (New York 1998), 13–15.

4 The term 'modernity' is used is very different ways across different academic disciplines, including history, cultural studies, literary theory and sociology. In this study the term is used to denote its traditional meaning in the field of Jewish history: the period after the Enlightenment (and its Jewish aspect, the *Haskalah*) and Jewish Emancipation.

5 D. Taylor, *British Chief Rabbis, 1664–2006* (London 2007), 239, 258, 311, 345, 370, 407.

6 C. Roth, 'Chief Rabbis', in Jung, *Jewish leaders* (Jerusalem 1953).

7 Taylor, *British Chief Rabbis.*

8 Ibid., 258, 331, 368.

9 M. Persoff, *Faith against reason: religious reform and the British Chief Rabbinate, 1840–1990* (London 2008).

10 T.M. Endelman, 'Introduction' in Persoff, *Faith against reason*, xxxi.

11 Alderman, *Modern British Jewry.*

12 I. Endelman, *Jews of Britain* (Berkley 2000).

13 Alderman, *Modern British Jewry*, 146.

14 Ibid., 108–109.

15 Ibid., 109.

16 Ibid.

17 Ibid., 147, 146.

18 Ibid., 148; G. Alderman, 'Power, authority and status in British Jewry: the Chief Rabbinate and shechita' in Alderman and Holmes (ed) *Outsiders and outcasts: essays in honour of William J. Fishman* (London 1993), 17.

19 Alderman, *Modern British Jewry*, 147.

20 Alderman, 'The Chief Rabbinate and shechita' 17.

21 Alderman, *Modern British Jewry*, 355, 359.

22 Ibid., 359.

23 Ibid., 361.

24 Ibid., 364.

25 Compare Ibid., 364 and Endelman, *Jews of Britain*, 251.

26 Endelman, *Jews of Britain*, 120.

27 D.B. Ruderman, *Jewish Enlightenment* (Princeton 2000), 5.

28 Endelman, *Jews of Britain*, 250.

29 Persoff, *Faith and reason*, 236, 247.

30 Ibid., 252.

31 Ibid., 253.

32 Ibid.

33 Ibid.

34 T. Endelman, 'Practices of a low anthropological level: a *shehitah* con-

troversy of the 1950s' in Kershen (ed) *Food in the migrant experience* (Aldershot 2002), 79.

35 W.D.Rubinstein, *Jews in the English-speaking world* (London 1996), 411, 414.

36 Endelman, 'A *shehitah* controversy of the 1950s', 88, 89.

37 Persoff, *Faith against reason*, 118.

38 V.D. Lipman, *History of the Jews in Britain* (Leicester 1990), 92.

39 I. Finestein, Anglo-Jewry in *changing times* (London 1999), 247.

40 Persoff, *Faith and reason*, 381.

41 B. Homa, *A fortress in Anglo-Jewry* (London 1953); J. Jung, *Champions of orthodoxy* (London 1974).

42 D. Englander, 'Anglicized not Anglican', 235–273.

43 M. Freud Kandel, *Orthodox Judaism in Britain since 1913* (London 2006), 52, 53, 64.

44 Ibid., 90.

45 Ibid., 68, 93.

46 Ibid., 90, 98, 100.

47 Ibid., 106, 109, 120.

48 Ibid., 108.

49 Ibid., 122.

50 Ibid., 116, 113.

51 Ibid., 116.

52 Ibid., 147, 150.

53 Ibid., 137, 138, 145, 135.

54 Ibid., 159.

55 Meirovich, *Vindication* ,13.

56 Ibid., 8.

57 Ibid., 10.

58 Ibid., 15.

59 Ibid.

60 Ibid., 14–18.

61 A. Newman, *Chief Rabbi Dr. Joseph H. Hertz, C.H.* (London 1973), 1–2.

62 Ibid., 20.

63 P. Shatzkes, *Holocaust and rescue* (London 2004), 224.

64 S.C. Reif, *Judaism and Hebrew prayer* (Cambridge 19993), 285.

65 N. Cohen 'Trends in Anglo-Jewish religious life' in Gould and Esh (ed) *Trends in Jewish life* (London 1964), 46.

66 Ibid.

67 N. Cohen, 'The religious crisis in Anglo-Jewry' *Tradition* 8:2 (Summer 1966), 46.

68 I. Jakobovits, 'An analysis of secular versus religious trends in Anglo-Jewry' in Lipman and Lipman (ed) *Jewish Life in Britain* (London 1977).

69 D. Ellenson, *Rabbi Esriel Hildesheimer* (Tuscaloosa 1990), D. Ellenson, *After Emancipation* (Cincinnati 2004), M. Breuer, *Modernity within tradition* (New York 1992), M.A. Meyer, *Judaism within modernity* (Detroit

2001), M.B. Shapiro, *Between the yeshiva world and modern orthodoxy: the life and times of Rabbi Jehiel Jacob Weinberg* (Oxford 1999), M. Davis, *Conservative Judaism* (Philadelphia 1963), J. Wertheimer, *Tradition renewed* (New York 1997), R.E. Fierstein, *A different spirit* (New York 1986), P. Cohen Albert, *The modernization of French Jewry* (Hanover, New Hampshire 1977), J.M. Berkovitz, *Rites and passages* (Philadelphia 2004), J. Frankel and S.J. Zipperstein (ed), *Assimilation and community* (Cambridge 1992).

70 Ellenson, *Hildesheimer*, 63–72.

71 E.H. Carr, *What is history?* (London 1961, 2nd edn 1987), 7ff.

72 G.R. Elton, *The practice of history* (Sydney 1967), *passim*; see L.B. Namier, *The structure of politics at the accession of George III* (London 1927) for insight into Namier's method and attitude to sources, particularly private letters and diaries.

73 Many of the points made either explicitly or implicitly in the works of Carr, Elton, Namier and others have been repeated more recently, for example by R. Evans in his *In defence of history* (London 2001) and J. Tosh in *The pursuit of history* (London 1991). Nevertheless, these earlier works remain the best expressions of the fundamental issues connected with the use of sources in the study of history.

74 Shapiro, *Weinberg*, 134.

75 Homa, *Fortress*, 14–15.

76 M. Joseph, *Judaism as life and creed* (London 1903), 27; Meirovitch, *Vindication*, 162.

77 J.H. Hertz, *Early and late* (Hindhead, Surrey 1943), 162.

78 J.H. Hertz, *Affirmations of Judaism* (Oxford 1927), 66.

79 For examples see Hertz, *Affirmations*, 47, 57, 64, 129, J.H. Hertz, *Sermons, addresses and studies* (London 1938), I 289, and Hertz, *Early and late*, 227.

Chapter 2

Historical context

RABBINIC JUDAISM EMERGED during the Second Jerusalem Temple period, following the return of the Jews from the Babylonian exile in 538 BCE. There followed a period of intense rabbinic activity, when the Jews' oral legal traditions, which the rabbis held were given to Moses on Sinai with the Written Law (Pentateuch), were collated. The rabbis also added a large number of new ordinances to protect the existing laws from being transgressed and to serve the needs of the time. For example, it was already forbidden to use money on the Sabbath; in the Second Temple period it became forbidden to move it, lest once it was moved it be used through absent-mindedness. Rabbinic legislation was extremely effective in preserving the Jewish people even after the destruction of the Second Temple and the ending of Jewish statehood by the Romans in 70 CE. Rabbinic regulations continued to develop and were codified in the Mishnah in approximately 200 CE.

Comments on the Mishnah were made later and redacted in the Gemara, which with the Mishnah formed the Talmud. This became the basis of Jewish law, and attracted numerous commentaries and rulings by subsequent generations of rabbis, who exercised a great deal of flexibility and creativity in their interpretations. Great figures such as Maimonides and R. Yosef Karo codified these legal conclusions in collections, which became authoritative, and were in turn commented upon, most significantly by R. Moses Isserles who – by adding glosses stating Ashkenazi custom – made the *Shulhan Arukh* acceptable to both Sefardi and Ashkenazi Jews.[1] In the pre-modern era, and for a while after, rabbis saw themselves and were seen as the heirs of this rabbinic tradition, whose role first and foremost was to rule on matters of religious law.

Before the Enlightenment and Jewish Emancipation in the eighteenth and early nineteenth centuries, the vast majority of Jews shared the same basic beliefs. There were small groups like the Karaites who rejected the principal tenets of rabbinic Judaism, primarily the authenticity of the Oral Law, and there were individual Jews who held heretical views, but these formed a tiny minority. Some Jews were more observant than others, some more pious than others, but there was little dispute about major issues of dogma. Everyone agreed that God created the world and gave the Torah.

That changed in the late eighteenth and early nineteenth centuries. In the view of scholars such as Jacob Katz, this was the result of the Enlightenment (which in its Jewish form is known as the *Haskalah*), which emphasised reason over tradition and stressed the universality of mankind. Jews found new intellectual resources to challenge the basic tenets of Judaism and did so in large numbers.[2] Starting in Germany, many Jews either abandoned their faith or sought to reform it so it reflected contemporary mores, informed by the concern that their religion distinguished them from their fellow citizens and prevented full integration. This presented tremendous challenges for the rabbinate. Rabbis could no longer expect automatic obedience; indeed, the bans they imposed upon the leaders of the Jewish Enlightenment, the *maskilim*, were ignored.[3] In the view of other historians, such as Endelman, Frankel and Zipperstein, the source of the changes can also be found in socio-economic developments, which might be grouped together under the term 'modernisation'. As Frankel has written, 'urbanization, industrialization, migration, market forces and the opportunities (educational, occupational, cultural) available all combined to undermine the traditional life of the Jewish people in nineteenth-century Europe'.[4] To cope with these new circumstances, rabbis were forced to move from being legal experts to being spiritual leaders who had to persuade their communities to adhere to classical Jewish belief and practice, based on the Thirteen Principles of Faith of Maimonides and the *Shulhan Arukh*, both of which had received wide acceptance.[5]

All varieties of Judaism which have emerged since the onset of modernity, from the apparently most traditional to the most radical, are, in fact, quite different from what came before. They each represent a different approach to meeting the challenges thrown up by the new circumstances created by modernity. As we shall see, some rabbis felt that an unprecedented strictness and inflexibility was the appropriate response; and, though such 'traditionalists' might claim they were merely perpetuating pre-modern forms of Judaism, they were departing from them as surely as those who sought varying degrees of accommodation to modernity.[6]

Approaches to this new task among traditional rabbis broadly fell between two poles. The highly traditional, led by Rabbi Moses

Sofer (1762–1840), forbade any concession to modernity, borrowing a Mishnaic statement to declare 'change is forbidden by the Torah'; this created small but strong communities.[7] Others, led by Esriel Hildesheimer (1820–99) promoted a form of Judaism that allowed some adaptation to the conditions of the time without compromising what they regarded as essential religious principle, an approach which created traditional communities that were larger but less intense.[8] Britain's Chief Rabbis were also attempting to respond to this new religious climate, and deployed a variety of tactics to achieve their aims. To bring this more sharply into focus we should turn to the unique context of English Jewry.

The first Jews probably came to England with William the Conqueror. Over the next two centuries the community grew into a minor, if not wholly obscure, outpost of Jewry, which came to an end in 1290 with Edward I's expulsion of the Jews. Some conversos filtered back, especially under the Tudors, but the Resettlement is usually dated to 1656 when Oliver Cromwell sanctioned the re-admittance of Jews. The first Jews to return were from Holland, the descendants of those who had fled from Spain and Portugal at the end of the fifteenth century.[9] By 1663 they had an organised community and a year later they appointed a rabbi (haham), Jacob Sasportas (1610–98).[10] These Sefardim were later joined by their central and eastern European co-religionists, the Ashkenazim, who formed their own synagogue in 1690. This synagogue, in Dukes Place in the City of London, eventually became the Great Synagogue.[11] The Chief Rabbinate evolved out of the rabbinate of the Great Synagogue, which remained the seat of the Chief Rabbi until it was destroyed by the Luftwaffe on 11 May 1941.[12]

By the middle of the eighteenth century the Ashkenazim formed about two thirds to three quarters of London's seven to eight thousand Jews and were largely from the population of Polish Jews living in Germany.[13] They appointed Aaron Hart as their rabbi in 1704, but as early as 1707 the Ashkenazi community began to fragment when Marcus Moses set up a synagogue in his home which eventually became the Hambro Synagogue.[14] In 1760 a synagogue was founded in Westminster which became the Western Synagogue, and in 1761 the congregation that would evolve into the New Synagogue was founded, in addition to a number of other small synagogues and prayer groups (*hevrot* and *minyanim*).[15]

Aaron Hart was recognised as the religious authority for all London Jews, as was his successor, Hart Lyon (rabbi 1758–64).[16] However, David Tevele Schiff (rabbi of the Great Synagogue 1765–91) had to compete with the Hambro's candidate, Israel Solomon, until the latter went to Russia in 1780.[17] In 1802 Solomon Hirschell, the son of Hart Lyon, was appointed rabbi after an eleven-year interregnum. The community that Hirschell found on his arrival was in a poor state. Although quite large numerically, with 22,500 Jews in England, including 5,000 outside London, it was religiously lax and ignorant. The Sabbath, dietary laws and Jewish learning were neglected.[18] The wealthiest removed themselves from the community and bought country houses outside London, where they adopted the mores of the non-Jews of the same economic stratum.[19] By 1800 the Jews of England were probably the most acculturated, secular and ignorant in Europe. Endelman has argued that this laxity was not driven by ideology, as was the case with the continental *maskilim*, but was simply a function of a desire for an easier existence and the ability to enjoy the pleasures around them.[20] Ruderman, on the other hand, argues that Jews in England 'were never inarticulate or nonreflective' and that, in fact, modernisation of Anglo-Jewish society was the result of a specifically Anglo-Jewish response to English conditions.[21] Either way, English Jews were able either consciously to reject tradition, or to slide into a non-traditional life, because unlike in Germany, for example, the rabbi could not call upon civil law to enforce his decisions and relied simply on his own authority. Perhaps one exception to the rabbi's powerlessness was his ability to issue a *herem* (excommunication) which would deny its object any contact with the Jewish community, or a Jewish burial. When Solomon Hirschell arrived in 1802 he threatened to excommunicate anyone who ate (non-kosher) game birds, and presumably he considered that the threat would carry some weight.[22]

Hirschell was the bridge between the office of rabbi of the Great Synagogue and the modern office of Chief Rabbi. His rabbinate lasted for 40 years and witnessed significant changes in the community. The Jewish population had grown to 35,000 by Hirschell's death, with the Ashkenazim forming an increasing majority.[23] The community moved from being made up mostly of Yiddish speakers to being essentially English-speaking and English-born. This demographic change was one of the factors which enabled the move led by the Goldsmids and others towards Emancipation.[24] In 1835 Jews were allowed to be sheriffs of the City of London, and bills for general Jewish Emancipation were passed by the House of Commons in 1830, 1834, 1836 and 1841, though all were defeated by the House of Lords.[25] Hirschell's authority was accepted throughout England, in the colonies and even in the United States. The communities in Portsmouth and Manchester sought his guidance.[26] In 1825 the B'nai Jeshurun synagogue in New York asked for Hirschell's advice, and in 1830 Hirschell sent one of the *dayyanim* (judges) of his religious court (Beth Din) to Australia to help establish Jewish life there.[27] Such was Hirschell's authority and the growth of English-speaking Jewry both in Britain and overseas, that he evolved into a Chief Rabbi over the course of his incumbency.

The most important event of Hirschell's Chief Rabbinate came almost at its end. From the 1820s onwards there had been an increasing desire on the part of the wealthier members of the community, particularly among the Sefardim, to introduce mild reforms to make the service more decorous, and to set up a branch of the synagogue in West London closer to their homes.[28] The Elders of the congregation allowed the *hazzan* (cantor) to wear robes and permitted a sermon in English rather than Portuguese, but refused to budge on other points, particularly the ban on the erection of any synagogue within six miles of Bevis Marks.[29] The result of this frustration of the wishes of much of the membership by the lay leadership was secession by some of the wealthy members of Bevis Marks, joined by a number of Ashkenazi families, led by the Goldsmids, and the foundation of the West London Synagogue of British Jews in 1840.[30]

It is instructive to examine the rationale given by the founders of the West London for their action. It shows that they were not revolutionaries – and, as Persoff remarks, not doctrinally motivated – but merely wanted moderate reforms.[31] They identified five reasons: 'the distance of the existing synagogues from our places of residence . . . the length and imperfections of the order of service . . . the inconvenient hour at which it is appointed . . . the unimpressive manner in which it is performed . . . the absence of religious instruction [sermons] in our synagogues'.[32] As Englander has noted, not a single one of those complaints touched on theology. They could have been accommodated had the religious and lay authorities of the community so decided.[33] The depth of the founders' traditionalism becomes clear when we examine the original ritual at the West London. The sexes sat separately, prayers were in Hebrew, and references to the Messiah and the return to Zion were retained.[34] The founders did not seek to alter the fundamentals of the service, merely to make it more seemly, more 'English'. Indeed Isaac Lyon Goldsmid had been contemplating founding a new synagogue for that very purpose since 1831.[35]

Radical change only arrived when the new congregation began to look for a minister. They came across a teacher of Hebrew at University College London, David Wolf Marks.[36] Marks' religious views were unusual to say the least. He had no patience for those, like the German reformers, who disputed that Moses received the Pentateuch on Sinai.[37]

However, he was, in Steven Singer's phrase, a neo-Karaite.[38] He denied
the authenticity and authority of the Oral Law and removed much from
the ritual that was rabbinic in origin, leading to some radical changes.[39]
For example, the second day of festivals was abolished because it had
no Biblical source and the organ was introduced because instrumental
music on the Sabbath is only rabbinically prohibited.[40]

This Bibliocentric theology and rejection of rabbinic Judaism
was heavily influenced by Anglican theology, notably the arguments
deployed by evangelicals against tractarians in support of the authority
of scripture over tradition.[41] Indeed Israel Zangwill called the members
of the West London 'the Protestants of Judaism'.[42] It enabled its followers to avoid the critique of Judaism propounded by Alexander McCaul
and others on the evangelical wing of the Church of England that
Judaism was merely soulless 'rabbinism'.[43] An inclination to promoting
the Bible over the Talmud may also have been a legacy of the converso
past of some of the founders.[44] Finally, as Liberles has argued, the
desire for Emancipation played a part.[45] Morris Joseph, Marks' successor at West London, said of the founders of the synagogue that 'they
had to prove that they deserved their liberties, and one of the proofs
was their ability to set free their own minds'.[46] Marks' views therefore
made him an attractive candidate, even for those who had no interest
in theology.

Hirschell and the religious leaders of the Sefardim (without a haham
at the time) now found religious objections to the new synagogue. Other
congregations who had broken away as a result of communal politics
were eventually recognised, but there could never be recognition of a
heretical congregation, even if it had become heretical almost acciden-
tally, without premeditation by the lay founders, who were largely uninterested in theology. The religious leadership issued a *herem* in January
1842. Hirschell wrote, 'certain persons calling themselves British Jews
. . . reject the Oral Law . . . any person or persons publicly declaring
that he or she rejects and do not believe in the authority of the Oral
Law, cannot be permitted to have any communion with us Israelites in
any religious rite or sacred act'.[47] The response to the *herem* was not
encouraging for Hirschell. It was rejected by the Western Synagogue
and the communities of Manchester and Liverpool.[48] In England, just as
in Germany, a *herem* was no longer accepted and obeyed. Hirschell had
used his ultimate weapon and found it to be powerless.

In the end, Moses Montefiore caused more problems for West London
than the Chief Rabbi. Under the Marriage Registration Act 1836 the
Board of Deputies of British Jews, led by Montefiore, had sole authority to certify a congregation as one made up of 'persons professing the

Jewish religion' to enable them to perform marriages valid in English law. Montefiore, a strict traditionalist, withheld the certificate, preventing the synagogue from solemnising marriages, but even this issue was soon resolved when the wealthy leaders of the West London sponsored the passage of a bill through parliament to enable them to appoint a marriage secretary. The whole affair showed up the Jewish community as intolerant and sectarian. The Jews were asking for tolerance and equal rights, but it seemed that they did not practise toleration themselves. This would have profound implications for the first of the Chief Rabbis we will consider in detail, Nathan Marcus Adler.

Hirschell died on 31 October 1842.[49] The lay leaders who sought his replacement were informed by the changes in the community and by the West London affair. An acculturated community searching for acceptance and Emancipation would not find a rabbi of the mould of Moses Sofer satisfactory. They looked for a new type of rabbi – with Jewish learning, but also with an appreciation for the world outside the synagogue – who could understand and even approve of their attraction to modernity. In 1845 a Committee of Delegates made up of the four London synagogues and the communities of nineteen English cities chose Nathan Marcus Adler.[50]

Adler was just what the committee was looking for. He was born in 1803 into a distinguished rabbinical family, and his great uncle was David Tevele Schiff.[51] He graduated in 1828 with both a PhD and rabbinical ordination, was appointed rabbi of Oldenburg in 1829, becoming Chief Rabbi of Hanover a few years later.[52] As a result of his mixed education, shared by few other rabbis (and even fewer traditional rabbis) in Europe at the time, he was able to engage in both traditional learning and modern scholarship, known as *Wissenschaft des Judentums* (the scientific study of Judaism). He published traditional Talmudic discourses and novellae, but his greatest work, *Netina lager*, a commentary on the Aramaic translation of the Pentateuch, the *Targum Onkelos*, both contained traditional explanations and used modern techniques, such as philology.[53] He made his views on *Wissenschaft* known in the wider European Jewish community too; when the Frankfurt-based founder of neo-orthodoxy, S.R. Hirsch, criticised D.Z. Hoffman, a rabbinical and scholarly leader of traditional Jews in Berlin, for quoting *Wissenschaft* scholars in his study of the Talmudic rabbi Mar Samuel, Adler came to his defence.[54] Adler delivered Talmudic *shiurim* (lectures) and presided over his Beth Din, but also gave regular sermons in English. He wore Western dress, often under clerical robes, and a respectable beard. English Jews could feel confident in his competence in traditional duties, and feel proud of his learning but not remotely ashamed of his manners. If the Christians had Dr Arnold and Dr Newman, the Jews had Dr Adler.

Nevertheless, the lay leadership was not prepared to trust him with all the powers enjoyed by his predecessors. There was concern among those campaigning for Emancipation that an attempt to use religious coercion against theological opponents would damage their campaign.[55] Adler's appointment was therefore on condition that the *herem* was not used.[56] Adler was therefore forced to promote his brand of Judaism using other methods.[57] His objections to West London were just as profound as those of Hirschell and Montefiore and he attacked what he regarded as their heresy and defended the Oral Law. For example, in 1854 he told his congregation 'our holy faith has two elements, the written and the oral law, both of which are divine'.[58] He also attacked Marks on his own ground, and argued that there was a Biblical basis for two days of Festivals.[59] Adler was uncompromising with individuals and bodies who shared West London's views, for example Solomon Schiller-Szinessy in Manchester, whom he effectively excluded from the traditional community.[60] However, his defence of those elements he considered to be the essentials of Judaism was accompanied by flexibility on matters he considered of lesser importance.

In 1847 Adler issued his *Laws and regulations*, which altered the synagogue service to increase its appeal to the Anglicised members of his flock. He hinted at the situation he faced, and that prompted the publication of *Laws and regulations*, in the introduction, which described 'deserted synagogues'.[61] In one regard at least Adler agreed with the agitators of 1840: a disagreeable service drove people from the synagogue. They had been ignored, had broken away and almost by chance they had become a heretical movement. As Black has noted, by permitting moderate changes, within a strict theological and legal framework, Adler hoped to avoid radical reform and heresy.[62] This is different to Persoff's claim that Adler conceded reforms under pressure from wealthy members of the community.[63] As Adler wrote – acknowledging, and attempting to replicate, the flexibility of pre-modern rabbis – 'the major cause of lack of religiosity is the absence of theological leaders who, by implementing leniencies which fit the needs of the time and the demands of religion, following the example of the rabbis of by-gone times, will prevent the nation from breaching the fences of the law'.[64] This tendency has been noted by, amongst others, Marc Shapiro, who argues that 'in the responsa literature there is always a tension between what the pure halachah is and what the community will accept' and halakhic jurists (or 'decisors') have deviated from their ideal positions, and sought leniencies, in order to preserve as much adherence to *hala-khah* as possible.[65]

Thus, for example, Adler banned the custom of 'knocking' during the recitation of the Book of Esther on *Purim* and the circling of the bridegroom by his bride because they were deemed indecorous and put people off attending the synagogue.[66] He insisted that clerical costume should be worn and that a 'solemn and reverential silence shall pervade the Synagogues'.[67] Adler stated that his reforms were 'in strict conformity with the Law', because fundamentally he was a traditionalist.[68] As Heilman has written, Adler 'was prepared to modify modernity if necessary to make it fit Judaism, but not the reverse'.[69] However, the changes Adler introduced also answered many of the complaints of those who had left Bevis Marks and the Great for the West London. Adler removed another major source of grievance, the absence of synagogues in the West End of London by allowing the establishment of the Central Synagogue in 1855 and the Bayswater Synagogue in 1865. He even accepted and adapted some of the reforms introduced at West London. Marks introduced a prayer to be said by a woman after childbirth; Adler took the idea and wrote his own.[70]

Adler's dual policy – of firmness on what he considered essentials and flexibility on matters to which he attached lesser importance – was extremely effective in keeping the synagogues which recognised his authority dominant in the community and restricting the growth of the West London.[71] A survey by the *British Weekly* found that, of the 2360 Jews who went to synagogue on Saturday 23 October 1886, only 81 went to the West London. If we compare attendance at West London with Adler's synagogues catering to the same social class we find that the figures are Bayswater 261, St John's Wood 247, New West End 161.[72] One reason that Nathan Adler's policy was so effective was that, unlike his successors, he faced only very mild demands for reform. His settlement of 1847 was able to hold sway until 1880 when he faced the first conference called to discuss alterations to the liturgy, a challenge he confronted with the close co-operation of his son, Hermann Adler. We will examine that conference when we look at Hermann Adler's religious policy.

The finely tuned religious policy Nathan Adler adopted could only work if he exercised strict religious control over the community. The *Laws and regulations* made him the community's sole religious authority; he even had the right of veto over the erection of new synagogues.[73] These powers were reinforced in 1870 when the United Synagogue was formed by five London congregations (the Great, the New, the Hambro, the Central and Bayswater) at Adler's prompting.[74] They were soon joined by other synagogues, including Borough in 1873, St Johns Wood

in 1876 and East London in 1877.[75] The United Synagogue's Deed of
Foundation and Trust made the Chief Rabbi the sole authority over all
religious matters, including the form of worship and the appointment
of ministers.[76] This provision highlights one of the distinctive features
of Anglo-Jewry in the nineteenth and for much of twentieth century; the
presence of ministers at the spiritual head of United Synagogue congregations, rather than rabbis. This was the result of the type of seminary
set up by Nathan Adler. In 1855 he founded Jews' College, which –
though led by great scholars, not least Michael Friedlander, Principal
1865–1907 – did not produce graduates of great traditional learning.[77]
They studied Bible and some Talmud but they did not receive a classical rabbinical education, probably because for the first 25 years of
its existence Nathan Adler and his *dayyanim* were the only rabbis the
community needed. Individual synagogues required men who could
lead services, preach and undertake pastoral duties, and that is what
Jews' College produced. Religious authority was to be exercised by the
Chief Rabbi and questions of religious law were to be taken to the Beth
Din, of which he was the active head.[78]

This brief account brings us to 1880, the start of the period which this
book will explore. This is a significant date for a number of reasons. It
was the year that Hermann Adler took over the day-to-day running of
the religious life of the community as Delegate Chief Rabbi. It marks
the approximate beginning of the great waves of immigration of eastern
European Jews who would eventually overwhelm the original Ashkenazi
community, which was drawn from western and central Europe. They
brought with them a greater religious stringency and different customs,
and would be a source of difficulties for the Chief Rabbis. The Jews
already in England were by 1880 highly Anglicised, and as Endelman
has observed, religion for them, as for their Anglican neighbours,
was a matter not of burning zeal but of decency and propriety.[79] They
had achieved Emancipation in 1858, there were a number of Jewish
Members of Parliament and Sir George Jessel had become the first government minister in 1871.[80] Later, Nathaniel Rothschild would be raised
to the peerage.[81] The leaders of these acculturated members of the community tried to pull the Chief Rabbis towards greater religious liberalism
and ritual reform, and the relationship between these pressures and
the theology of the Chief Rabbis is a major subject of this book. Before
we begin to investigate it we will sketch out the lives and careers of the
Chief Rabbis since 1880 beginning with Nathan Adler's son, Hermann.

Hermann Adler was born in Hanover in 1839 and came to England
with his father in 1845.[82] He was educated at University College School

and was then at the yeshivah (rabbinical seminary) of Solomon Judah Rapoport in Prague. Rapoport was, like Nathan Adler, a master of both traditional learning and *Wissenschaft*. Hermann received his doctorate from the University of Leipzig in 1862 and his rabbinical diploma from Rapoport and two others in 1863.[83] He thus emerged with an education like his father's, combining *Wissenschaft*, traditional learning and secular scholarship. He returned to England in 1864 and was appointed Principal of Jews College, a post which he held until he was appointed minister of the newly founded Bayswater Synagogue in 1865.[84] He was appointed Delegate Chief Rabbi in 1879 and Chief Rabbi in 1891; he served until 1911.[85]

Adler's thirty-two years as Delegate Chief Rabbi and Chief Rabbi witnessed a number of major events within the Anglo-Jewish community. We have already mentioned the ritual reform conference of 1880. Another was convened in 1891–92 just after Hermann became Chief Rabbi.[86] In 1892 the Hampstead Synagogue was founded after extensive negotiations over the ritual and the minister.[87] In 1901–02 C.G. Montefiore and Lily Montagu founded the Jewish Religious Union, which by 1910 had evolved into the Liberal Jewish Synagogue, a more radical movement than West London and similar to American and German Reform Judaism, especially in its emphasis on ethics over ritual. It was the first British movement to incorporate the findings of modern scholarship on the origins of the Pentateuch, and the contemporary veneration for Greece and Rome, into its theology.[88] In 1910 Adler faced religious agitation in the ranks of his own ministers, from Joseph Hochman of the New West End.

As we have noted, 1880 marked the start of the great wave of Jewish immigration from eastern Europe, which increased the size of the Jewish population from 60,000 to 300,000 by 1914.[89] These new immigrants were much more traditional, on the whole, than the Jews already settled in England. They did not feel at home in the United Synagogue and formed their own small synagogues, or *hevrot*. In 1887 the wealthy but traditional Samuel Montagu united many of these congregations into the Federation of Synagogues. The Federation accepted the authority of the Chief Rabbi but had its own Chief Minister, which had the potential to create tension with the Chief Rabbinate, based as it was on centralised authority.[90] Much more militant were the founders of Machzike Hadath which from 1891 until 1904 waged a war against the Chief Rabbi over the issue of his standards of *shehitah*, the ritual slaughter of meat, which Machzike Hadath claimed were unacceptable.[91] In 1911 the rabbinical leaders of the most traditional Jews took a step forward by meeting in Leeds to discuss issues of mutual concern.[92]

Among the synagogues that remained outside a strong institutional framework, many irregularities, particularly over marriage and divorce, took place, to which Adler had to respond.[93] The new immigrants did not just bring with them religious fervour, they also brought political radicalism. Adler had to cope with socialism and potentially destabilising ideology of Zionism in the mid to late 1890s.[94]

Adler was as honoured by non-Jewish society as any rabbi in the diaspora – Edward VII called him 'my Chief Rabbi' and appointed him a Commander of the Royal Victorian Order – but by the time Adler died in 1911 he was conscious that despite his high standing in the wider world he was having difficulty managing his own community. In his final message to the community he called for a successor who could appeal to the East End and West End Jews.[95] It took two years of searching before the election of J.H. Hertz.

Joseph Herman Hertz was born in Slovakia on 25 September 1872.[96] His father was a teacher and Hertz's first instructor in Bible and Talmud.[97] The family left Europe for New York in about 1883.[98] In 1887 Hertz entered the newly established Jewish Theological Seminary founded by traditionalist rabbis who were sympathetic to *Wissenschaft*.[99] Hertz graduated with ordination in 1894.[100] The day before, he had received his PhD from Columbia for his thesis on the ethical system of James Martienau.[101] Hertz's first rabbinical position was at Adath Jeshurun in Syracuse, where he became a founder member of the Orthodox Union, and which he held until 1898.[102] In 1898 Hertz became minister of the Witwatersrand Old Hebrew Congregation in Johannesburg.[103] He established a reputation as a masterful preacher and a defender of traditional Judaism and was an outspoken supporter of the British in the Boer War.[104] By 1911 Hertz was missing the scholarly opportunities afforded by New York, despite his position as Professor of Philosophy at the University of the Transvaal, and returned to America to become rabbi of Congregation Orach Chayim, a strictly traditional German synagogue, which only allowed Sabbath-observant individuals to become members.[105]

Hertz's stay at Orach Chayim lasted only two years, because in 1913 Hertz was appointed Chief Rabbi, a position he held until his death 33 years later.[106] During his time as a religious leader of Empire Jewry, Hertz saw two World Wars, the Balfour Declaration and the rise of the Nazis. He led the attack on the proposed calendar reform at the League of Nations which would have led to the Sabbath moving through the week, toured the Empire to inspect the congregations under his authority, published volumes of sermons, addresses and studies, compiled the

Book of Jewish Thoughts, edited his famous *Pentateuch and Haftorahs* and *Authorised Daily Prayer Book*.[107] Within the United Synagogue, agitation for reforms continued and Hertz got on very badly with his foremost lay leader, Sir Robert Waley Cohen. The Liberal Jewish movement continued to grow and its synagogues began to demand recognition from the Chief Rabbi so they could appoint marriage secretaries. The highly traditional also increased in number and confidence, and one group established their own synagogue organisation, the Adath Yisroel in 1926.[108] Weakened by the deaths of his wife and one of his sons, his long-running battles with Waley Cohen and the stresses brought on by the Second World War, Hertz died on 14 January 1946.[109] Dayan H.M. Lazarus was appointed Deputy for the Chief Rabbi until a successor could be appointed.[110] The Chief Rabbi who took office in 1948 was Israel Brodie.

Israel Brodie was born in Newcastle in 1895 the son of Lithuanian immigrants from distinguished rabbinical families.[111] He attended school in Newcastle and had private tuition in Talmud.[112] In 1912 he entered Jews' College, led by the *Wissenschaft* scholar, Adolf Buchler. He took his BA in Hebrew, Syriac and Arabic in 1915 and proceeded to Oxford where he started a BLitt, which he completed after service as an army chaplain in the First World War.[113] In 1923 Hertz awarded Brodie the rabbinical diploma and he left to be rabbi of the Melbourne Hebrew Congregation, Australia. In 1937 he returned to England to undertake a DPhil. at Oxford and teach at Jews' College.[114] He was offered a seat on the London Beth Din in 1939, but turned it down to take a post with the Board of Deputies.[115] However, he was soon conscripted to serve as an army chaplain. He joined the British Expeditionary Force and was evacuated from Dunkirk leaving his DPhil. notes behind. In 1944 he became Senior Chaplain to the Forces and at the end of the War he returned to his duties at Jews' College.[116] When Hertz died Brodie was the obvious choice to succeed; he was a fine preacher, English born, a product of Oxford as well as Jews' College, he had experience in the Empire and had served in two World Wars. He seemed the perfect candidate, but in case he was not, Waley Cohen ensured that the appointment of the new Chief Rabbi would terminate on his seventieth birthday.[117] Two religious controversies marked Brodie's Chief Rabbinate. In 1948 there was a fresh dispute with the Liberal Jewish Synagogue over marriage registration. The Jacobs Affair, a controversy over the origin of the Pentateuch, dominated the years 1959 to 1964 and the wounds were still raw in 1965 when Brodie retired and the search began for a successor.

It took two years and several attempts before Sir Isaac Wolfson, the President of the United Synagogue chose Immanuel Jakobovits. Jakobovits was born in Germany into a rabbinical family in 1921.[118] His father, Dr Julius Jakobovits was the rabbi of Konigsberg's and then Berlin's traditional synagogue.[119] In 1936 Jakobovits came to London and was soon joined by his father, who was appointed a dayyan of the London Beth Din. He was educated at the Etz Chayim yeshivah in London under traditional teachers, who ordained him a rabbi, and at Jews' College, where he received his BA in Semitics and his ministerial diploma. In 1942 he was appointed Minister of Brondesbury Synagogue, moving to South East London Synagogue in 1944. In 1947 he was appointed the minister of the Great Synagogue as the post was finally divorced from the office of Chief Rabbi.[120] In 1949 Jakobovits became Chief Rabbi of Ireland and in 1959 the founding rabbi of the Fifth Avenue Synagogue in Manhattan. He returned to London as Chief Rabbi in 1967.[121] Jakobovits was appointed to help heal the rifts in the community caused by the Jacobs Affair and we will examine his early attempts to address the problems it threw up before we close our study.

Notes

1 For a good overview of Jewish religious development from the Second Temple period to modern times see N. De Lange, *An introduction to Judaism* (Cambridge 2000).
2 J. Frankel, 'Assimilation and the Jews in nineteenth-century Europe' in Frankel and Zipperstein (ed) *Assimilation and community* (Cambridge 1992), 18; D. Ellenson, *Rabbi Esriel Hildesheimer and the creation of a modern Jewish orthodoxy* (Tuscaloosa, Alabama 1990), 8.
3 Ellenson, *Hildesheimer* 8.
4 Frankel, 'Assimilation and the Jews' in Frankel and Zipperstein (ed) *Assimilation and* community, 18.
5 There were those who questioned Maimonides' Principles of Faith, and Yemenite Jews never accepted the *Shulhan Arukh*, but a consensus in Europe did accept them. .
6 For a fuller analysis of this phenomenon see, for example, J. Katz, 'Orthodoxy in historical perspective' in P.Y. Medding (ed) *Studies in contemporary Jewry* (Bloomington, Indiana 1986), II: 3–17.
7 Ibid., 19. To declare that there should be no change was itself a change, as we shall see.
8 Ibid., 21–72.
9 For more detail see T. Endelman, *The Jews of Britain, 1656 to 2000* (Berkeley 2002), 15–30. In addition to this work, and G. Alderman, *Modern British Jewry* (Oxford 1992), the following studies are also important: D.

Cesarani (ed), *The making of modern Anglo-Jewry* (Oxford 1990); V.D. Lipman, *A history of the Jews of Britain since 1858* (Leicester 1990); C. Roth, *A history of Jews in England* (Oxford 1964); W.D. Rubinstein, *A history of the Jews in the English-speaking world: Great Britain* (London 1996).

10 Endelman, *Jews of Britain*, 31.

11 A. Newman, *The United Synagogue, 1870–1970* (London 1977), 1.

12 Ibid., 153.

13 Endelman, *Jews of Britain*, 51, 41.

14 Ibid., 51–52.

15 A. Barnett, *The Western Synagogue through two centuries (1761–1961)* (London 1961), 22.

16 Endelman, *Jews of Britain*, 54.

17 Ibid.

18 H.A. Simons, *Forty years a Chief Rabbi: the life and times of Solomon Hirschell* (London 1980), 21, 25.

19 Endelman, *Jews of Britain*, 57.

20 T. Endelman, *The Jews of Georgian England* (Philadelphia 1979), 121.

21 D.B. Ruderman, *Jewish Enlightenment in an English key* (Princeton 2000), 5–6.

22 Ibid., 55.

23 Simons, *Hirschell*, 21.

24 Endelman, *Jews of Britain*, 101.

25 Ibid., 102–3.

26 Simons, *Hirschell*, 49.

27 Ibid., 51, 66–67.

28 Ibid., 110–111.

29 Ibid., 111.

30 Ibid.

31 M. Persoff, *Faith against reason: religious reform and the British Chief Rabbinate, 1840–1990* (London 2008), 26.

32 Simons, *Hirschell*, 111–112.

33 D. Englander, 'Anglicized not Anglican: Jews and Judaism in Victorian Britain' in Parsons (ed), *Religion in Victorian Britain, I: Traditions* (Manchester 1988), 256.

34 Simons, *Hirschell*, 112.

35 Ibid.

36 Ibid., 113.

37 D.W. Marks, *Sermons* (London 1855), 18, 26–27.

38 S. Singer, *Orthodox Judaism in early Victorian London* (PhD Dissertation, Yeshiva University 1981), 78 .

39 Persoff claims that West London's neo-Karaite theology ensured its reforms were moderate – but as we shall see, this is to oversimplify; Persoff, *Faith against reason*, 97.

40 Marks, *Sermons*, 117.

41 G. Parsons, 'Reform, revival and realignment: the experience of Victorian Anglicanism' in Parsons (ed) *Religion in Victorian Britain* (Manchester 1988), 34. See D. Feldman, *Englishmen and Jews* (New Haven 1994), 62–65.

42 Englander, Anglicized not Anglican', 236; Singer, *Judaism in Victorian London*, 79.

43 M.A. Meyer, *Judaism within modernity* (Detroit 2001), 306.

44 Ibid., 307.

45 R. Liberles, 'The origins of the Jewish Reform movement in England' *AJS Review I* (1976), 121–150.

46 M. Joseph, 'The jubilee of political emancipation' *Transactions of the Jewish Historical Society of England* 6 (1912), 102. Meyer has discussed the relationship between tolerance for Jews and internal Jewish tolerance as a broader phenomenon: M.A. Meyer, 'Modernity as a crisis for the Jews' *Modern Judaism* 9:2 (May 1989), 155.

47 Simons, *Hirschell*, 96.

48 Ibid., 100.

49 C. Roth, 'Britain's three Chief Rabbis' in Jung (ed) *Jewish leaders* (Jerusalem 1953), 475.

50 Ibid., 479. There was no question of finding an English candidate for the post. England did not possess a community large or learned enough to produce men for the rabbinate, not did it have the educational infrastructure to train them. That is perhaps why one of Adler's early projects was Jews' College.

51 Ibid.

52 Ibid.

53 Ibid. *Netina lager* was published in *Torat Elohim* (Vilna 1875).

54 M. Breuer, trans. E. Petuchowski, *Modernity within tradition* (New York 1992), 186.

55 Persoff, *Faith against reason*, 62.

56 Simons, *Hirschell*, 100.

57 In the 1840s, at least, Adler did not oppose coercion in principle. He supported the Frankfurt rabbis who in 1842 wished to force a man to circumcise his son by threatening him with preventing him taking the *more Judaico*, which would mean that he would be unable to use secular courts: J. Katz, 'The changing position and outlook of halakhists in early modernity' in Landman (ed) *Scholars and scholarship in Jewish history* (New York 1990), 98.

58 N.M. Adler, *Solomon's judgement* (London 1854), 8.

59 Katz, 'Changing position and outlook of halakhists', 106.

60 B. Williams, *The making of Manchester Jewry* (Manchester 1976), 188, 211–217, 234–236, 241–247, 249–250. See also Persoff, *Faith against reason*, 28–9, for an account of Adler's refusal to allow a member of the West London Synagogue, Benjamin Elkin, to be buried in the Great Synagogue cemetery by the usual officiant. Adler wanted him to be buried

by the sexton. On the other hand, Adler did allow marriages between West London and Great Synagogue families (Persoff, *Faith against reason*, 33–34).

61 N.M. Adler, *Laws and regulations for all the synagogues in the British Empire* (London 1847), iii–iv. A religious census in 1851 found that only 16% of the Jewish community attended Sabbath services, compared to 40.5% of the Christian population; Englander, 'Anglicized not Anglican', 255.

62 E.C. Black, 'The Anglicization of orthodoxy: the Adlers, father and son' in Malino and Sorkin (ed) *From east and west* (Oxford 1990), 302.

63 Persoff, *Faith against reason*, 94.

64 J. Katz, *Divine law in human hands* (Jerusalem 1998), 331.

65 M.B. Shapiro, 'A response to Samuel C. Heilman's "How did fundamentalism manage to infiltrate contemporary orthodoxy?"' *Contemporary Jewry* (25 2005), 277.

66 N.M. Adler, *Laws and regulations for all the synagogues in the British Empire* (London 1847), 16, 19.

67 Ibid., 8, 9.

68 Ibid., iv.

69 S. Heilman, 'The many faces of orthodoxy, part 1' *Modern Judaism* 2:1 (February 1982), 39.

70 Meyer, *Judaism within modernity*, 308; S. Singer *The authorised daily prayer book* (London 1891), vii.

71 In this study whenever expressions such as 'essentials', 'matters of lesser importance', 'authentic Judaism' etc. are used, they describe the views of the figure being discussed, and are not an attempt to set out objective judgements or standards.

72 *British Weekly* (5, 12, 19, 26 November 1886).

73 Adler, *Laws and regulations*, 6.

74 Roth, 'Chief Rabbis', 482–483.

75 Newman, *United Synagogue*, 216.

76 Ibid., 89.

77 Endelman, *Jews of Britain*, 119.

78 The structures of the community, including Jews' College, the Beth Din and the United Synagogue are amplified below. In particular the chapters on Hermann Adler go into further detail about his father's incumbency.

79 T. Endelman, *Radical assimilation in English Jewish history, 1656–1945* (Bloomington, Indiana 1990), 86.

80 Ibid., 164.

81 Endelman, *Jews of Britain*, 164.

82 I. Finestein, *Anglo-Jewry in changing times* (London 1999), 215.

83 Roth, 'Chief Rabbis', 483.

84 Ibid.

85 Ibid., 484–485.

86 J. Jung, *Champions of orthodoxy* (London 1974), 25–26.

87 Finestein, *Changing times*, 247.

88 Meyer, *Judaism within modernity*, 313; Endelman, *Jews of Britain*, 168–169.

89 Finestein, *Changing times*, 242. For an overview of this period of Jewish immigration see L.P. Gartner, *The Jewish immigrant in England, 1870–1914* (London 1973). See also Feldman, *Englishmen and Jews*.

90 Endelman, *Jews of Britain*, 177. See G. Alderman, *The Federation of Synagogues, 1887–1987* (London 1987) for an account of the Federation, and D. Gutwein, *The divided elite* (Leiden 1992) for a contrasting view.

91 Endelman, *Jews of Britain*, 179. B. Homa documented the Machzike Hadath in his highly partial *A fortress in Anglo-Jewry* (London 1953). An alternative view of the dispute can be found in A.M. Hyamson, *The London Board for Shechita, 1804–1954* (London 1954).

92 Finestein, *Changing times*, 245.

93 Ibid., 219.

94 Roth, 'Chief Rabbis', 485. See W.J. Fishman, *East End Jewish radicals, 1875–1914* (London 1975).

95 Finestein, *Changing times*, 245.

96 E. Levine, 'Memoir' in Epstein (ed) *Joseph Herman Hertz, 1871–1946: In Memoriam* (London 1947), 1.

97 M. Freud Kandel, 'The theological background of Dr Joseph H. Hertz' *Le'eyla* 48 (2000), 25; S.M. Lehrman, 'Joseph Herman Hertz' in Gottlieb (ed) *Essays and addresses in memory of JH Hertz* (London 1948), 33.

98 Ibid.

99 R.E. Fierstein, *A different spirit: the Jewish Theological Seminary of America, 1886–1902* (New York 1990), 73.

100 Ibid., 95. Freud Kandel has written that Hertz received a basic ordination from the Seminary, but a higher diploma, the *hattarat horaah* from rabbis from outside the Seminary (Freud Kandel, 'Hertz's theological background', 32.) This is gleaned from a letter sent by Hertz to J. Goldreich in 1898 in which he states that he was a graduate of the Jewish Theological Seminary and that he received his *hattarat horaah* from six rabbis. However, copies of Hertz' ordination and *hattarat horaah* certificates in Southampton University Library (MS 175/70/3) show that both were granted under the auspices of the Jewish Theological Seminary; the former was signed by Joseph Blumenthal, the President of the Board and Sabato Morais, the President of the Faculty, and the latter by six rabbis, most of whom were associated with the Seminary (including Morais) but some of whom were not.

101 Levine, 'Memoir', 2.

102 I. Epstein (ed) *Joseph Herman Hertz, 1871–1946: In Memoriam* (London 1947), 74; M.Davis, *The emergence of Conservative Judaism* (Philadelphia 1963), 315.

103 Epstein, *Hertz*, 74.

104 Levine, 'Memoir', 3–4.

105 Hertz papers in Southampton University Library, 44/6; Epstein, *Hertz*, 74; Levine, 'Memoir', 4.
106 Epstein, *Hertz*, 74.
107 Levine, 'Memoir', passim.
108 Endelman, *Jews of Britain*, 221.
109 Levine, 'Memoir', 30.
110 Chief Rabbinate Papers, London Metropolitan Archives (CRP LMA), ACC/2172/15/2039.
111 J.M. Shaftesley, 'A biographical sketch' in H.J. Zimmels, J. Rabbinowitz and I. Finestein (ed) *Essays presented to Chief Rabbi Israel Brodie on the occasion of his seventieth birthday* (London 1967), xvi.
112 Ibid., xvii.
113 Ibid., xix.
114 Ibid., xx, xxiv.
115 CRP LMA, ACC/ 2172.15/1554.
116 Shaftesley, 'Biographical sketch', xxiv, xxvi.
117 Ibid., xxix.
118 M. Persoff, *Immanuel Jakobovits* (London 2002), 3.
119 Ibid., 5, 8.
120 Ibid., 12–13.
121 Ibid., 118.

Chapter 3

Jewish religious responses to modernity: a typology

THIS BOOK ARGUES that the Chief Rabbis' response to modernity should be viewed in the context of Jewish religious responses that emerged following the Enlightenment and Emancipation, some of which I have already mentioned. I will sketch out a possible typology of those responses, so that we can place the Chief Rabbis in that context. This typology does not presume to be a final scheme, nor does it seek to deny the massive variety of responses, many of which it does not include explicitly. It merely attempts to give the main flags around which Jews rallied, to a greater or lesser extent. I must also stress that this typology is merely my attempt to organise in a helpful way the many complex aspects of individuals' thought.

Those individuals did not see themselves as belonging to the groups I place them in; they had other labels for the parties they belonged to, labels which I have tried to avoid (as I have mentioned), because their imprecision and shifting meanings can obscure the important issues. Still less did the historical actors I discuss act in any sense because they belonged to the groups I divide them into. These groupings are descriptive, that is, people's thought and behaviour has led me to place them in different parts of the typology, not the other way around. I do not claim that the typology in itself explains why people behaved in certain ways. No one I discuss said 'I am a member of the scientific branch of the acknowledgement school', for example, 'and therefore I will hold such a view about such an issue'. I do argue, however, that these groupings organise individuals and movements in such a way that we can see more clearly what their reasons were.

Peter Berger constructed a typology of general religious responses to modernity in the 1960s, based around two ideal types: 'accommodators', who believed that peace could be made between tradition and modernity, and 'resistors' who rejected modernity as wholly negative.[1] In the 1970s Heilman developed the ideas of synthesis and nihilation to analyse the Jewish response to modernity. Synthesis seeks to make

Table 1 Four responses to modernity

Antipathy	Modernity is rejected as a threat to authentic Judaism
Acknowledgement	Modernity has positive aspects but the essentials of tradition must be retained
Adaptation	Modernity has much to teach and Judaism must be adapted to take account of those lessons
Acceptance	Modernity, flowing from Enlightenment and leading to Emancipation is to replace Judaism

harmonious the old and the new, while nihilation blocks out one or the other as much as possible.[2] Thus, the spectrum of the Jewish religious response to modernity can be seen as a continuum, with two nihilistic positions at each end, one abjuring modernity, and the other, tradition, while in the middle is an attempt to synthesise the two. The typology presented here follows from Berger's basic distinction and Heilman's spectrum and develops them further. It can be argued that there were four principal Jewish religious responses to the challenges and opportunities of modernity. I call these responses antipathy, acknowledgement, adaptation and acceptance.

The antipathy school denounced modernity, especially the Enlightenment and including Emancipation.[3] It is best summed up in the dictum of the German-born leader of Hungarian Jewry, Moses Sofer (1763–1839) who declared, quoting the Mishnah but reinterpreting it homiletically, *hadash asur min hatorah bekol makom* Everything new is forbidden by the Torah under all circumstances'.[4] Modernity was seen as a threat to Judaism so, as the physical ghetto walls were pulled down, the spiritual and intellectual walls were to be strengthened. This school did not believe that Judaism could withstand the onslaught of modernity, which therefore had to be kept out; there could be no accommodation or concession to modernity. As Ellenson has argued, Sofer feared that any concession to modernity would weaken the tradition fatally and therefore had to be resisted.[5] Katz contends that therefore Sofer placed increasing emphasis on tradition itself as a value.[6]

This rejection of all outside influences and of all halakhic development was actually a departure from Jewish tradition, which had previously embraced aspects of the non-Jewish world perceived as valuable, from Greek philosophy to Arabic poetry, and which had always developed organically, both in terms of *halakha* and philosophy.[7] As Heilman notes, while fundamentalisms claim that 'tradition' is pristine and unchanging, and must be defended against any deviation, but in fact this approach is itself a modern development which seeks to alter the tradition as it has been received, though its proponents deny it.[8] Moses Sofer's ethical will is an example of this new attitude. He warned his descendants: 'never engage in corruptible partnership with those fond of innovations . . . be warned not to change your Jewish names, speech and clothing . . . the order of prayer and synagogue shall remain forever as it has been up to now, and no one may presume to change anything'.[9] It is an irony that this insistence on no change was, itself, a change. Another example of this school's approach is the statement issued by a Hungarian conference of rabbinical followers of Sofer in 1866, which ruled that it was forbidden to preach or hear a sermon in a non-Jewish language, to erect a synagogue with a tower, for rabbis or cantors to wear clerical robes, for a choir to sing during the service or for a synagogue to have an organ, even if it was not played on the Sabbath. Indeed, they ruled that it was forbidden to change any custom or practice of the synagogue.[10]

The next group along the spectrum of traditionalism was the acknowledgement school, which was happy to acknowledge the positive aspects of modernity and incorporate them in their *weltanschauung*. This is the school to which the Chief Rabbis belonged, and which we will be examining in the greatest detail, so we will lay out its main features last.

The third group was the adaptation school. Members of this school possessed a very positive attitude towards modernity. They welcomed the Emancipation as an opportunity for Jews to play a full and active part with their non-Jewish fellow citizens in building a better society for all. This was to be combined with an effort to take full advantage of the benefits brought by the Enlightenment, to place society on a rational and scientific basis. Eisen argues that Judaism's particularism was identified as a 'barrier to acceptance' and attempts were made to minimise it.[11] That is why the German Reform leader Abraham Geiger (1810–74) said, 'in civic affairs [Jews] . . . will join with other elements and merge into the national life'.[12] Members of the adaptation school, such as Geiger, spoke about reforming Judaism on the basis of scientific explorations of its origins and development; they were thus among the leading proponents of the scientific study of Judaism, the *Wissenschaft des Judentums*.[13] This approach included the acceptance that the Pentateuch was a human and composite document, and that Jewish Law had changed and could continue to change to meet the demands of the time.[14]

For example, Geiger argued that the Pharisees had developed the laws of animal slaughter, and had set up their 'new halakha' in place of the Saducees' 'old halakha'.[15] However, as Heschel suggests, Geiger's contention that the Pharisees were in some sense 'liberals' attempting to reform the *halakhah* of the Sadducees was to a large extent an attempt to justify reforms in his own day.[16] For, as Altmann pointed out, although Geiger and others spoke of looking into the Jewish past to determine what was essential and what was expendable in Judaism, in fact they sought to adapt Judaism to contemporary, nineteenth-century religious and ethical thought, in a way essentially unconcerned with history.[17] As one of Geiger's colleagues, Samuel Holdheim (1806–60) wrote in 1847, 'the Talmud speaks with the ideology of its own time, and for that time it was right. I speak from the higher ideology of my time, and for this age I am right'.[18] Yet the leaders of this school were absolutely committed to preserving Judaism, albeit a changed and reformed Judaism, which they regarded as a positive spiritual force in the world. As Geiger put it, 'Israel is endowed with a vitality that ensures its survival . . . Israel's vitality has always consisted in the endeavour to fight for that which is Divine'.[19]

The final response belonged to the acceptance school, based around the children and disciples of Moses Mendelssohn. Mendelssohn welcomed the prospect of Emancipation warmly and sought to show that the doctrines of Judaism could be deduced from reason, even though the laws could only have come from Revelation. As he wrote, 'Blessed be the Lord who gave us the Tora of Truth. We have no principles that are contrary to, or above, reason. Thank God we add to natural religion nothing except commandments, statutes, and righteous ordinances'.[20] As Sorkin has written, through this combination Mendelssohn offered a Judaism that both revealed and was wholly rational'.[21] Mendelssohn was both a leading light both in European Enlightenment and an inspiration for the *Haskalah*.[22] Mendelssohn remained a believing and observant Jew, but his followers diverged from his path. They adopted Mendelssohn's love of the Enlightenment, but not his loyalty to Jewish tradition, and placed great emphasis on the winning of Emancipation. They accepted the ideologies brought by modernity to the exclusion of Judaism. Thus, famously, all of Mendelssohn's grandchildren died Christians. His leading disciple, David Friedlaender proposed the creation of a new religion of reason to replace both Judaism and Christianity, and only when he was rebuffed by the Christian authorities did he try to reform Judaism, removing ceremonial laws, leaving only the ethical content.[23]

All these responses are worthy of study, but they are not the focus of this book, which confines itself to the group to which the Chief Rabbis belonged, the acknowledgement school, bringing in other schools by way of comparison. The acknowledgement school is as complex as any other of the four schools, but (as Meyer, Liberles and Ellenson have noted) it has been neglected by historians.[24] Mordechai Breuer expressed it with great clarity when he wrote that this group is characterised by a desire to 'appropriate the positive values and acceptable norms of European culture and society. [It] was not only concerned with somehow coming to terms with modernity and possibly averting its dangers but also with internalising modernity and putting it in the service of traditional Judaism when this seemed beneficial'.[25] Samuel Heilman has characterised its post-War form as believing that 'much in popular culture and contemporary society was not a source of defilement, but rather a fertile environment for bringing ancient Jewish traditions and values into engagement with modernity . . . all the while maintaining fidelity to Jewish law and observance'.[26]

Many Jewish leaders, thinkers, rabbis and scholars adopted this programme. All Jews who valued tradition over modernity and were committed to preserving all of it essentials, while engaging with the positive aspects of modernity, belonged to the acknowledgement group. All members of the group affirmed the binding nature of *halakhah*, though not all members held that the Pentateuch was given on Sinai.[27] Their upholding of Jewish Law despite their views on the Pentateuch separated them from the adaptation school, just as their acceptance that there were valuable aspects of modernity placed them apart from the antipathy school.

However, as Mordecai M. Kaplan pointed out as early as 1934, the difference of opinion over the origin of the Pentateuch was an absolute dividing line within the acknowledgement school and within the Jewish religious response to modernity as a whole.[28] Those from the antipathy school may have disagreed with much of what members of the acknowledgement school thought, but they did not seek to delegitimise them entirely if they continued to hold to the traditional belief in the origin of the Pentateuch. Conversely, any member of the acknowledgement school who considered the Pentateuch a composite work was not only considered outside the bounds of acceptability by those in the antipathy school, but also by those in the acknowledgement school who maintained the traditional belief. This contention, that a gulf existed between what in this typology are called the traditionalist and non-traditionalist members of the acknowledge school is central to understanding the crisis with which this study ends, the Jacobs Affair.

Before we move on, it is worth adding a note on the use of the word 'traditional' in this study. In the context of the typology that is presented here, the terms 'traditional' and 'non-traditional' are simply shorthand for particular approaches to the Pentateuch. However, when I am not dealing with the typology, I use 'traditional' in a broader sense, not restricted to this one issue. When individuals or movements are described here as more or less traditional, outside discussions of the typology, it will be to make a statement about a whole range of the beliefs and behaviour, and indeed outlook. The Jews of Machzike Hadath will be called 'traditional', for example, and it is true that at least the vast majority of them believed the Pentateuch was given on Sinai, but the word, in that instance, will be used as shorthand for their highly observant and unacculturated lifestyle as much as their theology.

Those who held modern views on the Pentateuch, yet remained committed to the *halakhah* – such as Louis Jacobs, but also men like Morris Joseph, Joseph Hockman and Herbert Loewe – were as much part of the acknowledgement school as were the Chief Rabbis, there was a chasm within this school because because of differing attitudes to the Pentateuch. Although they all shared the same general response to modernity, wishing to acknowledge it, the Chief Rabbis did not regard these other figures as ideological allies. There is therefore no need to account for Jacobs' treatment under Brodie by positing a 'move to the right' among the Chief Rabbis, because in acting as he did Brodie was following the approach of his predecessors. The undue lack of emphasis by historians on the importance of individuals' attitude to the Pentateuch is not restricted to Britain and the Jacobs Affair; Ellenson, for example, does the same when analysing the Berlin member of the acknowledgement school, Michael Sachs, as I discuss later.[29] I argue that the entire Jewish religious response to modernity is divided in two, down the centre of the acknowledgement school, over the issue of the Pentateuch. Traditionalists on that issue were accepted as within the boundaries of acceptability even by those of much greater traditionalism, while anyone else was not. A greater stress on theology in general, and on the question of the authorship of the Pentateuch in particular, can improve our understanding of Jewish religious history since the advent of modernity, in Britain and elsewhere.

Aside from the issue of the Pentateuch, the acknowledgement group is highly complex because there were many different strands within the school. These disagreed with each other about what were the best aspects of modernity and what were the essentials of the tradition. Some differences concerned theology, but equally important were the different levels of power that leaders enjoyed and the organisational arrangements they regarded as appropriate, either pragmatically or as a matter of ideology. The theology of the different groups within the acknowledgement school expressed what they believed in theory; power and organisation determined how they were able to carry those ideas into practice. There was some overlap in individual cases, as I shall point out, but they are sufficiently distinct to remain useful sub-categories

The first axis is theology, and the three main theological approaches can be identified as romantic, scientific and aesthetic. The romantics, whom I have so named because of the influence of German Romanticism on their thinking, were led by S.R. Hirsch. He took the view that the divine could be found anywhere, including in non-Jewish sources. Hirsch stated unequivocally that if the Jewish scholars of the past had been able 'they would quickly have greeted what was true and good in general culture as something closely akin to the Jewish outlook, and they would have been the first to prepare a home for it in their circle'.[30] This led to his philosophy of *Torah im derekh erets* – which advocated the union of Jewish and Western thought into a harmonious whole.

The scientific group embraced *Wissenschaft des Judentums* as the best way to understand Jewish tradition and they sought to incorporate its methods and findings in their modes of study. It was amongst those who associated with this group that the issue of the authorship of the Pentateuch was most pressing, and some – like Frankel, Morais, Kohut, Hildesheimer, Hoffman, Weinberg and the Chief Rabbis – were advocates of *Wissenschaft* but also traditionalists on the Pentateuch. Others within the acknowledgement school, for example Louis Ginzberg and Louis Jacobs, did accept modern views on the Pentateuch.

The aesthetic approach was common to all western European communities and in North America, but was most developed in France, where demands for a Westernised, decorous service were the strongest. As Berkovitz observed, in France pressure for religious reform concentrated on means to improve the aesthetics of Jewish life.[31] This caused the French rabbinate to push the bounds of tradition very far in an attempt to satisfy the demands they faced, for example to allow an organ to be played on the Sabbath.[32] This temporarily placed them outside of the bounds of acceptability for many, but not on a permanent basis. In general, only a non-traditional approach to the Pentateuch could do that (although, as we have seen, the West London was regarded as beyond the pale because of its views on the Oral Law). An approach connected to the aestheticism of France took dominant form in North America. This did not arise from any thought-out ideological analysis; indeed North American Judaism, especially that practised in many United Synagogue of America congregations, was known for its lack of ideology. This approach comprised a desire to maintain 'tradition' but not at the expense of being 'thoroughly American, which meant late Friday services, a mixed choir and possibly an organ, decorum, an English sermon and family pews, which were combined with a traditional, predominantly Hebrew service.'[33] Followers of this approach sought a compromise that connected them to tradition but did not make them feel threatened by associating them with forms alien to American mores. This desire for unthreatening traditionalism can be thought of as nostalgic.

The second axis is power and is closely connected to the third axis, organisation. The authority of the religious leaders of the acknowledge-ment school varied depending on local conditions, including organisa-tion structures. First, individuals mould organisations and then they are moulded by them, so the lines of cause and effect between individuals, organisations and their context are very complex. Although no commu-nity can be understood as falling fully and exclusively within a single category, different approaches can be identified as dominant in particu-lar communities. Hirsch's community in Frankfurt was a small, strong community in which he and his successors had very considerable reli-gious control. It can be called a nuclear community, highly disciplined but numerically limited. This came about because Hirsch developed his community from a vanguard of a small number of highly commit-ted individuals, who broke all ties with other Jewish groups in order to maintain absolute charge over their religious standards, following the policy of *Austritt*. As Katz argues, for Hirsch, authentic Judaism might only possess minority appeal, but quality was far more important than quantity.[34] This approach was adopted by only a minority of even traditional Jews. Most traditional Jews belonged to a wider commu-nity that encompassed all denominations with separate synagogues serving each, the *Grossgemeinde*. The traditional groups within the *Grossgemeinde* were also small and highly observant, nuclear (even though they were not vanguard) communities. Rather they were co-operative, not rejecting links with other Jews that did not involve what they regarded as theological compromise. In total, traditionalist Jews in Germany comprised only 10–12% of the Jewish population.

In France and Britain, traditional (in the broader, rather than the narrow typological sense) religious leadership enjoyed the institutional allegiance of most Jews. In France, however, the power of the rabbis was heavily constrained by a powerful lay leadership. In Britain the Chief Rabbis also enjoyed a high level of nominal allegiance, which they fostered by an expansive approach, which sought to include as many as possible within the traditional community, by making the demands of Jewish Law as gentle as they could without breaking that Law. Hildesheimer's Berlin community was perforce nuclear but he took an expansive approach. Some of his students followed Hirsch and the vanguard model; others associated with the *Grossgemeinde* and were co-operative.

In the USA, organisations were much looser than in Europe. For many years most Jewish communities lacked rabbis, which made rabbinic control difficult to impose when rabbis did arrive; hence the failure to establish a successful Chief Rabbi of New York in the late nineteenth century. Englander has ascribed this resistance to centralised authority to the strength of Christian Congregationalists in the USA.[35] This context meant that American congregations within the acknowledgement school with high standards, which they did not want to compromise, could choose to remain unaffiliated and become nuclear-vanguard communities. If they desired to join with other congregations they could form only loose unions, the Orthodox Union and the United Synagogue of America, which made limited, sometimes very limited, demands on the synagogues that affiliated. They were loose confederations where power was driven centrifugally, away from the centre to the individual synagogues. These power and organisational structures help to explain the disparities between the theological statements of some leaders of the acknowledgement school and the actual practices of the communities they presided over. They also do much to explain the actions of the Chief Rabbis, and their effects.

One final point about the acknowledgement school remains to be made. The group claimed to be upholding tradition, and in the case of those members who accepted the Divine origin of the Pentateuch, their claim was accepted even by the antipathy school. This provokes an insight into the evolving nature of Jewish tradition. Members of the acknowledgement school accepted some views not in keeping with tradition – for example some asserted the existence of two authors of Isaiah and the late dating of some psalms – but they were not ostracised

Table 2 Intellectual and sociological streams within the acknowledgement school[36]

Theology	
Romantic	Hirsch; *Torah im derekh erets*
Scientific	Hildesheimer and others; *Wissenschaft*
Aesthetic	France; bringing Jewish ritual up to the standards of Western beauty
Nostalgic	USA; desire to preserve a familiar Judaism, less concern with theology
Power	
Nuclear	Germany; small, strong communities with powerful religious leadership
Constrained	France; central religious power in theory but overwhelmed by other factors
Hegemonic	Britain; religious leaders with substantial control and adherence
Centrifugal	USA; little central religious control and great congregational autonomy

for holding such views. How could they be considered traditional if they departed from established traditions? The answer seems to be that, when new ideas come along the traditional community comes to a consensus on them. They can be accepted more or less universally, although this is rare. They can be rejected as wholly unacceptable, for example Higher Criticism of the Pentateuch.

However, there is a third option: new ideas, such as the dual authorship of Isaiah, can be regarded as acceptable even if they are not widely adopted. In this way the tradition continues to develop and take on new ideas. The acknowledgement school amended the tradition as well as passing it on. This is part of what makes the acknowledgement school so fascinating, and the Chief Rabbis as part of that group so interesting and important to understand.

Notes

1 P. Berger, 'A sociological view of the secularization of theology' *Journal for the Scientific Study of Religion* 6:1 (1967), 3–16.
2 S. Heilman, 'Constructing orthodoxy' in Robbins and Anthony (ed) *In gods we trust* (New Brunswick, New Jersey 1981), 150–151.
3 Heilman calls this group 'rejectionist': S. Heilman, 'The many faces of orthodoxy, part 1' *Modern Judaism* 2:1 (February 1982), 26–27.
4 In context (Orlah 3:9) the Mishnah is referring to when new grain may be eaten.
5 D.Ellenson, *Rabbi Esriel Hildesheimer* (Tuscaloosa 1990), 19. The view of the dangerous nature of modernity was exacerbated by the speed with which it arrived in the Jewish world, an aspect which Meyer has noted: M.A. Meyer, 'Modernity as a crisis for the Jews' *Modern Judaism* 9:2 (May 1989), 154.
6 J. Katz, 'Religion as a uniting and dividing force' in Katz (ed) *The role of religion in modern Jewish history* (Cambridge, Massachusetts 1975), 11 .
7 Examples of halakhic development include Rabbeinu Gershom's ending of polygamy around the year 1000, the ending among Ashkenazi Jews of the practice of *yibum* (a man marrying his brother's childless widow) and the banning of the consumption of legumes on Passover.
8 S.C. Heilman, 'How did fundamentalism manage to infiltrate contemporary orthodoxy?' *Contemporary Jewry* (2005), 258. Lynn Davidman, who uses Berger's accommodators-versus-resistors typology in her comparative analysis of modern Orthodoxy and Lubavitch in the late twentieth century, made a similar point when she wrote 'religious traditions . . . respond to [modernity's] . . . pressures and continue to exist, re-form and even thrive in modern societies.' L. Davidman, 'Accomodation and resistance to modernity' *Sociological Analysis* 51/1 (Spring 1990), 37.
9 W.G. Plaut, *The rise of Reform Judaism* (New York 1963), 256–257.

10 Ellenson, *Hildesheimer*, 47–48. Aaron Schreiber has argued persuasively that Moses Sofer's attitude to modernity was more nuanced than is often thought and that the uncompromising stance attributed to him owed as much to some of his disciples' thought (such as those at the 1866 conference) as it did to Sofer's. A.M. Schreiber, 'The Hatam Sofer's nuanced attitude towards secular learning, *maskilim* and reformers' *Torah u-Madda Journal* 11 (2002–2003), 123–173.

11 A. Eisen, 'Theology, sociology and ideology: Jewish thought in America, 1925–1955' *Modern Judaism* 2:1 (February 1982), 92.

12 M.A. Meyer and W. G. Plaut (ed) *The Reform Judaism reader* (New York 2001), 8.

13 Ibid., 7.

14 S. Heschel, *Abraham Geiger and the Jewish Jesus* (Chicago 1998), 33, 37, 104.

15 Ibid., 43, 92.

16 Ibid., 104.

17 A. Altmann, *Essays in Jewish intellectual history* (Hanover, New Hampshire 1981), 266.

18 Meyer and Plaut, *Reform Judaism reader*, 13.

19 Ibid., 9.

20 A. Altmann, *Moses Mendelssohn, a biographical study* (London 1998), 249, 376.

21 D. Sorkin, 'The case for comparison: Moses Mendelssohn and the religious enlightenment' *Modern Judaism* 14:2 (May 1994), 128.

22 Mendelssohn's exact relationship to the *Haskalah* is disputed; see D.B. Ruderman, *Jewish Enlightenment in an English key* (Princeton 2000), 14.

23 H.M. Graupe, *Rise of modern Judaism* (Huntington, NY 1979) 107–108.

24 D. Ellenson, *After Emancipation* (Cincinnati 2004), 194. Meyer Liberles and Ellenson noted that while Hirschian neo-orthodoxy is well covered, and the Reform movement had received extensive attention, the Positive-Historical school of Sachs, Mannheimer and Joel 'has lain almost fallow'. Heilman did discuss the school and identified some members in two articles, calling them 'syncretists': Heilman, 'The many faces of orthodoxy, part 1', 23–52 and S. Heilman, 'The many faces of orthodoxy, part 2' *Modern Judaism* 2:2 (May 1982), 171–198.

25 M. Breuer, *Modernity within tradition* (New York 1992), 22.

26 Heilman, 'How did Fundamentalism infiltrate orthodoxy?', 261–262.

27 See S. Heilman, 'The many faces of orthodoxy, part 1', 30, where he argues that this group 'hold an ultimate loyalty to the *halakha*, the tradition and limit their modernity.'.

28 M.M. Kaplan, *Judaism as civilisation* (New York 1934), 126, 160.

29 Ellenson, *After Emancipation*, 221–222.

30 I. Grunfeld, *Judaism eternal* (London 1956), 207.

31 J.M. Berkovitz, *Rites and passages* (Philadelphia 2004), 192.

32 Ibid., 206.

33 M. Raphael, *Profiles in American Judaism* (San Francisco 1984), 90.

34 J. Katz, 'Sources of orthodox trends' in Katz (ed) *The role of religion in modern Jewish history* (Cambridge, Massachusetts 1975), 30.

35 Englander, 'Anglicized not Anglican', 238.

36 A full analysis of all the responses in this way is beyond the scope of this study, though it would be possible, particularly in the case of the adaptation school. For example, C.G. Montefiore's approach, which sought to incorporate Classical and Christian thought, could be seen as a radical form of Hirsch's romantic attitude, whereby non-Jewish wisdom is welcomed as containing spiritual truth. Geiger's programme was based on *Wissenschaft*, and was scientific. The form of Reform Judaism represented by Temple Emanuel in New York, with its emphasis on architecture and music, was in the aesthetic tradition, whereas Reconstructionism, which dispensed with a belief in God but nevertheless wanted to maintain Jewish practices, could be seen as based on nostalgic impulses.

Chapter 4

Intellectual context: theology and theologians

THIS BOOK SUGGESTS that the Chief Rabbis were members of the acknowledgement school, which contained a number of different theological currents: romantic, scientific, aesthetic and nostalgic. The Chief Rabbis were primarily members of the scientific stream, although – as they took conservative positions on certain matters, particularly the authorship of the Pentateuch – they were members of its traditional wing. However, the Chief Rabbis also adopted ideas from the romantic stream and thereby inhabited theological ground which some scholars have argued did not exist. In practice their ideologies were a synthesis of the approach of the *Wissenschaft des Judentums* scholar Zachariah Frankel, the more traditional exponent of *Wissenschaft*, Esriel Hildesheimer, and the romantic, *Torah im derekh erets* philosophy of S.R. Hirsch. Meirovich has argued that one could either be a follower of Hirsch and Hildesheimer on the one hand or of Frankel on the other, but not both.[1] But the Chief Rabbis were (not uncritical) followers of all three. They bridged the gaps that divided these schools of thought, for there were divisions between Hirsch and Hildesheimer as well as between them and Frankel. To make sense of this, we need to understand the *Wissenschaft* and *Torah im derekh erets* movements, their relationship to 'tradition' (a term we will have to define), how they were regarded by others in the Jewish, and particularly in the rabbinic community, and how those who followed these approaches regarded themselves.

Wissenschaft des Judentums (literally, the science of Judaism, although it is better understood as the application of modern scholarly methods to the study of Jewish texts) was founded in 1818 when Leopold Zunz (1794–1886) published a booklet entitled *Etwas ueber die rabbinische literatur* ('Something on rabbinic literature').[2] In this work Zunz pronounced 'here we are presenting Jewish literature in its fullest compass as a subject for research without concern for whether its entire content needs to be, or can be, also a norm for our own decisions.'[3] According to its earliest conceptualisation, then, *Wissenschaft* was the academic study of Judaism for its own sake, without any practical implications. In contrast to traditional Jewish scholarship, where the scholar considered himself to be part of the system he was analysing, the next link in the chain of tradition – the *Wissenschaft* scholar – regarded himself as outside the subject of his research, looking in from a supposed position of objectivity, however pious or irreligious he might be.

That is why after brief periods as a preacher in reformed synagogues, Zunz rejected any involvement with institutions, like the *Hochschule fuer die Wissenschaft des Judentums*, which combined *Wissenschaft* with the training of rabbis. For Zunz, *Wissenschaft des Judentums* was a branch of the Classics, without ideological objectives, which should not be taught in a seminary but in a university, as he wrote: '*Wissenschaft* needs first of all to emancipate itself from the theologians and raise itself to the level of historical understanding.'[4] That attitude reflected trends in German scholarship at the time, led by scholars such as von Ranke and von Humbolt who aimed to produce objective studies of the past, which revealed the 'truth'. This spirit of objectivity was brought to its peak by Moritz Steinschneider (1816–1907) who considered Judaism dead, and the purpose of *Wissenschaft* to give it 'a decent burial'.[5]

The attitudes of Zunz and Steinschneider were abhorrent to traditional Jewish scholars. They objected to this detachment from the subject, and the replacement of the traditional methods of Jewish study with the new methods of the university, which meant the treatment of sacred and secular texts in the same manner. To these rabbis Jewish texts were inherently different from secular texts and not susceptible to the modern tools of textual and historical criticism. Furthermore, *Wissenschaft* was declared useless to the strengthening and perpetuating of Jewish life, which critics held to be a major goal of Jewish scholarship; indeed, it was seen as undermining traditional Judaism.

The leader of the campaign in Germany against *Wissenschaft* was Samson Raphael Hirsch (1808–88). He called *Wissenschaft* 'a system for the theoretical extenuation of an actual apostasy' and claimed that its activities were 'more or less throwing sand or stones at Judaism'.[6] He dismissed the achievements of *Wissenschaft* scholars as building up a 'cabinet of curios for antiquarians' and taking Steinschneider at his own estimation, as the 'pathological anatomy of a dead and dying Judaism'.[7] For Hirsch, all study had to be directed towards action. Hirsch began his work *Horeb* with the statement 'the flower of knowledge is life.' Hirsch wanted a '*Wissenschaft des Lebens*', a living scholarship.[8] Ultimately,

Hirsch held that *Wissenschaft* failed because it did not 'inspire our sons and daughters to develop their own spiritual lives' because it did not interest 'our contemporary generation in drinking deeply . . . from the wellsprings of Judaism in order to enlighten their minds, warm their hearts, and gain sufficient energy and courage for vital, active, personal involvement'.[9]

Hirsch was not prompted entirely by traditionalism, but also by his own variety of innovation, deeply influenced by German Romanticism. He argued that Israel had a mission to spread justice and truth in the world and that non-Jewish values that affirmed these ideals are to be welcomed. Emancipation, feared by the leaders of the antipathy school, was to be celebrated as evidence that justice was in the ascendant. As Hirsch wrote, 'I bless Emancipation, when I see how the excess of oppression drove Israel away from human intercourse, preventing the cultivation of the mind, limited the free development of the noble side of character'.[10] Hirsch summed up this approach under the slogan *Torah im derekh erets* – 'Torah and the way of the world'.[11] Hirsch was therefore just as much of an innovator as Zunz, and was opposed to *Wissenschaft* not because it was new, but as a result of specific objections. This complex attitude is reflected in the fact that some of Hirsch's own views conflicted with tradition, just as those of *Wissenschaft* scholars did: for example Hirsch held that some Talmudic statements about medicine were scientifically wrong.[12]

Despite their bitter opposition to each other, Hirsch and Steinschneider more or less agreed what *Wissenschaft* was: a purely academic pursuit with no purpose in strengthening Judaism or increasing Jewish commitment. They simply disagreed about whether such a pursuit was valid. The largest *Wissenschaft* group, however, disagreed with both schools. They believed that *Wissenschaft* had a religious function and they founded seminaries to promote it as a basis of rabbinic education. This group spanned the religious spectrum, from the Reform leader Abraham Geiger (1810–74) a leader of the adaptation school, to the positive-historical school led by Zachariah Frankel (1801–75), a member of the acknowledgement school, to the most traditional exponents of *Wissenschaft*, led by Esriel Hildesheimer (1820–99). Geiger founded the *Hochshule fuer die Wissenschaft des Judentums* as an institute of higher learning ostensibly without denominational bias but with no restrictions on academic freedom and no dogmatic rejection of any conclusions that might be reached, including about the Pentateuch. But he also wanted it to serve as a training college for reforming rabbis and he hoped to harness *Wissenschaft* to his task. He said 'I was always concerned to study thoroughly the kernel [of Judaism] to draw results from it for reform.' Specifically, Geiger hoped that *Wissenschaft* would demonstrate the historical flexibility of Judaism to justify further changes for the future, which he regarded as vital for the survival of Judaism.[13] As Heschel has written, Geiger saw the Pharisees as a 'force for innovation' and 'asked for a revival of genuine Pharisaic principles in contemporary reforms of Judaism'.[14]

More traditional was Zachariah Frankel, who initially co-operated with Geiger and the German Reformers but broke with them in 1845 over certain proposals for reforms.[15] Frankel rejected the higher critical study of the Pentateuch, which he regarded as the unmediated Divine word and therefore beyond literary analysis, which placed him firmly in the traditional wing of the acknowledgement school.[16] Rabbinic literature was a different matter, and Frankel dedicated himself to the critical study of the Talmud, particularly the Mishnah, which he analysed in his *Darkhe hamishnah* ('Paths of the Mishnah', 1859). In that work, and elsewhere, he argued that some of the commandments described by the Talmud as *halakhah leMoshe miSinai* ('given to Moses on Sinai') were in fact created later by the rabbis and the Talmud's term merely implied great antiquity.[17] Contemporary traditionalist critics, such as Hirsch, argued that by this Frankel meant to deny the origin of the Oral Law on Sinai. However, the evidence does not support that contention. Frankel's view that some laws labelled *halakhah lemosheh misinai* were later in origin was in fact a restatement of a view held by the universally accepted medieval Talmudic authority, Asher ben Yehiel (*Rosh*).[18]

The attack on Frankel over his views on the Oral Law came in different forms: the technical assault was led by Tsvi Benjamin Auerbach (1808–72) who responded to Frankel in *Hatsofeh al darkhe hamishnah* (1861) where he marshalled authoritative sources which, he argued, contradicted Frankel's writings. Auerbach rejected any historical understanding of the Oral Law and insisted that the only acceptable approach was that the Mishnah was simply the writing down of the laws that Moses had announced after coming down from Sinai, and he considered Frankel's views heretical.[19] A more ideological critique was formulated by Hirsch, who demanded that Frankel state clearly his view of the origin of the Oral Law. Frankel refused to publish a detailed defence of his position, although he did say 'any thought of undermining and diminishing either the Torah or the tradition was far removed from my thoughts' and asserted the antiquity of '*hakabbalah vehamesorah*' (the original reception of the Torah and its subsequent transmission.)[20] Hirsch nevertheless concluded that Frankel denied the Divine

origin of the entire Oral Law and he condemned Frankel's journal, the
Monatsschrift fuer Geschichte und Wissenschaft des Judentums and
his seminary, the Judisch-Theologisches Seminar in Breslau.

Frankel founded his seminary because unlike Hirsch he believed
that *Wissenschaft* was vital to Jewish survival. According to Frankel,
Judaism 'decays when the love of its scholarly study disappears' and
his own researches often concentrated on what made Judaism unique,
and therefore necessary.[21] Frankel called his brand of Judaism 'historical' or 'positive-historical.' It was within the acknowledgement
school, but its scientific orientation differentiated it sharply from
Hirsch's approach, just as its halakhic and scholarly conservatism
separated it from the adaptation school. Frankel asserted the positive value of Jewish observance and claimed that his approach was
compatible with the essentials of Judaism and supported tradition.
Indeed he could argue that he recognised better than his opponents
the true dynamic of Judaism, which had changed in the past and continued to change, albeit in an evolutionary and semi-conscious way.[22]
Frankel could even argue that his approach was more traditional than
his opponents'. For example, the concern of *Wissenschaft* scholars to
establish accurate texts continued the work of such luminaries of the
traditionalist world as Rabbi Elijah Gaon of Vilna (1720–97) and his
predecessors going back to the Talmud, who proposed amendments
to the text, often as a means of solving difficulties in the received
wording. Solomon Schechter certainly regarded the Gaon as an early
proponent of *Wissenschaft*.[23] Accepting the text as presented in the
standard editions without consulting alternative readings was a nineteenth-century development following the production and dissemination of the Vilna edition of the Talmud, which became the dominant
version.

Seminaries based on Frankel's approach were founded in Vienna and
Budapest. There rabbinic literature was studied according to the latest
critical methods, but the Pentateuch was not subjected to modern
scholarship.[24] It has been argued that like Geiger, Frankel wanted to
use *Wissenschaft* to justify reforms.[25] The evidence for this contention come from a paper Frankel wrote about the proposal to remove
Hebrew as the language of prayer, where he wrote 'science . . . must
be the basis of any reform'.[26] However, this quotation comes from a
text in which Frankel was arguing against change, not in favour of it.
Further, there is no evidence that either Frankel or his leading followers favoured reforms, at least beyond the aesthetic changes that others,
including Hirsch, introduced. Indeed elsewhere Frankel argued that
changes could only emerge in an evolutionary, imperceptible way.[27]

The suggestion that Frankel sought to use *Wissenschaft* as a basis for reform is therefore unproven at most.

The most traditional practitioners of *Wissenschaft* were based around the Rabbinerseminar in Berlin, founded by Esriel Hildesheimer in 1873. Hildesheimer had previously opened a seminary in Eisenstadt in Hungary, where he trained a number of students including JH Hertz's father, Simon, but the seminary faced opposition from the members of the antipathy school who led Hungarian Jewry, and soon closed. Hildesheimer was not the first traditional Jewish scholar to engage in *Wissenschaft*. In Prague, Hermann Adler's teacher, Solomon Judah Rapoport (1790–1867), used modern scholarly techniques and defended Frankel against his critics.[28] Although Hildesheimer was an opponent of Frankel, he went further than Rapoport in his own studies and included *Wissenschaft* in the curriculum of his seminary.[29] Hildesheimer was convinced that the use of the methods of *Wissenschaft* would reveal more of the truth, which was the object of all study and a sacred undertaking. He declared that 'the second half of this century has brought several changes [in study]. *Wissenschaft des Judentums* has paved the road for these changes, and areas that have been known for a long time, i.e., Bible commentary, demand investigation from a new point of view and require the usage of valuable linguistic materials . . . In our desire to engage in these areas as our own, we will attempt to work in them with absolute academic seriousness and for the sake of, and only the sake of, the truth'.

Nevertheless, the Rabbinerseminar was criticised for not being wholly objective and for dogmatically rejecting some ideas *a priori*.[30] Hildesheimer did not see the problem because he was sure that modern scholarship would support the claims of tradition, and called the use of *Wissenschaft* to defend tradition a 'sanctification of God's Name.'[31] D.Z. Hoffman, who succeeded Hildesheimer as head of the seminary, expressed this most fully when he said 'the revealed truth cannot be in contradiction to the truths which have been researched by means of the human spirit, assuming these latter truths are the truths of reality and not just hunches and suppositions. Rather the former [revealed truth] will be supported by the latter [discovered truth] and lead to full clarity and complete understanding.'[32] For all this rhetoric, Hildesheimer's seminary did teach some untraditional ideas: Hildesheimer's son-in-law, Jacob Barth taught that there were two authors of the Book of Isaiah.[33] Hoffman argued that the development of the Oral Law was affected by the dispositions of the Talmudic sages, for example Mar Samuel's 'humanitarianism.' As Hoffman wrote, 'it is obvious that very many old *mishnahyot* have undergone . . . transformations through the diverging explanations of the later Tannaim' who transmitted teachings 'in the formulation that appeared fittest to him'.[34] He also quoted radical *Wissenschaft* scholars, like Zunz and Geiger, in his works.[35]

The existence of these attitudes in Hildesheimer's seminary prompted attacks from Hirsch.[36] Hirsch accused the Rabbinerseminar of being essentially the same as Frankel's seminary and therefore not to be regarded as 'orthodox', despite the fact that Hildesheimer and Hoffman both publicly declared their belief in the origin of the Written and Oral Law on Sinai; indeed, Hoffman wrote a book attacking Higher Criticism.[37] Despite the appreciation Hirsch had for the erudition and the personal piety of Barth and Hoffman he condemned their work as 'heresy.'[38] Some leading rabbis came to Hoffman's defence, for example Nathan Adler, but Hirsch also had strong allies.[39] Seligman Baer Bamberger, who opposed Hirsch on other issues, announced 'I hate Hildesheimer's seminary more than Geiger's' – presumably because Hildesheimer gave heresy respectability.[40] Isaac Halevy, who used *Wissenschaft* techniques to substantiate the tradition completely and to refute the work of those who questioned it, attacked the Rabbinerseminar as a place where 'it is unimportant whether a person writes for or against the Torah.'[41] That was a suggestion that Hildesheimer, Barth and Hoffman rejected. They held that their studies were sanctioned by tradition, which accepted that the Oral Law was fluid and had developed in the hands of the rabbis. They asserted the Divine nature of the Oral Law and of prophecy and they did not anticipate that their studies would undermine any commandments of Jewish Law.[42] The arguments between Hirsch and Hildesheimer and between Hirsch and Frankel are therefore comparable. There were important differences between Hildesheimer and Frankel, to the extent that Hildesheimer condemned Breslau. On the other hand Hirsch condemned both Breslau and Berlin, while both seminaries claimed to uphold the essentials of Judaism.

Outside Germany, and in later generations within Germany, many saw themselves as co-workers of both Berlin and Breslau, and even of Hirsch as well. For example, in 1879 Jews' College appointed S.A. Hirsch, who joined the faculty from Hirsch's school in Frankfurt.[43] Another member of staff was Hartwig Hirschfeld who was a graduate of Hildesheimer's seminary. In 1883 the college established a scholarship to send students to complete their education at the Rabbinerseminar.[44] In 1909 the college appointed Adolph Buchler, a graduate of Budapest and Breslau, as principal.[45] In France in the first half of the nineteenth century, when the conflict between Frankel and Hirsch, Auerbach and others was at its most intense, the faculty of the Ecole Rabbinique in

Metz contained both followers of Frankel and traditionalists aligned to the antipathy school.[46] Within Germany, the last rector of the Rabbinerseminar, Rabbi J.J. Weinberg, did not consider Frankel a heretic. He argued that Frankel was a profound scholar and referred to him using the traditional rabbinic honorifics, which he withheld from Geiger.[47] During his years in Berlin, Weinberg was also a passionate Hirschian. Another example of this synthesis is J.H. Hertz's alma mater, the Jewish Theological Seminary.

The Jewish Theological Seminary was founded in 1886 by American traditionalists who opposed the founders of the Hebrew Union College in Cincinnati, who had drafted the Pittsburgh Platform in 1885, which abrogated Jewish dietary laws and repudiated the belief in the return to Zion.[48] The leading founder of the seminary was Sabato Morais, who set the tone for the seminary in terms recalled by J.H. Hertz: 'we were thrilled', Hertz wrote, 'by the clear, clarion notes of his call to the Wars of the Lord; by his passionate and loyal stand that the Divine Law was imperative, unchangeable, eternal. He made rigorous demands upon him who would come forward as defender of the Judaism of our Fathers – piety and scholarship, consistency, and the courage to stand alone, if need be, in the fight against unrighteousness and un-Judaism.'[49] Another Sefardi who helped found the seminary was Henry Pereira Mendes, minister of New York's Shearith Israel synagogue. He was a graduate of Jews' College who later helped to found the Orthodox Union.[50] Two less traditional founders were Marcus Jastrow and Benjamin Szold, who accepted the composite authorship of the Pentateuch but who wanted to maintain Jewish practice and rejected the radicalism of the Pittsburgh Platform.[51] A founder at the other end of the religious spectrum was Henry Schneeburger, who received his ordination from Hildesheimer.[52]

In terms of the role of *Wissenschaft* the two most significant founders were Alexander Kohut and Bernard Drachman. Both were graduates of Breslau and venerated the institution. When Morais invited Drachman to help him found the seminary, Drachman replied 'I hope it will be modelled upon the Breslau Seminary.'[53] Although Drachman was a proud product of Breslau, he asserted the theological similarities between his alma mater and the *Rabbinerseminar*. He wrote: 'the Breslau and Berlin Seminaries were . . . in fundamental harmony on the basic concepts of Traditional Judaism and its adjustment to modern conditions'.[54] Drachman was also a Hirschian, and translated Hirsch's *The nineteen letters of Ben Uziel* while dean of the seminary.[55] Drachman thus represented a synthesis of Breslau, which he

considered to be theologically identical to Berlin, from which he took
a commitment to the modern, critical study of Talmud and to the
Divine origin of the Written and Oral Law and Frankfurt, from which
he adopted *Torah im derekh erets*. Kohut was a master of the critical
study of the Talmud, but, as one would expect from a Breslau graduate,
he opposed similar examinations of the Pentateuch and once declared,
'to us the Pentateuch is *noli me tangere*! Hands off! We disclaim all
honour of handing "the sharp knife that cuts the Bible into a thousand
pieces".'[56]

The Jewish Theological Seminary was therefore on the traditional
wing of the acknowledgement school with a special attachment to its
scientific branch. It was founded by graduates of Breslau and Berlin,
but there was a significant intellectual debt to Frankfurt. This may
seem inherently contradictory; indeed, in his study of Hertz, Meirovich
assumed it was impossible, and argued that individuals must have held
either an allegiance to Frankfurt and Berlin on the one hand, or Breslau
on the other.[57] Yet men like Drachman and his pupil J.H. Hertz found
a way to synthesise all three approaches. The ideologies of these men
refutes Meirovich's argument that the traditions of Breslau, Berlin and
Frankfurt could not be synthesised, as does the curriculum of the seminary, which was based on that of both Breslau and Berlin.[58]

Pentateuchal criticism was out of bounds at the seminary: as Morais
said, 'the icy cold criticism of the German and Dutch schools of
modern times shall not be permitted to blight the growth of religious
enthusiasm in the hearts of our pupils.'[59] A large amount of time was
devoted to Talmud, but also to Bible, Midrash, *halakhah*, philosophy
and homiletics.[60] The instructors, led by Kohut, were familiar with both
traditional and modern methods of Talmud study. One, Joshua Joffe,
was educated at both the great yeshivah of Volozhin and at Geiger's
Hochschule.[61] The first rabbinic graduate of the seminary, JH Hertz,
was examined not only by the seminary faculty but also by traditionalist rabbis, who joined with Morais, Joffe and others to sign Hertz's
hattarat horaah (traditional ordination.)[62] By doing so they not only
certified that Hertz was fit to be a rabbi; they signalled their approval of
the seminary itself.

We have now established a picture of the scientific (*Wissenschaft*) and
romantic (*Torah im derekh erets*) streams within the acknowledgement school and their complex relationship with each other and with
the antipathy school. It is already clear that the concept of 'tradition'
is fraught with complications. Although, as we have already noted,
terms such as 'Orthodox' and 'Conservative' are unhelpful and often

anachronistic, we will use the term 'traditional' a great deal, although we should acknowledge that term is problematic too, as 'tradition' is a historically constructed concept. Therefore, while we will use it, we should bear that caveat in mind. We will also establish its meaning and the difficulties associated with it. We also need to understand how traditional scholars like Hildesheimer and Hoffman did not allow *Wissenschaft* to affect *halakhah*.

The only figure we have encountered who can truly be called 'traditional' in his approach to Jewish learning is Auerbach, who rejected any historical aspect to halakhic development, was without a post-Enlightenment historical consciousness, and carried on studying texts as they had been studied in the previous 300 years.[63] 'Traditional' could not be used to describe *Wissenschaft*'s leading ideological opponent, SR Hirsch. Hirsch's neo-orthodoxy, with its celebration of secular culture as a tool for religious enhancement, was a departure from tradition and an acknowledgement of modernity, even if Hirsch's acknowledgement came in a romantic rather than a scientific form. Indeed, Hildesheimer took a more traditional line than Hirsch on this specific issue and did not place veneration for non-Jewish culture on a theological level, although he enjoyed it. Hildsheimer regarded Torah as complete and in need of no outside supplementation.[64]*Wissenschaft*, based as it was on the use of modern, critical methods, was inherently untraditional, whether the scholar applying those methods was Steinschneider or Hoffman, or even Halevy.

Despite his opposition to Frankel and Hildesheimer on the grounds of untraditionalism, Halevy was himself criticised by Rabbi Abraham Isaac Kook for using modern methods and non-traditional sources – for example, the writings of Josephus.[65] Even if Halevy used new techniques, he was wholly committed to coming to traditional conclusions; the same could not be said of Hildesheimer and Hoffman. They endorsed the theory of two authors of Isaiah and the influence of the personal attitudes of the rabbis on halakhic development, an idea alien to pre-*Wissenschaft* Jewish thought. So the concept of a 'traditionalist *Wissenschaft* school' is, strictly speaking, a contradiction in terms. One can either be traditional or acknowledge modernity by engaging in *Wissenschaft*, just as one can be traditional or acknowledge modernity through support of *Torah im derekh erets*. Nevertheless, there is a sense in which talking about 'traditionalists within the acknowledgement school' makes sense, because tradition is fluid and absorbs new ideas. Of course, one might argue that Reform Jews are also traditionalists for maintaining Judaism to the extent they do. However, here the social context of traditionalism become important, for traditionalist members of the acknowledgement were accepted as being sufficiently traditional to be regarded as authentic representatives of Judaism by those who rejected as much of modernity as they could, whereas Reform Jews were not.

Hildesheimer and his followers thought some new ideas could be assimilated into the tradition, and others could not. They were unmoveable on the issue of Divine authorship of the Oral as well as the Written Law, but on other issues they were flexible, such as authorship of Biblical books aside from the Pentateuch, including the Psalms and Isaiah. On the Oral Law, although they insisted that the Mishnah and Gemara were records of traditions going back to Sinai, they did not believe that the written form they took was set out at Sinai. For example, Hoffman argued that the Mishnah was composed and redacted over a long period, and was not written down by one sage at one time.[66]

The point that the Talmud and the Biblical books other than the Pentateuch have in common is that the tradition never claimed that the words were Divinely dictated. They were always seen as human records of Divine inspiration or communication. As they were human texts, Hildesheimer and his followers could argue (in common with Frankel and others) that they had a history, which could be studied. Hoffman expressed this distinction when he wrote that while the Mishnah 'is for the best part of Divine origin as far as its content is concerned . . . its form has only been fixed at a relatively later time. From Moses until the Tannaim the form of the Mishnah was fluid', but 'we consider the authenticity and integrity [of the text of the Pentateuch] to be absolute'.[67] This distinction was not universally accepted. Hirsch and Auerbach took a much more rigid line on both the text of the Mishnah and the authorship of the non-Pentateuchal Biblical books.

Significantly, these disagreements did not place Hildesheimer and his followers beyond the pale, even in the traditionalist centres of Lithuania, who accepted Hildesheimer and Hoffman as representatives of authentic Judaism, even if they diverged in their methods and conclusions.[68] Rabbi Israel Salanter of the antipathy school campaigned against the founding of modernised seminaries like Hildesheimer's in Russia, and said of Hildesheimer's practice of lecturing to women: 'if a rabbi in Lithuania would dare do this, he would be deposed, and rightly so' but also said, 'I wish I would receive the reward of the pious Rabbi Hildesheimer in the world to come'.[69] Even Hirsch worked with Hildesheimer despite his opposition to the Rabbinerseminar, and wanted him to support his Free Association for the Interests of Orthodox Jewry.[70] Auerbach and Hildesheimer disagreed fundamentally about *Wissenschaft*, yet Hildesheimer sent his son Hirsch to be taught by Auerbach, and Hirsch became one of Auerbach's favourite pupils.[71] Ultimately, the common position of these figures on the Pentateuch held them together despite their differences on other issues.[72] This set them apart from men such as Z.P. Chajes, who as upholders of *halakhah* were members of the acknowledgement school, but did not accept the Divine authorship of the Pentateuch and so were considered unacceptable by those who did, namely, the traditional wing of the acknowledgement school and the antipathy school.

The seeming contradiction in the traditional but scientific members of the acknowledgement school's separation of scholarship from practical halakhic decision-making in fact flows from their belief in the giving of the Pentateuch on Sinai. Hoffman held that the Oral Law was given on Sinai, at which point it passed into the control of the Jewish people, as the Talmud says in *Bava Metsia* in explaining the Biblical verse: 'it is not in Heaven' – that is, it is for people and not for God to render decisions on Jewish law. As such, *halakhah* went through a process of development, which can be studied scientifically; however, the steps along the way do not affect the practical conclusion. The sanction for practical *halakhah* comes from the decisions of the great authorities; how they reached their conclusions and the paths the tradition took to reach them is of academic but not of practical interest, just as learning the opinions of Shammai, though generally rejected in favour of those of Hillel, has religious value, but does not establish normative behaviour. In this view, any determination of the correct practice must be based on a reading of the standard codes and the opinions of the rabbis that have been accepted as authoritative, not on an analysis of variant texts or historical context.

Ellenson has analysed one example of this understanding being put into practice. Rabbi J.J. Weinberg argued in a responsum that, although recent studies had revealed that the meaning of a Talmudic text was different from that understood by Maimonides, they could not be taken into account because a contemporary ruling had to be based on precedent and the chain of tradition, not on textual investigation. He wrote, 'we have no right to change the rulings of *rishonim* [early authorities] even on the basis of reasoned assumptions'.[73] A contemporary Talmudist, David Weiss Halivni, has expanded on this reasoning. While the historian seeks to understand a text in its original context and recover the original meaning, the halakhist is interested in the meaning as determined by subsequent rabbinic literature, based on the principle that the law follows the most recent authority.[74]

This analysis is predicated on the belief that at Sinai authority over *halakhah* was placed in the hands of the Jewish people, and the decisions of its leaders were made binding. If that event did not take place, then the authority of contemporary rabbis to determine the law based on tradition falls away. Precedents to justify changes can be taken from anywhere; there does not need to be a supporting contemporary opinion. This difference of view explains why Hoffman did not believe historical research would affect practical decisions and why Geiger engaged in *Wissenschaft* precisely in order to justify his reforms. Those attitudes, which flowed from a view of the Pentateuch to an approach to *halakhah*, were some of the defining differences between the adaptation school and the traditional wing of the acknowledgement school. Some non-traditional members of the acknowledgement school such as Z.P. Chajes, Louis Ginzberg and Louis Jacobs denied that conclusions about the Pentateuch need have halakhic ramifications. The Chief Rabbis – as traditional, but scientific members of the acknowledgement school – rejected this approach, just as they rejected Geiger's and followed Hoffman instead. They asserted that the authority of *halakhah* depended directly on the origin of the Pentateuch.

Wissenschaft developed from a highly academic beginning, unconcerned with practicalities, into a central aspect of some schools of thought, which aimed in different ways to construct an approach to practical Jewish life. Some of these figures fell within the adaptation school, others within the acknowledgement school. The members of the acknowledgement school who used *Wissenschaft* faced the opposition of other members, like Hirsch, whose form of acknowledgement was romantic, not scientific. Hildesheimer perceived himself (and was perceived by others) as being within traditional Judaism, and was widely admired, even by those who were not inclined towards *Wissenschaft* themselves. This was because of Hildesheimer's traditional views on the Pentateuch. This attitude was not shared by all members of the acknowledgement school, some of whom adopted modern views on the question. Although they had much in common with traditional members they were not considered representatives of authentic Judaism by members of the antipathy school or by the traditional members, of the acknowledgement school, either scientific or romantic.

Outside Germany, where the debates about *Wissenschaft* were most intense, there were individuals and institutions with a common allegiance to both Hirsch and *Wissenschaft* –and, for that matter, to the Lithuanian leaders of the antipathy school. Meirovich has argued that such a synthesis was not possible and did not exist, but we can see that this was not the case.[75] Indeed, the Chief Rabbis belonged to this very group, the traditionalist part of the acknowledgement school, influenced by both its scientific and romantic branches.

Notes

1 H. Meirovich, *A vindication of Judaism* (New York 1998), 15.
2 H.M. Graupe, trans. J. Robinson, *The rise of modern Judaism* (New York 1978), 147.
3 M.A. Meyer, *Judaism within modernity* (Detroit 2001), 89.
4 Ibid., 134.
5 Ibid., 150.
6 M. Breuer, trans. E. Petuchowski, *Modernity within tradition* (New York 1992), 177–178.
7 Ibid., 180–181.
8 Ibid; Meyer, *Judaism within modernity*, 131.
9 M.B. Shapiro, *Weinberg* (Oxford 1999), 79.
10 S.R. Hirsch, trans. B. Drachman, *The nineteen letters* (New York 1899), 165.
11 Graupe, *Rise of modern Judaism*, 174–175.
12 Breuer, *Modernity within tradition*, 178–179.
13 S. Heschel, *Abraham Geiger and the Jewish Jesus* (Chicago 1998), 36; Meyer, *Judaism within modernity*, 133.
14 Heschel, *Geiger and the Jewish Jesus*, 97, 104.
15 M.L. Raphael, *Profiles in American Judaism* (San Francisco 1984), 86.
16 Meyer, *Judaism within modernity*, 133.
17 Ibid., 132.
18 C. Adler et al. (ed) *Jewish Encyclopaedia* (New York 1906), 424–425.
19 D. Ellenson, *Wissenschaft des Judentums, historical consciousness and Jewish faith*, Leo Baeck Memorial Lecture 48 (New York 2004), 6–7.
20 Ibid., 8.
21 Meyer, *Judaism within modernity*, 133.
22 Breuer, *Modernity within tradition*, 13–14.
23 S. Schechter, *Seminary addresses and other papers* (New York 1969), 183–184.
24 M. Carmilly-Weinberger, 'The similarities and relationship between the *Judisch-Theologisches Seminar* (Breslau) and the Rabbinical Seminary (Budapest)' *Leo Baeck Institute Year Book* XLIV (1999), 3–22.
25 R. Furst, *Hakirah or Mehkar: the religious implications of an historical approach to Limmudie Kodesh* (ATID, Jerusalem 2001), 17.
26 Ibid.
27 Z. Frankel, *On changes in Judaism* www.ucalgary.ca/~elsegal/363_Transp/ZFrankel.html.
28 Graupe, *Rise of modern Judaism*, 150.
29 Breuer, *Modernity within tradition*, 130–131.
30 D. Ellenson, *Rabbi Esriel Hildesheimer* (Tuscaloosa 1990), 144.

31 Ibid., 143–144.
32 M. Shapiro, 'Rabbi David Zevi Hoffman on Torah and *Wissenschaft*' *Torah u-Madda Journal* 6 (1995–96), 132 .
33 Ibid., 149.
34 D. Ellenson and R. Jacobs, 'Scholarship and faith: David Hoffman and his relationship to *Wissenschaft des Judentums*' *Modern Judaism* 8 (1988), 37.
35 Breuer, *Modernity within tradition*, 183–184.
36 Ellenson, *Hildesheimer*, 144.
37 Ibid., 145.
38 Ibid., 149.
39 Breuer, *Modernity within tradition*, 186.
40 Ellenson, *Hildesheimer*, 145.
41 Ibid., 146.
42 Ibid., 156.
43 A.M. Hamson, *Jews' College London, 1855–1955* (London 1955), 46.
44 Adler, *Jewish Encyclopaedia*, 298; I. Harris, *Jews' College jubilee volume* (London 1906), lxxxvii.
45 I. Epstein, 'Adolph Buchler' in Brodie and Rabbinowitz (ed) *Studies in Jewish history* (Oxford 1956), xiv.
46 J.M. Berkovitz, *Rites and passages* (Philadelphia 2004), 197.
47 M.B. Shapiro, 'Review essay: sociology and *halakhah*' *Tradition* 27:1 (Fall 1992), 80–81.
48 R.E. Fierstein, *A different spirit* (New York 1990), 18, 25–26.
49 J.H. Hertz *Sermons, addresses and studies* (London 1938), III:362.
50 Fierstein, *Different spirit*, 32–33.
51 Ibid., 25, 38.
52 Ibid., 38.
53 Ibid., 43.
54 B. Drachman, *The unfailing light* (New York 1948), 100. Of course, at the end of his life, as a leader of the Orthodox Union, Drachman would wish to stress his traditionalism and therefore to stress the traditionalism of his seminary. One way to do that was to assert its theological similarities with the *Rabbinerseminar*, the traditionalism of which was unquestioned.
55 Drachman, *Unfailing light*, 4; M. Davis, *The emergence of Conservative Judaism: the historical school in 19th century America* (Philadelphia 1963), 336.
56 A. Kohut, 'Secular and theological studies' *The Menorah* (13 July 1892), 49. See Babylonian Talmud, *Bava Batra* 111b.
57 Meirovich, *Vindication*, 15.
58 Fierstein, *Different spirit*, 80; D. Ellenson, *After Emancipation* (Cincinnati 2004), 282–283.
59 Fierstein, *Different spirit*, 72.
60 Ibid., 81–84.
61 Ibid., 87.

62 Hertz papers in the Hartley Library, Southampton University, MS 175/70/3.

63 Ellenson, *Wissenschaft, historical consciousness and Jewish faith*, 9. It is arguable that earlier scholars, active circa 1000–1500 were more sensitive to textual questions that their successors. See, for example, Rashi's (Rabbi Solomon ben Isaac of Troyes) frequent references in his Talmudic commentary to different versions of the text.

64 Sh.Z. Leiman, 'Rabbinic openness to general culture in the early modern period' in Schacher (ed) *Judaism's encounter with other cultures: rejection or integration?* (New York 1997), 209. Hildesheimer's relationship to Hirsch's thinking is not straightforward. He trained rabbis for both *Austritt* and traditional *Grossgemeinde* synagogues, but himself headed an *Austritt* congregation, the Adath Jeshurun of Berlin. He supported the secessionist law which allowed all *Austritt* communities to be established but gave, in Liberles' words, 'tentative approval' to the co-operative organisation the Gemeindebund; R. Liberles, *Religious conflict in social context* (Westport, Connecticut 1985), 197–198. He loved German culture, but did not make a theological niche for it.

65 Ellenson, *Wissenschaft, historical consciousness and Jewish faith*, 14.

66 A. Marx, *Essays in Jewish biography* (Philadelphia 1947), 206–207.

67 Ellenson and Jacobs, 'Scholarship and faith', 37.

68 Ellenson, *Hildesheimer*, 164.

69 E. Lederhendler, *Jewish responses to modernity* (New York 1994), 78; Breuer, *Modernity within tradition*, 125.

70 Breuer, *Modernity within tradition*, 186.

71 D. Strumpf, 'Hirsch Hildesheimer' in Jung (ed) *Guardians of our heritage* (New York 1958), 425.

72 As one correspondent to the newspaper *Zionswaecher* (set up by Hirsch's teacher, Ettlinger) wrote, whatever differences separated different strands 'we Orthodox believe that God revealed to Moses at one time the oral law as well as the written, that both together are only one Torah, each merely a part of the whole'; R. Liberles, *Religious conflict in social context* (Westport, Connecticut 1985), 77.

73 Ellenson, *After Emancipation*, 379.

74 Ibid., 380.

75 Meirovich, *Vindication*, 15, where he says that Hertz's theology 'stood in sharp contrast . . . to that of Rabbi Esriel Hildesheimer'.

Part II

Theology and policy, 1891–1946

Chapter 5

The theology of Hermann Adler

D URING HIS TIME as Chief Rabbi, Hermann Adler significantly raised the status of his office among the non-Jewish public. He was the first Chief Rabbi to become a national figure, well known to the non-Jewish as well as the Jewish community and the first to be honoured by the state and leading institutions.[1] Yet since his death he has receded from both popular and scholarly attention. Those historians who make some mention of him generally take a poor view of the man and his achievements; for example, Geoffrey Alderman wrote of Adler's 'intellectual limitations' and lack of 'circumspection and diplomacy.'[2] The view that Hermann Adler was not a serious thinker or a profound scholar has meant that historians have not considered him worthy of extensive research, and he has never been the subject of a book-length academic study. I do not suggest Adler was in the first rank of Jewish scholars in the nineteenth century, but the evidence that I present here suggests that this neglect has been unwarranted and that Adler was a respectable scholar, in both traditional and modern methods, and his thought contained interesting aspects. More importantly, it is impossible to understand Adler's communal policies, to be discussed in the next chapter, without a clear picture of his theology. I argue that, like other Chief Rabbis, Adler's religious policies were to a great extent motivated by his religious ideas. The way in which Adler led Anglo-Jewry is important in understanding its religious development as a whole, and that in turn requires an analysis of Adler's theology.

One reason why inaccurate judgements have been made about Hermann Adler may be the paucity of easily available primary sources. Adler published only two books, both collections of sermons, the first in 1869 at the beginning of his career and narrowly focused on refuting Christological interpretations of the Hebrew Bible, and the second to mark his seventieth birthday in 1909, just two years before he died.[3] Some of Adler's sermons and lectures were published individually or reported verbatim in the *Jewish Chronicle*, which also printed his letters to the editor. Finestein has described Adler's sermons as 'intellectually undemanding', but in fact they contain a number of interesting theological ideas and we will make extensive use of them.[4] In 1877 Bernard Spiers of the London Beth Din published a *Hagadah for Passover* with Hebrew comments by a number of rabbis, including Hermann Adler.[5] In 1878 and 1881 Adler contributed essays to the *Nineteenth Century*, rebutting Goldwin Smith's anti-Jewish essays published in that journal.[6] There are also manuscripts in London, Southampton, Jerusalem and New York, but until now these have not been closely examined.[7]

This chapter uses that material to discern Hermann Adler's attitudes to the essential issues of Jewish belief, notably the Torah, Written and Oral, and the authority of Jewish Law (*halakhah*). We will also look at issues which were of great importance to Hermann Adler as a leader of emancipated Jewry in western Europe in the late nineteenth and early twentieth century: the relationship between Jews and non-Jews and religions other than Judaism, the role of secular learning and modern methods in Jewish learning, and Zionism. Adler was a member of the first generation of rabbis to consider some of these issues, for example Zionism, and entered debates which were still raging in his time, such as that over Biblical criticism, which makes his contribution all the more interesting. We examine Adler's influences and intellectual opponents. Finally, we place Adler's thought in the context of our typology of the Jewish religious responses to modernity.

Hermann Adler's theology was a fusion of highly traditional beliefs and scholarly methods, and a more modernised approach that included openness to non-Jewish culture, *Wissenschaft* and a Westernised aesthetic. This was an inheritance from his father Nathan Adler, a master of both classical rabbinic and modern critical modes of study, and his teachers in Prague, both the unmodernised and Solomon Judah Rapoport, a founder of *Wissenschaft*. Adler received their ordination in 1863 and adopted aspects of both approaches which they represented. Adler's attitude to many issues resembled that of the moderate traditionalist leaders of German Jewry, S.R. Hirsch and Esriel Hildesheimer, although as they were active at around the same time and as Adler never quotes them directly, it is unclear whether they were a direct influence on Adler or whether they simply all responded to the same circumstances in the same way. Hermann Adler was also significant as a drawer of distinctions between what he considered to be the essential and the inessential, and between form and substance in Judaism. Once he had determined to his own satisfaction what aspects of Jewish life and thought were sacrosanct, he was relaxed about changing other features.

This represented a middle path between a radical reforming approach and a complete rejection of any change or development. Although, like his father, Hermann Adler thought many accommodations to modernity were both acceptable and desirable, he placed ultimate and uncompromising value on those parts of Jewish law and theology he thought could not be changed. He rejected the notion that any fundamental aspect of Jewish theology required change; as he once asked incredulously, 'does then Judaism, so sublime in its purity and so pure in its sublimity, teach dogmas which are repugnant to our common sense?'[8] That was what guided him throughout his life, as he wrote in his deathbed message to the community: 'I have tried to do my duty, to act in conformity with *Torah haketuvah vehamesorah* [the Written Torah and Jewish tradition]'.[9]

These attitudes place Adler in the acknowledgement school in our typology of Jewish religious responses to modernity. His *Wissenschaft* inclinations place him in the scientific branch, although his concern for the outward forms of Jewish life and worship and his openness to non-Jewish culture display a debt to the romantic and aesthetic branches too. His conservative theological views situate him in the traditional wing of the acknowledgement school, alongside figures such as Hildesheimer, Hoffman, Mendes and Drachman, but set him apart from non-traditional acknowledgement school members, such as two we examine in depth, Morris Joseph, candidate for the ministry of the Hampstead Synagogue in 1895, and Joseph Hochman, Minister of the New West End Synagogue, 1906–15. This helps us to understand the complex relationship between Adler and the leaders of French Jewry, who were conservative in dogma but made major concessions in practice. One of the themes that will emerge from our study of Adler and his successors is the complexity of the acknowledgement school and its internal relationships. An appreciation of its complexity is crucial to understanding many problems in modern Jewish religious history, in Britain and elsewhere. Before we turn to these substantive issues we should address the question of Adler's learning.

Hermann Adler was raised in the house of one of the outstanding Jewish scholars of western Europe, Nathan Adler, whose religious opinion was sought by leading rabbis throughout Europe and even North America, and whose writings were published in the great centres of eastern European Jewish scholarship.[10] Nathan taught his son Talmud from the age of ten, and in 1860 at the age of 21 Hermann went to Prague to complete his rabbinic education.[11] There he was taught by two members of the antipathy school, Rabbi Shimon Ausch and Rabbi Shmuel Freund, both scholars of international standing, and by a member of the scientific branch of the acknowledgement school, indeed one of the founders of *Wissenschaft des Judentums*, Solomon Judah Rapoport.[12] Adler immersed himself in intensive Jewish learning for eighteen months, even writing Talmudic *hiddushim* (novellae), the mark of a traditional rabbinic scholar.[13] In 1863 he received his rabbinical ordination from all three teachers.[14] He received a PhD from the University of Leipzig, a sure sign that he is rightly placed in the acknowledgement school, in 1862.[15]

Adler was offered the post of Chief Rabbi of Hanover, but declined it, and returned to England where his father appointed him Principal of Jews' College.[16] He did not remain principal for long, although he continued to teach at the college; in 1864 he became minister of the Bayswater Synagogue, a post he held until he was appointed Chief Rabbi in 1891.[17] His return to England did not mark the end of his learning and he began to study with Jacob Reinowitz, the extremely erudite dayyan of the London Beth Din.[18] When he was appointed Chief Rabbi in 1891, Adler appealed to the community: 'do not entirely deprive me of a few interspaces consecrated to those studies which are the rejoicing of my heart', which suggests a continued attachment to learning, as does his daughter's recollection of his enjoyment in Talmud study.[19]

Despite Adler's small literary output, there is some evidence of his learning. He edited parts of the medieval English halakhic work *Ets hayyim*, and intended to publish the entire work with critical notes.[20] A lecture he gave on the Talmudic sage Elisha ben Abuya quoted the Mishna in *Megillah*, tractates *Moed Katan*, *Shabbat* and *Sanhedrin* of the Babylonian Talmud and *Hagigah* in both the Babylonian and Jerusalem Talmud, the Midrash on Ecclesiastes and Ruth, the Ethics of the Fathers and the Ethics of the Fathers according to the House of Natan.[21] In his comments on the *haggadah* Adler explained an apparent contradiction in the opinion of the medieval commentator Rashi on the source of the obligation to drink four cups of wine at the *seder*, by making references to various other rabbinic writings including the Midrash in *Bereishit Rabbah* and the Jerusalem Talmud.[22] In a later discussion he quoted the early modern Polish authority the *Matteh Mosheh* and built on one of his explanations.[23] A third comment resolved a problem in the Tosefta, which is made up of statements excluded from the Mishna, and is less studied than the Talmud itself.[24] In his Hebrew correspondence Adler indulged in the traditional practice of paraphrasing Biblical verses, displaying a wide knowledge of the material.[25] Adler's citations show that in addition to Hebrew, Aramaic, Syriac, Yiddish, Judendeutsch, Greek, Latin, French and German, Adler also had command of Arabic.[26]

Contemporary reports also suggest that Adler was learned. In 1896 the *Jewish Chronicle* reported Adler's Talmudic discourse for the Sabbath between the New Year and the Day of Atonement, the *Shabbat Shuvah derashah*. The *Chronicle* reported that Adler's discourse was attended by the leading 'rabbis, dayanim and maggidim [traditional preachers] of the East End' in such numbers that a larger venue had to be found at the last minute. The *Chronicle* commented, perhaps with a touch of hyperbole, that 'the Chief Rabbi brought to bear an astonishing amount of abstruse Rabbinical lore . . . in really masterly fashion.'[27] Although only Ashkenazi Jews in the British Empire were bound to call upon him for his rulings, other rabbis did the same, especially in the United States. The Hirschian Congregation Orach Chayim, and the Sefardi Shearith Israel, both in New York, turned to Adler for rulings and Rabbi Yosef Aharon Taran of Argentina sought Adler's opinion alongside that of other leading European rabbis on whether the muscovy duck was kosher.[28] When Adler died, the leading German-Jewish historian Ismar Elbogen paid tribute to the 'ability which he displayed in his interpretations of Jewish law' and wrote that he was 'a man of deep scholarship and wide reading . . . he was like the rabbis of the old school in that he brought a rich store of knowledge to his office and was ever anxious to increase his learning.[29] Elbogen was, of course, writing in praise of Adler's memory, and we might suspect some exaggeration, although not complete fabrication. Whatever Adler's theological opinions were, therefore, they were based on learning and scholarship.

We begin our survey of Adler's theology with his attitude towards the central Jewish text, the Pentateuch. Adler was convinced that the Five Books of Moses were of supreme importance and relevance. In 1882 he called the Pentateuch 'the law of Sinai to which we owe the most valued achievements of civilisation, – the law of Sinai, which offers the only solution to the enigmas of life' and described it as 'eternal, immutable law.'[30] Adler's Judaism was centred on the Bible, particularly the Pentateuch. We should not be surprised, therefore, that Adler held strong views on the origin of the Pentateuch.

It is not difficult to find quotations from Adler's writings which demonstrate his belief in the revelation of the Pentateuch on Sinai. He spoke of 'the day when the Lord first vouchsafed us that Revelation three thousand five hundred years ago'.[31] Adler peppered his sermons with phrases like 'the Law of the Bible is the word of our God', 'the Book of books which in very truth has descended from heaven to us' and 'commandments revealed by God on Sinai'.[32]

The nature and frequency of Adler's references to this doctrine demonstrate that he not only held it to be true, in a strict historical and literal sense, but also that it was an important doctrine, in which it was vital to believe. This separated Adler from figures in the adaptation or acceptance schools, such as Geiger and Steinschneider, who held that the Pentateuch was a composite human document and who either sought to change Jewish practice, or abandoned it altogether. It also set him apart from some other members of the acknowledgement school, such as Zunz in Germany and Morris Joseph in England, and later leaders of Conservative Judaism such as Louis Ginzberg and Louis Jacobs, who accepted Biblical criticism but did not believe that Judaism need change as a result, and who continued to uphold *halakhah*.[33] We would place these figures on the non-traditional wing of the acknowledgement school, whereas Adler belongs on the traditional wing, which promoted the doctrine of a divinely revealed Pentateuch as the only solid foundation of Judaism and an absolute fundamental of faith.

The best evidence for this comes from very early in Adler's career. In 1863 a controversy arose following the publication by J.W. Colenso of *The Pentateuch and the Book of Joshua critically examined*, in which he argued against the Pentateuch's historicity and Mosaic authorship. The *Jewish Chronicle* published an editorial, which suggested that as Judaism was based on the Talmud not the Pentateuch such arguments would not destabilise Judaism.[34] Adler disagreed, and in article in the *Jewish Chronicle* attempted to refute Colenso point by point.[35] Adler's decision to challenge Biblical criticism through detailed refutation anticipated the efforts of his successor, J.H. Hertz, in Britain and David Hoffman in Germany who subjected Wellhausen's higher criticism of the Pentateuch to sharp scrutiny on a number of occasions.[36] Like Adler and Hertz, Hoffman saw Pentateuchal criticism not just as wrong, but as dangerous. In 1908 Hoffman wrote 'the high tide of destructive Bible criticism has swept away many students of Jewish theology and carried them into . . . apostasy, and denying the most important religious principles.'[37] Significantly for Adler's status as an original thinker, Adler formed this analysis and acted upon it over 40 years earlier, as one of the first generation of rabbis who confronted the issue.

As we have seen, the leaders of the West London Synagogue did not dispute the Divine origin of the Written Law, they merely objected to the Oral Law. The Jewish campaign for Judaism to take into account the findings of Biblical criticism therefore did not come from West London but from independent intellectuals led by C.G. Montefiore and Israel Abrahams, who founded the *Jewish Quarterly Review* in 1889 and published articles propounding critical theories and calling for Judaism to be amended in light of them.[38] One source for Montefiore's views was the Master of Balliol College Oxford, Benjamin Jowett, who was heavily involved in the *Essays and Reviews* controversy within the Church of England in the 1860s, when he argued that Anglicanism should incorporate the findings of modern Biblical scholarship.[39] Montefiore was educated at Balliol and described Jowett as 'one to whom in matters of religion I owe more than to any other living man.'[40] Montefiore and Abrahams became two of the founders of Liberal Judaism, the first Jewish movement in Britain to place Biblical criticism at the centre of its ideology.

Adler's response, which he formed when the theories were first published by non-Jewish scholars and continued to state as they were accepted by some members of the Jewish community, became the standard response for traditional Jewry: that the theories were wrong, it was important that they were wrong and they could be disproved point by point. As he told Jews' College in 1905, 'I conceive it to be one of the main duties incumbent upon the teachers of our College to show . . . that . . . the results of sound scientific research do not affect and assail that fundamental doctrine of Judaism – the belief in Divine Revelation', thus distancing himself in terms of both scholarship and theology from Montefiore, Abrahams and others, and associating himself with traditionalist leaders of Jewry, including in the antipathy school, who insisted upon that belief in the revelation at Sinai was essential.[41] Just as Adler's attitude on the Pentateuch set him apart from individuals in the acknowledgement school who did not accept the traditional doctrine, so it established a fundamental unity between Adler and those best understood as situated in the antipathy school, even though they disagreed on many other issues.

One such issue was the role of modern scholarship; we have just seen how Adler did not reject it, as the antipathy school did, but, in a manoeuvre typical of the group comprising the scientific branch of the acknowledgement school, wanted to deploy it to support traditional beliefs. Of course, just as today, the vast majority of modern Biblical scholars of Adler's day disagreed that objective scholarship upheld tradition, and concluded that the overwhelming evidence pointed to multiple human authorship of the Pentateuch. Like David Hoffman and JH Hertz, Adler did not bring an open mind to the issue; in common with the antipathy school, Adler was always going to conclude that the Pentateuch was the result of direct revelation. We can see another example of Adler's view – that, in cases of doubt, scholarship had to give way to dogma – in his discussion of Elisha ben Abuya. It is important to note, however, that Adler's fundamentalism on the origin of the

Pentateuch did not mean that he approached the text simplistically. For example, whereas other Jewish commentators downplayed any suggestion that the Patriarchs sinned, Adler adopted a more nuanced approach and argued that the great Biblical figures were human with weaknesses and failings, and did sin. When discussing Jacob's deception of his father Isaac in order to take his brother's blessing, Adler writes: 'he atones for the wrong of earlier years by the sufferings of a life, until, having been educated and purified by severe discipline, he is transformed from Jacob (*Hebr.* a Supplanter) into Israel (*Hebr.* a Prince of God)'.[42]

By calling the direct revelation of the Pentateuch the 'fundamental doctrine of Judaism' Adler signalled flexibility on other doctrinal issues, for example the authorship of books in the Prophets and the Hagiographa. Judaism never regarded these books as Divinely revealed, but rather as human documents written under the influence of Divine inspiration, so there is more room for manoeuvre within the tradition on questions of authorship and dating. Nevertheless, there was a traditional approach to the origins of some books, which the antipathy school continued to hold: Ecclesiastes was regarded as the work of King Solomon, Isaiah was seen as the product of one hand alone and the Psalms were held to have been written by David, Solomon and earlier authors, and not during or after the Babylonian exile.

Adler, however, argued that 'some of the views hitherto entertained on minor points must be somewhat modified.'[43] For example, he suggests that David might not be the author of all the psalms apparently ascribed to him: he hints heavily that Psalm 137 was written during the Babylonian exile, and not by David under the influence of prophecy.[44] This attitude placed Adler in the same group as the scientifically inclined figures within the acknowledgement school, such as Hildesheimer's son-in-law, Jacob Barth, who taught that there were two authors of Isaiah.[45] Adolph Buchler, who taught at Jews' College from 1906 considered that some of the psalms might date from Maccabaean times, an opinion that Hertz was also willing to consider.[46]

The other pillar of rabbinic Judaism alongside the Bible is the Talmud, which is a written record, built up over many centuries until about 500 CE, of the Oral Law. There is significant disagreement as to what the Oral Law actually is; we have already seen that it was the main point of theological difference between the West London Synagogue and its minister, David Wolf Marks, and the Chief Rabbi. It therefore might seem curious that Hermann Adler seems never to state explicitly his attitude to the Oral Law. However, by the 1880s the West London had ceased to be a threat. Israel Zangwill called it 'a body which had stood still for fifty years admiring its past self'.[47] It had barely changed and was no longer attracting new adherents; in 1886 it had the lowest attendance of any major London synagogue. Marks' views on the Oral Law were therefore of little concern and became even less so in 1893 when Morris Joseph, who did not reject the Oral Law, succeeded him as minister.[48] Hermann Adler was therefore not required to go into battle on behalf of the Oral Law as his father had been, hence the scanty dogmatic statements. However, we can discern Adler's attitude from less direct statements and from his use of sources in sermons.

In 1868, Hermann Adler told his congregants at Bayswater: 'study our Law by the help of the light shed upon it by our sages and commentators, those great and wise men who devoted their lives to the exposition of the Torah. Try to gain some knowledge of our wondrous literature, which, varied as it is, springs from, and revolves in wider or narrower circles around, one immutable centre – the Bible.'[49] This was a plea for the study of rabbinic records of the Oral Law and a rejection of the suggestion that the Bible could stand alone. In 1909 he wrote that the Jewish preacher must expound the Bible 'with the aid of the *Talmud, Midrash,* and the post-Biblical literature.'[50] Adler himself based many of his explanations on rabbinic texts.[51]

For example, Adler explained the legal parts of the Bible according to the rabbis' interpretations, and was careful to stress that they were merely explicating the text, not creating new legislation. When Adler described the institution of bar mitzvah, for example, he said 'the authorized expounders of the written law have ordained [*Ethics of the Fathers* 5:24] that an Israelite, on attaining the age of thirteen, has to take upon himself the observance of the precepts of Judaism. *Our teachers base this opinion on a careful analysis of certain Bible texts*' [emphasis added].[52] In other words, Adler held that rabbinical statements are based on authentic explanations of the Written Law. Adler's discussion of the four cups of wine at the *seder* was an attempt to link the practice, rejected by West London as rabbinic, with a Biblical source.[53] This is an example of establishing connections between the Written and Oral Law, something SR Hirsch specialised in.

Like his father, then, Adler regarded the Oral Law as indispensable, but how much, if any, of it was given at Sinai was an issue of fierce contention among Jews in the nineteenth century. In our typology, we would class Nathan Adler as a scientific member of the acknowledgement school, who held that the Oral Law developed in human hands after it was given. It follows that – when Hoffman was attacked by Hirsch for arguing that the Oral Law, while Sinaiatic in origin, developed partly as a result of the dispositions of the Talmudic sages – Nathan Adler came to Hoffman's defence. This was a case of one scientific member of the acknowledgement school coming to the aid of another when under attack from a non-scientific member of the same school. On the other hand, although neither Nathan nor Hermann Adler condemned Zachariah Frankel as Hirsch did, they withheld their approbation until they ascertained his precise attitude to the origin of the Oral Law, and were sceptical when Frankel was vague. As Hermann wrote to his father '[Frankel] writes that he never intended his words to be an attack on *halakhe leMoshe miSinai* yet his declaration does not read convincing[ly].'[54] Thus Nathan and Hermann Adler were scientific members of the acknowledgement school, but they were also traditional members. We examine more evidence later that places Hermann Adler in this group: those properly placed in the acknowledgement school, and inclined to a scientific approach to Jewish texts, but restrained by adherence to tradition.

The ultimate destination of the legal sections of Written and Oral Laws is *halakhah* – the day-to-day rules (*mitsvot*) of Jewish life. Adler was a stout defender of Jewish law. He declared that one of the functions of a rabbi was 'vigilantly to safeguard and jealously to defend' the *halakhah*.[55] In 1868 Adler rejected the idea that Jewish law was no longer relevant or binding, saying that 'no new dispensation has ever, can ever, come to supersede or abrogate the law given on Sinai.'[56] He stressed that the Bible itself called *halakhah* an 'eternal statute' – *hukat olam* – to be kept *l'dorotekhem* ('throughout your generations').[57]

In 1882 Adler derided the argument that mankind had progressed to a moral level such that it no longer needed the discipline of the *mitsvot*. He argued that the world was 'stained by crimes as huge and dark as ever disgraced those days when the "right of the fist" stalked triumphantly though the land' and it was only the 'restraints of religion' that prevented the 'terrible nightmare of a faithless world'.[58] In his campaign for *halakhah* Adler did not restrict himself to generalities. In 1889 he dedicated a sermon to urging greater Sabbath observance.[59] Elsewhere he made a plea for *kashrut*, daily prayer and honesty in business.[60] This allegiance to *halakhah* placed Adler firmly apart from the adaptation and acceptance schools.

This brings us Adler's philosophy of *halakhah*. The purpose of the *mitsvot* for Adler was to curb man's passions and so create a righteous world. Adler explained the *tefillin* as 'mementoes, reminding us . . . that the love of God must be the master passion of our life, curbing every unlawful desire, and restraining every sinful propensity'.[61] But *mitsvot* had to be performed in an intelligent manner. In 1868 he said 'theory and practice, study and action, knowledge and performance go hand in hand'.[62] In 1902 he attacked 'parrot-like' observance, so that a practice becomes a 'religious rite, with all the religion omitted'.[63] Rather, the Jew must understand 'the meaning of the various ordinances' because 'Judaism bids you learn, study, search and obey . . . We must search the meaning of each single precept'.[64]

Adler here adopted the same approach as Maimonides, who high-lighted 'the repeated assertion of our Sages that there are reasons for all commandments' although only a 'general purpose . . . and not to the object of every detail' may be discoverable.[65] Adler's philosophy of *mitsvot* has a great deal in common with that of Hirsch, who argued, like Adler, that the *mitsvot* guarded the Jew against temptation and that their efficacy was dependent on their being understood. As Hirsch wrote, 'Judaism turns to the intellect . . . to regulate the whole of our workaday, breadwinning life . . . and to subjugate it to God's law. Not feeling, only cognitive reason, bright with the rays of God's word, can fortify against life's trials and temptations'.[66] Hirsch sought to go further than Maimonides and explain in detail how the details of the *halakhah* were spiritually relevant. Although Hirsch went into detailed explana-tions in his *Nineteen letters* and *Horeb*, whereas Adler only expounded a few examples, their aim was the same. Olsberg's comment on Hirsch holds true for Adler; they both wanted to show that '*halakhah* is a meaningful, edifying system'.[67] Adler and Hirsch alike were operating in a post-Enlightenment world where reason was valued above all, and where Judaism could be respected by many only as a rational reli-gion. Adler and Hirsch acknowledged the changed sociological reality brought by modernity and both sought to rationalise Judaism.

Adler also emphasised practical benefits of *halakhah*. He told a congregation in 1900 that a religious home would be a happy home, for 'if God is there, then love will enter and abide there'.[68] He pointed to 'the wealth of peace and happiness which the Sabbath brings to the household'.[69] Adler identified *halakhah* as a force to bind the Jewish people together and distinguish them from other nations. He said 'every religious ordinance we perform, will strengthen the bond that unites us . . . with our brethren in faith throughout the world' and that one of the functions of the *mitsvot* is 'to preserve the purity of our race and the prevent our being absorbed among the peoples in whose midst we dwell'.[70] It is worth pointing out that Adler's use of the term 'race' was not biological. Adler wrote specifically that the charge that Jews 'regard non-Israelites as aliens in blood' was untrue and gave Ruth as an example of a convert welcomed into the Jewish people.[71] Adler saw

Jews as united only by their faith and practice, and not ethnically or as a nation in the modern sense. Adler's concern was that Jews could only fulfil their spiritual mission by remaining separate. We will delve further into these issues later.

While Adler was committed to *halakhah*, unlike the antipathy school he did not consider that everything Jews did was part of the *halakhah*, and therefore while *halakhah* could not be abandoned other practices could, if appropriate. This attitude was a defining feature of the acknowledgement school, for if Judaism objects to any change then the modern world cannot be acknowledged; this was the platform of the antipathy school. Whereas Moses Sofer objected to sermons in the vernacular, Adler was an enthusiastic supporter. For Sofer both the form and the substance were important, whereas for Adler what he regarded as the form could change, so the language of a sermon did not matter if the message was right. This is the key distinction Adler often made between form and substance. The substance, either theological or halakhic, was sacrosanct; the form, the package they came in, could change to suit the times. When we review Adler's religious policy we will see this inclination in practice; here we will analyse his attitude in theory.

In discussing the proposal that the prayers should be read in English he explicitly rejected the philosophy of the antipathy school when he remarked that 'there may be some Rabbis, who, at the bare mention of such a proposition could hold up their hands in pious horror . . . I do not approve of such unseasonable reticence' and cited the Talmud that prayer in the vernacular was permitted, even though it would be a departure from existing practice.[72] As it happens, Adler was opposed to the wide use of the vernacular in public worship for other reasons; crucially, however, he was open to the possibility of change. This echoes Esriel Hildesheimer who rejected the view that novelty in itself prohibited a practice, writing that the only appropriate criterion was the 'law according to its [Talmudic] source'.[73] This was also the view of Nathan Adler, who observed that 'the major cause of lack of religiosity is the absence of theological leaders who, by implementing leniencies which fit the needs of the time and the demands of religion, following the example of the rabbis of by-gone times, will prevent the nation from breaching the fences of the law'. In other words, that Judaism was to be preserved by allowing changes demanded by the times and permitted by the *halakhah*, and not by considering all change prohibited *a priori*.[74]

We should consider the forces that Adler was reacting to when he proposed his views on *halakhah*. We have already mentioned one such factor, the Enlightenment. Another factor which prompted Adler to defend Jewish law was widespread lack of adherence to *halakhah*. It is apparent from Adler's sermons that he was very conscious of this trend. He told the congregation at the Great Synagogue on the Day of Atonement 1894, 'If Isaiah were in our midst, how he would thunder forth his denunciations! "Sinners in Zion be afraid: tremble in fearfulness, ye hypocrites"'.[75] Elsewhere he lamented the 'apathy and materialism' that was threatening the survival of Judaism.[76] As we have seen, he sought to combat lack of observance both by exhortation to practice and also by following the approach of his father and of Hildesheimer, by allowing change when such a change would have positive results and not contravene the *halakhah*.

These two forces, the Enlightenment and religious apathy, endangered Judaism, but Adler was also conscious of even stronger threats to what he considered to be authentic Judaism, from both from without and within. The external threat came from Christian missionaries. When Adler protested that an all-knowing God would not give a law that would ever require revision, his argument was directed against the Christian doctrine, which claimed that Jesus brought a new dispensation. As Adler said 'how . . . dare Christianity assert, that a purer and more elevated morality than that contained in the Bible was preached by its founder? The word of God could not have been imperfect or incomplete so as to require either correction or development'.[77] The sermon that quotation comes from was included in a volume designed to combat the arguments of Christian missionaries. Adler contended that the surest weapon against their arguments was a thorough understanding of the Law, which provides a further reason for his assigning meaning to the *mitsvot*, because such an understanding would reduce conversions to Christianity.

The other attack, from within the Jewish community, came from the intellectual leaders of the adaptation school in Britain, C.G. Montefiore and Israel Abrahams. Not only did they attempt to integrate Biblical criticism into Judaism, but they also wanted to reduce its halakhic element. Montefiore placed emphasis not on rite, but on monotheism and the moral law. He held that ritual law was only of instrumental worth, and could be dispensed with if it did not perform its function of enhanced ethical behaviour.[78] We can see that Adler combated this challenge in two ways, first by arguing that the origin of the Law made it eternally binding, above and beyond any instrumental value, and secondly by showing that the *mitsvot* did indeed have great instrumental value, that they brought man closer to the Divine and improved him ethically. Adler's approach to *halakhah* was therefore based firmly on tradition but also took into account the contemporary social and intellectual pressures he faced, and he tailored his response accordingly.

Figures from the acknowledgement school were sympathetic to what they believed was wholesome in the modern world. This tendency appeared in three forms: first, the use of modern scholarly methods in Jewish study (*Wissenschaft des Judenums*), secondly, an appreciation of the value of non-Jewish literature and the truth of modern science and thirdly, an enthusiasm to alter the form of the synagogue service to bring it up to the standard of Western beauty, to create a ritual which Adler's acculturated community would find attractive.[79] These attitudes typified the responses to modernity of the scientific, romantic and aesthetic branches of the acknowledgement school respectively. To some extent Adler subscribed to all three of these attitudes.

As we have seen, as a traditionalist proponent of *Wissenschaft*, Nathan Adler can be called a member of the scientific branch of the acknowledgement school. His commentary to *Targum Onkelos* uses *Wissenschaft* techniques such as philology and comparative linguistics. Nathan sent his son to learn from one of the founders of *Wissenschaft*, S.J. Rapoport, in Prague. However Nathan was also a rabbinic scholar in the old sense who delivered traditional *derashot* and published *hiddushim* in the pre-*Wissenschaft* style. When he sent Hermann to Prague, it was not just to learn from Rapoport but also from the traditionalist rabbis of the antipathy school who taught there. Thus Nathan accepted *Wissenschaft* in addition to traditional study, not to replace it. Hermann Adler shared this attitude. He continued the practice of traditional rabbinic scholarship and wrote *hiddushim* while still a student in Prague, and as Chief Rabbi he gave the twice-yearly *derashot* which involved highlighting and resolving apparent problems in the Talmud and its commentaries using traditional techniques, without the help of source or historical criticism.

On the other hand there are hints throughout Adler's *oeuvre* which betray a historical-critical approach. As we noted, Adler was convinced and unconcerned that 'some of the views hitherto entertained on minor points must be somewhat modified in the light of sound scientific research'.[80] We have seen examples of this attitude in Adler's willingness to suggest that some psalms ascribed to David were not actually by him. Before he narrated a parable in a sermon in 1893 he pointed out that although it was a story found in the Talmud, it was actually an Indian story that had been adopted by the Jews and incorporated into their own literature'.[81] He asserted that the supposedly first-century-CE *Tanna deve rabi Eliyyahu* was a work actually assembled 900 years later.[82]

This position followed closely that of the Rabbinerseminar in Berlin, a centre of the traditional wing of the acknowledgement school's scientific branch, and its leaders, Hildesheimer and Hoffman. Hildesheimer believed that *Wissenschaft* was a valuable pursuit alongside traditional study and his successor, Hoffman, believed that a synthesis of traditional learning and *Wissenschaft* was the key to the achievement of true understanding.[83] They, therefore, pursued both types of study. Thus, at his yeshivah in Eisenstadt, Hildesheimer devoted most of the curriculum to the Bible and Talmud with rabbinic commentaries and Codes, and during his time in Berlin he delivered the twice yearly *derashot*.[84] However, he also authorised the teaching of the theory of the dual authorship of Isaiah.[85] Hoffman continued to compose *pilpul*, the uncritical pre-modern form of rabbinic discussion, but also pursued detailed critical studies of the Mishna, demonstrating its textual development.[86]

What of Adler's attitude towards Western civilisation: the art, literature and music of non-Jewish Europe? While the antipathy school denied the value of these achievements of non-Jews, Hirsch famously built up the appreciation of the cultural achievements of the West into a central plank in his theological platform *Torah im derekh erets*, which posited that a Jew should expose himself the best of non-Jewish culture and would be spiritually enhanced by doing so.[87] Hirsch attitudes to non-Jewish culture were profoundly influenced by German Romantic thought, which is why we have described Hirsch's branch of the acknowledgement school as romantic.[88] Adler did not seek to raise the status of non-Jewish culture to such a high theological level, but he did appreciate its value and found pleasure in it himself. Like his father, Adler entered the non-Jewish academic world and received a PhD. He praised the 'blossoms of art and the fruits of high intellectual culture' which the ancient Greeks gave to the world, despite the religious objections Adler had to Greek civilisation.[89] Although Finestein is not absolutely accurate that Adler's sermons were 'almost as likely to contain English or classical literary allusions as rabbinic or biblical citations' they are evidence of wide reading.[90] He quoted Thucydides, Dante, Shakespeare and Milton and expressed his admiration for Goethe.[91] He told the congregation at his installation as Chief Rabbi that he had 'endeavoured to draw my mental nurture from the rich store of our dear England's thought and learning'.[92] When he was a student in Prague, Adler took great pleasure in attending concerts and wrote home to his parents to describe his experiences.[93]

Adler was not afraid of the findings of science either. Unlike many contemporary churchmen, most famously Bishop Wilberforce, Adler did not perceive Darwinism as a threat and did not attempt to refute it.[94] As Zangwill wrote, whereas 'the evolution doctrine has been only one of a host of dissolvent influences [upon Christianity] . . . Judaism stands, so Jews assert, untouched'.[95] This is probably due to the long-standing Jewish tradition that does not insist upon the literal truth of the Biblical account of creation. Adler shared this approach with Hirsch and others who, as Shuchat has shown, accepted evolution and even used it to homiletical effect, to point out the greatness of God, who could create breathtaking diversity from the very simplest elements.[96] Although there is no evidence that Adler used evolution in his sermons, he did quote Kelvin's theory of 'strains and vibrations' to show the potentially huge effect of small forces, which he used to illustrate the point that individual moral actions could have huge ramifications.[97]

Although not all of London's Jews had secular learning many of them – especially in the West End – did, and these were the Jews whose loyalty to Judaism was most in need of strengthening. Adler himself identified this trend in 1868 when he told his West End congregation 'our children [are] well versed in the knowledge of art and science, skilled in every worldly accomplishment, but they lack what is better, nobler than any art or science . . . the knowledge of God's word'.[98] Jews with a high secular education would have no respect for a rabbi ignorant of Western civilisation – indeed, he would be wholly alien to them and therefore unable to influence them – so, although Adler's use of non-Jewish literature in his sermons was not merely instrumental, there were practical reasons for Adler's wide-ranging references.

In Britain, the acknowledgement school encompassed rabbis more traditionalist than Adler. Within Adler's Beth Din, Bernard Spiers, Polish-born and popular in the East End, was described at his death as having 'combined happily in his own person the old spirit of ultra-orthodoxy at its best with Western culture'.[99] The Federation of Synagogues was led from 1890 to 1894 by Rabbi Dr Mayer Lerner, a graduate of the Berlin *Rabbinerseminar* and Berlin University, who engaged in *Wissenschaft*. This places him in the acknowledgement school's scientific branch, while his marriage to Hirsch's grand-daughter connects him to those in its romantic branch.[100] As Feldman has pointed out, Machzike Hadath, which had many quarrels with Adler, was also a part of the acknowledgement school and agreed with Adler about secular learning, which they did not reject.[101] Dr Victor Schonfeld, the leader of the *Adath Yisroel* from 1909, said in 1912 that he wanted the boys at *Etz Chaim* yeshiva to improve their secular learning, albeit on the instrumental grounds that it would help them 'place the fruits of true Jewish spirit before their followers' more effectively, although we have seen that such considerations probably also played a part in Adler's thinking.[102]

Just as Adler held that Torah was superior to non-Jewish studies, he was certain that science and culture did not guarantee high ethical or spiritual standards. Prompted by the growing anti-Semitism espoused by the frustrated opponents of the Republic, which led to the founding of the newspaper *L'Anti-Juif* in 1881, Adler launched a barely concealed attack on France in 1882 when he criticised 'a country that boasts of its Enlightenment and superior intelligence . . . waving the white banner of culture and learning' while spreading 'malice and ill-will'.[103] He broadened this into a general point and said 'science can trace the path of the sun, foretell the appearance of a comet and the return of an eclipse. But in vain do we turn to science . . . to curb human passion, to restrain the sinful longing . . . Science may try to set up its system of ethics; it will never effectually influence the human heart'. Only religion could achieve that, and for Jews that meant Judaism.[104] Adler thus steered a middle course between the antipathy school and the romantic enthusiasm of Hirsch. His attitude was again similar to Hildesheimer's, who adored German literature and music (and used to sing German *lieder* to his children on Sabbaths and festivals), but was sceptical about giving it a theological place in his Judaism.[105]

If some aspects of modern thought were to be welcomed, the question inevitably arose what attitude to take if science (or philosophy) contradicted the teachings of Judaism. In a lecture on Elisha ben Abuya, Adler advised 'not to suspect science' but stressed 'do not permit intellectual doubt and difficulties lead you into mazy speculations, which end in confusion and darkness, but cling with unshaken confidence to the teachings of True Science, to your belief in God, the binding force of religion and the supremacy of virtue'.[106] For Adler, if science, or any aspect of modern scholarship, directly challenged the essential parts of the tradition it had to submit to faith. This attitude has a lot in common with that expressed by David Hoffman in his opening address to the *Rabbinerseminar* in 1919. On the one hand he argued that 'true science' did not pose a threat to Judaism because 'the revealed truth cannot be in contradiction to the truths which have been researched by means of the human spirit, assuming these latter truths are truths of reality and not just hunches and suppositions. Rather the former will be supported by the latter.[107] One the other hand, like Adler, he was of the opinion that that mere hypotheses could not be allowed to affect Jewish practice and decried the view whereby 'only those principles of belief which did not contradict the falsehood and illusion of established learning were granted the right to exist'.[108] For Hoffman and Adler, modern scholarship must be false if it contradicted essential traditions, and therefore had to be rejected. They are usefully understood as scientific members of the acknowledgement school, but only insofar as their traditionalism permitted.

The final aspect of this positive approach to modernity and non-Jewish culture is the beauty of the synagogue service. The antipathy school's view that anything new was proscribed applied as much to the synagogue and its service as anything else. Just as Adler rejected their condemnation of *Wissenschaft* and *Torah im derekh erets* he also differed with them on this aspect of Jewish worship. The acculturated section of his community equated decorous, dignified worship with genuine spirituality, and its members were repulsed by the lack of decorum found in traditionalist prayer services; such sentiments contributed to the establishment of the West London Synagogue in 1840. Adler responded to these attitudes, which threatened to drive many away from the synagogue, by urging his community to hold services characterised by 'solemnity and reverence'.[109] This was a continuation of his father's approach, who had insisted on dignified services in his *Laws and Regulations* of 1847, and it was an attitude shared by others in the acknowledgement school, like Hirsch and Hildesheimer. Later I examine in detail the reforms Hirsch introduced to his synagogue to improve its aesthetic, when I come to consider Adler's own policies more thoroughly; Hildesheimer for his part paid tribute to the great composer of synagogue music Louis Lewandowski at his death for his 'beautiful compositions . . . created for the ennoblement of the service'.[110] Above all, French Jews placed a high religious value on an aesthetically pleasing service.[111] They are the clearest example of figures to be placed in the aesthetic branch of the acknowledgement school, but Adler, Hirsch and Hildesheimer were also sympathetic to its programme.

Adler was opposed in principle to any change, however aesthetically pleasing, which contravened Jewish law, and even when the *halakhah* was not at stake Adler rejected what he saw as unnecessary adoptions of non-Jewish mores. One of his criticisms of the Jewish Religious Union's services was the 'exaggerated deference to the superficial customs of their non-Jewish neighbours' which could only lead to 'a service of repellent frigidity'.[112] For Adler, although some adoption of Western mores was acceptable, even desirable, hence his wearing of canonicals, there were limits to what he regarded as valid acculturation and the concept of *hukat hagoy* – following in the ways of gentiles – retained force.[113] A Westernised service could only be a means to an end, and was always secondary to other religious considerations. As he told members of the Brondesbury Synagogue in 1905, 'your services may be decorously and reverently ordered; and yet you may not have risen to the true purpose for which this house was erected'.[114] Adler wanted 'every Service to be characterised by dignity and reverence' but also by 'fervour and devotion'.[115] Just as Adler's traditionalism placed a curb on his scientific and romantic inclinations, so too they restricted his aesthetic leanings.

Although Adler viewed many aspects of the non-Jewish world positively, there were other aspects which, as a traditionalist, he could not approve – for example, faiths other than Judaism. He criticised Greek polytheism as 'a mythology which could not but corrupt and debase'.[116] He blamed Rome's lack of true religion for its 'luxury, cruelty and sensuality'.[117] These attacks on the classical inheritance were part of the wider debate sparked by Matthew Arnold and the chapter on 'Hebraism and Hellenism' in his *Culture and Anarchy*, published in 1869. Arnold argued that neither Hebraism nor Hellenism was superior to the other, but 'the aim and end of both . . . is . . . one and the same, and this aim and end is august and admirable'.[118] He later asserted that 'both Hellenism and Hebraism are profound and admirable manifestations of man's life, tendencies and powers'.[119]

This view was adopted by Benjamin Jowett, who in turn passed it to his disciple, Montefiore, and it became a central element of his thinking. He said 'Israel has something to learn from Greece. Both Greek and Hebrew spirituality are immortal, yet neither can exist in fullest potency without the other'.[120] The danger from this view was that it was balanced. Jews were not likely to accept that Greek ethics were superior to Jewish ethics, but an approach that celebrated both might incline Jews to attach more importance to Hellenistic morality than they otherwise might, and certainly more than Adler did. In his attack on the downgrading of Hebraism and elevation of Hellenism, Adler used Arnold's own writings against him, quoting his assertion that 'as long as the world lasts all who want to make progress in righteousness will come to Israel for inspiration' rather than Greece and Rome which were, in Adler's words, 'addicted to idolatry and the gratifications of the senses'.[121]

Looking more widely, Adler ridiculed the 'absurdly superstitious rites' of the Chinese and condemned the human sacrifices the 'savage South Sea islander' brought to his 'horrid idol'.[122] Of course, some of these attitudes were as Victorian as they were Jewish, and reflected attitudes that prompted Christian missionaries to attempt to convert the populations of distant outposts of the Empire, Adler, after all, was a Victorian. However, his statements also express typically Jewish theological concerns, such as the forceful opposition to idolatry or the rejection of any post-Mosaic revelation. For example, Adler pointed to the 'error' in Islam which 'though proclaiming "there is but one God" adds the false words "and Mahomet is His prophet"'.[123]

The main religious challenge from outside the community came from Christian conversionists, and was twofold. It was religious, attempting to lure Jews (without much success) away from Judaism, led by the London Society for Promoting Christianity among the Jews.[124] It was also political, in that the conversionists imagined a world without Jews, one where those of different faiths could belong to the same polity with equal rights. These attitudes echoed some of the debate on Emancipation of the 1840s and 1850s, when figures such as Sir Frederick Thesinger argued against giving Jews political rights on the basis that it was necessary to preserve the Christian character of the nation, and E.A. Freeman pursued his ideas about the need for communities of race.[125] By implication, therefore, conversionism questioned and threatened Emancipation. Leading conversionists, such as Sir Robert Inglis and Sir Robert Newdegate, were often strongly opposed to Jewish emancipation.[126]

Adler therefore had to meet its challenge, but his response was inevitably related to the concept of the chosenness of Israel, which implied Jewish separatism, and was seized upon by critics such as Goldwin Smith as evidence of lack of brotherly feeling towards non-Jews and a lack of loyalty to the countries in which Jews lived. Adler confronted this issue too. To do so, he condemned non-Jewish faiths, but not non-Jews themselves. He stressed the loyalty, even patriotism, of Jews to the countries in which they dwelt. This had further theological consequences. Adler based his claim that Jews were loyal citizens of the countries in which they lived on the premise that the Jews were a religious, not a political, unit. As this argument implied the rejection of Jewish nationalism, once political Zionism emerged Adler could not view it positively. However, a rejection of Zionism called into question Adler's belief in the Messiah and the ingathering of Israel. He therefore had to make his views clear on that matter also. Adler was sculpting new responses to new challenges, but he was not the only traditionalist leader to face these problems, and we will see how others responded.

Both of Adler's books contained withering critiques of Christianity and vicious personal attacks on conversionists, whom he called 'self-created dispensers of salvation'.[127] He described the Christian belief that Jesus died for the sins of the world as 'monstrous . . . repugnant to all that the Bible tells us of the righteousness of God, that an innocent and sinless man should suffer the punishment which the guilty have entailed upon themselves'.[128] Adler pointed out what he considered were logical problems with the Christian creed. If Jesus was the Messiah, who tradition held would usher in a period of universal peace, why was the world far from peaceful?[129] If Jesus was the Messiah he would have to be descended from King David, but the Gospels trace Jesus to the Davidic line via Joseph, husband of Mary. If Joseph was his father then Jesus could not be the Son of God; if not, then Jesus could not be the Messiah.[130] The Messiah was supposed to rule over Israel, yet Jesus did not.[131] The prophets predicted that the Messiah would uphold Mosiac law, yet Christianity seeks to replace the law of the Torah with a new dispensation.[132]

Adler's strongest language was reserved for the concept of the Trinity. He said of this doctrine in 1868 it 'is surely the most monstrous . . . God is dragged down from heaven and likened unto man! The Supreme Being (I shudder while I say it), is lowered to the level of one of those deities with which the mythology of Greece peopled their Olympus'.[133] In 1905 he wrote that the Trinity is 'in diametrical opposition to our pure Monotheism'.[134] Adler's hostility would have been sharpened by Montefiore, who suggested that the Trinity contained a 'certain truth' as part of his wider project to incorporate Christian teaching into Jewish theology.[135] It should be noted that Adler did not have a wholly negative view of Christianity, and for that matter Islam. Following Maimonides, and like Hirsch, he saw them as fulfilling an important role, to 'teach the worship of one God to a heathen world, and to promote the pure and lofty doctrines of the Bible.' Evidently, although Adler believed that Christianity's monotheism was compromised, it was still present in some form.[136]

Adler certainly did not denigrate the followers of other religions themselves. He stressed the brotherhood of humanity. This idea can be traced to Jewish sources but it was also a response to a contemporary impetus, in this case the assertion of Goldwin Smith and others that Jews lacked a feeling of brotherhood towards those outside their faith.[137] Smith found support in the writings of Montefiore, who argued that a deficiency of Judaism was that it asserted the superiority of Jews over gentiles, although it should be noted that Montefiore himself attacked Goldwin Smith, and defended Judaism, even of the traditional variety, as 'pure religious universalism'.[138] In answer to Goldwin Smith Adler asserted that 'he who, without being a Jew, fears God and keeps His commandments . . . may hope to win eternal bliss. "The righteous among the gentiles have a share in the world to come"'.[139] He highlighted the missions of Israel's prophets like Jonah to save not just Jews, but non-Jews as well.[140] As such, Jews 'should live on the terms of the utmost cordiality, goodwill and friendship with our Christian neighbours'.[141] Adler contrasted Judaism's 'truly Catholic spirit' with the exclusivity and divisiveness of Christianity.[142] He asked, how can it be claimed that 'Christianity taught the universal fatherhood of God, when we find it to be fundamental doctrine that salvation is in store exclusively for those who believe in the Son begotten of the Father from everlasting?'[143] According to Adler, it was Judaism's rejection of such exclusiveness and its belief that Jew and non-Jew alike could be saved, that provided the rationale for the mission of Israel.

Adler spoke explicitly about the election and mission of Israel. He called the Jews 'chosen of God' to stand apart from other nations 'unto the end of time.'[144] He warned worshippers in 1895 that 'we must never forget in our dealings with them [non-Jews] that we are Israelites. We must not fall into the dangerous error of imagining that, in order to gain favour with our fellow citizens, we may renounce the distinctive features of our faith . . . or intermarry'.[145] Adler regarded intermarriage as the 'first step on the road to desertion and eventual apostasy'.[146] Although he made it clear that intermarriage was forbidden by *hala-khah*, he did not put that forward as a reason to desist. Rather, he described the impossibility of domestic harmony when husband and wife followed different religions, that the children could not be brought up as loyal Jews and that misery would ensue.[147] These are practical rather than principled arguments against intermarriage. As such they are distinctly untraditional, albeit in defence of tradition.

The technique of deploying untraditional arguments to support tradition was one shared by others on the traditionalist wing of the acknowledgement school, such as Hildesheimer and Hirsch. When, in 1847, Hildesheimer attacked a reformist convention he did so partly on the grounds that the proceedings were undemocratic. For any traditionalist rabbi the voting procedures were the least objectionable aspect of the conference, but Hildesheimer deployed the argument that he believed would be most persuasive. For Jews steeped in the ideology of Enlightenment and Emancipation, that meant raising issues of democracy and representation.[148] Hirsch used contemporary German ideas in his defence of tradition, and although he never referred to them by name his audience would have been aware of concepts Hirsch borrowed from Hegel, Kant, Herder and others. For example, Hirsch argued that truly to understand the spirit of a text it was necessary to delve deeply into its language; in the case of Jewish texts, this was Hebrew. This idea was propounded in the German context by the Romantic thinker Schleiermacher, who argued that language was not just a transparent medium behind which sat the meaning of a text, but conveyed a message in itself.[149] Adler was adopting much the same approach when he discussed intermarriage. The most effective arguments against marrying out of Judaism, untraditional though they were, concerned domestic happiness and so they were the ones that Adler deployed. This technique has been given the term 'contemporizing' by Reiff. According to Heilman, it is the process which 'established rationally what faith postulates a priori, so that in place of what Durkheim referred to as "passive resignation" to tradition there is instead an "enlightened allegiance"'.[150]

Adler's support for Jewish particularism stemmed from his conviction that 'if we desire to ensure the immortality of Judaism, we must remain steadfast in our Judaism.'[151] But it was particularism with a purpose, to fulfil the Jews' 'mission of teaching goodness and truth to the world by our example'.[152] According to Adler 'the Israelites are to be . . . the teachers and instructors of mankind'.[153] Adler was proposing universalism through particularism, rejecting Goldwin Smith's accusation of tribalism while maintaining a form of Jewish separatism on the basis that the world still needed Jews to preach righteousness. He said 'while misery and ignorance still prevail on earth; while the deification of nature and of natural instincts is regarded as the sign of culture; while the fabric of social order is being gravely endangered by the dissemination of anarchist, communist and revolutionary doctrines; while religious persecution, fanatacism, and intolerance prevail in their most hideous aspects, it surely cannot be maintained that Israel need no longer preach his message'.[154]

This conception of Israel's mission to the rest of the world is rooted in the Jewish idea that the Jews should be 'a light unto nations' but it is also a response to the circumstances of Adler's times. Significant strands of Enlightenment thinking stressed universal brotherhood, and Emancipation was based on that premise. As we have already noted, some non-Jewish thinkers, for example Goldwin Smith, argued that the Jews determination to keep apart was incompatible with equal political rights.[155] In response to pressures such as these, Moses Mendelssohn laid out a modernised concept of the mission of Israel, and all sections of German Jewry stressed its centrality to Judaism.[156] The Reform group accepted the idea in its most radical form and looked towards 'the union of all nations into one peaceful realm to serve their one true God'.[157] This vision of a universalistic ethical monotheism without distinguishing ritual practices was imported into England by Montefiore, who maintained that the Jews needed to remain separate so they could fulfil their role, but that ethics and not ritual were central to the success of the Jewish mission.[158]

Adler took a different view and argued that Israel's mission could only be achieved if Jews were loyal to both the ethical and ritual aspects of Judaism.[159] Adler was convinced that Jews' achievements in the general community could only be of benefit if they were combined with religious observance. This approach to Israel's mission and its relationship to Emancipation is very reminiscent of that proposed by Hirsch and Hildesheimer. Unlike the antipathy school they both saw Emancipation as a positive development which would help Jews achieve their mission, but on the proviso that new political rights did not undermine religious standards.[160] As they held the views that cause us to place them in the acknowledgement school they welcomed Emancipation, but as traditionalists they wanted to guard against negative religious consequences.

Adler's assertions that Jews and non-Jews were brothers, that non-Jews could find salvation and that Jewish separateness was intended partly for the benefit of non-Jews and was not a mere cliquishness, did much to answer Goldwin Smith, but he had also made the specific accusation that – although they took advantage of Emancipation – Jewish separatism made Jews disloyal to the countries they lived in.[161] To answer Goldwin Smith, Adler had to put Jewish patriotism beyond doubt, indeed raise it to the level of a religious obligation.

We should recall that Adler was already nineteen when Jews were granted full Emancipation; it was for him a relatively new luxury and he was therefore very sensitive to anything which might undermine it. After all, in other European countries political rights had been given to the Jews only to be withdrawn again.[162] In response to arguments casting doubt on the loyalty of British Jews, Adler sought to distinguish the traditional Jewish idea of peoplehood from the modern concept of nationality. He stated emphatically 'ever since the conquest of Palestine by the Romans, we have ceased to be a body politic: we are citizens of the country in which we dwell. We are simply Englishmen, or Frenchmen, or Germans, as the case may be . . . having the same stake in the national welfare and the same claim on the privileges and duties of citizens . . . What is the political bearing of Judaism? It has no political bearing whatever'.[163] These statements had sound Jewish sources, as he told a congregation on one occasion: 'we must . . . fully share the civic and political life of our nation, and work zealously for its welfare. We must render a ready and cheerful obedience to its laws, in accordance with the Rabbinic teaching *dina demalkhuta dina* – "the law of the realm binds us".' Adler did not deny the bonds between Jews of different lands, but insisted that 'the interest we feel in our oppressed brethren in foreign countries is then wholly a matter of sympathy' and certainly not based on any commercial or financial consideration.[164]

Adler stressed British Jews' patriotism. He asserted that 'to the English nation we feel ourselves with heart-whole loyalty to belong'.[165] He delivered sermons to mark great national occasions, such as Queen Victoria's Diamond Jubilee.[166] In 1899 he prayed for the British troops in the Boer War and told the congregation 'our minds are absorbed, even as it becomes loyal Englishmen and Englishwomen, by the critical position of a portion of Her Majesty's forces'.[167] Adler went so far as to claim that 'under Divine Providence the future of the British Empire is assured'.[168] Of course, not all strands of British opinion supported the Boer War, and in doing so Adler was associating himself with a Tory rather than a Liberal patriotism.[169] Nevertheless, Adler was in no doubt that the expression of such sentiments helped to safeguard the position of British Jews. He said 'I maintain that a portion of the triumph that has been achieved [Jewish Emancipation] is due to the influence exercised by . . . [the Great] Synagogue and its rulers . . . Whatever the event that moved the hearts of England's sons – when a great victory evoked national rejoicing, when a sovereign had been stricken down by an illness, and when it pleased the Lord to send him healing, when a joyous national Jubilee was kept, and when death entered our palaces – every event was commemorated here with the voice of prayer and supplication, of praise and thanksgiving, proving that the Israelite, then as always, was "steeped to the very lips" in loyalty'.[170]

In his protestations of loyalty Adler was therefore following the practice of his predecessors, including his father and Solomon Hirschell, who preached a special sermon to celebrate victory in the Battle of Trafalgar.[171] He also shared this approach with German Jewry. Indeed, Hirsch went further than Adler and argued that not only were the Jews a nation no longer, they were never intended to be so in the usual sense. Hirsch's position was close to that of Reformers like Geiger and Holdheim, however much he might deny it.[172] Hoffman wrote 'Judaism has already existed for a long time as nothing but a religion'.[173] All were responding to the need to silence attacks on Jewish loyalty. They came to the same solution – denial of a Jewish political identity and a noisy assertion of patriotism.

Adler, then, argued fiercely that British Jews were loyal only to Britain, thus disproving Goldwin Smith's contention and protecting the position of British Jews. However, in the 1890s a new threat to this assertion emerged. Zionism directly challenged this argument, because it claimed that the Jews remained a political nation and wanted to establish a new state to which they could attach their loyalties. Adler was a member of the first generation of rabbis to respond to this challenge. He pointed out the nature of the difficulty which in his view was raised by Zionism, saying that it was 'calculated to revive the false charges of . . . lack of loyalty to our native country'.[174] Therefore, although Adler supported Jewish settlement in Palestine, visited Palestine and stressed the centrality of Zion in Jewish thought, he was a staunch opponent of political Zionism.[175] There were some English Zionists, even among Jewish ministers, for example Simeon Singer. Moses Gaster, Haham of the Spanish and Portuguese Jews in London was a tireless worker for Zionism.[176] Adler shared his attitude with most contemporary English Jews, and with Hildesheimer in Germany, who was also a dedicated supporter of the Jews of Palestine.[177]

Adler made both a religious and a practical case against Zionism. He argued it was 'opposed to the teaching of Judaism' to seek to hasten the redemption which was to be in God's good time, and was not to be brought about by man's 'precipitate action'.[178] According to Adler the only way to bring redemption was 'by seeking to . . . realise the high ideals which our religion sets before us', a traditional Jewish answer, and the corollary to the text in the festival prayers, 'on account of our sins we have been exiled from our land'.[179] Unlike some contemporaries, such as Morris Joseph, Adler held the traditional belief in the Messiah as an actual person who would deliver the Jews and return them to their land. He was not, in Joseph's words, 'an ideal' that 'tinges the soul . . . with a radiance of the sublime' – he was flesh and blood, and would rebuild the Jerusalem Temple and reign over the Jews.[180]

As Israel Zangwill pointed out, Adler's rejection of Zionism but retention of the belief in the Messiah was discordant.[181] Adler himself stated clearly that in the hope for such a redemption 'every believing and conforming Israelite must be a Zionist'.[182] As a traditionalist Adler could not abandon his belief in the Messiah, yet he wanted to stress the exclusive loyalty of British Jews to Britain, lest the position and political rights of British Jews be weakened. He was therefore left in the uncomfortable position of claiming that for all practical, political purposes the belief in the coming of the Messiah was irrelevant, for it was in God's hands, not man's. European contemporaries of the same theological attitudes shared Adler's position. Rabbi H. Plato of Cologne expressed the same ideas, saying 'until the Ruler of the fate of nations calls us home, we are and remain faithful sons of our German fatherland' and claimed the belief in the Messiah was 'absolutely not a factor that interfered with loyalty to the state'.[183] Hirsch went further to depoliticise Messianism, and argued that the Jewish longing for redemption was not primarily

about sovereignty: 'the Jew mourns for the lost sanctuary of the Torah
. . . not for the lost land'.[184]

There remain a number of issues which Adler addressed and which we
ought to consider. The first regarded a matter which was of great importance to acculturated Jews of Adler's time: sacrifices. In 1892 one of the
demands of the founders of the Hampstead Synagogue was that references to sacrifices be omitted from the liturgy. The man they wanted
to serve as their minister, Morris Joseph, said of the sacrificial rite 'our
souls revolt at the thought. The God who loves Sacrifice is not He whom
we worship.'[185] Britain was not the only place where this issue was of
major concern. The German Reform leader Abraham Geiger omitted
references to sacrifices in his prayer books of 1854 and 1870, while the
Breslau Seminary professor Manuel Joel printed both traditional and
expurgated texts in his prayer book, but only translated the reformed
text.[186] The answers of traditionalists, of Hirsch and Hoffman in
Germany and Adler in Britain, were very similar, to stress the symbolic
aspect of sacrifices.[187] Just as these German rabbis regarded sacrifices
as means to raise the spirituality and ethics of those who offered them
up, so Adler said of sacrifices 'these acts in themselves were not effica-
cious, but were to serve as symbols and admonitions to the people' and
he quoted Maimonides: 'all these rites were calculated to impress the
soul of the worshippers and to stimulate them to repentance'.[188] This
answered Joseph's claim that the sacrifices implied that God desired
'the slaughter of sheep and oxen for His greater glory'.[189] According to
Adler these arguments misunderstood the purpose of sacrifices.

Another area of Jewish thought that caused Adler's contemporaries difficulty was mysticism. Hirsch was resolutely anti-mystical. He
declared 'Judaism has no secrets' and referred to 'amulet junk'.[190] Adler
was more nuanced. He made scant references to mysticism, and gave
rational interpretations to ideas that seemed mystical. For example,
when he related the ancient custom to discover the solution to a national
crisis by asking a schoolchild to repeat the verse they had just learnt in
school, Adler said 'think not. . .that this was a superstitious practice, or
a kind of divination. Our Synagogue fathers knew well that, in a time of
national stress, the wise schoolmaster would teach his young charges
such Bible texts as would afford some comfort, guidance and wise
practical counsel how to meet the crisis'.[191] Obviously, this rationalism
was a product of the Enlightenment for Hirsch and Adler alike, but it
was also the result of an older tradition. Adler received this double
influence from his teacher, Rapoport, whom Schischa has described
as a 'Maskil/Mithnaggid' – an Enlightenment-influenced opponent of

mystical hassidim.[192] However, Adler does seem to have been more enthusiastic about mysticism than Rapoport. He studied mystical writings, for example *Sefer yetsira*, which he quoted in an 1885 sermon.[193] This may be due to the mystical tradition within his family. His father's great-uncle, Nathan Adler of Frankfurt, was a famous kabbalist.

Adler was roused to tackle the eternal question of why the virtuous suffer by the sinking of HMS *Victoria* in 1893. It is noteworthy that it was a British tragedy that prompted Adler's response. This has to be understood in the context of his patriotism, but also because the suffering of Jews could be explained by the fact that they were in exile, whereas the suffering of innocent non-Jews required a different answer. Adler gave a rationalist answer, arguing that the world required laws in order to function, but that all laws in this finite world were inevitably imperfect and allowed for disaster.[194] He then deployed the ancient argument that, if God intervened to prevent disaster every time it was imminent, man would lose his free will.[195] However, Adler also argued that many tragedies were the result of human error caused by neglect or overwork, and that they were therefore avoidable and were the result not of God's but of man's failure.[196]

In 1885 a clerical symposium was held on immortality in which Adler was the only Jewish participant. Some contributors argued that the Jewish belief in immortality was a late development. Adler argued for the traditional view that 'the immortality of the soul formed an integral portion of Jewish belief from the most ancient times'.[197] Indeed he argued it could 'be inferred from the very first page of the Pentateuch' because the statement that man was created 'in the image of God' could only refer to the immortal soul, for God has no physical appearance.[198] He then traced the idea through Biblical texts referring to Enoch, Abraham, Moses and David.[199] This begged the question as to why the idea was only mentioned explicitly relatively late, in Maccabaean times. Adler answered by quoting Maimonides, that the Jews who left Egypt were of such a low spiritual state that they could only comprehend the idea of earthly reward, and the idea of the afterlife was not stressed until the Jews had developed sufficiently to appreciate it.[200] Adler himself subscribed to the traditional idea of the world to come: as he told one congregation, on death each person 'will have to stand before the Judgement throne of God' and although, with normative Jewish tradition, he rejected a belief in 'the endless bodily torture of a Gehenna' he did believe in an 'unending remorse. . .judgement and eternity'.[201]

We have now analysed all the major elements of Adler's theology, those who influenced and shared his ideas and those who disagreed with and opposed them. Adler's views place him on the traditionalist wing of the acknowledgement school, because he felt (like others we would place in the same part of our typology) that there was no alternative, indeed a positive virtue, in acknowledging the modern world and accepting its best aspects. This acknowledgement encompassed different aspects of modernity. There was acceptance of new scholarly methods and some of the conclusions deduced using them, which led to Adler support-ing *Wissenschaft*. There was a recognition of the spiritually positive aspects of the non-Jewish world, which grew out of a Romantic sen-sibility and made Adler sympathetic to the *Torah im drekh erets* of Hirsch; and there was an appreciation of the beauty of some examples of non-Jewish expression, especially religious expression, which moti-vated Adler to make aesthetic considerations a feature of his Judaism.

However, the traditionalist wing of the acknowledgement school was restrained by its traditionalism from accepting modernity completely or uncritically, and first and foremost Adler was a traditionalist. Although Adler adopted modern attitudes and methods, they did not dislodge his traditional views. He encouraged *Wissenschaft* but also wrote *pilpul*, and interpreted sacrifices symbolically but also looked forward to carrying them out in practice. In this regard he was the spiritual and intellectual successor of his father, who combined the old learning of the pre-modern era with university training, the halakhic expertise of a traditional *rav* with the refinement and dignity of a modern cleric. It was also an inheritance from Hermann Adler's teachers. The tradition-alist influence of Ausch and Freund is detectable alongside that of the enlightened Rapoport.

Adler was immoveable on the Pentateuch, like all traditionalists in the acknowledgement school and the antipathy school leaders of Hungary and eastern Europe. He also stood firm on the Divine nature of the Oral Law, as all of these scholars did, although they disagreed on the extent to which it had developed. Adler followed his father on this issue and stood with the scientific Hildesheimer and Hoffman, rejecting the unhistorical approach of Hirsch, Auerbach and Moses Sofer. Alongside Hildesheimer and his students, Adler was not theologi-cally concerned about the dating and authorship of the Biblical books outside the Pentateuch, which were, after all, considered Divinely inspired rather than Divinely dictated. He was a dedicated upholder of *halakhah*, but like Hildesheimer and others he did not believe that it stood still, or should stand still, or that it was all-encompassing. Aspects of Jewish behaviour could change if necessary, as long as hala-khic sources did not proscribe such a change. In other words, the exter-nal forms of Judaism could adapt to the times but what he considered to be the substance was unchangeable. Non-Jewish learning and beauty were welcome, but Torah came first. As Adler said in his lecture on Elisha ben Abuya, if science contradicted Torah, then Torah must be upheld until 'true science' was found which did not contradict Torah. Greece and Rome contributed much, but were also gravely morally deficient. Jewish prayer should be beautified but never at the expense of *halakhah*.

This theological approach separated Adler from men like Morris Joseph who – despite wishing to hold on to much more tradition than, say, Geiger, and who therefore should be placed in the acknowledgement school – differed with Adler on decisive issues, especially the Pentateuch, and therefore occupied the school's non-traditional wing. On the other hand, although Adler's attitude towards issues such as the value of secular literature and the dating of some psalms was never shared by the antipathy school, it was regarded at least as acceptable by them, hence the admiration which we have seen eastern European rabbis had for Hildesheimer. As a traditionalist within the acknowledgement school, who accepted some views which others did not, Adler belonged to the school of Jewish thought which developed the tradition, which like all traditions can never be static, as well as transmitting it.

Adler's thought bears the mark of the theological, political and social pressures to which he was responding. As Montefiore and others in the adaptation school were questioning doctrines such as the Divinely revealed Pentateuch and the necessity of *halakhah*, Adler had to speak out all the more forcefully in favour of them, and develop new defences and lines of attack, alongside and at the same time as other traditionalist Jewish leaders of his generation. As the acculturated Jews he ministered to worried about sacrifices and what they regarded as the irrational nature of Jewish mysticism, Adler interpreted them in certain ways. As some non-Jews questioned Jewish loyalty to the state, Adler had to stress the universalistic aspects of Judaism and the patriotism of the Jews, and to repudiate Zionism. This latter placed Adler in a difficult position, especially regarding the idea of the Messiah, from which he extricated himself only with difficulty. In this Adler wrestled with the same problem as those contemporaries who sought to make the same case for Jewish patriotism without sacrificing any item of Jewish faith, or even denying the bond that united all Jews.

This analysis of Adler's theology and its context leads us to a revised understanding of the man. Although Adler was not a great original theologian, he was learned and thoughtful, and developed intellectual responses to the challenges of his time, when Judaism was struck by the collapse of rabbinic authority and the implosion of traditional belief in the wake of Enlightenment and Emancipation.[202] Adler's position of leadership is what makes these views important, because they determined how he guided his community, and therefore left their mark on Jews throughout Britain and its Empire, both in his own tie and subsequently. The respect he accrued was demonstrated at his death not only by tributes from Anglo-Jewry, but from leading foreign scholars such as Elbogen. As Adler was not simply or even primarily a religious thinker but an active and dedicated religious leader we must now investigate whether, and how, he implemented his abstract religious ideas and used them to shape practical communal policy.

Notes

1 He was appointed a Commander of the Royal Victorian Order by Edward VII and was given an honorary doctorate by Oxford University.

2 G. Alderman, *Modern British Jewry* (Oxford 1992), 147.

3 H. Adler, *Niftulei Elohim* (London 1869); H. Adler, *Anglo-Jewish memories* (London 1909).

4 I. Finestein, *Anglo-Jewry in changing times* (London 1999), 226.

5 B. Spiers (ed), *Hagadah for Passover* (London 1954).

6 H. Adler, 'Jews and Judaism: a rejoinder' *Nineteenth Century* (1878), 133–150; (1881), 813–829.

7 At the London Metropolitan Archives, the Anglo-Jewish Archives, Southampton University, the archives of the Jewish and National Library, Jerusalem, and the Jewish Theological Seminary, New York.

8 H. Adler, *The old paths* (London 1902), 6.

9 Adler Archives at the Jewish Theological Seminary, New York (AA JTS) 3, 1/9.

10 For example, by Rabbi Seligman Bamberger (the Wurzburger Rav), the leading German Talmudist of his generation, the leading traditionalist exponent of *Wissenschaft*, Rabbi David Hoffman, and Rabbi Yissakhar Dov Illowy of New Orleans all sought Nathan Adler's approbation or religious ruling; *Netina lager* was published in *Torat Elohim* (Vilna 1875).

11 E.C. Black, 'The Anglicization of orthodoxy: the Adlers, father and son' in Malino and Sorkin (ed) *From east and west* (Oxford 1990), 296.

12 A. Schischa, 'Adler, yeshiva bahur, Prague, 1860–1862' in Shaftesley (ed) *Remember the days* (London 1966), 242, 244.

13 AA JTS 3, 1/5.

14 Schischa, 'Adler in Prague', 257.

15 C. Roth, 'Britain's three Chief Rabbis' in Jung (ed) *Jewish leaders* (Jerusalem 1953), 483.

16 Black, 'Anglicization: the Adlers', 312.

17 Roth, 'Chief Rabbis', 483.

18 E. Newman, 'The responsa of Dayan Jacob Reinowitz, 1813–98'6 *Jewish Historical Studies* 23 (1969/70), 23.

19 Adler, *Anglo-Jewish memories*, 90; Schischa, 'Adler in Prague', 241.

20 I. Brodie, *The strength of my heart* (London 1969), 123.

21 H. Adler, 'Elisha ben Abuya' *Jewish Chronicle* (22 March 1878), 11–12.

22 Spiers, *Hagadah*, viii.

23 Ibid.

24 Ibid., 17.

25 See, for example, Adler's correspondence with Samuel Isaac Hillman, Hillman Archive Jewish and National Library Jerusalem (HA JNL), 9b/284.

26 *Jewish Chronicle* (11 August 1865), 6.

27 *Jewish Chronicle* (8 September 1896), 16–17.

28 Chief Rabbinate Papers, London Metropolitan Archive (CRP LMA) ACC 2805/2/1/133; A.Z. Zivotofsky and A. Amar 'The halakhic tale of three American birds, turkey, prairie chicken and muscovy duck' *Journal of Halakhah and Contemporary Society* 46 (2003), 81–104.

29 M. Breuer, trans. E. Petuchowski, *Modernity within tradition* (New York 1992), 195; *Jewish Review* (September 1911), 194, 202.

30 Adler, *Anglo-Jewish memories*, 227, 229.

31 Adler, *Niftulei Elohim*, 163.

32 Ibid., 170, 172; Adler, *Anglo-Jewish memories*, 222.

33 Hermann Adler's obituary of Zunz in the *Jewish Chronicle* (26 March 1886), 9; M. Joseph, *Judaism as life and creed* (London 1903), 24; M.L. Raphael, *Profiles in American Judaism* (San Francisco 1984), 102; L. Jacobs, *We have reason to believe* (London 1957), 80–81.

34 D. Feldman, *Englishmen and Jews* (New Haven, Connecticut 1994), 124.

35 *Jewish Chronicle*, (2 January 1863), 6.

36 A. Marx, *Essays in Jewish biography* (Philadelphia 1904), 199.

37 Breuer, *Modernity within tradition*, 204.

38 M.A. Meyer, *Judaism within modernity* (Detroit 2001), 313.

39 G. Parsons, 'Reform, revival and realignment: the experience of Victorian Anglicanism' in Parsons (ed) *Religion in Victorian Britain, I:Traditions* (Manchester 1988), 40.

40 C.G. Montefiore, *The Hibbert Lectures 1892* (London 1897), xi.

41 H. Adler 'The sons of the prophets' in Harris (ed) *Jews' College jubilee volume* (London 1906), 15–16 .

42 H.Adler, Some recent phases of Judaeophobia' *Nineteenth Century* (1881), 818 .

43 Ibid.

44 H. Adler, *Hebrew, the language of our prayers* (London 1885), 9.

45 Adler, *Niftulei Elohim*, 149.

46 L. Jacobs, *Helping with inquiries* (London 1989), 77; J.H. Hertz, *The Authorised Daily Prayer Book* (New York 1948), xiii.

47 T. Endelman, *The Jews of Britain, 1656 to 2000* (Berkeley 2002), 114.

48 An interesting indication of Joseph's attitude to the Oral Law and

rabbinic legislation so forcefully rejected by Marks and the West London is his observance of the second day of festivals, when he attended the Bayswater Synagogue. O.S. Phillips and H.A. Simons, *The history of the Bayswater Synagogue, 1863–1963* (London 1963), 14.

49 Adler, *Niftulei Elohim*, 174.

50 Adler, *Anglo-Jewish memories*, xi.

51 Ibid., *passim*.

52 Ibid., 252.

53 Spiers, *Hagadah*, viii. I would like to thank Oliver Harris with whom I first studied these comments.

54 Schischa, 'Adler in Prague', 247–248.

55 Adler, *Anglo-Jewish memories*, 87.

56 Adler, *Niftulei Elohim*, 163.

57 Ibid., 164.

58 Adler, *Anglo-Jewish memories*, 224, 227, 228.

59 H. Adler, *The Sabbath and the synagogue* (London 1889).

60 H. Adler, *Is it well with thee?* (Birmingham 1893), 7; Adler, *Anglo-Jewish memories*, 173; H. Adler, *Home worship* (London 1894), 5–6.

61 Ibid., 255.

62 Adler, *Niftulei Elohim*, 174.

63 Adler, *Anglo-Jewish memories*, 253.

64 Ibid., 253–255.

65 Maimonides, *Guide of the perplexed*, ed M. Friedlander (London 1904) chapter 26.

66 Breuer, *Modernity within tradition*, 63.

67 M. Olsberg, unpublished undergraduate dissertation (2005), 17.

68 Adler, *Anglo-Jewish memories*, 191.

69 Ibid., 191.

70 Ibid., 192; Adler, *Is it well with thee?*, 7.

71 Adler, 'Jews and Judaism: a rejoinder', 136.

72 H. Adler, *Hebrew, the language of our prayers* (London 1885), 3.

73 D. Ellenson, *Rabbi Esriel Hildesheimer and the creation of a modern Jewish orthodoxy* (Tuscaloosa, Alabama 1990), 49.

74 J. Katz, *Divine law in human hands* (Jerusalem 1998), 331.

75 Adler, *Anglo-Jewish memories* (London 1909), 174–175.

76 Ibid., 205.

77 Adler, *Niftulei Elohim*, 170–171.

78 Meyer, *Judaism within modernity*, 313.

79 These are, of course, subjective judgements, and each individual's view of what is wholesome or beautiful, and how much incorporation of outside influences is compatible with authentic Judaism, will differ. Here we are discussing Adler's view.

80 Adler, 'Sons of the prophets', 15–16. Adler considered these to be 'minor points'; others did not.

81 H. Adler, *A good heart* (London 1893), 6.

82 Adler, *Anglo-Jewish memories*, 283.
83 Breuer, *Modernity within tradition*, 181–183.
84 Ellenson, *Hildesheimer*, 131; Marx, *Jewish biography*, 218.
85 Ellenson, *Hildesheimer*, 149.
86 Marx, *Jewish biography*, 218–219.
87 M.B. Shapiro, *Between the yeshiva world and modern orthodoxy: the life and times of Rabbi Jehiel Jacob Weinberg* (Oxford 1999), 102–103.
88 Olsberg, dissertation, 9.
89 Adler, *Anglo-Jewish memories*, 272–273.
90 Finestein, *Changing times*, 226.
91 Adler, *Anglo-Jewish memories*, 143, 218; Adler, *Niftulei Elohim*, 173; Adler, *Anglo-Jewish memories*, 112; H. Adler, *This book of the Law* (London 1891), 6–8.
92 Adler, *Anglo-Jewish memories*, 81.
93 Schischa, 'Adler in Prague', 266.
94 G. Parsons, 'Reform, revival and realignment' in Parsons (ed) *Religion in Victorian Britain, I: Traditions*, 26.
95 Meyer, *Judaism within modernity*, 319.
96 R. Shuchat, 'Attitudes towards cosmogony and evolution among rabbinic thinkers in the nineteenth and early twentieth centuries', *Torah u-Madda Journal* 13 (2005), 15–49; S.R. Hirsch, *Collected writings* (New York 1988), volume 7, 263.
97 Adler, *Anglo-Jewish memories*, 256.
98 Adler, *Niftulei Elohim*, 173.
99 *Jewish Chronicle* (3 January 1902), 9.
100 J. Jung, *Champions of orthodoxy* (London 1974), 1.
101 Feldman, *Englishmen and Jews* (New Haven 1994), 336.
102 *Jewish Chronicle* (16 August 1912), 14.
103 Adler, *Anglo-Jewish memories*, 223.
104 Ibid., 225.
105 Ellenson, *Hildesheimer*; Sh.Z. Leiman, 'Rabbinic openness to general culture in the early modern period' in (Schachter ed) *Judaism's encounter with other cultures: rejection or integration?* (New York 1997), 209.
106 *Jewish Chronicle* (5 April 1878), 12.
107 M. Shapiro, 'Rabbi David Zevi Hoffman on Torah and *Wissenschaft*' *Torah u-Madda Journal* 6 (1995–1996), 132.
108 Ibid., 133.
109 *Jewish Chronicle* (1 July 1892), 17.
110 Breuer, *Modernity within tradition*, 162.
111 P.C. Albert, *The modernization of French Jewry* (Hanover, New Hampshire 1977), 53.
112 H. Adler, *The old paths* (London 1902), 10; Adler, *Hebrew, language of our prayers*, 12.
113 *Hukat hagoy* was never an absolute; indeed, another point of dispute between the antipathy and the acknowledgement school concerned the

extent of its application. The antipathy school would apply it even to dress, whereas the acknowledgement school did not. Historically Jews had always adopted the customs of their surroundings. For example in terms of languages, scholars such as Maimonides wrote some of their works not in Hebrew but in Arabic.

114 Adler, *Anglo-Jewish memories*, 237.
115 Ibid., 87. 'Dignity' as understood at the time, of course.
116 Ibid., 273.
117 Ibid., 227.
118 M. Arnold, *Culture and anarchy* (London 1869), 145.
119 Ibid., 148.
120 C.G. Montefiore, *Liberal Judaism and Hellenism* (London 1918), 185.
121 Adler, 'Jews and Judaism: a rejoinder', 141.
122 Adler, *Niftulei Elohim*, 142.
123 Ibid., 158, 143.
124 Endelman, *Jews of Britain*, 86.
125 Feldman, *Englishmen and Jews*, 28–30, 113–114, 91.
126 Ibid., 57.
127 Adler, *Niftulei Elohim*, iii, 2.
128 Ibid., 34. See also Adler, *Anglo-Jewish memories*, 243–244.
129 Adler, *Niftulei Elohim*, 140–141.
130 Ibid., 130.
131 Ibid., 147.
132 Ibid., 165–166.
133 Ibid. 62–63.
134 Adler, *Anglo-Jewish memories*, 264.
135 S. Bayme, 'Claude Montefiore, Lily Montagu and the origins of the Jewish Religious Union' in *Jewish Historical Studies* 27 (1978/80), 65; Montefiore, *Hibbert Lectures*, 550–551.
136 Adler, *Niftulei Elohim*, 159; S.R. Hirsch, trans. B. Drachman, *The nineteen letters* (New York 1899), 63.
137 Finestein, *Changing times*, 229.
138 Montefiore, *Hibbert Lectures*, 548; C.G. Montefiore, 'Is Judaism a tribal religion?' *Contemporary Review* (1882),9–16.
139 Adler, 'Jews and Judaism: a rejoinder', 138.
140 Ibid., 282.
141 Ibid., 284.
142 Ibid., 283.
143 Adler, Jews and Judaism: A rejoinder,143.
144 Adler, *Anglo-Jewish memories*, 270.
145 Ibid., 285.
146 Ibid., 266.
147 Ibid., 261–269.
148 Ellenson, *Hildesheimer*, 34.
149 Olsberg, dissertation, 9.

150 S. Heilman, 'Constructing orthodoxy' in Robbins and Anthony (ed) *In gods we trust* (New Brunswick, 1981), 144–145.

151 Adler, *Anglo-Jewish memories*, 287.

152 Ibid., 257.

153 Ibid., 270.

154 Ibid., 274.

155 See Adler, 'Jews and Judaism: a rejoinder'. The next chapter discusses in detail the contemporary political circumstances of the Adler–Goldwin Smith dispute.

156 Meyer, *Judaism within modernity*, 313.

157 G.W. Plaut, *The rise of Reform Judaism* (New York 1963), 135.

158 Meyer, *Judaism within modernity*, 313.

159 Adler, *Anglo-Jewish memories*, 288.

160 Breuer, *Modernity within tradition*, 286, 294.

161 The full context of this argument, especially its relationship to the Eastern Crisis of 1878 and the personal antipathy between Goldwin Smith and Disraeli, will be discussed when we consider Adler's religious policy.

162 D. Sorkin, 'The impact of Emancipation on German Jewry' in Frankel and Zipperstein (ed) *Assimilation and community: the Jews in nineteenth-century Europe* (Cambridge 1992), 184.

163 Adler, 'Jews and Judaism: a rejoinder', 134.

164 Adler, *Anglo-Jewish memories*, 155; Adler, 'Jews and Judaism: a rejoinder', 135.

165 Adler, 'Jews and Judaism: a rejoinder', 136.

166 Adler, *Anglo-Jewish memories*, 98–99.

167 Ibid., 107.

168 Ibid., 123.

169 On the other hand, Hayim Zundel Maccoby identified with the Liberal Party but still supported the Boer War. Jung *Champions*, 59.

170 Adler, *Anglo-Jewish memories*, 74–75.

171 H.A. Simons, *Forty years a Chief Rabbi: the life and times of Solomon Hirschell* (London 1980), 35.

172 Ibid., 289.

173 Ibid., 307.

174 H. Adler, *Religious versus political Zionism* (London 1898), 13.

175 S.A. Cohen, *English Zionists and British Jews* (Princeton 1982), 186.

176 Ibid., 191.

177 Endelman, *Jews of Britain*, 188–189; Breuer, *Modernity within tradition*, 370.

178 Adler, *Zionism*, 7.

179 Ibid., 15.

180 M. Joseph, *The ideal in Judaism* (London 1893), 41.

181 Finestein, *Changing times*, 229.

182 Adler, *Zionism*, 8, 7.

183 Breuer, *Modernity within tradition*, 287.

184 Ibid.
185 Joseph, *Ideal in Judaism*, 43.
186 D. Ellenson, *After Emancipation* (Cincinnati 2004), 208–209, 216–219.
187 Marx, *Jewish biography*, 202–203 .
188 D. Ellenson, 'A vindication of Judaism: the polemics of the Hertz Pentateuch: a review essay' *Modern Judaism* 21 (2001), p. 73; H. Adler, *Anglo-Jewish memories* (London 1909), 246.
189 Joseph, *Ideal in Judaism*, 42.
190 Breuer, *Modernity within tradition*, 66.
191 Adler, *Anglo-Jewish memories*, 1. This explanation is problematic because it implies that a simple teacher of small children would know better than the great sages which text to consult for guidance.
192 Schischa, 'Adler in Prague', 250.
193 Adler, *Hebrew, language of our prayers*, 15.
194 H. Adler, *The loss of HMS Victoria* (London 1893), 10.
195 Ibid., 11.
196 Ibid.
197 H. Adler in *Immortality: a clerical symposium* (London 1885), 88.
198 Ibid., 90.
199 Ibid., 90–92, 96.
200 Ibid., 94–96.
201 Adler, *Anglo-Jewish memories*, 175.
202 His trailblazing attack on Biblical criticism in 1868s, his wrestling with the relationship between Jewish peoplehood and British patriotism, his response to the new challenges of Zionism and of scholarship, both on non-Pentateuchal Jewish texts and in science, are particularly significant in this regard.

Chapter 6

The religious policy of Hermann Adler

WE HAVE ANALYSED Adler's theological position in theory, but we can only achieve a proper understanding of his religious position by examining how he operated as an active religious leader, dealing with the day-to-day management of a community. From the age of 25 until his death 48 years later Adler served the Jewish community: as Principal of Jews' College (1864–65), minister of the Bayswater Synagogue (1865–91), Delegate Chief Rabbi (1879–91) or Chief Rabbi (1891–1911).

Adler attempted to uphold his principles in the face of pressure exerted from all sides of his community. He held firm on some issues and conceded on others, but only after he had analysed whether *halakhah* tolerated concession. Although Adler generally followed his father's example, he did deviate in some cases, and employed innovative means to achieve aims he shared with his predecessor. Adler operated in a post-Enlightenment and post-Emancipation context, in which affiliation to the Jewish community was voluntary. Members of Adler's community could either take or leave his rulings, while the *herem* (excommunication) was put beyond his use by the lay leadership.[1] In any case, the *herem* issued by Hirschell against West London had been ineffective and created a poor impression of the Jewish community amongst the non-Jewish public, displaying it as intolerant and sectarian, so that even if Adler had still been able to use it, he would have been wise not to.

In this chapter, I examine the new methods Adler had to employ to achieve his aims. Adler used the spoken and the printed word to encourage and to condemn. He used his powers as ecclesiastical authority for the United Synagogue to impose discipline, and worked to extend and deepen his religious authority, as part of a policy of religious centralism that has come to be known as Adlerism. Where he lacked formal power he used his moral and spiritual authority, and his connections with the great and the good both inside and outside the Jewish community, to influence and cajole. Adler also had to look outwards from his community. Jews had to be seen to be fulfilling the responsibilities that came with Emancipation: loyalty to the nation and a willingness to contribute to its well-being. It fell to Adler as a leader of Anglo-Jewry to show that they were.

When we examine Adler's policies in the context of those of other religious leaders, they again demonstrate that Adler is correctly sited in the traditionalist camp within the acknowledgement school. In his policies Adler had much in common with other members of that group, such as Hildesheimer and Hirsch, while he differed from the antipathy and adaptation schools, and crucially, with those in the non-traditionalist group within the acknowledgement school. Although this latter group shared Adler's broad analysis, they differed with him on how far the boundaries of tradition could be pushed to acknowledge modernity. In terms of power and organisation, Adler was expansive and hegemonic. He allowed change within *halakhah*, as he interpreted it, in order to maintain allegiance to his brand of Judaism, and he succeeded.

Adler's principal device for achieving his objectives was the spoken word. The sermon was central to Anglo-Jewish practice in Adler's time, and his title of 'lecturer' at the Bayswater Synagogue expressed the role expected of a modern religious leader.[2] In 1909 a Jews' College committee placed the ability to 'preach efficiently' at the top of the list of requirements for a synagogue minister, and therefore the college taught elocution and homiletics.[3] Adler identified preaching as one of the prime duties of the minister, and said, 'his voice will be heard . . . awakening the careless, and stirring up the slothful, seeking to kindle in his hearers' hearts the enthusiasm that stirs and quickens his own soul'.[4] He set an example, speaking in synagogues around the country.[5] If necessary, in order to transmit his message effectively, he spoke in Yiddish, although he encouraged the use of English.[6]

This emphasis on the sermon was influenced by the popularity of sermons in contemporary English society, where they were published and read on a wide scale.[7] Jewish enthusiasm for the sermon had first emerged among those with reformist tendencies (an English sermon was one of the demands of the founders of West London in 1840), as part of their answer to the charge that Judaism lacked spirituality. Nathan Adler appropriated the sermon for the purposes of tradition, as a useful medium for transmitting his message. Adler's publication of his sermons was therefore an expression of a general trend, but there was a traditional Jewish aspect to Adler and Anglo-Jewry's enthusiasm for the sermon. In eastern Europe the *maggid*, or itinerant preacher, was a familiar figure, and the leaders of the established community brought him to England in the person of Hayim Zundel Maccoby, the Kamenitzer Maggid.[8] Naturally, the *maggidim* of Europe spoke in Yiddish, and leaders of the antipathy school declared in 1866 that it was forbidden to preach in a non-Jewish language. Adler, like his father (and Maccoby) disagreed with the antipathy school and spoke in English.[9] Their decision to preach in the local vernacular followed the example of the early leaders of the acknowledgement school, Isaac Bernays and Jacob Ettlinger, and was shared by their student Hirsch.[10] Here is another example of Adler deviating from the antipathy school and altering outward forms in order to convey his message. However, the content of Adler's sermons was traditional, making the distinction between Adler and the antipathy school one of form, but between him and the adaptation and acceptance schools one of substance.

Adler used his public utterances both to guide and to defend his community. Thus he preached the usual rabbinical messages: he urged his listeners to accept Jewish teachings and to follow *halakhah*, including Sabbath observance, synagogue attendance, marriage within the faith, giving children a Jewish education, honesty in business and so forth;[11] he asserted the Divine origin of the Pentateuch and the necessity of Jewish particularism.[12] But he also touched on more complex issues and addressed them in an interesting way. He discussed the problem of evil, argued that science need not undermine religious faith, celebrated Hebraism and criticised Hellenism.[13] Although Adler's favoured medium was the spoken word, either as a sermon or lecture, he also wrote letters to the editor of the *Jewish Chronicle*, for example in 1863 to refute Colenso's argument that the Pentateuch was a composite, human work.[14]

Adler was very conscious of the threat from Christian conversionists, not necessarily because he feared many Jews would convert, but because their arguments that Judaism was inferior to Christianity were an intellectual affront and because missionaries were imagining an end to Britain as a multi-religious polity, thereby implicitly questioning Emancipation.[15] He was convinced that the best defence was to educate Jews and refute conversionist arguments, and especially their readings of the Hebrew Bible.[16] Thus he delivered and published a series of sermons attempting to demolish Christological interpretations of the Hebrew Bible in 1869.[17] It was still a priority forty years later and Adler published another anti-missionary sermon in 1909.[18]

An interesting aspect of these sermons is the harshness of the attacks on missionaries, who were respected members of the general community, and often representatives of the Established Church. He called their arguments 'illogical utterances of soul-hunters'.[19] This language displays a confidence that was the fruit of Adler's work stressing

Jewish loyalty to Britain. It also contrasts with the very cautious and circumspect approach followed by other Jewish leaders – for example, the very discreet, and in some cases ineffective, work of the Board of Deputies, and the appeals of the *Jewish Chronicle* to members of the community to avoid ostentatious displays of wealth or vulgarity, so as not to draw unsympathetic attention.[20] Adler therefore offers an interesting counter example to evidence which might be brought to support the argument that the Jewish community suffered from timidity, brought, for example by Alderman when he wrote 'emancipation and its achievement also had a prolonged and passive effect upon British Jewry's perception of its own public image'.[21]

Adler used sermons to intervene in religious controversies within the Jewish community. When there was agitation to remove Hebrew from the service Adler retaliated with a sermon, published as *Hebrew, the language of our prayers*, which affirmed the value of Hebrew prayer and appealed to the congregation to learn the language.[22] When the Hampstead Synagogue voted to install an organ to play on the Sabbath, Adler went to the synagogue and preached a sermon denouncing the idea, which was then not implemented.[23] When the Jewish Religious Union began to hold services, which Adler regarded as unacceptable, he condemned them in a sermon entitled *The old paths*.[24] This continued Nathan Adler's policy. He had combated the West London Synagogue's antagonism to the Oral Law by preaching sermons stressing its validity.[25] Like his father too, Adler used sermons to appeal to the community on issues that concerned him but were not specifically religious. He preached against political radicalism, to which poor Jews were thought to be vulnerable.[26] He delivered a sermon in Yiddish urging his listeners to learn English and to Anglicise.[27] During the 1905 persecutions of Russian Jews, Adler requested money to help refugees, just as his father had appealed for funds in 1881–82.[28] Adler particularly wanted money to fund emigration to the United States, and thereby to achieve two objectives: to help the refugees and to keep them out of Britain.[29]

This raises the issue of Adler's attitude towards immigration and immigrants, which, as Black has noted, was ambiguous.[30] As a Western Jew, no less than as an English Jew, he found what he considered the low cultural level of the immigrants distasteful. He referred to them as 'uncultivated and uncivilised'.[31] For their part, the religious section of the immigrant community did not hold Adler in great esteem as a rabbi and deprecated his level of learning. Like his father, Adler sought to discourage Eastern European Jews from coming to Britain, from staying if they came, from staying in London even if they remained in Britain, and if they did remain in England to Anglicise as quickly and thoroughly as possible.[32] His great concern was that the arrival of immigrants should not undo all the work of the previous half century in advancing the position of Jews politically and culturally in British society.

On the other hand, he campaigned against legal restrictions on immigration, declaring, 'we have declared an almost unanimous opinion that England's door should not be closed and that we regard an Alien Bill as unnecessary and unwise'.[33] Adler was concerned for the welfare of immigrants and respected their piety.[34] He believed, nevertheless, that wide-scale immigration could cause anti-Semitism, especially as it raised the fear of socialism and anarchism.[35] Adler would have been aware of comments like those of the Christian social worker Henry Walker in 1896, who wrote of the East End 'the English visitor feels himself one of a subject race in the presence of dominant and overwhelming invaders'.[36] Limiting immigration was therefore one way to ensure that legal restrictions were not imposed. If America could provide opportunity as well as Britain, he was keen that refugees should go there instead. That is why he urged a congregation in 1898 'to provide for these new-comers, either by finding them means of subsistence or by sending them to other hospitable lands'.[37] It is likely that it was the same considerations that prompted the man seen as the great friend of the immigrants, Samuel Montagu, to found the Jewish Dispersion Committee, to send immigrants to towns around Britain.[38]

Adler knew that his sermons would be published and reach a wider audience than the Jewish community. It is apparent, for example, that Christian theologians read Adler's *The Jewish doctrine of atonement*, because they published replies justifying the Christian concept of vicarious atonement, which Adler had attacked.[39] His sermons to mark great national occasions, such as the Jubilee and the death of Queen Victoria, were delivered to Jews, but signalled Jewish patriotism to the wider community.[40] Adler was sure that these demonstrations of loyalty benefited Jews.[41]

Adler's supposedly academic lectures also served as propaganda. In one, he highlighted the debt owed to Ibn Gabirol by non-Jewish philosophers.[42] He made a case for what he called the 'remarkable contributions to historical science' made by the Talmud.[43] He highlighted other Jewish contributions to European civilisation in terms of ethics, philosophy, science, medicine and even art.[44] In his lecture to the Church of England Sanitary Association in 1893, *Sanitation as taught by the Mosaic law*, Adler defended Jewish slaughter.[45] He attempted to deflect public criticism by condemning the East End Jews' irregular marriages before a Royal Commission on Divorce and Matrimonial Causes.[46]

Adler's lengthiest defences of his community were articles published in the journal *Nineteenth Century* in 1878 and 1881 entitled 'Jews and Judaism: a rejoinder' and 'Some recent phases of Judaeophobia' in which he combated the anti-Semitic arguments put forward by Professor Goldwin Smith.[47] Goldwin Smith was particularly dangerous because he had originally been a supporter of Jewish Emancipation, granted only twenty years earlier, but had changed his mind and had come to the conclusion that Jewish loyalty could not be relied upon. This issue was particularly sensitive in 1878 because of the Eastern Crisis, which persuaded many that the Jews were attempting to pull Britain into a war for their own purposes. In particular, Disraeli was looked upon with great suspicion, and the Liberal Goldwin Smith and Disraeli had a personal feud.[48] Meanwhile Jewish Emancipation was vulnerable elsewhere in Europe, for example in Germany.[49] Strikingly, Adler occasionally castigated the non-Jewish population. In his 1905 sermon on the Russian persecutions, Adler asked 'does it not then behove the leaders of Christian thought and action . . . to arise and offer their solemn protest against the atrocities committed and left unrebuked in a Christian country', something which Adler felt that the British population had failed to do sufficiently.[50] Adler's outspoken censuring of the general population is another reflection of the freedom of speech Adler's protestations of British loyalty afforded him.

The Chief Rabbi's power had a number of sources. First, the Chief Rabbi was *ex officio* President of Jews' College and of the London Beth Din (the Court of the Chief Rabbi), with ultimate responsibility for their administration and the Beth Din's decisions. The United Synagogue's Deed of Foundation and Trust appointed the Chief Rabbi as its religious authority. This included control over the form of services and the appointment of ministers, who had to possess his certificate to take up a post in the United Synagogue.[51] The second source of authority was the constitution of the Board of Deputies of British Jews. Under the Marriage Registration Act 1836 the Board had sole authority to certify that a congregation consisted of 'persons professing the Jewish religion' to enable them to perform marriages valid in English law. The Board of Deputies placed the decision as to whether a congregation met the criteria in the hands of the Haham for Spanish and Portuguese Jews, and the Chief Rabbi for Ashkenzim.[52] As Feldman has observed, this relationship, based on recognition by the state, brought the Board and the Chief Rabbi into a close alliance in which each derived authority from the other.[53] The power the Chief Rabbi gained from this arrangement was profoundly resented by those who chafed under it, for example the West London Synagogue, whose leaders complained publicly about it.[54] Adler was involved in many battles over the use of these extensive powers.

The death of Nathan Adler released what Hermann Adler called 'a great deal of discontent and dissatisfaction that was latent' on the part of the Anglicised members of the community, which his father's prestige had kept under control.[55] Adler bore the brunt of this previously suppressed frustration and faced major challenges within his first year as Chief Rabbi. The Ritual Reform Conference met to discuss reforms to the United Synagogue liturgy. It requested a number of changes to make the service more acceptable, both to congregants with a modern sensibility and non-Jewish observers. The conference was prompted partly by plans to establish a new synagogue in Hampstead, which was prepared to join the United Synagogue if the service was modified. As Apple has written, 'the founders of the [Hampstead] Synagogue had wanted a modified service and only on that condition had they agreed to join the United Synagogue'.[56] Some members of the founding committee ultimately joined the West London Synagogue when they felt that not enough of their requests had been approved.[57] The Hampstead Synagogue's founders also revived the issue of mixed choirs that had first arisen in 1880. Finally, they requested that Morris Joseph should become their first minister. This prompted a crisis because of Joseph's theological views. These were the difficulties to which Israel Levi referred after Adler's death, as 'circumstances which demanded of the new Chief Rabbi energy, ability, self denial of which the lamented Nathan Adler was not called upon to give proof in like degree'.[58] How he faced them reveals a great deal about how he translated his principles into action.

Most of the agenda of the Ritual Reform Conference came from the highly acculturated New West End Synagogue where there was overwhelming support for changes, and the Hampstead Synagogue, which would only join the United Synagogue if it could reform the service.[59] The conference consisted of synagogue ministers, who passed the reforms they endorsed to the Chief Rabbi for his sanction. Englander, following Singer, has argued persuasively that those who requested changes had come to see the Chief Rabbi not as a halakhic authority, but as a bishop who could grant dispensations, following the Anglican model.[60] We can see from Adler's Reply, published in July 1892, that he rejected that notion. He set out the two criteria he adopted to determine which reforms to sanction and which to forbid. He made clear his inclination to be permissive, writing, 'I have endeavoured, where at all possible, to give effect to the recommendations of the conference . . . in consequence of the communication you have made to me which was emphatically endorsed by a majority of your Ministers, that such modifications in the ritual were earnestly desired by a majority of your members'.[61]

Adler's words 'where at all possible' were significant, because he also wrote that he had only 'given my sanction to those alterations which do not violate any statute (*din*) of traditional Judaism' which meant that in some cases 'I have felt it my duty to refrain from adopting the opinion of the majority of the members'.[62] However, Adler added the caveat that 'I shall be gratified to learn that they [congregations] continue to hold their Service in strict accord with ancient usage'.[63] In other words, Adler was prepared to accede to permit changes when they were desired by a majority of members, but only when such changes were in accordance with *halakhah*, although personally he did not wish to see any changes at all. As Adler wrote to his mother in the 1880s, when he was deputising for his father, 'my own affairs do not look so bright as I could have wished. A certain section of the community would wish me to give pledges regarding Reforms, and this I look on as Simony'.[64] Jung's suggestion that Adler supported the changes is therefore too crude.[65] In a sense he did support them, and in a sense he did not. Ideally, Adler would have liked to have seen the service unchanged, but he realised that in order to keep as many as possible within the fold of traditional Judaism, and worshipping in conformity with *halakhah*, he had to be flexible and make changes where possible. On the other hand, he did not insist that changes were made; and the Great Synagogue, where there was little desire for change, did not take advantage of Adler's concessions. Importantly, for the most part, neither did Bayswater.[66]

One could infer that Adler was lukewarm on *halakhah* by examining what he permitted to be done at Hampstead and seeing it as representing his personal inclination. In fact, Bayswater exemplified his personal preference. One might expect Bayswater, socially very similar to the New West End, to be at the forefront of calls for change, but as its minister for 25 years Adler impressed it with his own ideology, which combined the 'solemnity and reverence' that fitted the Victorian conception of religion with a fundamental traditionalism: Judaism that was modern in form but unchanged in substance (as defined by Adler), an attitude Adler inherited from his father.[67] Thus Bayswater retained the medieval liturgical poems that had crept into the service (*piyyutim*), the synagogue had its own *mikvah*, the ritual bath in which ritual immersions take place, including by women after menstruation, a practice only common amongst the most observant. There was even a Talmud class, something more associated with an immigrant than an acculturated synagogue.[68]

A good example of the Adlers' concern with aesthetics is their attitude towards synagogue singing. Nathan Adler's *Law and regulations*
of 1847 gave a formal role to the choir, which was to sing the responses
to the cantor's prayers, a duty which would fall to the congregation only
when there was no choir.[69] In 1889 a *Handbook of synagogue music for
congregational singing* was published with Nathan Adler's sanction. It
included modern compositions and traditional melodies, and attempted
to set the Hebrew grammatically.[70] As Finestein has observed, this was
partly a reaction to the West London Synagogue and the churches,
many of which were at that time producing new hymnals containing
both old tunes and new melodies, which itself was a reflection of the
Anglican revival of ceremony in ritual that took place from the 1830s
onwards.[71] In 1899 *The voice of prayer and praise* was published with
the sanction of Hermann Adler as Chief Rabbi.[72]

These volumes represent the core of the Adlers' religious policy,
because they attempted to increase synagogue attendance by enhanc-
ing the beauty of synagogue worship without affecting the content
of the service. The traditional text was retained in full, but was to
be sung attractively, just as the minister was to preach traditional
Judaism dressed in non-Jewish clerical garb, in order, as the minister
of Hampstead, A.A. Green, wrote, to 'show the Christian world . . .
the foreign Jews . . . [and] English Jewish boys and girls that a Jewish
minister had the bearing, the position and the educational standing of
ministers of other denominations'.[73] The encouragement of the choral
service was not only influenced by Anglican practice, but was designed
to have the same effect, for as Parsons has written 'the choral service
is a near perfect vehicle for the religiously lukewarm and passive – it is
familiar, ordered, comfortable, offers the opportunity to join in, yet has
the choir to lead and instigate. Not a little of the Church of England's
relative success in retaining at least some hold over the lukewarm
. . . may be related to this development'.[74] However, as Englander has
written, although the aesthetic of the Church undoubtedly affected
the United Synagogue, ultimately 'acceptance of Anglicanism touched
externals rather than essentials'.[75] However, many members of the
United Synagogue were not content with mere cosmetic changes,
hence the calling of the 1892 conference.

Hermann Adler ruled on some requests, either positively or negatively
without comment. A third group was apparently composed of borderline cases, which he permitted, but for which he provided halakhic
rationales. Adler's audience for these explanations was presumably
traditionalists, to whom he wanted to demonstrate that he was acting

within *halakhah*. He insisted that the blessing recited by men thanking God for not making them a woman should be recited, and he insisted on retention of the priestly blessing. He refused to allow the text of the marriage contract to be changed, for the organ be played on Sabbaths and festivals, for the shofar to be blown on the New Year when it fell on the Sabbath, and changes to the text of *Kol nidre*.[76] These were radical proposals, involving either a direct departure from the *halakhah* (for example, the playing of the organ on the Sabbath) or sharp deviations from ancient tradition (the text of the marriage contract and *Kol nidre*). Adler's decisions are therefore unsurprising.

Adler refused to give permission for a number of apparently more minor changes. For example, he refused to allow the text of the hymn *En kelohenu*, which ends in the Ashkenazi ritual with a reference to the incense offered in the Temple, to be changed to the Sefardi text, which made no such reference. Adler ruled that the selection of psalms recited after the Sabbath afternoon service in the summer, and the Ethics of the Fathers in the winter, be retained. He insisted that the traditional excerpts from rabbinic writings be said as part of the morning service and that the Song of Solomon, Ruth and Ecclesiastes be recited on festivals. Adler's stringency concerning these parts of the service, which do not form the core of liturgy, is unexpected given his general eagerness to allow requests. However, support for their exclusion was not as strong as that for other changes, and therefore declining to sanction them would only have a minor impact.

Apart from *En kelohenu*, where the request only concerned a few words, none of these proposals affected the central portion of the service, which was best attended, especially by the most acculturated. Only traditionalists would be present at the beginning of the service, or attend the Sabbath afternoon service. If a festival fell on a weekday many Anglicised members would go to work rather than the synagogue. They would therefore be unaffected by the recitation of the Biblical books on festivals. This suggests that Adler retained even non-essential parts of the traditional ritual if he could do so without generating significant discontent, and is further evidence that while he was firm where he felt there was no room for manoeuvre, even where he regarded change as permissible he personally preferred no change at all.

Adler allowed a number of omissions from the service – for example, some of the *selihot*, the penitential prayers recited on fast days and between the New Year and the Day of Atonement, the regulations for lighting Sabbath candles in the Friday night service (*bameh madlikin*) or the description of the Temple incense from the Sabbath morning service (*pittum haketoret*). Adler permitted congregations to discard both the recitation of the Levites' 'psalm of the day' (*Shir shel yom*) and the first Aramaic prayer for the scholars of Babylonia (*yekum purkan*).[77] These passages seem to be on a par with others that Adler wanted retained, for example, those from the early morning service. However, more congregants would be present when these texts were read, and the impact of refusing changes would have been greater and potentially more damaging to his authority. It is relevant that Adler urged that if possible they should be recited in the early morning service, or in the Sabbath afternoon service, when traditionalists would be present, rather than deleted altogether. Thus although pressure could not make Adler sanction what he thought was forbidden, even when he considered changes to be halakhically permissible he drew back from them, to a default position of 'no change' if he felt he could do so without generating excessive unrest.

Hermann Adler allowed more major alterations. The times of services were unpopular. Nathan Adler had ruled that the Sabbath morning service should begin at eight o'clock in the summer and half an hour later in the winter.[78] This was determined by the concern that the *Shema* should be read before the fourth hour of the day, a halakhic requirement. Hermann Adler permitted two different changes to the timings of Sabbath services. He allowed the service to begin at a quarter to ten o'clock and proceed uninterrupted, or for it to begin at eight o'clock (or half an hour later) with a break until eleven o'clock when the Torah was read. The first option made it easier to attend the entire service, but difficult for the *Shema* to be recited before the fourth hour. Adler therefore urged that care should be taken that the *Shema* should be read at the proper time.[79] A split service did not raise problems about the *Shema* and was probably Adler's preferred solution; indeed he instituted it at Bayswater in 1864.[80]

The final group of changes that Adler permitted were those for which he provided halakhic support. The Sabbath additional service contains references to the restitution of sacrifices. This was deeply controversial and there were demands for the cantor not to repeat the prayers aloud after the congregation had recited them silently. Adler permitted synagogues to adopt the Sefardi custom, sanctioned by Maimonides, for the additional service to be repeated only in part, which meant, in practice, that the repetition did not refer to sacrifices.[81] Adler only allowed this custom to be adopted once he had received confirmation from the Haham that this was indeed their custom and it had rabbinic support.[82] Some congregations, especially Hampstead, wanted the Ten Commandments to be read publicly each Sabbath. Rabbinic tradition generally disapproved of singling them out, as it implied that they were more binding than other commandments. Adler, however, found support for a public recitation in the writings of the early modern authority, the Maharshal, and approved it on that basis.

To retain decorum following the conclusion of the Day of Atonement, the blowing of the shofar – which signals the end of the fast and tended to prompt a stampede to the exits – was transferred from before to after the evening service following the fast. Adler found support for this in the fifteenth-century authority, the Tur.[83] The rabbinic system does not approve of relying on minority opinions or adopting customs merely for convenience; however, it does recognise that in exceptional circumstances such action is possible. Faced with intense communal pressure, including the threat of defection, Adler was in such a situation. Thus Alderman's contention that Hermann Adler's rulings of 1893 were only just acceptable is misleading. Alderman is quite right that 'on some matters Hermann stood firm . . . but on others he gave way' but the judgements were more considered than Alderman gives credit for.[84] Adler was conservative on some points, and provided halakhic support for controversial decisions, which were often less radical than those of contemporaries, like Hildesheimer.

Not everyone agreed with Adler's analysis or actions. The Chief Minister of the Federation of Synagogues, Rabbi Dr Mayer Lerner, violently objected to liturgical changes. Although he is best understood as belonging to the acknowledgement school and open to *Wissenschaft* and *Torah im derekh erets*, he was a strict traditionalist when it came to Jewish practice. He condemned the changes permitted by Adler and wrote, 'all who are faithful adherents to God and His doctrine will act entirely in harmony with His desires and feelings by holding fast to the existing order of prayer. We know from experience that all those who commence with alterations of the ritual of prayer have ended by shaking off the yoke of God's commandments and destroying all the foundations of Judaism'.[85]

There was also disquiet within the Chief Rabbi's own camp. Dayan Jacob Reinowitz expressed his concerns to the Principal of Jews' College, Michael Friedlander. Friedlander's reply encapsulated Adler's expansive approach. He wrote, 'I too am displeased with the young who wish to break down the fence and destroy the vineyard of the Lord. I have no share in them. But this I must say before my master. We have to investigate and examine each problem . . . they submit to the Chief Rabbi . . . and rule according to the Din . . . At this age and especially in this country it is impossible . . . to say "this is my will and this you shall do'.' If we do we shall . . . drive many away from us and put to shame the Torah and men of Torah . . . It is better to walk the middle way. I do not wish to help those who transgress but only to help them to return to the fold'.[86]

In other words, circumstances made it impossible to resist all demands for change if a high degree of allegiance to traditional Judaism was to be maintained. Rather, it was necessary to permit alterations that would attract outsiders to the United Synagogue and retain those tempted to leave; only this expansive policy could achieve hegemony. As Hildesheimer also concluded, only *halakhah* could determine decisions, not a blanket rejection of all change. Strict adherence to tradition could be encouraged, but it was impossible to insist upon it. That this analysis was understood is perhaps why Adler was not condemned by eastern European rabbis, who continued to correspond with him and recognise him as a representative of what they regarded as authentic Judaism.[87]

Here we see how and why Adler's approach and Lerner's diverged. Although they were both within the acknowledgement school theologically, which is why Lerner accepted Adler's spiritual authority, in policy Adler was expansive whereas Lerner adopted a vanguard approach. Adler wanted to reach out to as many people as possible and create a ritual within *halakhah* with which they felt comfortable; otherwise many would remove themselves from his jurisdiction, and he would lose all control over and contact with them. Lerner took a different approach. He was determined to safeguard the traditional order of prayer in every detail, and was content to lead a limited if more committed group. Although he wanted to reach out to the less religious members of the community, he was determined to do so on what he considered the terms of authentic Judaism.[88] He thought that a small pious group was preferable to a large following, which had deviated from tradition.

These different approaches led to different organisational outcomes. Adler achieved a position of hegemony in Anglo-Jewry, in which he enjoyed the allegiance of the vast majority of British Jews of many different levels of observance, but who adhered to *halakhah* in their communal and institutional practices. Lerner, on the other hand, led the federation of Synagogues, a nuclear community, based on a small but more traditional group and just one of those which accepted Adler's spiritual leadership. The members of the Federation were less acculturated and therefore less anxious for changes, and so Lerner was under much less pressure to make changes. As a result he formed a community that suited its members but had limited appeal for those outside, unlike Adler's community, which pulled outsiders in.

Adler's hegemonic-expansive policy continued his father's, as reflected in Nathan Adler's *Laws and regulations*, his response to an 1880 ritual reform conference and the text of the *Authorised daily prayer book*, which he sanctioned just before his death in 1890. Jung has argued that Nathan Adler opposed liturgical change, writing that when he was presented with proposals for alterations he 'resisted them manfully and, in the main, successfully' and that it was 'a pity that he [Hermann Adler] did not follow in the footsteps of his distinguished father'.[89] The evidence, however, does not support Jung's analysis. In 1847 Adler introduced a number of changes of his own accord, so that 'the Synagogue should not be deserted'.[90] He limited the *selihot* on the Day of Atonement and the elegies on the fast of the Ninth of Av.[91]

In 1879 the Central Synagogue proposed a number of changes. In 1880 United Synagogue delegates attended the Conference of Delegates to Consider Modifications in the Service of the Synagogues to discuss them, before presenting their conclusions to Nathan Adler. Adler rejected a number of the recommendations which Hermann Adler later permitted, for example the omission of *bameh madlikin, yekum purkan* and *pittum haketoret*. He would not allow any change to the text of *Kol nidre* or the moving of the reading of the Biblical books on festivals. On the other hand, he allowed more *piyyutim* to be omitted than the conference itself requested. Hermann Adler worked closely with his father to respond to the 1880 conference and drafted the introduction to his father's rulings. In it Nathan Adler declared, as Hermann would in 1892, that he had only sanctioned 'those modifications which do not impair the integrity of the prayerbook and which do not infringe upon *dinim*'.[92] Just as in 1892, but unlike 1847, Nathan Adler was permissive, not prescriptive, and hoped in particular that the liturgy of the Great Synagogue would remain unchanged, although even the Great adopted some minor changes.[93] So while there were differences of detail between the responses of father and son in 1880 and 1892, the approach was broadly the same: a desire to preserve tradition but a willingness to concede within *halakhah* if there was demand. Detailed differences might be due to Nathan Adler's greater traditionalism, or to the context. When he made his rulings following the submission of the recommendations, they were simply accepted by congregations. In 1892 Hermann Adler could not be assured of such obedience.

Some differences between father and son were matters of principle – for example, the playing of the organ in a weekday service. Hermann Adler opposed the playing of an organ on the Sabbath, but a weekday service was potentially a different issue. In 1888 the Great Synagogue planned a Hanukkah service at which an organ would be played. Nathan

Adler had previously ruled against the playing of an organ at any synagogue service. Hermann rebuked the organiser of the service for ignor-
ing the Chief Rabbi's ruling and the service was cancelled. Nathan Adler
wrote later 'the use of an instrument on the occasion referred to did
not and could not receive my sanction'.[94] Lord Rothschild supported
the use of the organ, but that did not lead either Adler to temper their
stance, throwing doubt on Newman's assertion that 'the Adlers had
been willing to accept domination by the Rothschilds'.[95]

Hermann Adler's attitude in this instance is particularly interesting
because just two years later he arranged for an organ to be played at his
installation as Chief Rabbi. This suggests that he himself did not object
to the organ playing, provided it was a weekday, but was determined to
uphold his father's authority. Hermann Adler's differing attitude to the
organ being played on a weekday and on the Sabbath demonstrates how
he balanced aesthetics and *halakhah*. Adler appreciated the aesthetic
advantages of the organ, but where he considered *halakhah* to be at
stake – namely, when it would involve Sabbath desecration – *halakhah*
took priority. As he said, 'mere attractiveness would be too dearly pur-
chased if it infringed in the slightest degree on the rest prescribed for
the Sabbath'.[96]

The *Authorised daily prayer book* received Nathan Adler's sanction
just before his death and was published just after it, in 1890. Its size
and binding were reminiscent of the Book of Common Prayer, also
an 'authorised' work. Its attractive appearance was another reflection
of Adler's concern to acculturate Jewish life and worship. Although
the text was overwhelmingly traditional, as Reif has written, some
changes were 'smuggled' in.[97] The prayer book did not include the liturgical poems for special Sabbaths that Nathan Adler had allowed to be
omitted in 1880 and it edited some prayers to shorten them and remove
mystical references, for example in the service for the blessing of the
new moon – although excerpts from the mystical work, the Zohar, were
not excluded entirely.[98] Nathan Adler composed a prayer based on that
written for the West London Synagogue by David Wolf Marks for the
recovery of a mother from childbirth, and Hermann Adler composed
prayers to celebrate significant occasions, such as the consecration of a
home.[99] We mentioned the concept of 'contemporisation' in our discussion of Adler's arguments against mixed marriage. These new prayers
are an example of a related technique identified by Reiff, 'traditioning',
in which 'a new practice is invested with all the authority and character
of an age old ritual' so that an innovation is sanctified 'through a perceived nexus with previous holiness' and a sense of continuity is maintained by the way 'the present is reconceived in terms of the past'.[100]

Reif argues that there was a deliberate policy to exclude festival prayers, for example, the welcome to the spiritual visitors on Tabernacles and the blessing that enables the preparation of food on the festival for a Sabbath that follows it immediately. He suggests that the possession of a separate festival prayer book could not have been assumed, because otherwise the festival *amidah* would not have been included. He posits that its isolated inclusion implies that congregants were only expected to attend the synagogue for this central part of the service.[101] It is also possible, however, that the Adlers wanted to provide the bare essentials for worship for the entire year, in case their prayer book was the only one an individual owned, but they had no room to include every prayer. As the vast majority of Jews owned a festival prayer book, their attitude was not unreasonable, and their exclusion of festival prayers was dictated not by theology but by practicality.

The *Authorised daily prayer book* is comparable with *Das Gebetbuch der Israeliten* published in 1855 by the leading German figure of the period (whom we would place in the acknowledgement school), Michael Sachs, who was Hermann Adler's uncle and a profound influence on him.[102] Sachs' prayer book was aesthetically pleasing and well translated but did not amend the traditional text.[103] This was in contrast to another German acknowledgement-school prayer book, published by Manuel Joel of Breslau, who either altered controversial passages or printed both a traditional and reformed text. Joel was operating in particular circumstances. His predecessor in Breslau, the leader of the adaptation school, Abraham Geiger, had published a highly reformed prayer book which Joel was attempting to make more traditional, hence the compromise of printing two versions.[104]

Ellenson has argued that as the Sachs and Joel prayer books are from the two wings of the positive-historical school (part of the acknowledgement school), they foreshadow the two wings of American Conservative Judaism in the twentieth century: on the one hand the traditional faculty of the Jewish Theological Seminary, which maintained the established liturgy, and on the other the Conservative congregations that made major changes.[105] However, the split within the acknowledgement school, between its traditional and non-traditional wings, broke it into two parts, only one of which formed Conservative Judaism. Sachs and Adler were just as concerned as Joel about aesthetics, but the traditionalism of their prayer books, beneath the Westernised surface, demonstrates the fundamental difference between their approach and Joel's. They were eager to make changes to form but not to substance, whereas Joel altered both. Their prayer books are better seen as forerunners of Modern Orthodox editions, such as that by De Sola Pool, as opposed to Joel's, which foreshadowed Conservative works. Once again, the divisions within the acknowledgement school were just as important as its differences with other schools.

The other major issue in the synagogue service during Adler's tenure as Chief Rabbi concerned mixed synagogue choirs, which are halakhically problematic because a man should not be able to hear a woman's voice, at the very least while he recites the *shema*.[106] However, the Hatan Sofer, grandson of Moses Sofer, ruled in the 1880s that mixed choirs, as opposed to female solos, were permitted, because of the Talmudic principle that 'two voices are not heard' as individual voices, but only as an amalgam. Thus someone listening to a mixed choir is not actually listening to a woman's voice, because he cannot distinguish an individual voice at all.[107] Evidence suggests that Hermann Adler was aware of this opinion.[108]

In 1880 the Central Synagogue requested permission from Nathan Adler for a mixed choir. He 'declined to give his assent' and the matter was dropped; as a member of the synagogue wrote to the *Jewish Chronicle*, the Chief Rabbi's objection was 'incontestable'.[109] Similarly, in 1883 the Borough Synagogue moved to adopt a mixed choir, but when word came through that Nathan Adler objected, the issue was again dropped.[110] However, after Nathan Adler died in 1890, Stepney Green Synagogue adopted a mixed choir and in 1892 Hampstead Synagogue was formed with a mixed choir, and others followed. Finestein argues that Adler permitted mixed choirs and so compromised the adherence of the United Synagogue to Jewish law.[111] Lipman has written that 'the admission of female voices into the choir . . . permitted by Dr. Hermann Adler, did contravene rabbinic codes'.[112]

However, Hermann Adler did not sanction mixed choirs. In 1896 Adler wrote to Joseph Jacobs to refute the idea that he had done so, stating that 'the Chairman of the Choir Committee [of the East London Synagogue, which had just formed a mixed choir] is in error in supposing that I have sanctioned the formation of female choirs in synagogues. It is true that there are female voices in the choir of Hampstead Synagogue, but my sanction for this arrangement was never asked'.[113] In fact Hermann Adler publicly declared that he disapproved of mixed choirs and had denied them his sanction; as he wrote to the East London Synagogue 'if the present arrangement continues there is reason to apprehend that . . . solos will be sung by ladies of the choir – a display which I have uniformly deprecated as being contrary to the rules which regulate our Divine Service'.[114]

Whereas, in 1880, as soon as Nathan Adler intimated his opposition the matter was dropped, in 1896 a letter from Hermann Adler explicitly stating his personal dislike of the innovation prompted an audacious reply: 'the Board [of the East London Synagogue] notes with satisfaction that you do not declare the introduction of ladies' voices to be contrary to Jewish law'.[115] This is another example of how attitudes to Nathan and Hermann Adler differed. In the context of Hermann Adler's expansive policy, the halakhic room for manoeuvre offered by the Hatan Sofer and the danger of Hampstead leaving the United Synagogue, we can see why Adler took the approach he did. There were other issues at stake too.[116] Synagogues in the West End often paid Jewish choirboys to travel from the East End on the Sabbath, in contravention of *halakhah*.[117] Turning a blind eye to women replacing boys might involve a near-infringement of Jewish law, but it would prevent a clear contravention.

Significantly, Adler's personal standards remained rigorous. When he officiated at the foundation-stone laying ceremony for Hampstead he insisted on an all-male choir.[118] Further, when Adler was certain he would be listened to, he did stop mixed choirs. When the Great Synagogue held a service with a mixed choir in 1897 at the behest of the warden, Abraham Rosenfeld, but against the wishes of the congregation, Adler forced Rosenfeld's resignation and the experiment was not repeated.[119]

The case of mixed choirs therefore shows Adler's expansive policy, based on concession within *halakhah* when requested, pushed to its limit. Adler could countenance the omission of some *piyyutim* although he would have preferred them to be retained. However, other issues (like the organ playing on the Sabbath) involved unambiguous violations of the *halakhah* and Adler opposed them. Mixed choirs were on the borderline of acceptability, and an aggressive campaign to ban them would have had negative effects. Adler's approach was therefore put under extreme strain, hence his disapproval of mixed choirs but failure to stamp them out. The policy was successful in this case as well, because Hampstead stayed within the United Synagogue, achieving Adler's objective of hegemony, but his position was certainly uncomfortable.[120]

Adler not only controlled synagogue ritual, he also determined who could preach and lead services. Adler's refusal to allow ministers of the West London Synagogue to preach in his synagogues caused some resentment in the community. As one anonymous letter to the *Jewish Chronicle* complained in 1893, 'there are many synagogues in London now who would readily ask a sermon from the talented clergy of

Berkeley Street [West London], but that they know that the Chief Rabbi would certainly intervene with his veto'.[121] Adler's refusal followed the precedent set by his father, who in 1884 protested to the Western Synagogue, an acculturated but traditional independent synagogue, which accepted the authority of the Chief Rabbinate voluntarily, when it invited David Wolf Marks to preach.[122] On the other hand, in 1904 Hermann Adler allowed a West London Synagogue minister to conduct a funeral at the United Synagogue cemetery in West Ham.[123] Adler may have given his permission in this case because the service would have taken place outside the synagogue, the minister was unlikely to discuss theology and the deceased may have been a member of the West London Synagogue as well as the United Synagogue.[124] Adler even attended the memorial service at the West London Synagogue for David Wolf Marks, along with the *dayyanim*.[125] Importantly, however, the service was on a weekday and the sexes sat separately, so Adler would not have been present for infringements of *halakhah*.

More serious were questions of permanent ministers of congregations. The biggest ministerial problem Adler faced came, again, from Hampstead, and concerned Morris Joseph. I have said that I would attempt to add to our understanding by taking theology seriously. My analysis of this episode concentrates on the theological issues being debated, in addition to matters of religious style, in order to cast fresh light on events. The Hampstead synagogue grew out of the Hampstead Sabbath Afternoon Services of 1890–1892, which were regularly addressed by the Rev. Morris Joseph.[126] When the supporters of the afternoon services decided to found their own synagogue they invited Joseph to become minister and he accepted.[127] Before he could take up his post he had to receive the Chief Rabbi's certificate, which Adler withheld. He gave his reasons in May 1892, writing that Joseph's 'opinions are not in accord with the teachings of traditional Judaism. I have therefore no alternative but to withhold my sanction'.[128]

Adler objected to three of Joseph's views. First, he supported the use of an organ on the Sabbath, secondly he opposed the restitution of sacrifices and thirdly, he denied that the Pentateuch was given as a whole to Moses, or in the case of the final few verses, to Joshua.[129] Adler's veto caused great disquiet amongst the synagogue's supporters, and there was talk of the congregation affiliating not with the United Synagogue but with West London.[130] Nevertheless, Adler held firm. Part of the problem was that the public did not understand why Adler took his stand. One letter writer expressed the confusion in these terms: 'how many of our so-called "orthodox" ecclesiastics in the inner temples of their hearts worship the same image of Progressive Judaism as Mr. Joseph?'[131] If by this the author meant Simeon Singer of the New West End or J.F. Stern of the East London Synagogue, they were right, but there were two crucial differences. First, Singer and Stern were in post, and removing a sitting minister was a different matter to blocking an appointment. Secondly, whatever their private opinions, unlike Joseph, Singer and Stern never made their views public. Nevertheless, the attitudes of ministers like Stern and Singer did affect Adler's policy in other ways, as we shall see later.

If the letter writer was referring to Adler himself, they were quite wrong, but their lack of understanding of Adler's theology is itself interesting. First, it shows that sections of the Anglo-Jewish community always complained about what they perceived as the excessive strictness of the Chief Rabbis. Secondly, at the core of this misunderstanding is the fact that Joseph and Adler had enough in common that they should both be viewed as belonging to the acknowledgement school: they approved of a dignified service, were enthusiastic exponents of the vernacular sermon and were open to modern scholarship. Both were committed to *halakhah*, for – although they disagreed about individual issues, such as the organ – they both upheld the importance of Jewish Law. As Joseph wrote, 'the Jew, as the necessary consequence of his Judaism, assumes obligations from which the rest of mankind are free'.[132] However, there was a crucial difference of opinion between them: the source of *halakhah* – the Pentateuch. As Kaplan observed, this issue cut the acknowledgement school into two irreconcilable parts.

Adler's traditional group could not recognise the validity of the other. Kaplan termed this latter group (the non-traditional wing of the acknowledgement school) 'Conservative Reformism' and identified Joseph as a leading proponent. He argued, as we have argued here, that by their rejection of the belief in the Revelation at Sinai, but their continued insistence on *halakhah*, their approach was effectively 'identical with that of unqualified reformism [adaptation school]. It is only in the matter of religious practices that Conservatism [the non-traditional wing of the acknowledgement school] refuses to accept the logical consequences of that philosophy'.[133] That is why Adler could not include Joseph in the United Synagogue. Although they had much in common, the issue of the Pentateuch was decisive. Joseph understood this himself. He wrote that while he had 'hoped I could preach liberal doctrines from an orthodox pulpit' he realised he was wrong, and reflected 'my only wonder is that I ever allowed myself to dream it'.[134] Joseph understood why Adler had acted as he did, and why he was compelled to do so if he was to be faithful to his theology. Joseph, being faithful to his, became minister of the West London Synagogue in 1893.[135]

A similar ministerial crisis arose at the end of Adler's tenure, and was, again, essentially a theological dispute. The Rev. Dr Joseph Hochman became minister of the New West End Synagogue in 1906, and in 1910 began to make statements which caused Adler concern. On Jewish New Year, Hochman preached a sermon denying the Mosaic authorship of the Pentateuch. He said 'the Bible cannot be what Jewish orthodoxy would make it' and made other remarks provocative to traditionalists, such as 'orthodoxy has no place in the religion of the modern world'.[136] At this stage, in 1910, it appears that Hochman's views no longer justify us placing him in the traditionalist acknowledgement school (in which he had been trained at Jews' College and the Hildesheimer Seminary) and show he had moved into the non-traditionalist wing of the acknowledgement school, the same territory that Joseph occupied. One phrase is particularly telling, as it reveals that classic feature of non-traditionalist acknowledgement-school thought that Joseph also subscribed to: a commitment to *halakhah* without a belief in the giving of the Torah on Sinai.

Hochman called for a 'faith which seeks God's voice rather in the purpose than in the origins of His commandments'.[137] Adler instructed Hochman to retract his statements in his Day of Atonement sermon and 'explain that it had not been your intention to impugn traditional Judaism'. He told him 'you will in future be careful in your sermons to refrain from anything that might be interpreted as being antagonistic to traditional Judaism'. Adler was only partly successful, as Hochman later published the offending sermon. This prompted another letter from Adler requiring Hochman to show him the sermon he would deliver the next week with the threat that if he did not, Adler would preach himself in Hochman's place.[138] That did not happen, suggesting that Hochman complied, and indeed he survived as minister for the rest of Adler's incumbency, although his views and behaviour became more radical after Adler's death and he did not last long under Chief Rabbi Hertz.

As *ex officio* President of Jews' College and Chairman of the College Council, Adler was responsible for the training of ministers, with particular responsibility for staff and curriculum. The Principal of Jews' College when Adler became Chief Rabbi was Michael Friedlander, the product of both a traditional and a university education, known for his piety, who had occupied the office since 1865.[139] For a time Adler had been Theological Tutor and the two worked together on the college staff for 17 years.[140] Friedlander was a typical traditionalist *Wissenschaft* scholar, who was unshakable on the authorship of the Pentateuch, but accepted the late dating of some psalms and the developing nature of the Oral Law.[141] He was thus, like Adler, best understood as part of the scientific branch of the acknowledgement school. He also subscribed to Adler's expansive-hegemonic approach of conceding where *hala-khah* permitted, in order to keep as many within the fold as possible.

In 1906 Adler appointed Adolf Buchler as assistant to the 72-year-old Friedlander.[142] Buchler was born in Slovakia in 1867 and attended the Budapest Rabbinical Seminary from 1887.[143] The Budapest Seminary was founded in 1864 and was modelled on Frankel's Breslau seminary.[144] The Rector of the Seminary in Buchler's time was Wilhelm Bacher, a Breslau graduate who encouraged students to spend time there, as Buchler did, although he returned to Budapest to be ordained.[145] At Budapest, as at Breslau, Pentateuchal criticism was rejected, but Talmudic studies followed Frankel's critical method.[146] The year after receiving ordination, Buchler was appointed a lecturer at the similarly aligned Vienna Jewish Theological Seminary.[147] Buchler was appointed to Jews' College as a Talmudist, effectively as Principal-elect, and succeeded Friedlander in 1907.[148] Buchler amassed an enormous knowledge of Biblical and rabbinic literature, and contemporary non-Jewish material, and mastered both traditional and modern methods of study.[149] His particular project was to demonstrate that rabbinic texts should be taken seriously as historical documents. Previously, where Jewish and non-Jewish sources clashed, the Jewish source was disregarded as unreliable. Buchler uprooted what had been axiomatic in the study of Jewish history. This drew the attention of Ahad Ha'am, who described Buchler's 'spiritual battles for Israel'.[150]

Buchler combined modern scholarship with profound piety. According to a tribute written after Buchler's death (and therefore to be read with caution) by Isidore Epstein who succeeded Buchler as principal, 'he cherished every custom, law, and precept of the Jewish people, and was most scrupulous in the observance of all the minutiae of Jewish religious life and tradition'.[151] Another student described him as 'exceedingly orthodox'.[152] This combination of *Wissenschaft* and religiosity was a feature of many of the great traditionalists of the scientific branch of the acknowledgement school, including Frankel, Hildesheimer, Hoffman and the Adlers, who saw no contradiction between the two. Their belief in the Divine origin of the Pentateuch gave a firm theological foundation for *halakhah* as the direct expression of God's will, which was unaffected by any investigations into the development of *halakhah*.

An example of Buchler's attitude to *halakhah* comes from his evidence to the New West End Synagogue committee of 1912, which, at

Hochman's prompting, looked into replacing the annual cycle of Torah readings with a cycle of smaller readings that would spread over three years, called the Triennial Cycle. The Triennial Cycle had been used in ancient Palestine, but the Babylonian custom of an annual cycle had taken hold. Buchler did not deny that the Triennial Cycle had an historical basis, indeed he had established the exact details of the divisions.[153] However, for Buchler, practice was a different matter to history. He told the committee 'it is against our codified law' and that if you introduce the Triennial Cycle 'you act against the Shulchan Aruch' the authoritative code of Jewish Law.[154] When Adler appointed Buchler he thereby placed at the head of his theological seminary a man who shared his own scholarly and religious attitudes.

Other appointments by Adler showed the same tendency, for example, Arthur Marmorstein and Samuel Daiches. Daiches was a graduate of the Hildesheimer Seminary and both of these men, and especially Marmorstein, were first-rate critical scholars who held that there had always been significant halakhic development, but neither doubted an original revelation at Sinai.[155] As Emile Marmorstein wrote of his father, 'he accepted without reservation the doctrine of the Divine Revelation of the Written and Oral Law from Mount Sinai'.[156] The presence of these men, and their regular production of scholarly works, such as Marmorstein's *The old rabbinic doctrine of God* and Daiches' 'The meaning of "sacrifices" in the Psalms' in *Essays presented to J.H. Hertz* – together with that of their colleagues in the 'Jews' College Publications Series – suggests that Endelman's verdict that Adler's policies made Britain a 'cultural backwater' is not a completely fair assessment.[157] London was certainly not the equal of Berlin, Breslau or Frankfurt in the west, nor of Vilna, Volozhin or Warsaw in the east, but it was no wasteland either.

The other major issue was the college's curriculum. There was less stress on Talmud and Codes than at the Breslau or Berlin seminaries (let alone the traditional *yeshivot* of eastern Europe) and more on grammar, history, philosophy and homiletics. There was, however, some traditional content to the curriculum, especially after it was revised in 1879.[158] Originally the college did not train for rabbinic ordination, as rabbis were not considered necessary to the community, which was still small enough to be able to rely on the Chief Rabbi and the Beth Din, but in 1881 it introduced a scheme which led to ordination. However, it was not encouraged, students had to seek out their own tuition, and no one received ordination until Asher Feldman and Moses Hyamson in 1899.[159] Some did not lament this failure of Jews' College to produce rabbis.

In 1895 Claude Montefiore, doubtless invited because of his generous financial support, addressed the college prize-giving.[160] He told the
audience that the knowledge required for the rabbinical diploma 'has
now become obsolete, the possession of which would be of no value
to a minister whose task it is to influence the lives of modern English
Jews and Jewesses'.[161] He advocated instead the 'broad and human',
but less traditional, education that the college already provided.[162]
The traditional education, which Montefiore considered unnecessary,
equips a rabbi to render halakhic decisions. This attitude demonstrates
Montefiore's attitude towards *halakhah* and its details, which was to
regulate it to secondary importance. This placed him in the adaptation
school, which did not emphasise the importance of *halakhah*. Neither
Adler nor Montefiore thought it necessary to provide rabbinic education, but their views came from different sources, Montefiore's from his
opinion that the knowledge of the rabbi was irrelevant to the community, but Adler's from the belief that he and his *dayyanim* could fulfil
all rabbinic functions for the community. However, even in this regard
Adler changed his views over time.

After 1899 Adler placed a new emphasis on ordination. In 1903
examinations were held, and in 1905 F.L. Cohen was ordained.[163] In
1905 Adler formally announced a change of mind on the question of the
need for rabbis. He conceded that although previously the community
only required the Chief Rabbi and Beth Din, more rabbis had become
essential, especially as the number of immigrants grew. Adler wanted
to supply them with spiritual leaders who had a Jewish education they
could respect and a secular education to encourage acculturation, in
other words, rabbis of the acknowledgement school.[164] Although Adler
wanted to control ordination, the argument that he was determined to
deny his ministers rabbinical status is flawed, as we will see when we
consider the cases of Simeon Singer and Hermann Gollancz.

As the college was becoming more traditional some were trying to
make it less so. In 1907 there was an attempt to make Jews' College
part of the University of London, which failed because the university
insisted that Jews' College would have to teach some New Testament,
and Adler, whose views on Christianity we know, refused. This enraged
some supporters of Jews' College, like Israel Abrahams, who had taught
at the college until he was appointed Reader of Rabbinics at Cambridge
in 1902, and who later became a supporter of the Jewish Religious
Union founded by Montefiore and Lily Montagu.[165]

In 1908, Abrahams condemned Adler to a United Synagogue committee and asked that he be removed as Chairman of the College
Council.[166] Adler resigned as chairman that year.[167] The disputes over

the New Testament and traditional rabbinic training were related to funding. Jews' College was chronically under-funded. Until about 1903, the United Synagogue gave only £200 a year, when it raised its annual donation to £300.[168] The first decade of the twentieth century also saw Jews' College lose income as some of its most generous traditionalist supporters died, including Charles Samuel (who gave £200 a year), Fredereick David Mocatta and Alfred Louis Cohen.[169] The college therefore increasingly relied on money from outside the traditional community, for example the occasional donations given as a sign of goodwill by the West London Synagogue and individuals like Montefiore, who wanted men such as Israel Abrahams to be influential in college policy.[170] This placed the college, its staff and Adler in a difficult position, and had the potential to compromise its theological position. This may be part of the reason why despite its learned and pious faculty, Jews' College did produce ministers of questionable traditionalism, who fitted Norman Cohen's description of them, as lax in dietary and Sabbath laws.[171]

The final major institution for which Adler was responsible was the London Beth Din. From 1876 the Beth Din consisted of Nathan Adler, Hermann Adler and Bernard Spiers, a rabbi from Poland of traditional background, but with openness to secular learning.[172] When Nathan Adler retired to Brighton in 1879 and appointed Hermann Delegate Chief Rabbi he also appointed Jacob Reinowitz to the Beth Din. Reinowitz was eastern European, born in 1818. He was the religious leader of Vilkovisk in Poland when in 1876 he was appointed rabbi of a traditional congregation in the East End. Here he came to the attention of Nathan Adler, who appointed him as the leading halakhic authority on the Beth Din. Reinowitz corresponded with great authorities, including Naftali Tsevi Yehudah Berlin of Volozhin and Isaac Elhanan Spector of Kovno, who endorsed his rulings. He published responsa and Talmudic analyses. When Nathan Adler wanted a responsum on the acceptability of machine-made *matsot* in 1882, he asked Reinowitz. Furthermore, unlike Hermann Adler, Reinowitz lived in the East End and was accessible when individuals had religious questions. According to Michael Friedlaender, Reinowitz once answered 95 ritual questions in one day. From his appointment in 1879 until his death in 1893 all major halakhic issues before the Beth Din were referred to Reinowitz, although rulings were approved by the Chief Rabbi before public judgments were given.[173] Hermann Adler was therefore accustomed from the start of his Chief Rabbinate to working with a senior halakhist to whom he passed major questions.

Hermann Adler's satisfaction with this arrangement can be seen from his decision following Reinowitz's death in 1893 to appoint Reinowitz's son-in-law, Susman Cohen as dayyan. Cohen, like his father-in-law, was a halakhist of distinction who published responsa, and he became the leading authority.[174] From 1879, then, the Beth Din consisted of Adler and two traditionally educated European rabbis whose origin were in the antipathy school. We can see from Reinowitz's concern about Adler's response to the Ritual Reform Conference that he still shared some of its outlook. Nevertheless, they were willing to work with an expansive-hegemonic figure within the acknowledgement school. In this sense they can perhaps be described, using Heilman's term, as 'tolerators' of modernity, members of a group falling between the antipathy and the acknowledgment schools, who were not convinced of the positive value of modernity, but did not feel the need actively to oppose it. Rather they tolerated it, accepted it as a fact and worked on that basis.[175] Adler was happy to work with them, though they differed in ideology, because they gave the Beth Din the expertise and prestige it required to uphold *halakhah*.

The small size of the Beth Din created problems, because all members needed to be present if a full court of three *dayyanim* was needed. In 1898 a scheme was developed to place the Beth Din on a firmer footing. There would be three full-time *dayyanim*, one dayan would always be available to answer queries and the court would sit more regularly, to encourage litigants to come before the Beth Din rather than civil courts.[176] This policy of encouraging the use of the beth din for civil disputes was the subject of contention within the acknowledgement school. While Hirsch did not attempt to maintain Jewish judicial auton-omy or promote the use of the beth din, Hildeshiemer encouraged his followers to use the beth din instead of German courts.[177] Interestingly, this placed Adler and Hildesheimer of the acknowledgement school in the same group on the issue as the antipathy school, which also pro-moted the beth din.[178]

However, the motivation was different. The antipathy school wanted to retain a role for the beth din in order to preserve as much as pos-sible of pre-Emancipation Jewish life. Adler and Hildesheimer, on the other hand, were primarily worried about cases in the secular courts making the Jewish community look bad by airing acrimonious disputes between Jews and highlighting some Jews' questionable business prac-tices.[179] Hirsch may have disagreed because he was more concerned about Jews becoming wholly emancipated, which required them to be a purely religious group, with no pretensions to civil autonomy. Another interesting aspect of the scheme was to create an attractive new facility to learn in, a *beth hamedrash*, which was conceived of specifically as an alternative to the conversionist reading rooms sponsored by missionaries, to help combat Christian proselytising.[180]

When Spiers died in 1902, this plan was acted upon and Adler appointed Moses Hyamson and Asher Feldman as *dayyanim*. This decision caused disquiet in the East End and a protest meeting was held against the appointment of two English-educated young men instead of an experienced Talmudist from eastern Europe.[181] Jung, Alderman and others have identified this meeting as a sign that the East End rejected Adler and his foolish attempt to impose Englishmen on the immigrants.[182] However, the *Jewish Chronicle* reported that the meeting 'could hardly be said to have had the sympathy of East End Jewry as a whole'.[183] Neither Feldman nor Hyamson resigned from the Beth Din and both enjoyed distinguished careers. Feldman became its administrative head and served until 1938. He also published *The parables and similes of the rabbis* which demonstrated an encyclopaedic knowledge of rabbinic sources.[184] Hyamson was a candidate for the Chief Rabbinate in 1913 losing to Hertz. He went to New York and was appointed Professor of Codes at the Jewish Theological Seminary, joining Solomon Schechter's distinguished faculty.[185]

Whatever the personal merits of Feldman and Hyamson, the reaction to their appointment made it plain that a significant element in the East End wanted a distinguished eastern European scholar to sit on the Beth Din and, following the protests, Adler recognised he needed such a halakhist of high reputation. Moshe Avigdor Chaikin was born in Russia 1852, received his rabbinic ordination in 1877 from Isaac Elhanan Spector and others, and came to England in 1890. Adler was very active in developing Chaikin's career. First he recommended him to the Sheffield Jewish community, then, in 1901 Chaikin became Chief Minister of the Federation of Synagogues, again on Adler's recommendation. After the controversy following the appointments of Feldman and Hyamson, Adler invited Chaikin to join the Beth Din. Officially he was assistant dayyan but as Sussman Cohen's health declined Chaikin became the senior dayyan.[186] The Beth Din now had five members including Adler himself, of which two, Feldman and Hyamson, were full-time *dayyanim* and two distinguished halakhists. It was not a court of the low standard Alderman has suggested.

When Sussman Cohen retired in 1906 Adler would have liked to appoint Chaikin as a full dayyan, thus creating a Beth Din of three full-time members including a distinguished halakhist, enabling Adler to concentrate on other duties.[187] However, communal politics intervened. The United Synagogue refused to make Chaikin a full dayyan;

the federation refused to allow him to spend half of his time working for the United Synagogue and withdrew Chaikin from the Beth Din. It returned to the position of 1879, being composed of the Chief Rabbi and two colleagues.[188] This was unfortunate for three reasons. First it burdened Adler with regular attendance at the Beth Din, secondly it meant that a full court could only sit when all three members were available and thirdly it reduced the prestige of the Beth Din because, although learned, Adler was not a halahkist of the calibre of Reinowitz, Cohen or Chaikin. This situation continued for the rest of Adler's life, and it was only after his death that the United Synagogue, which now had only two *dayyanim*, which was too few to maintain the Beth Din, made an accommodation with the federation and reappointed Chaikin as dayyan.[189] Despite the setback of 1906 we can see that Adler wanted to create a strong Beth Din (which after the protests of 1902 he realised had to contain a recognised eastern European scholar, in order to be credible) which could uphold *halakhah*, either by rendering decisions as a court, or through a dayyan answering individual halakhic questions. He came closest to this between 1893 and 1906 before circumstances rendered it impossible. Adler's foreign-born *dayyanim* came from a strictly traditional background and had no involvement in *Wissenschaft* or engagement with secular culture. Their views would not justify their placement in the acknowledgement school, but this did not concern Adler. They were tolerators who did not oppose the acknowledgement school, and were happy to work with Adler, who was more interested in their halakhic expertise than in their religious philosophy.

Other issues that arose during Adler's time also demonstrated his attitude to *halakhah*. In 1905 the French rabbinate attempted to resolve the problem of *agunah*, by which a married man disappears leaving his wife 'chained' to him, because in *halakhah* both parties have to consent to a divorce. They wished to place a clause in the marriage contract stating that, if the civil authorities divorced the couple in French law, their Jewish marriage became retrospectively invalid. Retrospective invalidation is not unknown to Jewish Law, but this plan made halakhic status dependent on status in civil law, and gave non-Jewish judges power to determine who was married by Jewish Law. It caused widespread opposition among rabbis throughout the world, including Adler, who enlisted the support of the Haham, Moses Gaster.[190]

Adler was also deeply preoccupied with more day-to-day issues. He sent instructions to rabbis around the country on the correct procedures to approve slaughterers, and the care that should be taken over the production of *matsah* for Passover.[191] Adler advised colleagues not to trust the *kashrut* of the French rabbinate, but that they could rely on the certification of Rabbi Meir Hildesheimer of Berlin.[192] Adler advised that the flour for *matsah* produced in Carlisle was acceptable, but expressed concern about standards in Edinburgh and Leeds.[193] These detailed and technical discussions were usually conducted privately, but famously a dispute over *shehita* (slaughter) developed into a massive controversy with one group of London Jews, the Machzike Hadath. This in turn raises important issues about Adler's relationships with the highly traditional section of Anglo-Jewry and his general policy of religious centralisation, which deserve separate examination.

In 1890 the Machzike Hadath Society was formed by a number of immigrants who were concerned about the halakhic standards of the meat supervised by the Chief Rabbi and Beth Din. The two biggest concerns concerned kidney suet, which is not kosher, but was sold in Beth Din butchers, and hindquarter meat, which requires the removal of the sciatic nerve if it is to be kosher, in a procedure known as porging. Although a Beth Din employee (*shomer*) was present to porge the meat, his services were often not called upon, and non-kosher meat was sold in supposedly kosher butchers. According to Homa, representatives of the Machzike Hadath asked Adler to address their concerns, but he rebuffed them. This forced them to set up independent slaughtering arrangements outside Adler's jurisdiction. Adler resented this undermining of his office, and the greater learning of their rabbis, and declared their meat non-kosher.

In the battle that followed, the two sides each enlisted the support of foreign rabbis, Isaac Elhanan Spector and Shmuel Mohilever for Adler, and Michael Yehiel Epstein, Israel Meir Kagan and others for Machzike Hadath.[194] Endelman has argued that Adler first bullied and then cajoled Machzike Hadath in order to reassert his authority, over them and other breakaway movements in Liverpool and Manchester.[195] Homa even accuses Adler of bribery and deception in order to obtain support from foreign rabbis.[196] Alderman argues that 'Adler's condemnation of the rebel shechita went unheeded', suggesting that Adler did not prevail over Machzike Hadath.[197] Homa describes how in 1904 an agreement was reached whereby the Chief Rabbi accepted that the Machzike Hadath could have their own slaughterer and butchers under their independent religious control, but with Adler's Board for Shechita handling administration, the Chief Rabbi thereby effectively capitulating to the Machzike Hadath.[198]

The situation was more complicated than Homa or Alderman has described. There is no doubt that non-kosher meat was being sold in Beth Din butchers, that Adler and his *dayyanim* were turning a blind eye to it, and that Adler was ultimately forced to compromise with forces he initially thought he could defeat easily. However, such a bald assessment ignores much complexity – for example, the presence of the highly observant Samuel Montagu at the head of the Board for Shechita, who was very concerned with halakhic standards, as his daughter reports.[199] In fact, although there were religious issues, they were complicated by finance, the possibility that Jewish slaughter would be banned, and the power of the butchers.

As early as 1864, Beth Din butchers sold unporged meat, and Nathan Adler banned the practice. However, butchers began to operate under the licences of foreign rabbis who did not object, such as the Chief Rabbi of Rotterdam. The resulting dispute led to expensive legal action to restore Beth Din control.[200] It was in this context that the selling of unporged meat increased. When Machzike Hadath expressed their concerns to Adler, he banned the sale of kidney suet and supported their desire for their own butchers, slaughter yard and slaughterers. They also asked for the Board for Shechita to pay their rabbi, Abraham Werner, £3 a week to supervise.[201] The board opposed any comprise with Machzike Hadath on a number of grounds. First the butchers were opposed, and they were important financiers of the board and the Beth Din. If they rebelled, the board would lose its hard-won monopoly and a great deal of money, and they had already complained about Adler's prohibition of the sale of kidney suet.[202] There was also concern that the Machzike Hadath slaughter yard might not meet the humanitarian standards expected by the general population, leading to renewed attempts to ban Jewish slaughter altogether.[203] It is also likely that Adler and his *dayyanim* thought that Machzike Hadath did not pose a serious threat and that it would be easily suppressed, and therefore they did not strain themselves to accommodate its members' wishes.

Followed the decision of the board, Adler declared Machzike Hadath meat to be non-kosher, the standard practice of a beth din establishing its authority, but he continued to search for a compromise whereby the Machzike Hadath could have their own butchers and send a representative occasionally to check that everything was done in accordance with *halakhah* before meat reached their shops. Although Machzike Hadath agreed that Beth Din slaughterers were acceptable in theory, and wanted to place their slaughter under board jurisdiction, they were insistent on employing their own slaughter men and rejected the compromise. They opened their own slaughterhouse, which charged lower fees than the Beth Din, starting a price war, and the dispute reached its bitterest stage.[204] The dispute was deepened in 1899 when the Machzike Hadath synagogue refused to accept Hermann Adler's spiritual jurisdiction.[205]

The breach remained open for a further five years, during which time both sides suffered financially, but of course that was felt more by the poorer party, Machzike Hadath. That contributed towards their willingness to reach a compromise, while increased external criticism of the humanity of Jewish slaughter encouraged both disputants to present a united front. In 1904 a comprehensive agreement was finally reached, which involved compromise by both sides. Machzike Hadath kept its own slaughterers and butchers, but the board employed the supervisors, and any new slaughterers required Adler's approval. The Machzike Hadath synagogue joined the Federation of Synagogues, which accepted Adler's authority although it had its own Chief Minister, at that time Adler's friend, Avigdor Chaikin. Adler had the right to veto the appointment of any rabbi to replace Werner as supervisor. Adler was to issue the certificates for all marriages conducted by Machzike Hadath, which had to refer all divorces to the Beth Din.[206] The stipulation that Adler had to act in accordance with the *Shulhan arukh* was somewhat humiliating, but he was prepared to accept it to achieve reconciliation.[207]

Adler did not have as much control over Machzike Hadath as over the United Synagogue, but he and the Board for Shechita had re-established their authority. This was solidified in 1908 when the Local Government Board approved a form of bye-law, swiftly adopted nationally, that made only those slaughterers with the Chief Rabbi's approval exempt from the requirement to pre-stun animals, a procedure that would render them non-kosher according to most opinions.[208] The religious problems arose because of many pressures facing Adler, including the threat to the legality of Jewish slaughter and the board's concern for its income if butchers broke away. These issues were of greater concern to Adler as an expansive rabbinic leader than to Machzike Hadath, which was content to be a nuclear community. As Feldman has pointed out, Machzike Hadath concerns were not just religious. Werner's attitudes, such as his view that there is 'no reason why secular education should alienate Jews from their own literature', place him in the acknowledgement school.[209] However, they wanted religious leaders who shared their background and sensibilities, not the acculturated Adler. They resented being forced to accept the leadership of the Anglo-Jewish elite, either religious or lay.

The distance between Adler and the immigrants has often been commented upon, and has been attributed to the laxity of Adler versus the stringency of the immigrants. Nicknames for Adler quoted by Endelman and Englander – 'Chief Reformer' and 'West End *goy*' – suggest that the immigrants' attitude was beyond merely differing with Adler on specific halakhic decisions, but went as far as denying him legitimacy as a halakhic leader.[210] However there are also examples of co-operation. The Federation of Synagogues was the principal attempt to bring the Chief Rabbinate and the immigrants closer together. It was founded by Samuel Montagu in 1887 from the small synagogues (*hevrot*) of the East End, to place them on a sound financial footing and encourage the use of English, while preserving their intense religiosity.[211] Montagu's aim was mild acculturation without religious compromise or political radicalisation. Indeed, one reason why Montagu brought Maccoby to London to be the federation's *maggid* was to reinvigorate immigrants' piety, and combat socialism and anarchism.[212] That was also why he founded a non-socialist tailors' organisation, the London Tailors' and Machinists' Society in 1886.[213]

Gutwein has argued that the federation was part of Montagu's campaign against the United Synagogue in order to wrest control of the leadership of Anglo-Jewry from Lord Rothschild.[214] However, the argument made by Alderman and Endelman that the federation was designed to co-operate with the United Synagogue, rather than compete with it, finds better support in the evidence.[215] Although Montagu was the primary organiser, Lord Rothschild was President of the Federation, as well as President of the United Synagogue, and the federation accepted the Chief Rabbi's authority, and he consecrated most of its new synagogues.[216] Adler's role was no formality. Just as Bayswater, not Hampstead, reflected Adler's agenda for his acculturated followers, so the federation, which aimed to combine tradition with decorum and sound finances, represented his vision for the immigrants, much more than the East London Synagogue, which was within the United Synagogue, but introduced a mixed choir despite Adler's opposition. Indeed, had Adler enjoyed more supportive lay leaders, allowing his own preferences to be fully realised, synagogues under his authority would not have looked like the *hevrot*, but they would have been more like Bayswater and, say, the Federation's New Dalston Synagogue (depending on their position in the spectrum of acculturation) than either Hampstead or East London.

There were conflicts between the two bodies, for example over the United Synagogue's East End Scheme of 1889 to build a colossal synagogue in Whitechapel, which Montagu thought would not appeal to immigrants, and over the federation's acceptance of the New Dalston Synagogue, which was not a *hevra*, and which the *Jewish Chronicle* interpreted as an encroachment onto United Synagogue territory.[217] Mayer Lerner, Chief Minister of the Federation 1890–94, opposed Adler's concessions on Ritual Reform, and in 1908 the federation withdrew from the Jewish Religious Education Board, which it had joined in 1894, when a representative of the West London Synagogue became president.[218] Nevertheless, Hermann Adler co-operated with the federation's religious leadership. He became a friend of Maccoby, and was the *sandek* at the circumcision of one of his sons.[219] Adler invited Maccoby to join the Beth Din and, although Maccoby declined, because he was a vegetarian, he preached in Adler's synagogues and joined the Visitation Committee.[220] That did not mean that Adler and Maccoby agreed on all points – for example, Maccoby opposed the United Synagogue's hiring of a hall used by missionaries for most of the year as a venue for high holiday services.[221]

Yet these specific disagreements should not distract from the generally close relationship, which also existed between Adler and another leader of the federation, Chaikin, who joined the Beth Din. Indeed the closeness of Adler to Maccoby, Lerner and Chaikin should not come as a surprise, because of their common membership of the traditional wing of the acknowledgement school. Lerner was a *Wissenschaft* scholar, Maccoby was keen to learn English and become naturalised, and he sent his children to study to become teachers at schools run by the London County Council.[222] At his death the *Jewish Times* remarked that Maccoby was respected by the traditional for his learning, but that also 'the secularist appreciated his views and *weltanschauung*'.[223] Chaikin was also known for his familiarity with secular culture.[224] The differences between Adler and these rabbis concerned non-theological issues. Adler favoured an expansive approach whereas Lerner was vanguardist. As there was little demand for concessions among the Jews of the federation, its leaders could adopt this approach, whereas Adler had to work with the Anglicised leaders and members of the United Synagogue. That is why the United Synagogue and the federation complemented each other. Each had its own constituency but there was little or no theological difference amongst the leaders.

Adler's good working relationship with immigrants and their religious leaders extended beyond the formal. We have seen how the East End turned out in force to hear Adler's *Shabbat Shuva derasha*. In 1908 Samuel Isaac Hillman became the rabbi of Glasgow and immediately began to consult Adler on religious and communal matters. Hillman complained to Adler about his evidence to the Royal Commission on Divorce and Matrimonial Causes, in which Adler had argued that some halakhically permitted marriages should be prohibited by British law.

These were marriages involving an individual divorced in Jewish but not in British law from their first spouse, which resulted in one of the partners committing bigamy in British law. This was considered to demonstrate a lack of respect for *halakhah*. Adler replied that his only wish had been to defend the Torah and demonstrate Jewish respect for British law. He could justifiably claim that he never suggested that Jews break *halakhah*, merely that they should not take advantage of a permissive regulation, which would bring them into conflict with British law. Contrary to Feldman, it was therefore not the case that for Adler 'when Jewish law and English law came into conflict he was content for the former to give way'.[225] Despite this incident Hillman and Adler continued to co-operate; indeed, Hillman used the *Agudat rabbanim uvaale vatim haharedim bemedinat britanya* – the Association for Furthering Traditional Judaism in Great Britain – as a vehicle for disseminating Adler's instructions to provincial rabbis, such as for licensing slaughterers. He also repeatedly asked Adler to attend their conference in Leeds in 1911, which Adler was unable to do because of ill health.[226] This conference has been identified as a challenge to the Chief Rabbinate by more traditional rabbis.[227] Their concern that he should be present at the conference rather shows their desire to work with him, not against him.

A final interesting point about the Hillman correspondence is that Adler addresses the letters to '*harav hagaon Shmuel Yitshak Hillman*' – in other words, to Rabbi Hillman. Jung and others have written that Adler would not allow any one other than himself to be called rabbi, possibly excepting those to whom he had personally given ordination.[228] Adler's method of addressing Hillman in their Hebrew correspondence suggests rather that Adler's use of title depended on the context. In rabbinic letters he used traditional forms of address, but in English he used the English form 'reverend'. That explanation works for figures outside the United Synagogue. Within it, both Simeon Singer and Hermann Gollancz possessed ordination from recognised European authorities. However, neither was permitted to call himself 'rabbi'.[229]

The explanation goes to the heart of Adler's expansive-hegemonic approach to religious leadership. Adler's policy of conceding within *halakhah* required the walking of a very narrow path and was dependent on Adler reserving to himself and his Beth Din all rabbinic decisions. We have seen the untraditional stances taken by Joseph and Hochman. J.F. Stern, the minister of the East London Synagogue introduced a mixed choir, while Gollancz favoured the Triennial Cycle. A.A. Green of Hampstead was discreet, but seems to have wanted to abrogate prayers for sacrifices and to count women towards a quorum for prayer.[230] Perhaps hoping to bring to the United Synagogue some of the religious pluralism that had developed in the Church of England, Singer and Stern worked with the Jewish Religious Union, until Adler instructed them to disassociate themselves.[231]

One might ask why Adler did not impose his authority more forcefully on wayward ministers. This is a difficult question, to which one response is that Adler was not as concerned with theology as I have argued, and was willing to sacrifice his principles under certain circumstances, especially if pressed to do so by the lay elite. Alternatively, the answer may be that he had to choose the battles he could win, especially if his opponents had wealthy and influential supporters. While Adler could not tolerate clear breaches of what he considered essentials of belief and practice by his ministers, he would not go out of his way to create conflict if at least official allegiance to these norms was maintained.

Of course, once issues of primary importance to Adler were at stake, wealthy and influential opponents could not dissuade him. We have already seen this approach in Adler's attitude towards the liturgy. His responses to the Ritual Reform Committee's requests were affected by the strength of feeling each request aroused. If Adler could refuse consent to a proposal without causing excessive offence he would do so (e.g. his refusal to allow changes to the early morning service), but if there was considerable support for a change (e.g. the reading of the Ten Commandments) he would go to great lengths to find reasons to permit. However, if he could not conscientiously permit a change (e.g. the omission of the blessing made by men 'who has not made me a woman'), he was undeterred by the communal or financial power of those pressing for reform.

To return to the questions of ministers, as we have noted, as long as they did not publicise untraditional views, they were left unmolested. Adler no less than his successors, Hertz, Brodie and Jakobovits, did not demand a confession of faith from his ministers.[232] Silence was taken as acceptance of the official position. As Taylor has noted, if Adler gave individuals like Stern and Green rabbinical authority, he would have even less control over ministers and would lose sway over the religious character of the United Synagogue, and the halakhic institution he wanted and had managed to create would have been lost.[233] That is why Nathan Adler imposed religious centralism. Hermann Adler upheld it in his father's name, submitted to it himself – he never used the title 'rabbi' until his father's death – and continued as Chief Rabbi, because expansive-hegemonic leadership requires powerful central authority.

Adler shared the traditionalist wing of the acknowledgement school with the German religious leaders Hirsch, Hildesheimer and Hoffman, as well as the official French rabbinate. We will gain further insight into Adler's approach by comparing his religious policies with theirs, and with those of other comparable rabbis, because like Adler they took into account scholarly and cultural developments in the non-Jewish world, and post-Enlightenment and post-Emancipation changes in attitudes to rabbinical authority amongst Jews. There were, of course, many Jewish leaders of both significantly greater and lesser traditionalism, within the antipathy and adaptation schools, who either refused to sanction any change however minor or who happily made any number of reforms to make Judaism relevant to the times, as they saw it. But these individuals are of less interest to us. Their policies arose out of a quite different theology from Adler's. Our interest is in how other individuals of similar views translated those views into action.

The official theology of the French Rabbinate was very close to Adler's, but the differences in its religious policies are instructive. In theory the French religious leadership was powerful. The *Consistoire* was led by a Grand Rabbin and, as with the British Chief Rabbi all changes had to have his approval.[234] In practice, the way in which Emancipation had come about in France severely limited the power of the French rabbinate. The French state narrowly confined the concept of religion and thus the field of activity of the rabbinate. The French-Jewish lay leaders kept the rabbis within their restricted role, made them subservient to the laity, and felt themselves entitled to disagree with rabbinic decisions.[235] As Albert has observed, 'the attitude of Jewish leaders towards the rabbinate was one of employer to employee'.[236] This placed the rabbinate in a weak position in which they constantly needed to please their lay leaders, and their ability to uphold *halakhah* was much more constrained than Adler's in England. Thus, although the French community claimed to represent authentic, traditional Judaism, it pursued policies that Adler found unacceptable, for example, on the organ playing on the Sabbath and festivals. Whereas Adler was firmly opposed, Grand Rabbin Salomon Ullman allowed the organ to be played by a non-Jew and believed that this conformed to *halakhah*. As he stated in defence of his decision, 'let us say about a prohibition that it is prohibited, and about that which is permitted that it is permitted'.[237] Some French rabbis, like Salomon Klein disputed that the organ was halakhically permitted, although unlike the antipathy school, Klein did not oppose all change *a priori*.[238] The difference with Adler and Klein on the one hand, and Ullman on the other, was therefore not one of principle but of degree.

French Jewry acknowledged modernity primarily through aesthetics. The French rabbinate faced powerful pressures for acculturation, especially in the cause of aesthetic improvements, and bent under them. In 1831 a consistorial commission in Strasbourg proposed liturgical and ritual innovations to enhance the beauty of public worship.[239] In 1838 the Paris *Comité de Secours et d'Encouragement* reported that 'the forms of the *culte* must be in harmony with our mores . . . the Jew of our day should not need to turn away from the synagogue for fear of rediscovering there a semblance of the Middle Ages'.[240] In 1841 Gerson Levy identified as the cause of religious indifference the 'lack of concern for synagogue music, solemnity and majestic ceremonies'.[241] Parts of the French rabbinate were sympathetic to these views. As Ullman wrote to Rabbi Samuel Dreyfus, 'I agree with your views on the need to render greater dignity to the public service and the means to accomplish this.[242] However, there was little principled opposition to *halakhah*. Gerson Levy proposed a service in French, but supplied rabbinic sources to justify praying in the vernacular and retained separate seating.[243] Later the proponents of changes dropped the demand for a service in the vernacular, and took traditional stances on other issues, such as liturgical references to the Messiah, the dietary laws, circumcision and intermarriage.[244]

The French rabbinate therefore adopted an expansive approach based on conceding as much as possible within *halakhah*. As Berkovitz has written 'Ullman's strategy for bolstering rabbinic authority was unambiguous. He affirmed the adoption of halakhically sanctioned changes . . . coupled with his vehement resistance to reform'.[245] The French rabbinate officially enjoyed significant authority but in practice was severely constrained, and therefore conceded more than Adler did in Britain. The leniency of the French rabbinate was also a function of its sympathy to the demands made of it, but the attitude of the community and power of the laity remain the crucial factors. Thus, in balancing demands for change with *halakhah* they came to different conclusions than Adler. These conclusions were so different that Adler could not regard them as different but equally valid opinions, but as outside normative Judaism. This is possibly why Adler did not trust French *kashrut*. It is undeniable, however, the French rabbinate's strategy of making concessions to maintain loyalty to the official community was successful. It maintained a profound hegemony among French Jews, and kept the Liberal movement in France small.[246] As Berkowitz has observed, 'the organisation of French Jewry within the consistorial system precluded the emergence of a radical reform ideology' because 'minor reforms introduced by the *consistories* effectively undercut the prospects of a successful movement to reform the Jewish religion'.[247]

Rabbis who shared Adler's traditionalist acknowledgement ideology in theory, but who also adopted similar expansive policies, included Hirsch in Frankfurt, Hildesheimer and Hoffman in Berlin, and the early leaders of the Orthodox Union in America. Emancipation had a particularly powerful effect in Germany because from the beginning of the 1700s the rabbis lost their civil authority, which unlike their British colleagues they had enjoyed in medieval German society, and which was withdrawn as Jews became individual citizens of the state, rather than a nation within a nation.[248] The Jews' civic identity ceased to be as Jews, but as Germans, and this was disastrous for what Ellenson has called 'unmodified medieval rabbinic Judaism'.[249] Until the 1840s there was significant fear and hostility to Emancipation among the traditionalist leadership, which felt Emancipation had been discredited by its association with Reform, although this fear died away as the traditionalists 'became more combative and self-assured in the fight against Reform' and were 'able and eager to show the non-observant how one could be emancipated and observant at the same time'.[250]

Germany was at the centre of the Enlightenment and its Jewish equivalent, the *Haskalah*. German rabbis were faced with a new phenomenon and their initial reaction was to condemn, not to acknowledge or adapt. This uncompromising stand only further weakened the traditionalist position, as it came to be seen as increasingly out of touch and irrelevant.[251] These factors contributed to the main difference between Britain and Germany in the modern period, which was the proportion of Jews who affiliated to traditionalist communities. In Britain it was the vast majority, but in Germany it was only around 10% of the Jewish population.[252] All that the German traditionalists could hope for was to arrest the decline and create small, strong communities, in the nuclear model. However, although Hildesheimer and his successors were attempting to preserve a small remnant, and Adler was trying to perpetuate the hegemony of tradition, they used similar approaches.

Hildesheimer, like Adler, did not regard Emancipation as necessarily a bad thing; instead, he wanted to show that Judaism was compatible with a modern political and cultural ethos.[253] This project was important for maintaining support for traditional Judaism among Jews who wanted to take advantage of Emancipation. In his approach to internal Jewish matters, Hildesheimer came to the same conclusion as Adler, that in a world in which only persuasion could maintain Jewish allegiance it was vital for traditional leaders to appeal to Jews effectively. Against the opposition of many he was an enthusiastic supporter of

1 Nathan M. Adler, Chief Rabbi 1845–1890 (author's collection)

2 Hermann Adler, Chief Rabbi 1891–1911 (courtesy of the London School of Jewish Studies)

3 Joseph Herman Hertz, Chief Rabbi 1913–1946 (author's collection)

4 Israel Brodie, Chief Rabbi 1948–1965 (courtesy of the London School of Jewish Studies)

5 Immanuel Jakobovits, Chief Rabbi 1967–1991 (Courtesy of the London School of Jewish Studies)

sermons in the vernacular. According to Ellenson, 'Hildesheimer felt that an Orthodox rabbi had an obligation to preach in the vernacular' because only then could he effectively combat Reform.[254] Hildesheimer did not consider the question of preaching in the vernacular to be a halakhic issue, unlike some who considered any change to be hala- khically forbidden. When considering matters he did believe required halakhic analysis, his policy was to find 'a way which finds assent and favour in the eyes of the majority of the people'.

In other words, like Adler, Hildesheimer favoured the expansive model.[255] This led Hildesheimer to adopt positions that appear extremely liberal. He allowed Jewish children to attend school on the Sabbath, although not to write, and instituted a Torah reading in his synagogue on Sabbath afternoon in the format of the traditional Sabbath-morning reading to accommodate schoolchildren. David Hoffman later upheld this ruling despite widespread opposition.[256] Hildesheimer gave permis- sion to eat in the house of a Jewish woman whose husband profaned the Sabbath.[257] When he was faced with the case of a man asking for a religious divorce from his missing first wife (who could therefore not give her consent as demanded by Jewish Law), he permitted the divorce to be granted because the man threatened to marry again anyway.[258] On the other hand, Hildesheimer ruled it was forbidden to enter a syna- gogue with either mixed seating or an organ.[259] Indeed the rabbinical ordination at Hildesheimer's seminary was conditional on the recipient not accepting a position at a synagogue with an organ.[260]

Like Adler, Hildesheimer conceded where he thought it was possible and desirable to do so, but was firm when he felt he had to be. Hoffman continued his teacher's approach. Gordis has written about Hoffman's attitude towards civil marriage: the latter's aim was to 'strike a delicate balance' between 'boundary maintenance' (the upholding of *halakhah*) and 'constituency rentention' (keeping as many within the fold as pos- sible). Gordis argues that Hoffman 'would push halakhic precedents, even in seemingly self-contradictory directions, in order to include as many Jews as he possibly could within the parameters of the traditional community'.[261] Hildeshiemer and Hoffman's greater halakhic expertise enabled them to be bolder than Adler in some cases, but their motiva- tions and basic strategies were the same.

Hirsch broadly followed the same approach as Hildesheimer and Hoffman, For example, in 1839 he removed *Kol nidre* from the liturgy to show that Jews could be trusted to keep their promises.[262] In this case Hirsch was more radical than Adler, who, as we saw, refused even to amend the text of *Kol nidre*. However, there was an important dif- ference between Frankfurt and Berlin; while Hirsch, like Hildesheimer, was willing to make his community attractive to a large group, he refused to have any official relationship with any non-traditional Jewish group, the policy known as *Austritt* – complete institutional separation. Although Hildesheimer was rabbi of an *Austritt* synagogue himself and supported the law that allowed secession, he gave his blessing to students who led traditional synagogues that were part of the general Jewish community, financed from a central fund, the system known as *Grossgemeinde*. He was also happy to co-operate with individuals with whom he had theological disagreements on non-religious matters; thus he worked with Graetz to establish an orphanage in Jerusalem.[263]

This practical difference was the result of alternative analyses of the best way to preserve tradition, either through a vanguard approach, whereby a small, strong group went its own way, or whether co-operation with the non-traditional was possible without theological sacrifice. Adler's expansive-hegemonic approach contained aspects of the analyses that produced both the vanguard and co-operative approaches. He refused to allow the ministers of the West London Synagogue to preach in his synagogues, and he vetoed a proposed meeting in 1890 between the United Synagogue, the Federation, the Sefardim and West London.[264] However, he was willing to work with them in some contexts, for example on the Jewish Religious Education Board. There were therefore commonalities between Hirsch and Adler, but Berlin provides the better German comparison with Adler in both theology and practice.

A final comparison comes from America. In the late nineteenth century two rabbinical organisations emerged, the *Agudat harabbanim* and the Orthodox Union.[265] The *Agudat harabbanim* insisted upon the teaching in Yiddish of a highly traditional curriculum and the preservation of an unchanged synagogue service.[266] The Orthodox Union, by contrast, were convinced that the best way to preserve Jewish tradition was to engage with the secular authorities to make Sabbath observance easier, to modernise Jewish educational techniques with an emphasis on English, and to infuse the synagogue with American manners appealing to the young.[267] The members of the Orthodox Union were products of the European schools of Jewish thought that Adler was most closely associated with, namely those from the traditionalist wing of the scientific branch of the acknowledgement school. Bernard Drachman studied at Breslau, Henry Schneeberger received his rabbinical ordination from Hildesheimer, H. Pereira Mendes was educated at Jews' College and J.H. Hertz attended the Jewish Theological Seminary, led by a leading figure advocating the views of the acknowledgement school, Sabato Morais.[268] Just as Adler thought Jewish tradition could be combined with British values and loyalties, the Orthodox Union believed it could be harmonised with American values. The *Agudat harabbanim* rejected that analysis. As Gurock has written, 'ultimately the *Agudat harabbanim* was less concerned that American law respect the immigrant Jews and more interested that the new American continue to respect Jewish law'.[269] Another source of division was the Orthodox Union's co-operative approach, for example with Reform leaders who sat on the board of its Uptown Talmud Torah.[270] The Orthodox Union was confederate, and member congregations enjoyed a high degree of independence. There were even synagogues with mixed pews.[271]

Using Berger's terminology, Gurock has described the *Agudat harabbanim* as being made up of 'resistors' to Americanisation and the Orthodox Union as being comprised of 'accommodators' – in other words, the former represented the antipathy school and the latter the acknowledgement school. However, Gurock has difficulty in explaining why Philip Hillel Klein, a graduate of the Hildesheimer Seminary and the holder of a PhD, should be a leader of the *Agudat harabbanim*, especially as he co-operated with Drachman, Mendes and others on other communal bodies. Gurcok ascribed Klein's apparently irregular alignments to a desire to maintain a power base in all religious camps.[272] However, having examined Lerner in England, we can detect other factors. Drachman, Mendes, Schneeberger and their colleagues should be seen as aligned like Adler, to that part of the acknowledgement school that favoured an expansive policy. Klein, like Lerner, held acknowledgement school views, but he was a vanguardist, committed to uncompromising traditionalism on ritual and practice, notwithstanding relatively progressive views on theological questions, even if that might limit his appeal to the religiously lukewarm. Klein therefore worked within the *Agudat harabbanim* alongside the antipathy school, even though he had more in common intellectually with the members of the Orthodox Union, and worked with them in other contexts. Again, splits within the acknowledgement school were just as important as splits between the acknowledgement and other schools.

Adler, the leaders of the Hildesheimer Seminary in Germany and the Orthodox Union in America conceded in their religious policies on the points where they believed there was room for manoeuvre, sometimes in quite radical ways, but where they felt the *halakhah* did not allow leniency they were firm. This was part of an expansive policy to make traditional Judaism as palatable as possible to as many as possible, and was a far cry from mere latitudinarianism. This attitude separated Adler's group from the uncompromising members of the *Agudat harabbanim* in America, whether they were from the acknowledgement school or not, and from Paris where the religious leadership was powerful in theory, but severely constrained in practice, and in an effort to be expansive and hegemonic made rulings that Adler regarded as unacceptable.

Our analysis of Adler, in theory and practice, and our contextualisation of his thought and actions as he responded to modernity cast doubt on many of the current historiographical conclusions. I have shown how Alderman, Endelman, Freud Kandel and others held that Adler was, or was regarded by the more traditional section of the community as, theologically suspect and lax in his enforcement of *halakhah*.[273] We can see now that although there was tension and mistrust the situation was more complex. Adler's theological views were traditional, his concern for *halakhah* profound and this was recognised, at least by the immigrants who attended his *Shabbat Shuva derashah* and their religious leaders, including Chaikin, Hillman, Spiers and Reinowitz who worked with him. The dispute with Machzikei Hadath was significant, but was not wholly religious and culminated with acceptance of Adler's authority via the Federation of Synagogues, to which the majority of immigrants had affiliated in any case.

Adler combined his traditional views and values with an appreciation for what he considered the best of modern culture, alongside figures such as Hirsch and Hildesheimer. He adopted the same expansive approach to policy as Hildesheimer, which helped to establish his hegemony in Anglo-Jewry. For all the tensions between the East End and West End, by the end of his life Adler enjoyed the allegiance in some form or another of a large spectrum of the community, from Hampstead and the New West End through the traditional wing of the United Synagogue including the Great and Hambro Synagogues, to the Federation of Synagogues and Machzikei Hadath, and even to figures such as Samuel Isaac Hillman. One Sabbath morning in 1895, by contrast, the West London Synagogue, outside Adler's jurisdiction, attracted just 18 worshippers.[274] That was his legacy to his successor as Chief Rabbi, J.H. Hertz.

Notes

1 H.A. Simons, *Forty years a Chief Rabbi: the life and times of Solomon Hirschell* (London 1980), 100.

2 I. Finestein, *Anglo-Jewry in changing times* (London 1999), 217.

3 London Beth Din Papers, London Metropolitan Archive (LBDP LMA) ACC 2712/15/1392; I. Harris, 'History of Jews' College' in Harris (ed) *Jews' College jubilee volume* (London 1906), lvii–lviii, lxxxvi, cc.

4 H. Adler, *Anglo-Jewish memories* (London 1909), 87.

5 See where the sermons in Adler, *Anglo-Jewish memories* were delivered.

6 *Jewish Chronicle* (26 May 1893); Finestein, *Changing times*, 222; I. Brodie, *The strength of my heart* (London 1969), 120.

7 R.H. Ellison, *The Victorian pulpit* (Susquehanna, Texas 1998), chapter 3.

8 J. Jung *Champions of orthodoxy* (London 1974), 43. Adler asserted the connection between his role as preacher and the traditional *maggidim*. Adler, *Anglo-Jewish memories*, ix–x.

9 D. Ellenson, *Rabbi Esriel Hildesheimer and the creation of a Modern Jewish Orthodoxy* (Tuscaloosa, Alabama 1990), 47–48; Jung, *Champions*, 53.

10 M. Breuer, trans. E. Petuchowski, *Modernity within tradition* (New York 1992), 153.

11 Adler, *Anglo-Jewish memories*, 192, 209, 238, 262, 171.

12 Ibid., 222.

13 H. Adler, *The loss of HMS Victoria* (London 1893), 11; Adler, *Anglo-Jewish memories*, 273, 256.

14 *Jewish Chronicle* (2 January 1863), 6.

15 Smith has shown that very few Ashkenazim converted to Christianity in the period, and fewer still for religious reasons, so few in fact as to make the conversionists' 'efforts meaningless'; R.M. Smith, 'The London Jews' Society and patterns of Jewish conversion in England, 1801–1859' *Jewish Social Studies* 43 (1981), 275; D. Feldman, *Englishmen and Jews* (New Haven, Connecticut 1994), 28–30, 91, 57, 113–114.

16 H. Adler, *Niftulei Elohim* (London 1869), 3.

17 Adler, *Niftulei Elohim*.

18 Adler, *Anglo-Jewish memories*, 242–250.

19 Ibid., 243.

20 T. Endelman, *The Jews of Britain, 1656 to 2000* (Berkeley 2002), 171.

21 G. Alderman, *Modern British Jewry* (Oxford 1992), 69.

22 H. Adler, *Hebrew, the language of our prayers* (London 1885).

23 H. Adler, 'The Sabbath and the organ' in *Jewish Chronicle* (11 January 1895), 13.

24 H. Adler, *The old paths* (London 1902). The praise Adler received from the immigrant community for this sermon is interesting evidence for a more positive attitude of the immigrants towards Adler than has sometimes been suggested. S.A. Cohen, *English Zionists and British Jews* (Princeton 1982), 185.

25 N. Adler, *The Jewish faith* (London 1848), 12.

26 Finestein, *Changing times*, 228.

27 Ibid., 222.

28 Adler, *Anglo-Jewish memories*, 11.

29 Ibid., 155.

30 E.C. Black, 'The Anglicization of orthodoxy: the Adlers, father and son' in F. Malino and D. Sorkin (ed) *From east and west* (Oxford 1990), 316.

31 B. Homa, *A fortress in Anglo-Jewry* (London 1953), 13.
32 D. Englander, 'Anglicized not Anglican: Jews and Judaism in Victorian Britain' in Parsons (ed), *Religion in Victorian Britain, I: Traditions* (Manchester 1988), 266–267.
33 Adler, *Anglo-Jewish memories*, 199.
34 Ibid., 92.
35 Hermann Adler condemned the 'pestilential opinions' of East End socialists; B. Williams, 'East and west in Manchester Jewry, 1850–1914' in Cesarani (ed) *The making of modern Anglo-Jewry* (Oxford 1990), 30.
36 Endelman, *Jews of Britain*, 157.
37 Adler, *Anglo-Jewish memories*, 199. See E.C. Black, *The social politics of Anglo-Jewry* (Oxford 1989), 91, V.D. Lipman, *A century of social service* (London 1959), 92–96, and Feldman, *Englishmen and Jews*, 302–306.
38 L.H. Montagu, *Samuel Montagu, Baron Sawythling* (London undated), 44.
39 *Jewish Review* (July 1910), 117–124.
40 Adler, *Anglo-Jewish memories*, 95, 117.
41 Ibid., 74.
42 *Jewish Chronicle* (4 and 11 August 1865).
43 Ibid. (7January 1870), 3.
44 Ibid. (7 January 1870), 31.
45 H. Adler, *Sanitation as taught by the Mosaic law* (London 1893).
46 Royal Commission on Divorce and Matrimonial Causes, *Evidence* (1912–1913), 408.
47 H. Adler, 'Jews and Judaism: A rejoinder' *Nineteenth Century* (1878), 133–150, H. Adler, 'Recent phases of Judaeophobia' *Nineteenth Century* (December 1881), 813–829.
48 W.D. Rubinstein, *A history of the Jews in the English-speaking world: Great Britain* (London 1996), 110.
49 Feldman, *Englishmen and Jews*, 91–92.
50 Adler, *Anglo-Jewish memories*, 153.
51 Ibid., 89.
52 Endelman, *Jews of Britain*, 113.
53 Ibid., 294.
54 D Englander (ed) *A documentary history of Jewish immigrants in Britain, 1840–1920* (London 1994), 50–52.
55 I. Finestein, *Jewish society in Victorian England* (London 1993), 335.
56 R. Apple, *The Hampstead Synagogue* (London 1967), 12.
57 Ibid., 14–15.
58 *Jewish Review* (September 1911), 198.
59 Jung, *Champions*, 25; United Synagogue Papers, London Metropolitan Archive (USP LMA) ACC 2712/WES/1.
60 Englander, 'Anglicized not Anglican', 261.
61 Jung, *Champions*, 25–26.
62 *Jewish Chronicle* (1 July 1892), 17; Jung, *Champions*, 25–26.

63 *Jewish Chronicle* (1 July 1892), 17.

64 Adler papers, Jewish Theological Seminary (AP JTS), 5, 2/4.

65 Jung, *Champions*, 25, 28.

66 Ibid., 27.

67 *Jewish Chronicle* (1 July 1892), 17.

68 O.S. Phillips and H.A. Simons, *The history of the Bayswater Synagogue, 1863–1963* (London 1963), 12, 15.

69 N.M. Adler, *Laws and regulations for all the synagogues in the British Empire* (London 1847), 12.

70 F.L. Cohen and D.M. Davis (ed) *The voice of prayer and praise* (3rd edn, London 1933), v.

71 Finestein, *Changing times*, 231; G. Parsons, 'Reform, revival and realignment: the experience of Victorian Anglicanism' in Parsons (ed) *Religion in Victorian Britain* (Manchester 1988), 50.

72 Cohen and Davis, *Voice of prayer and praise*, i.

73 Englander, 'Anglicized not Anglican', 251.

74 Parsons, 'Reform, revival and realignment, 51.

75 Ibid., 261.

76 *Jewish Chronicle* (1 July 1892, 17–18. *Kol nidre* nullifies vows, and gave the impression that one could not trust a Jew's promise. Many Jews wanted to remove it from the liturgy for that reason.

77 Ibid.

78 Adler, *Laws and regulations*, 8.

79 *Jewish Chronicle* (1 July 1892), 18. This is the current situation in the vast majority of British synagogues, both inside and outside the United Synagogue, where the service usually begins at 9.15 am, requiring worshippers to recite the *shema* at home before they attend public prayer, in order to have said it during the halakhically approved time.

80 Phillips and Simons, *Bayswater Synagogue*, 12.

81 *Jewish Chronicle* (1 July 1892), 17.

82 Chief Rabbinate Papers, London Metropolitan Archive (CRP LMA) ACC 2805/03/2/40. Requesting this confirmation from the Haham was rather odd. Adler surely knew the established custom of the Sefardim, and its halakhic justification.

83 *Jewish Chronicle* (1 July 1892), 18.

84 Alderman, *Modern British Jewry*, 107.

85 Jung, *Champions*, 28.

86 E. Newman, 'The responsa of Dayan Jacob Reinovitz, 1818–1893' *Transactions of the Jewish Historical Society of England* 23 (1969–70), 29.

87 For example Isaac Elhanan Spector in the dispute with Machzike Hadath. Homa, *Fortress*, 44–45; A.M. Hyamson, *The London Board for Shechita, 1804–1954* (London 1954), 47. Note that Homa argues that Adler used deception and financial pressure to procure the support of foreign rabbis.

88 Jung, *Champions*, 29.

89 Ibid., 24, 25.

90 Adler, *Laws and regulations*, iii.

91 Ibid., 15, 16.

92 CRP LMA ACC 2805/2/1/8.

93 AP JTS 5, 1/5; CRP LMA ACC 2805/2/1/8.

94 CRP LMA ACC 2805/2/1/29.

95 A. Newman, *The United Synagogue, 1870–1970* (London 1976), 157.

96 Adler, 'Sabbath and the organ', 13 .

97 S. Reif, *Judaism and Hebrew prayer* (Cambridge 1993), 285.

98 Ibid., 286; S. Singer (ed), *Authorised daily prayer book of the United Hebrew Congregations of the British Empire* (London 1890), 143, for example. This policy can be traced in the standard Anglo-Jewish festival prayer books, edited by Hermann Adler's brother, Herbert. See, for example, A. Davis and H.M. Adler (ed), *Service of the synagogue, Pentecost* (London 1909) where the traditional text is retained and faithfully translated. Liturgical poems are not included in the main text, but placed at the end, so that those who wished to do so were able to recite them. That volume is also notable for Herbert Adler's *Wissenschaft*-influenced 'Note on the festival of Pentecost', 206–207.

99 Ibid.

100 S. Heilman, 'Constructing orthodoxy' in Robbins and Anthony (ed) *In gods we trust* (New Brunswick, 1981), 152–153.

101 Reif, *Hebrew prayer*, 286–287.

102 D. Ellenson, *After Emancipation* (Cincinnati 2004), 220; A. Schischa, 'Hermann Adler, yeshiva bahur, Prague, 1860–1862' in Shaftesley (ed) *Remember the days* (London 1966), 270; Black, 'Anglicization: the Adlers', 316.

103 Ellenson, *After Emancipation*, 221.

104 Ibid., 214–216.

105 Ibid., 221–222.

106 S. Berman, 'Kol Isha' *Rabbi Joseph H. Lookstein Memorial Volume* (New York 1980), 45, 56–57. The prohibition is generally held to extend more widely, but this is the bare minimum.

107 Ibid.

108 See note 111 for evidence for this assumption.

109 *Jewish Chronicle* (5 March 1880), 11; (12 March 1880), 11; (9 April 1880), 6.

110 Ibid., (3 August 1883), 7.

111 Finestein, *Changing times* (London 1999), 247.

112 V.D. Lipman, *A history of the Jews in Britain since 1858* (Leicester 1990), 92.

113 *Jewish Chronicle* (15 May 1896), 10.

114 Ibid. (17 April 1896), 10 This reference to solos suggests Adler was familiar with the opinion of the Hatan Sofer.

115 Ibid.

116 R. Apple, *Mixed choirs in Jewish worship* (unpublished 1987), 7.

117 *Jewish Chronicle* (18 May 1900), 24. The matter was brought up at a meeting of the members of St John's Wood Synagogue where the practice took place. The following exchange took place: Mr. Blainbury: 'How do other West End synagogues manage [to get boys]?' Mr Arnholz: 'Pretty much as we do.' In other words the practice of paying choirboys to travel and break the Sabbath was common.

118 Apple, *Hampstead*, 21.

119 Finestein, *Changing times*, 233.

120 For a full analysis, see B.J. Elton, 'Did the Chief Rabbinate move to the right? A case study: the mixed choir controversies, 1880–1986' *Jewish Historical Studies* 39 (2004) 121–151.

121 *Jewish Chronicle* (22 September 1893), 8.

122 CRP LMA ACC/2805/2/1/46.

123 USP LMA ACC 2712/7/3/21.

124 These are the sort of factors which have traditionally led to a more lenient attitude by the Chief Rabbinate to Reform ministers officiating at funerals. Interview with Alan Greenbat, (22 August 2005).

125 M. Persoff, *Faith against reason: religious reform and the British Chief Rabbinate, 1840–1990* (London 2008), 138.

126 See M. Joseph, *The ideal in Judaism* (London 1893).

127 *Jewish Chronicle* (3 June 1892), 6.

128 Apple, *Hampstead*, 25.

129 J.M. Shaftesley, 'Religious controversies' in Levin (ed) *A century of Anglo-Jewish life* (London 1970), 102.

130 *Jewish Chronicle* (10 June 1892), 7.

131 Ibid. (1 July 1892), 9.

132 M. Joseph, *Judaism as life and creed* (London 1903), 153.

133 M.M. Kaplan, *Judaism as a civilisation* (New York 1934), 127.

134 *Jewish Chronicle*, (3 June 1892), 6.

135 *Jewish Chronicle* January 26 1912.

136 J. Hochman, *Orthodoxy and religious observance* (London 1910), 7, 11.

137 Ibid., 1.

138 CRP LMA ACC 2805/1/1/71.

139 A.M. Hyamson, *Jews' College London, 1855–1955* (London 1955), 33, 84; J.H. Hertz, *The Authorised daily prayer book* (New York 1948), 532–533.

140 Hyamson, *Jews' College*, 34, 46.

141 M. Friedlander, *The Jewish religion* (London 1922), 49, 91, 137.

142 Hyamson, *Jews' College*, 33.

143 I. Epstein, 'Adolph Buchler' in Brodie and Rabbinowitz (ed) *Studies in Jewish history* (Oxford 1956), xiii–xiv.

144 M. Carmilly-Weinberger, 'The Breslau and Budapest seminaries' in *Leo Baeck Institute Year Book* XLIV (1999), 7–8.

145 Epstein, 'Buchler', xiv.

146 Carmilly-Weinberger, 'Breslau and Budapest', 14–15.

147 Epstein, 'Buchler', xiii–xiv.

148 Hyamson, *Jews' College*, 82.

149 Epstein, 'Buchler', xiv–xv.

150 Ibid., xvi.

151 Ibid., xxi.

152 Epstein, 'Buchler', xv, xxi; Interview with Dr Isaac Levy, May 21 2004.

153 A. Buchler, 'The reading of the Law and the Prophets in a triennial cycle' *Jewish Quarterly Review*, 1893, 420–468; 1894, 1–73.

154 *Report on the Sabbath reading of the Scriptures in a triennial cycle* (London 1913), 9.

155 I. Levy, *History of the Sunderland Jewish community* (London 1956), 225.

156 E. Marmorstein 'My father, a memoir' in Rabbinowitz and Lew (ed) *Studies in Jewish theology* (London 1950), xxiii; S. Daiches, *Essays and addresses* (London 1955), 59, 82–83.

157 Endelman, *Jews of Britain*, 120.

158 Harris, 'Jews' College', viii, lvii.

159 Ibid., lxxvii, cxx–cxxi.

160 Hyamson, *Jews' College*, 64.

161 Harris, 'Jews' College', civ.

162 Ibid., cv.

163 Ibid., cxliii, clxxxv.

164 H. Adler, 'The sons of the prophets' in Harris (ed) *Jews' College jubilee volume* (London 1906), 16–17.

165 Hyamson, *Jews' College*, 78, H. Meirovich, *A vindication of Judaism: the polemics of the Hertz Pentateuch* (New York 1998), 153.

166 LBDP LMA ACC 2712/15/1392.

167 Hyamson, *Jews' College*, 83.

168 Ibid., 78.

169 Ibid., 77.

170 Ibid., 59, 78, 81, 73–74.

171 N. Cohen, 'Trends in Anglo-Jewish religious life' in Gould and Esh (ed) *Trends in Jewish life* (London 1964), 46; interview with Graeme Morris, 5 February 2006. The Rev. Isaac Livingstone of the Golders Green Synagogue carried his umbrella on the Sabbath.

172 *Jewish Chronicle* (3 January 1902), 9.

173 E. Newman, 'The responsa of Dayan Jacob Reinowitz' *Jewish Historical Studies* 23 (1969/70), 22–33.

174 Ibid.

175 S. Heilman, 'The many faces of orthodoxy, part 1' *Modern Judaism* 2:1 (February 1982), 26–27.

176 P. Orenstein, *Historical sketch of the Beth Hamedrash* (London 1905), 11.

177 Ellenson, *Hildesheimer*, 63.

178 Ibid.

179 Ibid., 64; Black, 'Anglicization: the Adlers', 318.

180 Orenstein, *Beth Hamedrash*, 13.

181 *Jewish Chronicle* (7 March 1902), 13.

182 See, for example, Jung, *Champions*, 84.

183 *Jewish Chronicle* (28 March 1902), 13.

184 A. Feldman, *Parables and similes of the rabbis* (Cambridge 1924).

185 J.S. Gurock, 'Yeshiva students at the Jewish Theological Seminary' in Wertheimer (ed) *Tradition renewed* (New York 1997), I: 491.

186 Jung, *Champions*, 71–84.

187 Ibid., 86.

188 Ibid., 85–88.

189 Ibid., 88–92.

190 CRP LMA ACC 2805/3/2/40. Gaster was a graduate of Breslau, and his support for Adler in this affair is further evidence of his alma mater's halakhic conservatism.

191 Hillman Papers, Jewish and National Library, Jerusalem (HP JNLJ) 4/1516/0284.

192 Ibid., 4/1516/0284/6583.

193 Ibid., 4/1516/0284/4549; 8883.

194 B. Homa, *Orthodoxy in Anglo-Jewry* (London 1969), 37–38, 19–20.

195 Endelman, *Jews of Britain*, 179.

196 Homa, *Fortress*, 44–45.

197 G. Alderman, 'Power, authority and status in British Jewry: the Chief Rabbinate and shechita' in Alderman and Holmes (ed) *Outsiders and outcasts: essays in honour of William J. Fishman* (London 1993), 18.

198 Homa, *Orthodoxy in Anglo-Jewry*, 21.

199 Montagu, *Samuel Montagu*, 20.

200 Hyamson, *London Board for Shechita*, 29.

201 Ibid., 45; Homa, *Fortress*, 31.

202 Hyamson, *London Board for Shechita*, 46; Homa, *Fortress*, 32.

203 Hyamson, *London Board for Shechita*, 46–47.

204 Ibid.

205 CRP LMA ACC/2805/03/2/40.

206 Ibid; Hyamson, *London Board for Shechita*, 47–48.

207 Lipman, *Jews in Britain*, 98; CRP LMA ACC/2805/03/01/20.

208 Alderman, 'Chief Rabbinate and shechita', 20.

209 Feldman, *Englishmen and Jews*, 337.

210 Endelman, *Jews of Britain*, 176.

211 Ibid., 177; Englander, 'Anglicized not Anglican', 265.

212 Jung, *Champions*, 49; W.J. Fishman, *East End Jewish radicals* (London 1975), 157 .

213 M. Goodman, 'Vice versa: Samuel Montagu, the first Lord Swaythling' *Jewish Historical Studies* 40 (2005), 86.

214 D. Gutwein, *The divided elite* (Leiden 1992), 146.

215 G. Alderman, *The Federation of Synagogues, 1887–1987* (London 1987),
     17–18; Endelman, *Jews of Britain*, 177.
216 Jung, *Champions*, 176; J.E. Blank, *Minutes of the Federation of Synagogues*
     (London 1912), 72. Indeed in at least one case Montagu made his funding
     conditional on Adler opening the synagogue: Feldman, *Englishmen and
     Jews*, 323.
217 Gutwein, *Divided elite*, 229, 210.
218 Blank, *Federation of Synagogues*, 46. Note that the Federation maintained
     its membership of the Board although there were Reform members; it was
     only when one became president that it withdrew.
219 Jung, *Champions*, 54.
220 Ibid., 51–52.
221 Ibid., 54.
222 Ibid., 53, 59.
223 Ibid., 65.
224 J.H. Hertz, *Sermons, addresses and studies* (London 1938), I: 111–112.
225 Feldman, *Englishmen and Jews*, 296.
226 HP JNLJ 4/1516/0284.
227 Finestein, *Changing times*, 245.
228 Jung, *Champions*, 72–73.
229 Ibid., 73.
230 *Jewish Chronicle* (4 September 1908), 9. 'Tatler' was A.A. Green.
231 Endelman, *Jews of Britain*, 168; Parsons, 'Reform, revival and realign-
     ment', 47.
232 Ministers suspected of untraditional views and practices were not per-
     secuted by Brodie and Jakobovits, for example, Isaac Levy and Isaac
     Livingstone, who both served during their tenures. If Adler let sleeping
     dogs lie, then so did they. Only when the minister involved went public,
     and therefore made their private views into a public issue did the Chief
     Rabbis, from Adler to Jakobovits, act.
233 D. Taylor, *British Chief Rabbis, 1664–2006* (London 2007), 320.
234 P.C. Albert, *The modernization of French Jewry* (Hanover, New
     Hampshire 1977), 314.
235 Ibid., 285.
236 Ibid., 297.
237 J.M. Berkovitz, *Rites and passages* (Philadelphia 2004), 206.
238 Ibid., 210.
239 Ibid., 191.
240 Ibid., 192.
241 Ibid., 193.
242 Ibid., 209.
243 Ibid., 194.
244 Ibid., 195–196.
245 Ibid., 208.
246 Albert, *Modernization of French Jewry*, 314.

247 Berkovitz, *Rites and passages*, 197.

248 Ellenson, *Hildesheimer*, 8.

249 Ibid., 10.

250 Breuer, *Modernity within tradition*, 284–285.

251 Ellenson, *Hildesheimer*, 10–11.

252 Breuer, *Modernity within tradition*, 397; D. Sorkin, 'The impact of Emancipation on Germany Jewry: a reconsideration' in Frankel and Zipperstein (ed) *Assimilation and community: the Jews in nineteenth-century Europe* (Cambridge 1992), 177; S. Sharot, *Judaism: a sociology* (Newton Abbot 1976), 108.

253 Breuer, *Modernity within tradition*, 285; Ellenson, *After Emancipation*, 20–21.

254 Ellenson, *Hildesheimer*, 49.

255 Ibid., 51. Of course, saying that an issue is not a matter for halakhic judgment is itself a halakhic judgment. .

256 Ibid., 65.

257 Ibid., 68.

258 Ibid., 68–69.

259 Ibid., 51.

260 M. Persoff, *Immanuel Jakobovits: a prophet in Israel* (London 2002), 11.

261 D.H. Gordis, 'David Zevi Hoffman and civil marriage: evidence of a traditional community under siege' *Modern Judaism* 10 (1996), 85, 88, 98.

262 Breuer, *Modernity within tradition*, 32. *Kol nidre* cancels vows, and therefore can make it seem that a Jew's word could not be relied upon.

263 Ellenson, *Hildesheimer*, 169.

264 Goodman, 'Montagu', 96.

265 J.S. Gurock, 'Resisters and accomodators' in J. Rader Marcus and A.J. Peck (ed) *The American rabbinate* (Hoboken, New Jersey 1985), 22.

266 Ibid., 23.

267 Ibid., 23–24.

268 Ibid., 10, 17, 30–31; M. Davis, *The emergence of Conservative Judaism: the historical school in 19th-century America* (Philadelphia 1963), 315.

269 Gurock, 'Resisters and accommodators', 2.

270 Ibid., 32.

271 J.S. Gurock, 'Twentieth-century American orthodoxy's era of non-observance, 1900–1960' *Torah u-Madda Journal* 4 (2000), 92.

272 Gurock, 'Resistors and accomodators', 30.

273 G. Alderman, *Modern British Jewry* (Oxford 1992), 108–109; T. Endelman, *Jews of Britain*, 176, 179; M. Freud Kandel, *Ideology forsaken* (PhD Thesis, University of Cambridge 2000) and *Orthodox Judaism in Britain since 1913* (London 2006).

274 *Jewish Chronicle* (8 November 1895), 9.

Chapter 7

The theology of J.H. Hertz

J.H. HERTZ'S THEOLOGY placed him in the traditional group within the acknowledgement school, although he was influenced by its scientific, romantic and aesthetic branches. We can see this in Hertz's attitude to the major issues of Jewish belief: the Pentateuch and the rest of the Hebrew Bible, the Oral Law, the development of *halakhah*, his philosophy of *mitsvot*, Jewish mysticism, the Messiah and the afterlife. We examine Hertz's position on secular learning, non-Jews and non-Jewish religious movements, and on Jews and Jewish movements other than his own. Finally I look at see how Zionism fitted into Hertz's theological outlook. Having established Hertz's religious attitudes, I trace their origins, identify Hertz's religious and intellectual inspirations, and then contrast Hertz's views with those of Jewish religious leaders with different attitudes and see how Hertz's approach can be seen as a reaction to those attitudes and as interventions in an ongoing debate within Judaism. As with Adler, we examine Hertz's theology for two reasons: first, because it is worthy of study in its own right, but secondly and more significantly because Hertz's religious policies were very important in shaping Anglo-Jewish religious history, and, as we shall see, Hertz's religious thought was the greatest factor in determining the way in which he led his community.

I argue that, like Adler before him, Hertz was a member of the group of traditionalists who wished to acknowledge what they considered to be the valuable aspects of modernity. Although Hertz was part of the scientific branch, he was also influenced by Hirsch – a position which Meirovich regards as impossible, but as others, like Drachman, were before him. Hertz adopted this position as a result of his education at the Jewish Theological Seminary (JTS). Although Hertz obviously continued to develop throughout his life, the basis of his religious thought was the values he internalised at the JTS: it is possible to trace all of Hertz's major attitudes back to the seminary and its teachers. Throughout his career he pursued the mission set by the President of the Seminary, Sabato Morais, a Westernised but traditional Jewish leader. Hertz wrote of himself and his fellow seminary students 'we were thrilled by the clear, clarion notes of his call to the Wars of the Lord; by his passionate and loyal stand that the Divine Law was imperative, unchangeable, eternal. He made rigorous demands upon him who would come forward as defender of the Judaism of our Fathers – piety and scholarship, consistency, and the courage to stand alone, if need be, in the fight against unrighteousness and un-Judaism'.[1]

Hertz centred his Judaism around the Torah. In his graduation sermon from the JTS in 1894 he told his fellow students 'we will follow Elijah who is now calling us to be zealous for Israel's Law, because we love Israel, because we love its Law' and he spoke of 'the lofty aim of drawing men nearer to the Torah'.[2] When he was installed as Chief Rabbi in 1913 he expounded the text 'Remember ye the word of Moses'.[3] In 1943, towards the end of his career Hertz again called for 'loyalty in life and death to the Torah and Tradition of Israel'.[4] The meaning of 'Torah' varies according to context. It can mean just the Pentateuch, or the Bible, or the Bible and Talmud, or the whole corpus of Jewish teaching. Nevertheless the core of 'Torah' is the Pentateuch, and that is where we begin our analysis of Hertz's views.

Hertz remains best known as the twentieth century's most active proponent of the view that the whole of the Pentateuch is the unmediated word of God, handed directly to Moses, or (in the case of the last few verses of Deuteronomy which describe the death of Moses) to Joshua. In his commentary to the Pentateuch, Hertz repeatedly asserts the claim. The preface to the first edition declares 'my conviction that the criticism of the Pentateuch associated with the name of Wellhausen is a perversion of history and a desecration of religion, is unshaken'.[5] A third of the Additional Notes at the end of each Book (nine out of 27) attempt to refute biblical criticism. Hertz deals with all the major problems raised by Higher Criticism; the two accounts of creation, the historicity of the Exodus from Egypt, the possibility that the Code of Hammurabi was the source of Biblical law and the age of the books of Leviticus and Deuteronomy. In each case Hertz argued for the traditional position, that Moses (or in the case of the final verses, Joshua) received all five books between the Exodus from Egypt and the entry into the Land of Israel and that, although Deuteronomy was lost, it was subsequently rediscovered and restored to its place in the canon, in the same pristine form in which it had first been given. Hertz even discussed the process of the revelation itself. He spoke of God revealing His word to Moses through 'continuous, unintermittent Light' stressing that Moses received the Pentateuch in a pure and unmediated form, without any human contribution.[6]

Not only did Hertz hold that the Pentateuch was Divine he also argued that the belief in its divinity was essential. He wrote 'Judaism stands or falls with its belief in the historical actuality of the revelation at Sinai'.[7] Therefore, Hertz had to argue that the Pentateuch was given in a direct revelation in order to maintain Judaism, but he also opposed the Documentary Hypothesis on scholarly grounds and planned his *Pentateuch* as a rational demolition of Biblical Criticism. For example, when Hertz discussed Exodus 6:3, often used as evidence by the critics, he sought to show they had misunderstood the text, and brought comparable Biblical passages as proof.[8] This pattern is repeated throughout the *Pentateuch*. Hertz's conclusion (whether accurate or not) was a scholarly one: 'Moses, the Exodus and the Legislation at Sinai all belong to strict history,' whereas he argued the Wellhausen hypothesis was 'unscientific'.[9]

Hertz's concentration on this question in his *Pentateuch* was the climax of his 'holy war on behalf of the Torah' to defend the traditional belief in its origin.[10] As early as 1898 he told his congregation in South Africa of 'that Law which Moses gave as an eternal inheritance to the Congregation of Israel . . . .the Torah and the whole Torah'.[11] In 1914 he attacked the 'blasphemous vagaries of that form of Higher anti-Semitism called Biblical Criticism'.[12] Thirty years later he was still speaking of 'the Law of Sinai'.[13] The passion with which Hertz repeatedly expressed these views throughout his career undermines Meirovich's suggestion that Hertz was motivated by pragmatism rather than principle.[14] As part of his case that Hertz was a 'Conservative Jew', Meirovich argues that Hertz advocated the dogma of the Divine origin of the Pentateuch because he believed only a Judaism based on that belief could endure – in other words, for tactical reasons.[15] For Hertz to devote so much of his life and writings to the defence of dogma he believed to be untrue would make him an immense cynic and hypocrite. We can see cases where Hertz may have made statements for tactical reasons (such as on the value of other faiths), but the argument that Hertz was dishonest about his views on a subject he campaigned consistently about requires more evidence that Meirovich supplies, if it is to be accepted.

Hertz acquired his view on the origin of the Pentateuch from his father and his teachers at the JTS, all of whom were aligned to the traditional but scientific branch of the acknowledgement school. Hertz's father, Simon, attended Hildesheimer's seminary in Eisenstadt. Hildesheimer taught the Mosaic origin of the Pentateuch, and Simon Hertz doubtless passed that on to his son. The three leading founders of the JTS, Sabato Morais, Alexander Kohut and Bernard Drachman, all believed that the Pentateuch was given on Sinai.[16] Hertz described Morais as 'the most potent religious influence in my life'.[17] Both Kohut and Drachman were graduates of the intellectual centre of traditional *Wissenschaft*, Zachariah Frankel's Breslau Seminary. Hertz called them both his 'beloved teacher' and Drachman signed Hertz's rabbinical ordination.[18] Kohut once declared, 'to us the Pentateuch is *noli me tangere!* Hands off! We disclaim all honour of handing "the sharp knife that cuts the Bible into a thousand pieces"'.[19]

The other great influence on Hertz's attitude to the Pentateuch was Solomon Schechter. Hertz called Schechter the 'Master' and his 'best friend on earth'.[20] In his memorial address he called Schechter 'the undisputed leader in the "Holy War" to rescue Judaism's Sacred Heritage from the profanation of the enemy'.[21] Schechter called Higher Criticism 'Higher Antisemitism' as Hertz was fond of quoting.[22] In the context of the British Chief Rabbinate, Hertz was also following in the footsteps of Hermann Adler, who we have seen placed great importance on the revelation at Sinai.

Hertz's defence of the Divine origin of the Pentateuch was partly prompted by the activity of the adaptation and acceptance schools in the Jewish community. He repeated the attacks on Reform rabbis he had made in America, soon after arriving in England. In 1914 he lambasted the leaders of the 'founders of the Jewish Reformed Church of America' who, he said, acted 'in defiance of . . . the spiritual laws of the universe'.[23] Hertz identified the Liberal Jewish Synagogue and its leaders Claude Montefiore and Israel Mattuck as the British equivalent of American Reform. Montefiore's book *The Bible for home reading* was a polemic for Biblical Criticism, and prompted Hertz to write his *Pentateuch* as a polemic against Biblical Criticism.[24]

For Hertz every word of the Pentateuch was Divine, but, like others whom we would place in the scientific branch of the acknowledgement school, his attitude to the rest of the Bible was more nuanced and he did not consider the questions of date and origin as important in terms of dogma. He described as 'liberating' the 'recognition that the supposed date or historical background behind a psalm, hardly affects the meaning of the psalm itself'.[25] Similarly, Hertz wrote that the dating of the second part of Isaiah 'touches no dogma, or any religious principle in Judaism', a view we have seen was shared by Hildesheimer.[26] In the case of Isaiah, Hertz sided with tradition, but in some cases he did deviate from the recognised tradition or took advantage of room for manoeuvre within the tradition. He highlighted the rabbinic opinion that the Book of Job was a parable rather than history.[27] Although Hertz rejected the theory that some psalms dated from Maccabean times, he did not refer to David as the editor of the psalms and (apart from Solomon) the last of the psalmists, as the Talmud teaches, but rather as 'the founder of the Psalter' and wrote that some psalms date from the Babylonian Exile'.[28] Hertz described the Song of Songs, traditionally attributed to King Solomon, as a 'collection of ancient lyrics of the springtime and youthful love'.[29] This attitude is typical of the traditionalist *Wissenschaft* approach of Hertz's father and teachers, represented in England by Nathan and Hermann Adler, Michael Friedlaender and other rabbinical leaders such as Mayer Lerner of the Federation of Synagogues.

Hertz described the Oral Law as 'the soul of Judaism' and its aim, purpose and achievement as 'the sanctification of human life'.[30] Hertz, however, was vague on the origin of the Oral Law. He described it as 'oral traditions current from time immemorial concerning the proper observance of the commandments of the Torah' which formed the 'authoritative interpretation and immemorial custom of Judaism'.[31] Hertz wrote that Ezra 'brought with him all the oral traditions that were taught in the [Babylonian] Exile'.[32] He suggested that these were combined with the deliberations of the Men of the Great Assembly whose 'teachings and ordinances received the sanction of popular practice and came to be looked on as halacha'. These statements leave some ambiguity. Was the Oral Law given with the Pentateuch on Sinai or was it developed by the Jewish people and its leaders subsequently?

Hertz elsewhere removed this ambiguity. In his comment on the first *mishnah* in the Ethics of the Fathers, 'Moses received the Torah on Sinai', Hertz wrote, 'the reference is to the Oral Tradition. To the Rabbis the real Torah was not merely the Written Text of the Five Books of Moses; it also included the meaning enshrined in that text as expounded and unfolded by the interpretation of successive generations of Sages who made its implicit Divine teachings explicit. This Oral Tradition was handed down from the earliest days by word of mouth, until it was codified in the Mishnah'.[33] He went on, quoting Abraham Cohen, 'the Judaism of today is in the direct line of descent from the Revelation on Sinai, the intervening generations of teachers forming links in an unbroken chain of Tradition'.[34]

In other words, in Hertz's theology, the Pentateuch requires the Oral Law to complete it: some parts were given with the Pentateuch and the rest lies within the Pentateuch, in potential. As Hertz wrote elsewhere, 'every shade of meaning which Divinely inspired interpreters discover in the Law merely states *explicitly* what is implicitly and organically contained in it from the very beginning'.[35] Hertz gave the example of Rabbi Akiva whose 'penetrating intellect enabled him to find a Biblical basis for every position of the Oral Law' implying that such a basis existed and just needed to be found. Hertz expressed the same idea (and referred to *midrash*) when he declared that the second set of tablets Moses brought down from Sinai were accompanied by 'a Heavenly commentary on that Law'.[36] Hertz even hinted that the Oral Law predated the Written. He quoted a statement by Cyrus Adler that 'the Oral Law is as old as the Bible; and if we may draw an inference from comparative studies, it is older than the Bible'.[37] That was Hirsch's view, who described the Written Law as crib notes to the pre-existing Oral Law.[38]

Hertz's vague statements that the Oral Law was 'sacred, immemorial custom' make more sense when they are understood in context.[39] Hertz's comments about the Oral Law as the record of ancient practice were not directed to those who believed it was the direct word of God transmitted on Sinai. Rather, he was speaking against those in the adaptation school who argued that the Oral Law was not binding. In his Inaugural Sermon at Orach Chayim, in which he referred to the 'liberalizing, revolutionary wing of our faith' and the three sermons delivered against the London Liberals in 1925–26, *The new paths*, he was not disputing the origins of the Oral Law, he was emphasising its importance, to increase its observance, not to convert observant Jews to a more sophisticated theology.[40]

Nevertheless, although Hertz believed that the Oral Law originated on Sinai he also held that it developed subsequently. He wrote of the Pentateuch being 'expounded, interpreted, and unfolded in ever greater fullness by successive generations of Sages'.[41] In other words, the regulations of the Oral Law were not just presented to the Jewish people, they had to be derived by the rabbis, using, for example, the 13 exegetical principles of Rabbi Yishmael.[42] So, while on the one hand Hertz spoke of 'God's holy and unchanging Torah', he also pointed to areas in which the Oral Law had developed.[43] For example, he spoke of 'the Sabbath as perfected by the Rabbis' whom he called the 'builders of the Sabbath Day in the life of the people' through their additions to it.[44]

Even that is not particularly radical, as everyone accepts that the rabbis added their own legislation, but Hertz seems to go further, to suggest that the rabbis were not just motivated by a desire to protect the ordinances of the Torah through a system of 'fences' but that they also sought to implement their own, original idea of the Sabbath: 'before the soul of the Rabbis there rose a vision of a Sabbath Day as a day of rest and joy, of pleasure and delight'.[45] Similarly, Hertz argued that in their alterations to the laws around divorce 'the uniform aim of the Rabbis . . . was to develop the law in the direction of greater equality between the man and the woman'.[46] That developmental view, while rejected by some, for example, in the antipathy school, was held by those in scientific branch of the acknowledgement school, including traditionalists like Hildesheimer and Hoffman.[47] Like them, Hertz depicts an active and thoughtful development by the rabbis, partly through the realisation of what was always implicit in the revelation at Sinai, but also partly through innovations by the rabbis to realise their own vision for the Jewish people.

Hertz held that much *aggadah*, the non-legal traditions included in the Talmud, should not be taken literally. He wrote that the Talmud contains 'facts and fancies of science by the learned; Jewish and heathen folklore, and all the wisdom and unwisdom of the unlearned'.[48] He called it 'legend pure and simple. Its aim is not so much to give the facts . . . as the moral that may be pointed' and he held with Maimonides that aggadic passages 'posses no general and binding authority'.[49]

Traditionalist *Wissenschaft* scholars were most active in the area of scientific analysis of the Talmud. The method of study pioneered by Frankel was transmitted to Hertz by a number of teachers, for example Joshua Joffe, a graduate of both the highly traditional yeshivah of Volozhin in Lithuania and the *Hochshule fur die Wissenschaft des Judentums* in Berlin. However, the greatest master of *Wissenschaft* to teach Hertz was Alexander Kohut, who as a graduate of Breslau adopted Frankel's ideas on the development of the Oral Law. Morais expressed similar views when he called the idea that the text of the Talmud was given on Sinai 'monstrous'.[50] However, Kohut, Morais and Hertz all held that there had been a revelation of the core of the Oral Law alongside the Pentateuch on Sinai and that it was therefore Divine and binding. That is why they must be placed on the traditional wing of the acknowledgement school and not on the non-traditional wing or in the adaptation school.[51]

Meirovich has argued that Hertz's association with Frankel placed him in a non-traditional camp. Meirovich defines this group as untraditional because of their willingness to apply critical methods to the study of post-Biblical material, particularly the Talmud. This, argues Meirovich, placed Hertz in opposition to Hildeshiemer and Hirsch. We have seen that Hirsch was a strong opponent of the *Wissenschaft* movement. He attacked Frankel and his views bitterly. Even Hildesheimer called Frankel a heretic.[52] On the other hand, Hildesheimer applied modern scholarly methods to the study of Jewish texts. Hildesheimer's successors at the Berlin Seminary eventually adopted many of Frankel's techniques. We have noted that Hirsch attacked Hoffman for referring to Frankel and his followers in his doctoral thesis.[53] So, although Hirsch rejected *Wissenschaft*, Hildesheimer and Hoffman adopted it. Meirovich's dichotomy between Hirsch and Hildesheimer on the one hand, and Hertz and Frankel on the other is therefore fallacious. There were important intellectual connections between Hildesheimer and Frankel and significant ideological tensions between Hildesheimer and Hirsch.[54]

Meirovich's insistence on placing Hertz and Hirsch in opposing camps led him to understate the influence of Hirsch on Hertz. This influence is difficult to ignore when we have a statement from Hertz that Hirsch was 'the greatest Jewish scholar and the most ardent defender of Traditional Judaism in the nineteenth century'.[55] A specific point of influence we have already encountered is the view that the Oral Law preceded the Written, an idea which underpinned much of Hirsch's thought.[56] Another example is Hertz's attitude to sacrifices; following Hirsch (and Hoffman and Adler), Hertz regarded sacrifices as tools to increase the moral standing of those who brought them.[57] Nor was Hertz the first or only thinker to be influenced by both Hirsch and Frankel. Drachman was the epitome of a synthesis between the two: a Breslau graduate and a devotee of Hirsch, indeed the first translator into English of Hirsch's seminal work *The nineteen letters of Ben Uziel*. J.J. Weinberg became both a Hirschian and a *Wissenschaft* scholar. English examples of this synthesis include Mayer Lerner and Hermann Adler.

Hertz's genuine ideological opponents were not Hirsch and his followers, but came from the adaptation school, led in England by CG Montefiore. Montefiore did not despise the Talmud, indeed he co-edited a volume of Talmudic extracts, *A rabbinic anthology*, but he did not ascribe any binding authority to the Talmud nor did he assert its Divine origin. Like Geiger and Holdheim he was a radical proponent of *Wissenschaft*. Further, he valued the statements of the rabbis alongside those of Jesus and the ethical thinkers of Greece and Rome.[58] For Hertz that was unacceptable, for reasons we examine further later.

Hertz's approach to the Oral Law was based around two themes: its importance and its developing nature. These two themes also shaped his attitude towards *halakhah*, which Meirovich has also identified as untraditional. Meirovich argues that as Hertz understood the evolving nature of Jewish law he therefore denied the final authority of the *Shulhan Arukh*.[59] Meirovich quotes Morais as saying in 1875 that a new code, taking into account changed conditions, needed to be written.

Meirovich also points out Hertz's belief in the sanctifying power of history and tradition. Although Meirovitch does not cite it, we can see Hertz's commitment to this idea from his comment on the second day of Festivals, 'the Second Day . . . has now been hallowed by over fifteen centuries' observance. It has therefore attained the force of religious law, and cannot be abrogated by any individual community or Jewry'.[60] We can test Meirovich's thesis by examining Hertz's statements on *halakhah* and its development.

Hertz declared 'what a Divine and eternal thing the halacha is in Israel's spiritual universe' and 'only in the faithful observance of these commandments is the secret of our deathlessness'.[61] This commitment goes back to the start of Hertz's career. At his graduation from the JTS he described the Jewish life adhered to by Jews of earlier generations that he felt was disappearing and wanted to recover. He quoted 'the formula which so strikingly expresses their religious life, viz "to dwell within the four cubits of the Holachah [*sic*]'.[62] In the same address he declared that the duty of graduates of the seminary was to bring back the 'loyal and intelligent observance of the duties demanded by our Sacred Faith'.[63] Like Hermann Adler, he emphasised the importance of *intelligent* observance. In his commentary to the Pentateuch he wrote 'only when there is *intelligent* conformity to the letter of the Torah does its spirit become a transforming power in the lives of men'.[64] But Hertz also held that ultimately it was action that counted: 'no amount of knowledge' he said 'can ever dispense a man from religious duty'.[65] He stressed the details of the *halakhah* as well as the broad ethical sweep of Jewish values and in 1941 he appealed to the listeners to his Passover broadcast to 'observe . . . the coming Festival according to ancient precept and immemorial custom'.[66] Hertz supported the observance of *halakhah* even when it came into conflict with the law of the land. He wrote in 1930 'when religion and [English] law clash it is religion that must come first'.[67]

This commitment to the observance of *halakhah* was combined with an understanding that it had always developed, hence Hertz's attitude to the second day of festivals as a development of the *halakhah*, but binding nevertheless.[68] Hertz argued that the process was ongoing and under certain circumstances changes could take place. He seems to give his support to a change in the text of the morning benediction, from blessing God for not making the worshipper a heathen to blessing Him for making him a Jew, converting the blessing from a negative to a positive formulation. Hertz claims that this would in fact be a return to an older form, another example of Hertz recognising that *halakhah* had a history. However he held that history alone was an insufficient basis for change and quoted contemporary authorities to support the alteration. Even so he did not actually change the text in the body of the *siddur*. As a matter of general policy Hertz only countenanced gradual change with the support of contemporary authorities, nothing which represented a break in the tradition or a deviation from fundamental Jewish values. This was the attitude taken at Breslau and by other traditionalist *Wissenschaft* scholars such as Hoffman.[69] Meirovich's placing of Hertz in a non-traditional camp must therefore, by his logic, be applied too to Hoffman, which is untenable.

Hertz's attitude to halakhic change is an example of his 'progressive conservatism', a phrase that Meirovich has argued is a sign of Hertz's non-traditional outlook.[70] Hertz defined it as 'religious advance without loss of traditional Jewish values and without estrangement from the collective consciousness of the House of Israel', stressing the balance to be struck between tradition and development.[71] On the one hand he said 'new occasions teach new duties' but also that 'when I am asked for a Judaism that is "in accordance with the times", two great utterances come to my mind. One of them is Zunz's . . . "Let us reform ourselves, not Judaism." And the other is the reply of Samson Raphael Hirsch to the same demand "Was Judaism ever 'in accordance with the times'? . . . When the Temple at Jerusalem was destroyed by the Romans . . . when our fathers suffered in all lands? And yet we would make the aim and scope of Judaism to be always 'in accordance with the times'!"[72] 'Progressive conservatism' was therefore identical with the attitude of the traditionalists within the acknowledgement school including Hildesheimer, Hoffman, Morais and Adler.

This appreciation for the dynamic nature of *halakhah* did not detract from the allegiance Hertz felt to the system of rabbinic authority that administered *halakhah*, which the traditional wing of the acknowledgement school upheld. Although Hertz believed *halakhah* could change, he did not believe that anyone could change it at whim. Contrary to Meirovich, he was fully committed to the rulings of Joseph Karo's sixteenth-century code *Shulhan Arukh*. He wrote, 'the *Shulchan Aruch* in which all the laws of Jewish life still in force at the present day are classified, [is] the last authoritative codification of the *halacha*'.[73] However, Hertz did not invalidate the rulings of later rabbinic figures and wrote that 'every interpretation of the Law given by a universally recognised authority is regarded as given on Sinai'.[74] Of course, in that last statement there is also a nod towards the complex relationship between tradition and development.

We can clearly recognise the voice of the acknowledgement school in Hertz's commitment to an authoritative but developing *halakhah*. Zunz was part of the acknowledgement school (at least at the end of his life) but he was, by its standards, a radical, who did not accept the Divine origin of the Pentateuch, yet even he was opposed to radical halakhic change. Hertz also adopted a specific limiting factor from Schechter. Hertz's warning against 'estrangement from the collective consciousness of the House of Israel' is undoubtedly a reference to Schechter's theory of 'Catholic Israel' or the 'Universal Synagogue' which posited that *halakhah* could change, but change had to come from a general movement of the entire Jewish people, not just one group or faction.[75] Judaism could only move forward if all Jews (at least all committed Jews) moved forward together. This position is itself a development of Frankel's view that the Jewish community was the body that authorised and sanctified innovation, not consciously but by their actual practice, and the *halakhah* that resulted was binding.[76]

As Schechter said in 1902, 'Judaism is not a religion which does not oppose itself to anything in particular. Judaism is opposed to any number of things and says distinctly "thou shalt not." It permeates the whole of your life. It demands control over all of your actions, and interferes even with your menu. It sanctifies the seasons, and regulates your history, both in the past and in the future. Above all, it teaches that disobedience is the strength of sin. It insists upon the observance of both the spirit and of the letter'.[77] This approach does not conflict with Morais' call for a new code of Jewish Law to update the *Shulhan Arukh*, cited by Meirovich; after all, that precise task was carried out by Y.M. Kagan, in publishing the *Mishnah berurah* between 1883 and 1907, a work which achieved almost universal acceptance in traditional Ashkenazi Jewry.

Hertz's rhetoric about *halakhah* formed part of his campaign against the adaptation school led by Reform in America and Montefiore in London. Hertz objected to the Liberals' relaxed attitude towards the central elements of traditional Jewish life: the dietary laws, the Sabbath and circumcision. Hertz sought to combat their arguments against *halakhah* in two ways. First, as we have just seen, he asserted its authority on the basis of its origins and secondly by emphasising its value in spiritualising everyday life. Like Adler and Hildesheimer, Hertz contemporised – that, is he used non-traditional arguments to justify tradition.[78] The traditional argument for *halakhah* is that it is the Divine will. Hertz used that argument, but he also used non-traditional, utilitarian arguments.

This dual approach underpinned Hertz's philosophy of *mitsvot*. For Hertz, *mitsvot* draw the Jew closer to the Divine through self-discipline and sacrifice, and foster unity amongst the Jewish people. As Hertz said in 1894, the *mitsvot* 'spiritualise the life, the everyday life', and elsewhere: 'laws are aids to holiness . . . They were not given because the climate required them; they were not given because the times required such legislation . . . the Almighty gave these laws to purify man by their means; to teach him obedience'.[79] The *mitsvot* achieve their effect through 'discipline and self-restraint'.[80] Christian thought held that obedience to detailed regulations is a barrier to spirituality. This attitude was adopted by David Friedlaender who wished to strip Judaism of its ritual, by his followers among the German Reformers, and in England by the Liberal Jewish movement, particularly by Lily Montague who felt untouched, and even alienated, by Jewish ritual.[81] Hertz, like Hermann Adler, argued rather that the details of the *halakhah* were the tools whereby true spirituality could be achieved.

The final aspect of Hertz's halakhic philosophy concerned not the relationship between man and God but between the Jew and his people, and as such was sociological as much as theological. In a sermon delivered in 1926, Hertz quoted Mordechai Kaplan by name when he asserted Kaplan's central idea that 'Judaism is a religious civilisation'.[82] Hertz's ideas on this sociological aspect of *halakhah* are related to views Kaplan later developed that Jewish practice was made up not of Divine commands, but of folkways which bound Jews together.[83] That was a radical development of Frankel's and Schechter's ideas of the halakhic importance of the Jewish people – and Frankel, Schechter and Hertz would all have rejected Kaplan's final conclusions – but Hertz quoted Kaplan's ideas in the 1920s, before they had fully developed. Kaplan later denied the existence of a personal God, which Hertz would have considered heretical. Nevertheless, in 1940 Hertz made this sociological case again, and quoted W.M. Haffkine who said 'if a Jew, at the time of partaking of food, remembers the identical words used by his fellow-Jews since time immemorial and the world over, he revives in himself, wherever he be at the moment, communion with his imperishable race'.[84]

Hertz's theology encompassed views on mysticism, the Messiah and the afterlife. Meirovich has suggested that Hertz began as a critic of Jewish mysticism.[85] Evidence is brought from a sermon Hertz delivered in 1914 in which he inveighed against those who had deviated from traditional Judaism, including 'the Kabbalists . . . the Sabbathians of modern times, and the Liberals of our own day'.[86] But only two years later Hertz wrote an article on mysticism (reissued in 1938 in the same publication as the 1914 sermon), which suggests that Hertz only opposed sham mystics As Hertz wrote, 'no system admits of as much charlatanism as a speculative mystical system'.[87] Hertz's general view of mysticism was more nuanced. He did not subscribe to the view that the Zohar, the basic text of Jewish mysticism, was written by the Talmudic sage Shimon bar Yohai.[88] He attributed its authorship to the Spanish rabbi Moses de Leon (1250–1305).[89] This approach can be traced to Morais and his own mentor, Samuel David Luzzatto.[90] In terms of Western European influences, Adler and Hirsch both wished to make Judaism appear rational and so were also sceptical towards mysticism – although, whereas Hirsch did not translate kabbalistic passages in his edition of the prayer book, Adler and Hertz did so in the *Authorised daily prayer book*.[91]

Notwithstanding Hertz's modern view of the Zohar, he argued that the themes of Jewish mysticism have far deeper roots, and de Leon merely collected pre-existing traditions. He wrote 'Jewish mysticism has its sources in Jewish antiquity . . . its beginnings go back to the Bible' in which he said could be found 'the *starting-point* and *beginnings* of every form of Jewish mysticism'.[92] He argued that 'it runs parallel to, and in constant interaction with, the other currents of Jewish life'. Hertz went on to trace the development of mysticism through the Talmud and subsequent Jewish intellectual development.[93] His conclusion was not to berate the mystics, but their modern critics. He wrote: 'the highest bearers of the mystic doctrine deserve quite other treatment than the condemnation coupled with contempt and hatred which most Jewish scholars have shown towards the personalities and productions of mysticism'. He singled out the German Jewish historian Heinrich Graetz as particularly culpable.[94] Hertz himself quoted from the Zohar, not only in his commentary to the Pentateuch, published in the 1930s, but also in his *Book of Jewish thoughts*, first prepared in 1915.[95]

Hertz's attitude to the doctrine of the Messiah and the restoration of the Jerusalem Temple was entirely conventional. He wrote in his commentary to Maimonides' thirteen principles of faith, 'to the overwhelming majority of the House of Israel in every generation the Messianic Hope has meant the belief in the coming of a Messiah – an exalted Personality, upon whom shall rest the spirit of the Lord. He will restore the glories of Israel in Israel's ancient land . . . He is but a mortal leader who, through the restoration of Israel, will usher in the regeneration of mankind'.[96] With the advent of the Messiah traditionally comes the return of animal sacrifices in the Temple. The Liberal Jewish Synagogue rejected the idea of a Messiah and a return to national Jewish independence entirely, hence its anti-Zionism and its rejection of the belief that the Temple service would be restored. They therefore omitted references to the return of animal sacrifices in the liturgy. Even some United Synagogue congregations, for example Hampstead, relegated them to silent recitation. As Hertz faced dissent on this point not just from groups outside his jurisdiction, but also inside it, he had to approach the issue with tact. He therefore praised those who prayed for a restoration of sacrifices as those who 'yearn for the opportunity of fulfilling Divine commandments which they cannot observe at present'.[97] Nevertheless, Hertz did quote a tradition which teaches that 'in the Messianic era, all offerings will cease, except the thanksgiving offering, which will continue forever' and the thanksgiving offering was not an animal offering.[98]

Hertz held that the belief in the immortality of the soul was not always accepted by all Jews, but pointed out that 'since the time of the Maccabees [c. 165 BCE], the belief in immortality had become well nigh universal among the masses of the Jewish people'.[99] He went on to argue that the statements of the Talmudic rabbis – such as Rav's 'in the world to come there is neither eating not drinking . . . but the righteous enjoy the radiance of the Shechinah' – contained 'new spiritual conceptions'.[100] This belief (that the idea of immortality was a late development) is not the mainstream rabbinical interpretation – which we have seen typified by Hermann Adler, who argued that the immortality of the soul was a familiar concept from the time of Adam – but it does find support in the writings of the medieval rabbi Bahya ibn Pakuda, about whom Hertz wrote an early study.[101] However, Hertz's personal view was traditional. He wrote that 'this world is but the ante-chamber to the Future Life – man's true home'.[102] This belief was rejected by some leaders of the adaptation school, for example the American Reform rabbis Emil Hirsch and James Wise. Although the belief in an afterlife was not universally rejected in the Liberal Jewish Synagogue, as Hertz made clear, he still used it a stick with which to beat the movement.[103]

We have seen, then, that Hertz took his positions on the basic questions of Jewish dogma from his teachers at the JTS. He was uncompromising on the unity and Mosaic authorship of the Pentateuch, but was more relaxed on questions of composition of other Biblical books. He regarded the Oral Law, and its culmination, *halakha*, as Divine in origin, authoritative and binding, but held that it had developed in human hands. Hertz did not accept that the Zohar was written in the Talmudic period, but neither did he dismiss its worth or that of mysticism in general. He believed in the Messiah and the afterlife in the traditional Jewish senses.

We now pass from questions of belief to more intricate questions of the relationship between dogma and scholarly methodology, and look in more detail at Hertz's relationship with *Wissenschaft*. Hertz was an enthusiastic supporter of the critical, scientific study of Jewish texts, which he called the 'New Jewish Learning.[104] Hertz called the founding of the Breslau Seminary 'nothing less than epoch-making in modern Jewish spiritual history . . .. Its Director was the renowned Talmudic scholar Zacharias Frankel, the leader of those who stood for "positive historical Judaism" in the groping and religiously unsettled generation'.[105] He praised the leading *Wissenschaft* scholar in England, Adolph Buchler, Principal of Jews' College as 'Master of those who know, *rosh hamedabrim bekol makom* [head of those who speak anywhere] in all things that relate to Jewish learning'.[106]

Hertz's positions on a number of scholarly questions, for example on the dating and authorship of the Psalms, *Shir hashirim* and the Zohar, are further evidence of his sympathy with *Wissenschaft*.[107] Hertz did not only accept the findings of other *Wissenschaft* scholars, he also used their methods in his own work. He wrote a short article for the *Jewish Quarterly Review* urging an amendment to the traditional text of Ethics of the Fathers VI:3 on scholarly grounds.[108]

More significant was Hertz's willingness to use archaeological, etymological and anthropological evidence to support his arguments in his *Pentateuch and Haftorahs* [hereafter Pentateuch].[109] Like other traditional but scientific figures whom we would place in the acknowledgement school, including Hildesheimer, Hoffman and Adler, Hertz believed that genuine scholarship supported the essential claims of tradition. Whatever evidence Hertz brought in his *Pentateuch*, it was always directed towards a traditional conclusion – for example, when he argued for the absence of contradictory accounts of Creation in Genesis, the Mosaic authorship of Leviticus and Deuteronomy, and the lack of debt of the Mosaic Code to the Code of Hammurabi. As Ellenson has written, for Hertz '*Wissenschaft* could serve the cause of traditional Judaism. It could never be used against it'.[110]

This analysis deepens our understanding of Hertz's statement 'Moses, the Exodus and the Legislation at Sinai all belong to strict history,' and his dismissal of the Wellhausen hypothesis as 'unscientific'.[111] This poor view of scholarship that produced non-traditional conclusions on the Pentateuch led Hertz to comment in his memorial address for Chief Rabbi Z.P. Chajes of Vienna, 'I did not share some of his religious views, nor subscribe to some of his critical methods or results'[112] Hertz, then, was not an uncritical supporter of *Wissenschaft*, and was very much a member of the wing within the scientific group that put tradition first. In theory, Hertz would have claimed he was only swayed by the strength of the scholarship; in practice, he always drew the line (between what he considered acceptable and heretical) at the foot of Mount Sinai.

Nevertheless, Hertz's analysis led him to the conviction that the revival of traditional Judaism and the intellectual defeat of the Higher Critics could only be achieved by *Wissenschaft* scholars.

As Freud Kandel has observed, Hertz placed his faith in the future of his brand of Judaism in a particular education programme. In 1913 he told Jews' College that the defeat of 'Higher Anti-Semitism' (Higher Criticism) could only come from 'institutions of University rank . . . not cheder or Beth Hamidrash, the Yeshibah or even the older type of Seminary'.[113] This restated the mission Hermann Adler had set the college in 1905 when he said 'I conceive it to be one of the main duties incumbent upon the teachers of our College to show and to prove that . . . the results of sound scientific research do not affect and assail that fundamental doctrine of Judaism – the belief in Divine Revelation'.[114] Hertz's statement was echoed in America two years later by a young JTS graduate, Herbert Goldstein, who was assistant to the highly traditional Rabbi Moses Zevulun Margolies at New York's Kehilath Jeshurun synagogue. Goldstein declared that 'the Judaism of the future' could only be secured by 'the young, university-trained Orthodox rabbi' because only they could hope to influence the 'scientifically trained, sceptical young Jew'.[115] Frankel, Hildesheimer and Hoffman shared this view, which is why they worked in seminaries founded to produce rabbis who could sustain Judaism in the modern world. So for Hertz, as for Adler, Frankel, Hildesheimer and Hoffman (although not Hirsch), *Wissenschaft* was not only compatible with traditional Judaism, it was vital for its survival.

We have examined Hertz's views on the use of Western scholarly techniques in the study of Jewish material, and now we look at his opinion of non-Jewish learning and wisdom in its own right. We should distinguish two types of non-Jewish intellectual activity: secular and religious. Hertz greatly respected non-Jewish secular scholarship, such as science, and loved non-Jewish art and literature.

Hertz was most concerned with science when it appeared to contradict the Bible, especially the theories of creation and evolution, although the latest science on these did not trouble him *per se*. He dismissed concerns about conflicts between the account of creation in Genesis and modern scientific theories by quoting the great medieval authorities Rashi and Maimonides, who both cautioned against a literal reading of the Biblical creation narrative.[116] Of evolution he wrote 'there is nothing inherently un-Jewish in the evolutionary conception of the origin and growth of forms of existence from the simple to the complex, from the lowest to the highest'.[117] Hertz identified the will behind development, and not the process, as important. He insisted that 'each stage is no product of chance, but is an act of Divine will, realizing the Divine purpose'.[118]

Once Hertz was content that evolutionary theory did not present a theological problem he incorporated it into his theology and used it homiletically. He remarked in one sermon that 'the nineteenth century . . . discovered that we came from the beast' in order to excoriate the twentieth century for 'trying to convince us that it was only natural for us to return to the beast' by attempting to overthrow morality.[119] Hertz tried to use science to support the Bible. For example, in *Pentateuch* he quoted the astronomer Halley's theory of nebulae to explain how light could have been created before the sun, even though, as Meirovich points out, by the time he wrote his commentary the theory had been discredited.[120] Hertz's willingness to interpret the Torah allegorically in places shows that – although he advocated fundamentalism, which is concerned with the origins of the text, and asserts its origin on Sinai – like Adler and Hirsch, he did not espouse literalism, an approach to how the text should be understood.

Another feature common to Hirsch, Adler and Hertz was a love for secular literature. According to Ephraim Levine, Hertz was 'omnivorous in reading' and quotations from the great authors abound in his sermons.[121] There are references to Homer, Virgil, Shakespeare, Milton, Coleridge, Heine, Schiller, Omar Kayam and many others. This attitude reflects Hirsch's philosophy of *Torah im derekh erets*. Like Hirsch, Hertz's relationship with non-Jewish learning went further than respect or enjoyment. He felt the need to engage deeply with it and, as Freud Kandel has argued, to create a synthesis of Jewish and non-Jewish wisdom.[122] Hertz's commitment was demonstrated by his doctorate on an entirely non-Jewish theme, the *Ethical system of James Martineau*, an English philosopher, and by his service as professor of philosophy at the University of the Transvaal, 1906–08. When he consecrated the Cambridge Synagogue in 1937 he composed a prayer for the university, in which he praised it as 'a never-failing fountain of wisdom; and men from far and near draw from it knowledge'.[123] Just as Hirsch wrote, 'Judaism . . . least of all things could be regarded as being opposed to anything that is genuinely good and true in the culture of any age', so Hertz defined the Judaism he represented as 'the life consecrated by Jewish religious observance . . . in indissoluble union with the best thought and culture of the age.[124]

Within London, Hertz shared his positive orientation towards *Torah im derekh erets* with the leaders of the highly traditional communities, Rabbi Dr Victor Schonfeld, rabbi of the Adath Yisroel congregation from 1909, and Rabbi Mayer Jung who led the Federation of Synagogues from 1912. Freud Kandel has argued that Schonfeld was more concerned with institutional separatism, *Austritt*, than *Torah im derekh erets*, but in fact Schonfeld's sermons brim with references to modern scholarship, science and literature.[125] Mayer Jung's son, Moses, wrote that his father's two major influences were 'the Torah and the university, each strengthening and complementing the other'.[126] Jung admired Goethe and Kant and studied philosophy, history and *Wissenschaft* at universities in Germany.[127] He founded a school in Moravia that taught both Jewish and secular subjects.[128]

As Freud Kandel has noted, Hertz respected secular learning in its own realm, not where it could have a negative impact on Jewish teaching.[129] Hertz's response to non-Jewish intellectual activity in that sphere was more complicated, for just as the acknowledgement school was happy to take advantage of what was positive in the non-Jewish world they were equally firm in their rejection of what was not. One of the central thrusts of Hertz's commentary in *Pentateuch*, which Meirovich has analysed extensively, is his critique of paganism and Hellenism, prompted by the intellectual development of his time, which sought to elevate the worth of the classical moral and ethical inheritance to the same level as the legacy of the Hebrew Bible, a project derived from the work of Matthew Arnold. We have seen how Adler sought to combat the setting up of any moral equivalence between Hellenism and Hebraism, which some in the Jewish community, particularly Montefiore, seemed to be advocating. Hertz renewed the attack.

As Breuer has written, Hertz set out to attack what he regarded as 'the insidious effects of the moral and ethical values of Western (read Christian) culture'.[130] Far from being the moral equals of Judaism, Hertz argued that Hellenism and paganism were barbarous, ethically bankrupt and morally repugnant. He cited the midrash which describes how the pre-Abrahamic builders of the Tower of Babel were heartbroken by the loss of a brick, but were unperturbed when a worker fell to his death.[131] In a lengthy study Hertz condemned the slight value placed on human life by the Code of Hammurabi.[132] Greek and Roman civilisation was held up as unjust and inhuman. For example, Hertz asserted that the gladiatorial fights of ancient Rome took place because the Romans did not possess the heart to recognise and stop the cruelty. This was contrasted with Judaism's commitment to justice, charity, hospitality and humanity.[133]

Hertz asserted that the modern heir to pagan Greco-Roman civilisation in all its moral deficiency was Christianity, the teachings of which we have seen Montefiore wanted to incorporate into Judaism.

Hertz pointed out that the classical subjugation of human rights under property rights continued into the nineteenth century, when Christian European societies still executed thieves.[134] Hertz traced the torture common in Christian lands to classical roots, and pointed out the right of a man in English common law to beat his wife, and the treatment of runaway slaves in the pre-Civil War American South.[135] Like Adler, Hertz even cast doubt on Christianity's monotheism, writing that 'the Shema excludes the trinity of the Christian creed as a violation of the Unity of God'.[136] He boldly attacked Jesus himself and quoted with approval the assessment by the German-Jewish philosopher Hermann Cohen, '[his] whole life was one of enmity and warfare against the foundations of our Faith as well as of amazing vilification of the Rabbis'.[137] Hertz's conclusion was that 'in religious things Israel has nothing to learn from the Western peoples. Long before Oxford, Israel was; and long after Oxford shall have ceased to be, Israel will endure'.[138] The limits Hertz, like Brodie and Jakobovits later, put to synthesis of Jewish and non-Jewish thought were therefore just as important as his commitment to what he regarded as its positive aspects. This is an important point to bear in mind in considering Freud Kandel's argument that Hertz's successors abandoned his synthesis and turned away from the non-Jewish world.

But there was a problem, which Hertz expressed in 1912: 'the spiritual quarantine forced on us throughout the Middle Ages down to recent times can no longer be maintained'. Damaging though non-Jewish value systems might be, they could not be ignored. This was an explicit rejection of the analysis of the antipathy school that the modern world could simply be shut out. Hertz had a solution: having compared other religious teachings to the song of the Sirens, he said 'we must fill the hearts of our children with the melody of the Shema and all it connotes . . . and then we need dread no sirens'.[139] Hertz went further than this, however, and celebrated that Judaism 'bears the impress of every culture. This civilisation has taken feely from others'.[140] This, however, refers not to fundamental issues of faith, but to cultural matters: food, music, art and literary style, which Hertz welcomed as enriching Judaism without compromising it. Indeed, in one sermon Hertz referred to the danger of 'religion without culture' a danger which, he told the Spanish and Portuguese Synagogue in London, Sefardim had managed to avoid.[141] Therefore modernity must be acknowledged, and its best aspects incorporated, but Judaism was not to be adapted wholesale to conform with the values of the non-Jewish world, and steps had to be taken to protect Jews and Judaism from malign external influences.

One of the aspects of the Sefardic religious approach that Hertz most admired was the beauty and refinement of its worship. Hertz regarded incorporating a Western aesthetic into Jewish life as very important. As early as 1891 his adoption of Western form alongside strictly traditional content was noted, and the *American Hebrew* called him 'the only Jewish Rabbi in this country who is thoroughly American in all his ways and yet is thoroughly orthodox'.[142] Temkin described the United Synagogue service under Hertz's leadership as 'something that was reasonably acculturated to contemporary society without infringing Jewish law'.[143] Hertz himself regarded acculturation, including dignified services, as important for maintaining Jewish tradition, and credited it with holding back Reform Judaism in America.[144] For Hertz, then, bringing a Western aesthetic into Jewish worship was not at the expense of tradition but, like *Wissenschaft*, was its great hope. Again Hertz's views were opposed to those of the antipathy school, who regarded any change to the synagogue service, including the introduction of choirs or 'non-Jewish' architecture, as proscribed.

As with so many aspects of his thought, it was an approach Hertz acquired at the JTS. Morais, a Sefardi, was convinced that Jewish worship had to combine tradition with decorum, dignity and good taste so that 'the young feel their faith is based on civilising principles'.[145] Drachman placed great emphasis on the beauty of the synagogue and its service, and wrote that those at his own synagogue, Zichron Ephraim, were of a particularly high standard and 'constituted a most significant demonstration for American Orthodox Judaism'.[146] This was an attitude they shared with Hirsch and Hildesheimer in Germany, and Hermann Adler in Britain. It was also the attitude of the religious leaders of French Jewry, although they were prepared to go much further to accommodate aesthetic demands than Hertz, Adler, Drachman, Morais, Hirsch or Hildesheimer, as we have seen.

Hertz's critique of Greece and Rome, and the identification of Christendom as their spiritual successor, was another legacy from Morais (inspired by Luzzato), Kohut (following his teacher the German-Jewish historian Graetz), and H. Pereira Mendes, another founder of the JTS. Luzzatto claimed that the Western Christian nations were unable to 'strip from themselves the soiled garments, the ways of Greece and Rome'.[147] Kohut declared that 'the poetry as well as the philosophy of Greece shrink before the single sentence [of the *Shema*.]'[148] Graetz's monumental *History of the Jews* is replete with anti-classical and anti-Christian polemic.[149] Pereira Mendes too attacked the immorality of Greece and Rome.[150]

Hertz's moral condemnation of paganism, Hellenism and Christianity was combined with religious tolerance. This was partly a pragmatic position. Like Adler, Hertz was keenly aware of the resentment the general population would feel towards British Jews if they were seen to be attacking Christianity. Nevertheless, Hertz's commitment to religious tolerance was fundamentally one of principle. He was fond of the Rabbinic saying 'the righteous of all nations have a share in the world to come'.[151] He went further and – following a strong stream of Jewish tradition, expressed by Maimonides amongst others – argued that 'the worship of the heathen nations forms part of God's guidance of humanity . . . Hence the amazing tolerance shown by Judaism of all ages towards the followers of other cults . . . Thus the prophet Malachi declares even the sacrificial offering of heathens to be a glorification of God (Malachi 1:11). . .. In their religious life these heathens merely followed the traditional worship which they had inherited from their fathers before them and they could not therefore be held responsible for failure to reach a true notion of the Unity of God. Such followers of other faiths were judged purely by their moral life'.[152] Hertz paid tribute to non-Jewish religious leaders, including Cardinal Hinsley, whose memory he said 'will remain a blessing in the world'.[153]

In this attitude Hertz remained a follower of Luzzatto, whose major objection to non-Jewish religions was their low level of morality, and who was keen to stress that 'all human beings, according to Judaism's teachers, are brothers, children of the same Father and are created in the image of God'.[154] Moreover, like Adler, Hertz emphasised the universalistic aspect of Judaism's particularism. He conceived that Jews could only be a blessing to the world by being good Jews. For example, when he encouraged the learning of Hebrew he said 'a Hebrew-less Jewry . . . would be a sin against humanity'.[155] After Hertz's death, Dayan I. Grunfeld of the London Beth Din identified this same attitude and said 'every day of his life belonged to Judaism and its world-historic task – the Emancipation of humanity. For him to work for Israel was to work for mankind. He made no difference between the two'.[156] This is a hagiographic tribute, but it remains significant that Grunfeld chose to highlight this aspect of Hertz's thought.

Hertz included many quotations by non-Jews in his edition of *The Pentateuch and Haftorahs*. They included J. Travers Herford and the Christian Oxford theologian S.R. Driver. Even Wellhausen, the leader of the Higher Critical movement, is quoted approvingly.[157] However, Hertz's quotations from non-Jews did not indicate sympathy with their religious outlook. Hertz as a great champion of the Mosaic authorship of the Pentateuch perceived Wellhausen as his greatest opponent, yet he quoted him when he agreed with him. As Hertz wrote in the preface to the first edition of *The Pentateuch and Haftorahs*, quoting

Maimonides, 'accept the true from whatever source it come'.[158] In this he followed Bahya ibn Pakuda, of whom he made a special study, and who used many quotations from non-Jews in his works, and Hoffman, who quoted Dillman, a non-Jewish scholar and proponent of higher criticism, in his commentary on Leviticus.[159]

Hertz's condemnation of aspects of the theological and ethical content of religions other than Judaism combined with tolerance has long characterised the Jewish response to other faiths. However, towards the end of his life Hertz stepped beyond this position. In his address to the World Congress of Faiths in 1943 Hertz quoted with approval a statement of Dr Inge, Dean of St Paul's Cathedral, 'every great Faith has its own contribution to make to the symphony of civilisation, its own instrument to play in the great hymn of humanity to the Creator'. Hertz continued, 'but be it noted that, if the individual instruments are not properly played upon, or if they are altogether silent, there can be neither symphony nor hymn. Therefore, what are called the 'barriers between the religions' cannot be dismissed as 'artificial'; for the power of a religion lies not so much in what it has in common with others, as in what is peculiar to itself. That constitutes its special contribution to the spiritual treasure of mankind'.[160]

This was a radical statement and difficult to reconcile with classical Jewish sources. How can idolatry, which it is a commandment to drive out according to the *Shulhan Arukh*, make a positive contribution to man's service of God? Moreover, Hertz seems to be contradicting himself. We have seen how he condemns paganism and Christianity, even doubting Christianity's commitment to monotheism, yet here he celebrates its 'special contribution to the spiritual treasure of mankind'. This assertion even conflicts with Hertz's statement, at the start of the very same address, that 'Israel has, throughout the ages, refused all entangling alliances with other Faiths. Like every sincere religionist, the true Jew of to-day deems is to be as much the mission of his Faith to proclaim there *are* false gods, false prophets and false philosophies, as it is to bring men nearer to its own vision of God'.[161]

Obviously we have to understand that Hertz was speaking to a non-Jewish audience at a World Congress of Faiths in the exceptional circumstances of the Second World War. Hertz naturally wanted to secure as much sympathy and support for the Jewish people and as strong a front against Nazism as possible. As he said elsewhere in his address, 'co-operation between the Faiths is not only possible, but becomes an ineluctable duty, whenever times call for united testimony to some everlasting truth. Ours is such a time'.[162] We might want to conclude that in an attempt to appeal to his audience in desperate times Hertz contradicted himself and said more than he believed. Nevertheless Hertz did say it, and later published it.

We have seen how the theology of the adaptation school, led in Britain by the Liberal Jewish Movement, prompted Hertz to state his own religious position, in order to attack and undermine their views. We will now look further at Hertz's relationship with the adaptation school. Hertz was convinced that it was heretical and had to be fought. In 1912 he told his new congregation in New York, 'I shall look to you for your help in my conflict with illiberal liberalism'.[163] He brought this message to London and told a congregation in 1914 that non-traditional Judaism 'may be dazzling' but asserted that 'at a nearer view, its light is seen to be a phosphorescent screen, the accompaniment of disintegration and decay'.[164] His called Liberal Judaism 'a revolt against Jewish Law, the Jewish life, the whole historic Jewish outlook. . ..dry rationalism – irreverent and disintegration. Above all it is devoid of faith, of fructifying belief. And therefore spiritual sterility is its portion'.[165] He told the Liberal Jew, 'You have dethroned God; and you have put your own reason in His place. You pick and choose among His precepts, retaining only those which suit your inclination or expediency'.[166]

Hertz's critique of Liberal Judaism begins with an examination of the Liberals' attitude to what Hertz called 'institutions'. He pointed out that Liberal Jews did not insist on circumcision for converts and anticipated that it would be dispensed with for infants. Hertz stated that circumcision was 'infinite' in its 'significance and influence in Israel's life'.[167] He criticised the Liberals for their attempts to abolish festivals such as Passover, the fast of the ninth of Av and above all the Sabbath, which he accused the Liberals of wanting to move to Sunday, just as the early Jewish Christians did.[168] This association of Liberal Jews with early Jewish Christians is a central rhetorical plank of Hertz's attack; indeed, he went so far as so say that Liberal Judaism must lead 'ultimately into Christianity' – in other words, that a major flaw of the adaptation school was that its followers ultimately ended in the acceptance school, abandoned Judaism and accepted another belief system in its place.[169] This critique, including the parallel drawn with early Christianity, echoed that of Schechter who said 'we must leave off talking about freeing the conscious by abolishing various laws . . . if we do not want to drift slowly but surely into Paulism, which entered the world as the deadliest enemy of Judaism'.[170]

Hertz argued that the concrete developments he had identified were symptomatic of a general attitude which rejected 'the binding character of the Torah and the sacredness of the Scriptures'.[171] He quoted

Montefiore, who wrote that 'we recognise no binding authority between us and God, whether in a man or in a book'. [172] For Hertz this meant that every practice was at the mercy of 'momentary whim'.[173] The result was the 'uprooting of sacred immemorial institutions that are interwoven with the very existence of Israel'.[174] Hertz explained that all attempts to try to philosophise the whole of Judaism and divest it of its outward signs, its 'immemorial rites, customs and ceremonies', along the lines of David Friedlaender's attempt, left Jews 'with nothing to live by, nothing to die for' and soon disappeared.[175] He predicted, quoting Josephine Lazarus, that such a course would lead to Jews remaining an ethical people, but ceasing to be a religious people.[176]

Having attacked the Liberals' willingness to adapt Jewish practices, Hertz turned his attention to their eagerness to accept non-Jewish norms and values. He accused them of laying 'the axe at the very roots of the Tree' of Judaism: the belief in God, the revelation to Israel, the immortality of the soul.[177] Specifically, Hertz attacked the Liberals for their adoption of the 'barbarous vivisection of the Torah by the Higher Critics'.[178] Hertz argued that this left the Liberal unable to answer 'the hosts of immoralist authors, artists and social revolutionaries' because the Liberals and the revolutionaries were essentially in agreement, that all laws were made by man, and could therefore be unmade by man.[179] Finally Hertz criticised Liberal Jews for their trumpeting of the ethical teachings of Christianity, while at the same time attacking their fellow Jews.[180] He identified Liberals as the leading agitators against *shehita*, as supporters of the calendar reform proposed at the League of Nations (which would have resulted in the Sabbath moving throughout the week, causing massive disruption to traditional Jews), and as opponents of measures to enable Jewish shopkeepers to close on Saturday instead of Sunday.[181] Hertz's objective was to construct a damning critique. He was arguing that Liberal Judaism's eagerness to adapt Judaism to modernity led to a negation of Judaism, the creation of an escalator into Christianity, and meant its proponents were acting against the interests of the Jewish people.

Hertz's attitude was tempered by his assertion of the unconditional love he felt for the whole Jewish people. Hertz quoted a tale of the founder of Hasidism, the Baal Shem Tov, in this regard. 'The later followers of Sabbethai Zevi, under the leadership of the notorious Jacob Frank, attacked Jews and Judaism far more bitterly that ever did Liberals in Berlin, Chicago or London. Yet, the Chassidic legend relates when Frank and his followers publicly left Judaism and joined the Catholic Church, the great Israel Baalshem wept the whole night through and refused to be comforted. "A man's arm may be paralysed or sorely diseased" he exclaimed, "still there is always hope that it will regain its health and vigour. But if it is amputated, all hope of healing is gone forever." It is needless to point the moral or the application of this beautiful legend'.[182] This was an essentially religious attitude. Hertz said 'we who believe in the God of Israel and in the Torah of Israel . . . believe in the People of Israel, in its perpetuity, unity and spiritual power'.[183] Hertz's warmth was not confined to generalities. Hertz called Marcus Jastrow, who was not a fundamentalist on the Pentateuch, 'my revered teacher' and in 1912 referred to Jastrow and Benjamin Szold (who was even more radical) as 'great teachers in Israel . . . who have gone to their eternal reward'.[184] Neither did Hertz advocate complete institutional separation from non-traditional Jews, along the lines of Hirsch's *Austritt* model. For example, Hertz had no objection to co-operation on 'national, social and educational questions'.[185]

Finally we come to Hertz's attitude to Zionism. Hertz was a Zionist from the beginning. One of his first publications, written in 1897, was a report of the Zionist Congress of that year.[186] At his seventieth birthday celebration he again referred to his Zionism.[187] He praised non-religious Zionist leaders, such as Herzl and Jabotinsky, but above all he was a religious Zionist, a member of the Mizrahi movement.[188] In his welcome for the Balfour Declaration in 1917, Hertz said 'only on its own soil can the Jewish people live its own life, and make, as in the past it has made, its characteristic and specific contribution to the common treasury of humanity. A land focuses a people and calls forth, as nothing else can, its spiritual potentialities; and the resurrection of the Jewish nation on its own soil will reopen its sacred fountains of creative energy'.[189] In other words a Jewish National Home in Palestine would enable Jews to be better Jews. Hertz therefore called for support for Zionism as a religious duty, and encouraged Jews 'to join in the sacred task of turning Palestine into Eretz Yisrael'.[190]

Hertz celebrated Herzl's declaration that 'the return to Zion must be preceded by our return to Judaism'.[191] Hertz criticised secular Zionists for not appreciating that Zionism was only possible because of the survival of Judaism, and Judaism could only survive as a religion, not as a national movement. As Hertz put it, 'where there is no *Shema Yisroel* there is no Jewish consciousness'.[192] Elsewhere he expressed his point more strongly: 'Torah-less nationalism, no less than Torah-less universalism ends in the arms of the Church' and 'nationalism that is Torah-less and decadent . . . is the loathing of my soul'.[193] He called extreme secular Zionists 'Hebrew speaking heathens'.[194] That is why, without a hint of anti-Zionism, he could attack those who accord 'primacy of place not to the Shema but to the *Hatikvah*'.[195] Ephraim Levine grasped this point when he wrote that for Hertz '*Torah*, Israel and Eretz Yisrael were . . . ideas woven into one, and if he had made his confession it would have been *Torah* first. Without *Torah* nothing is worth achieving'.[196]

Religious considerations affected Hertz's Zionism in two further ways. First, he placed support for Zionism above support for the policies of the British Government, just as he valued *halakhah* above British law. That is why he criticised British officials in 1929 for interfering in the Jewish prayer area in front of the Western Wall on Yom Kippur. He called it an 'outrage' and attacked 'British compliance with religious persecution'.[197] These were very strong words for a man who was so keen to praise Britain and its leaders, but were perhaps prompted by shock at the new and less sympathetic line the recently arrived High Commissioner, Sir John Chancellor, was taking towards the Zionists in Palestine, especially in comparison with Herbert Samuel, High Commissioner 1920–25.[198]

Hertz placed ethical values above those of political Zionism. He asserted that Zionism could not be at any price. As Levine wrote, 'he was not an unswerving political Zionist nor would he have approved of some of the zealot methods which in many quarters threaten [1947] to alienate sympathy from the true ideals of Zionism'.[199] Hertz demanded that in the new Palestine 'there will be no domination of Arab by Jew, just as there will be no domination of Jew by Arab'.[200]

For Hertz's inspiration again came from the JTS. Many of its lay and religious founders were Zionists, including Pereira Mendes, Solomon Solis-Cohen, Marcus Jastrow and Benjamin Szold, although Morais was not.[201] Hertz's Talmud teacher at the seminary, Joshua Joffe, who signed Hertz's ordination, was himself ordained by Rabbi I.J. Reines, one of the founders of Mizrahi. Among Hertz's friends, Schechter and the Stephen Wise were both staunch Zionists, as were leading Anglo-Jewish ministers and rabbis including the Jews' College graduates Ephraim Levine, S.M. Lehrman and H.M. Lazarus, and the European-trained Isaac Herzog and Issur Unterman, both later Chief Rabbi of the State of Israel.[202]

We have now seen all of Hertz's major theological views set out in their intellectual context. Hertz was a traditionalist of the acknowledgement school. Within that group he was most strongly associated with the *Wissenschaft*-inclined scientific branch. However, he was more influenced by the romantic strain associated with Hirsch than most members of the scientific branch, and he shared the concerns of those who wished to import a Western aesthetic into Jewish practice.

Furthermore, Hertz adopted this position from his teachers at the JTS for, although Hertz's thought obviously continued to develop throughout his life, it is possible to trace all of Hertz's major attitudes back to the seminary and its teachers. Those attitudes had much in common with other Jewish leaders of similar outlook, particularly Hildesheimer and Hoffman. It is also important to note the continuity of thought between Adler and Hertz. Freud Kandel argues that Hertz's enthusiasm for synthesis was something new in Anglo-Jewry, designed to bridge the gap between the East and West Ends, but in fact Hertz's approach was very much a continuation of Adler's, although – like Adler, and indeed Brodie and Jakobovits – Hertz set strict limits to synthesis.[203] Much of Hertz's impetus to state his views came from the radical theology of the British thinkers of the adaptation school, Montefiore, Montagu and the other leaders of the Liberal Jewish Synagogue.

Hertz's views on the origin of the Pentateuch, the core of the Oral Law and its further development, together with a more flexible approach to the origins of books of the Bible aside from the Pentateuch, place him in the tradition of Zachariah Frankel, whose views were adopted, in whole or in part, by Hertz's teachers, Morais, Kohut, Joffe and Drachman, all of whom were traditionalists aligned to the acknowledgement school. Indeed, JTS was founded as an American version of Breslau and based its curriculum on Breslau.[204] Hertz shared his niche in the traditional wing of the acknowledgement school and his scientific leanings with a number of contemporaries including Adolf Buchler, the Principal of Jews' College 1906–39, and J.J. Weinberg, Rector of the *Rabbinerseminar* in the 1930s. What united them all was their belief in a Divinely dictated Pentatuch, the accessibility of the documents of the Oral Law to critical study and an acceptance that *halakhah* moved forward, combined with caution about permitting or supporting specific reforms. Hertz then, like Adler, was part of that section of the traditionalist group which accepted some views which others did not. He was not just a transmitter of the tradition; he was also involved in its development, by holding and teaching new and minority views.

Hirsch's influence included his views on the Oral Law, secular literature, the proper approach to scientific developments such as evolution, and Jewish mysticism. It seems likely that Drachman was the conduit for those views. We noted that something seems a little odd about Hertz's admiration for both Frankel and Hirsch, but we have seen that Hertz was not the first or the only Jewish thinker to contrive such a combination; indeed, Drachman himself represented such a synthesis. Hertz's critical views on classical and Christian culture were another legacy of the JTS, and in particular Hertz's teacher's own mentors,

Luzzato and Graetz. The men who taught at the JTS during Hertz's time there also seem responsible for Hertz's religious Zionism, even though Morais, Hertz's great role model at the seminary, was not himself a Zionist.[205]

As well as identifying Hertz's ideological friends, we have seen who his ideological opponents were. Hertz's primary target for attack was the adaptation school, known as Reform in the United States and as Liberal in Britain. Hertz inherited this campaign from his teachers too.[206] Hertz's detailed critique of the London Liberals centred on what he perceived as their excessive willingness to adapt Jewish belief and practice to modernity. He took particular exception to their denial of the Divine origin of the Pentateuch, their dismissive attitude towards the Oral Law and their dispensation with ritual laws.[207] What appear to be Hertz's positive theological statements make best sense when they are seen as a reaction to these views and as part of an ongoing debate with them. For example, calling the Oral Law the 'authoritative interpretation and immemorial custom of Judaism' was not to query its Divine origin, but rather to ballast its authority.[208] When the Liberals claimed that practices such as circumcision and ritual slaughter were no long necessary, Hertz responded by asserting that they were vital for Jewish survival.[209] Hence, his statement that 'when the immemorial rites, customs and ceremonies go . . . we are left without God in our lives', was not intended to oppose those who regarded them as Divine laws rather than 'customs and ceremonies', but an attempt to stress their importance, in opposition to those who thought they could be abandoned.[210]

This analysis significantly revises the assessment of Hertz's theology made by Alderman, Meirovich, Endelman and Freud Kandel. They depict it as untraditional in many respects and in opposition to Hirsch's 'true traditionalism'; or they overstate Hertz's enthusiasm for synthesis of Jewish and non-Jewish thought. Hertz's regime has been depicted as characterised by latitudinarianism and a concern for civility and unity. We have seen that Hertz did belong to the traditional camp, was not tolerant of those who differed, such as the London Liberals, and was unconcerned with civility when he challenged them. That does not mean that Hertz did not belong to a very specific part of the traditionalist camp, which he shared with Hildesheimer, Hoffman, Weinberg and others of unquestioned standing within traditional Jewry.

Hertz's theology, like theirs, was rooted in tradition, but it was also interesting and original. His critique of Greece and Rome, his nuanced approach to other faiths, his attitude to the findings of modern science and his religious Zionism were all based on the ideas of his teachers but he developed them significantly. Above all, his method of expressing his traditional beliefs – by using modern arguments, whether drawn from archaeology, sociology or cosmology – represents the continuation of an approach began by Adler, Hildesheimer and Hirsch to ensure continued support for tradition in the context of modernity, after the disappearance of unquestioned rabbinic authority. They all came to the view that if Judaism was to survive it had to acknowledge the best of the modern world, and that the attempt to shut it out, as proposed by the antipathy school, would be in vain.

The final and most fundamental point is that Hertz's position within the traditionalist camp was always secondary to his identification with it in general. In a sermon delivered in 1919 he said he upheld 'the teachings and practices which have come down to the House of Israel through the ages; the positive Jewish beliefs concerning God, the Torah and Israel; the sacred Festivals; the holy resolve to maintain Israel's identity; and the life consecrated by Jewish observances'.[211] Of course, for a communal rabbi, beliefs are only half the story. Equally important is how he acts upon those beliefs, how he seeks to implement them in practice. How Hertz applied his theology as a rabbi and as Chief Rabbi is the subject of the next chapter.

Notes

1 J.H. Hertz, Sermons, addresses and studies (London 1938) [henceforth *SAS*], 362.
2 J.H. Hertz, *Early and late* (Hindhead, Surrey 1943) 125.
3 Hertz, *SAS*, I:11.
4 Hertz, *Early and late*, 182.
5 J.H. Hertz, *Pentateuch and Haftorahs* (London 1960) [hereafter Pentateuch], vii. Interestingly, the phrase 'perversion of history and a desecration of religion' comes from a Reform theologian, Emil Hirsch.
6 Hertz, *Early and late*, 263.
7 Hertz *Pentateuch*, 402.
8 Hertz, *Pentateuch*, 397–399.
9 J.H. Hertz, *Affirmations of Judaism* (Oxford 1927), 50; Hertz, *Pentateuch*, 399.
10 Hertz, *Affirmations*, 41.
11 Hertz Papers, Hartley Library, Southampton University Library (HP SUL): MS 175 25/4, cf. Deuteronomy 33:4.
12 Hertz *SAS*, I:310, borrowing Schechter's phrase, of course.
13 Hertz, *Early and late*, 19.
14 H. Meirovich, *Vindication of Judaism* (New York 1998), 8.
15 Ibid., 13.

16 Ibid., 88–89.

17 Hertz *SAS*, I:310.

18 Meirovich, *Vindication*, 14; Hertz, *Early and late*, 125; HP SUL MS 175/70/3.

19 A. Kohut, 'Secular and theological studies' *The Menorah* (13 July 1892), 49. The quotation is from the Babylonian Talmud, *Bava Batra* 111b.

20 Hertz, *Affirmations*, 14, 18.

21 Hertz *SAS*, I:86.

22 Ibid., I:86.

23 Hertz, *SAS*, I:309.

24 Meirovich, *Vindication*, 5.

25 Hertz, *The Authorised Daily Prayer Book (ADPB)* (New York 1948), xiii.

26 Hertz, *Pentateuch*, 942.

27 Hertz, *Early and late*, 34.

28 Hertz, *ADPB*, xiii, 594.

29 Ibid., 790.

30 Hertz, *Affirmations*, 58–59.

31 Hertz *SAS*, III:243; Hertz, *Early and late*, 129.

32 Hertz, *SAS*, III:242.

33 Hertz, *ADPB*, 613.

34 Ibid.

35 Hertz, *Pentateuch*, 322.

36 Hertz, *Affirmations*, 133–134.

37 Ibid., 130.

38 S.R. Hirsch, trans. I. Levy, *Pentateuch* (London 1959), II 287–288.

39 Hertz, *ADPB*, 345.

40 Hertz, *Early and late*, 126–139; Hertz, *Affirmations*, 149–185.

41 Hertz, *ADPB*, 35.

42 Ibid.

43 Hertz, *Affirmations*, 67.

44 Ibid., 62.

45 Ibid.

46 Hertz, *Pentateuch*, 933.

47 Some rabbis argue that the whole of the Talmud was given on Sinai, but many agree that significant development took place to produce the contents of the Talmud.

48 Hertz, *SAS*, III:248.

49 Ibid., 249–250; Maimonides, commentary to the Mishnah, preface to *Helek* in *Sanhedrin*.

50 S. Morais, 'The Talmud' *The Occident* (26 July 1868), 165.

51 Meirovich, *Vindication*, 6. As we have discussed, a belief that the Pentateuch was given in full at one time implies a belief in some accompanying oral tradition, as otherwise the Pentateuch is incomprehensible in parts. The Documentary Hypothesis has no need for a contemporaneous oral tradition to explain problems in the text.

52 Ibid., 15.

53 Ibid., 173.

54 Meirovich's overlooking of the fineness of some of these distinctions led Breuer to criticise his analysis as 'somewhat flat footed.' E. Breuer, Review of Meirovich, *Vindication of Judaism* in *Jewish Quarterly Review* 91 (January–April 2001), 448.

55 Hertz, *Affirmations*, 65.

56 Hirsch, *Pentateuch*, II:287–288 .

57 D. Ellenson, 'A *Vindication of Judaism: the polemics of the Hertz Pentateuch*: a review essay' *Modern Judaism* 21 (2001), 73.

58 C.G. Montefiore, *Hibbert Lectures 1892* (London 1897), 550–551.

59 Meirovich, *Vindication*, 10.

60 Hertz, *ADPB*, 775.

61 Hertz, *Early and late*, 105; Hertz, *SAS*, I:201.

62 Hertz, *Early and late*, 122.

63 Ibid.

64 Hertz, *Pentateuch*, 489.

65 Ibid., 112.

66 Hertz, *Early and late*, 4.

67 Chief Rabbinate Papers, London Metropolitan Archive ACC/2865/4/5/44.

68 Hertz, *ADPB*, 775.

69 B. Drachman, *The unfailing light* (New York 1948), 100.

70 Meirovich, *Vindication*, 15.

71 Hertz *SAS*, I:258.

72 Hertz, *Affirmations*, 65–66, 7.

73 Hertz, *SAS*, I:257.

74 Hertz, *Pentateuch*, 322. Of course, for all the rhetoric about the final authority of the *Shulhan Arukh*, in practice no Jew of Hertz's time followed the *Shulhan Arukh* completely, nor were they expected to. For example the *Shulhan Arukh* bans the use of sugar on Passover, but this ruling is universally set aside among Jews today.

75 S. Schechter, *Studies in Judaism* (New York 1958), 16–17, 15.

76 Z. Frankel, *On changes in Judaism*, www.ucalgary.ca/~elsegal/363_Transp/ZFrankel.html.

77 S. Schechter, *Seminary addresses and other papers* (New York 1969), 22.

78 D. Ellenson, *Rabbi Esriel Hildesheimer and the creation of a modern Jewish orthodoxy* (Tuscaloosa, Alabama 1990), 22.

79 HP SUL MS 175/44/3; Hertz, *Early and late*, 122. See also Hertz, *Affirmations*, 59, quoting Moses Jung.

80 Hertz, *ADPB*, 381.

81 E. Umansky, 'Lily Montague: religious leader, organiser, prophet' *Conservative Judaism* 34: 6 (July/August 1981), p. 18.

82 Hertz, *Affirmations*, 35.

83 M.M. Kaplan, *Judaism as Civilisation* (New York 1935).

84 Hertz, *Affirmations*, 158.
85 Meirovich, *Vindication*, 12.
86 Hertz, *SAS*, I:307.
87 Hertz, *SAS*, III:317.
88 Ibid., 308.
89 Ibid.
90 Meirovich, *Vindication*, 12.
91 S.C. Reif, *Judaism and Hebrew prayer* (Cambridge 1993), 282.
92 Meirovich, *Vindication*, 279.
93 Ibid., 300–301.
94 Ibid., 317–318 .
95 Hertz, *Pentateuch*, 480; J.H. Hertz, *A book of Jewish thoughts* (New York 1939), 189.
96 Hertz, *Early and late*, 264.
97 Hertz, *ADPB* (New York 1948), 533.
98 Hertz, *SAS*, III:185. See Leviticus and Leviticus Rabbah 7:9.
99 Hertz, *Pentateuch*, 925.
100 Ibid., reprinted in Hertz, *ADPB*, 122.
101 Bahya ibn Pakuda, *Hovot HaLevavot, Shaar HaBitahon*, chapter 4.
102 Hertz, *ADPB*, 1079. Again, the presence of two seemingly contradictory statements in the same book argues that they are actually not in disagreement. Having said that, the *ADPB* was produced towards the end of Hertz's life, when his editorial eye may have lost some of its sharpness.
103 Hertz, *Affirmations*, 165–166.
104 Hertz, *SAS*, II:46.
105 Ibid., 48.
106 Hertz, *Early and late*, 109; Meirovich, *Vindication*, 29.
107 Hertz, *SAS*, III:249–250; 308; 790; Hertz, *ADPB*, 589.
108 Hertz, *SAS*, III:261–265.
109 Hertz, *Pentateuch, passim*.
110 Ellenson, review of *Vindication*, 75.
111 Hertz, *Affirmations*, 50; Hertz, *Pentateuch*, 399.
112 Hertz, *Early and late*, 97.
113 HP SUL MS 175/61/6.
114 H. Adler, 'The sons of the prophets' in Harris (ed) *Jews' College jubilee volume* (London 1906), 15–16.
115 J.S. Gurock, 'Twentieth-century American orthodoxy's era of non-observance, 1900–1960' *Torah u-Madda* Journal 4 (2000), 34.
116 Hertz, *Pentateuch*, 194.
117 Ibid.
118 Ibid.
119 Hertz, *Affirmations*, 27.
120 Meirovich, *Vindication*, 163.
121 I. Epstein (ed), *Joseph Herman Hertz, In Memoriam* (London 1947), 29.

122 M. Freud Kandel, *Orthodox Judaism in Britain since 1913* (London 2006), 52.

123 Hertz, *Early and late*, 152.

124 S.R. Hirsch, *Judaism eternal*, ed Grunfeld (London 1959), I:206–207; Hertz, *Affirmations*, 151.

125 Freud Kandel, *Orthodox Judaism in Britain*, 81; V. Schonfeld, *Judaism as life's purpose* (London 1930).

126 G. Bader and M. Jung 'Meir Tsevi Jung' in Jung (ed) *Jewish leaders* (Jerusalem 1953), 298.

127 Ibid., 298–299.

128 Ibid., 304.

129 Freud Kandel, *Orthodox Judaism in Britain*, 53.

130 E. Breuer, Review of Meirovich, *Vindication of Judaism in Jewish Quarterly Review* 91 (January–April 2001), 447.

131 Hertz, *Pentateuch*, 197.

132 Ibid., 404–405.

133 Hertz, *SAS*, II:221–222.

134 Hertz, *Pentateuch*, 404.

135 Ibid., 935; 848.

136 Ibid., 921.

137 Hertz, *Affirmations*, 93.

138 Ibid., 100–101.

139 Hertz, *Early and late*, 132. Hertz's metaphor was very apt. In the Odyssey, the Sirens offer Odysseus not wealth or pleasure, but knowledge, in order to lure him onto the rocks.

140 Hertz, *Affirmations*, 36.

141 Hertz *SAS*, I:311.

142 HP SUL MS 175/25/4.

143 S. Temkin, 'Orthodoxy with moderation: a sketch of J.H. Hertz' *Judaism* (Summer 1975), 288.

144 Hertz, *Affirmations*, 151.

145 M. Davis, *The emergence of Conservative Judaism: the historical school in 19th-century America* (Philadelphia 1963), 211.

146 B. Drachman, *The unfailing light* (New York 1948), 211.

147 Ibid., 110.

148 Meirovich, *Vindication*, 176–177.

149 H. Graetz, *History of the Jews* (Philadelphia 1956).

150 Meirovich, *Vindication*, 177.

151 See, for example, Hertz, *Early and late*, 121.

152 Hertz, *Pentateuch*, 759.

153 Hertz, *Early and late*, 121.

154 M. Gopin, 'An orthodox embrace of gentiles? Interfaith tolerance in the thought of S.D. Luzzatto and E. Benamozegh' *Modern Judaism* 18 (1998), 176.

155 Hertz, *SAS*, I:8.

156 Epstein, *Hertz*, 48.

157 Hertz, *Pentateuch*, 562; 96; 559.

158 Ibid., vii.

159 D. Ellenson and R. Jacobs, 'Scholarship and faith: David Hoffman and his relationship to *Wissenschaft des Judentums*' *Modern Judaism* 8 (1988), 32.

160 Hertz, *Early and late*, 198.

161 Ibid., 197.

162 Ibid., 198.

163 Ibid., 132–133.

164 Hertz, *SAS*, 310.

165 Hertz, *Early and late*, 6.

166 Hertz, *Affirmations*, 175–176.

167 Ibid., 152.

168 Ibid., 154–157.

169 Ibid, 161.

170 Schechter, *Seminary addresses*, 23.

171 Hertz, *Affirmations*, 163.

172 Ibid.

173 Ibid.

174 Ibid. .

175 Ibid., 158.

176 Ibid.

177 Ibid., 165.

178 Ibid., 175.

179 Ibid., 175–176.

180 Ibid., 179.

181 Ibid., 181–184.

182 Ibid., 127.

183 Ibid.

184 Ibid., 32; Hertz, *Early and late*, 126.

185 Hertz, *Affirmations*, 175.

186 A. Newman, *Chief Rabbi Dr. Joseph H. Hertz C.H.* (London 1972), 10.

187 Hertz, *Early and late*, 143–144.

188 Hertz, *SAS*, I:119–126; J.H. Hertz, *Early and late*, 111–115.

189 Ibid., III:358.

190 Ibid.

191 Ibid., II:124.

192 Ibid., 125.

193 Hertz, *Affirmations*, 180; I. Jakobovits, *If only my people* (London 1984), 220.

194 Jakobovits, *If only my people*, 220.

195 Ibid., 18.

196 Epstein, *Hertz*, 28.

197 Hertz, *SAS*, II:366–367.

198 T. Segev, *One Palestine, complete: Jews and Arabs under the British Mandate* (London 2000), 334–335.

199 Epstein, *Hertz*, 28.

200 Hertz, *Early and late*, 114.

201 N.W. Cohen, 'Disaspora plus Palestine, religion plus nationalism: the Seminary and Zionism, 1902–1948' in Wertheimer, *Tradition renewed*, 115–116.

202 HP SUL MS 175 30/2.

203 Freud Kandel, *Orthodox Judaism in Britain*, 68.

204 R.E. Fierstein, *A different spirit* (New York 1990), 80.

205 Cohen, 'Disaspora plus Palestine', 115.

206 Hertz, *SAS*, 125.

207 Hertz, *Affirmations*, 158, 163.

208 Hertz, *Early and late*, 129.

209 Hertz, *Affirmations*, 174; 183.

210 Ibid., 158.

211 Ibid., 151.

Chapter 8

The religious policy of J.H. Hertz

WE HAVE SEEN where J.H. Hertz stood on issues such as the origin of the Pentateuch, the authority of the Oral Law and the binding force of *halakhah*, although his views on these issues were not crude and he possessed a nuanced understanding of the way Jewish Law developed. He was very critical of less traditional views within the Jewish community, of the doctrines of other religions and of the veneration of the moral legacy of Greece and Rome, and assailed them with sometimes original and interesting arguments. He combined these attitudes with a belief in the value of modern scholarly methods in the study of Jewish texts, a relaxed stance towards such issues as evolution and an enthusiasm for the best aspects of non-Jewish culture. These views place him in the traditional grouping within the acknowledgement school, with a particular affiliation to its scientific branch, alongside other *Wissenchaft*-influenced traditionalists, such as Hildesheimer, Hoffman, Morais and Hermann Adler.

However, Hertz differed profoundly from some others within the acknowledgement school. For while everyone we would identify as part of the acknowledgement school sought to combine the best in modernity with essential Jewish traditions, there was massive dispute over what aspects of modernity should be incorporated and which parts of the tradition could be dispensed with. There was a general consensus on the binding nature of Jewish Law based on a system of rabbinic authority, albeit one which contained flexibility and was capable of change. The fundamental line of demarcation between the traditionalists and the non-traditionalists within the acknowledgement school was the issue of the origin of the Pentateuch. Just as this question divided the acknowledgement school, so it united its traditional wing with the antipathy school. Despite disagreements over certain points, the importance of which neither group denied, unanimity on this issue bound together figures such as Hildesheimer from the acknowledgement school and Salanter from the antipathy school. Hertz's theology, with its insistence that 'Judaism stands or falls with its belief in the historical actuality of the Revelation at Sinai', places him in this wider alliance.[1] This attitude was also reflected in his religious policy.

Hertz put his theology into practice in his communal religious policy, which was mostly concerned with *halakhah* and its implementation. Like Adler, Hertz faced great pressure to sanction changes. How he reacted to these pressures tells us much about his fundamental attitude towards *halakhah*. The picture that emerges is of a religious leader attempting to uphold his principles but having to decide which battles were worth fighting, where he could concede while leaving his religious integrity intact and where he had to stand firm. Before we examine particular instances we should restate a general point about the freedom of action available to Hertz and to the other Chief Rabbis since Nathan Adler. They operated in a post-Enlightenment and post-Emancipation context, where Jews could only be persuaded to affiliate; the age of religious coercion was over. As Hertz said himself, the only means of enforcing his will was 'moral influence' which could be either accepted or rejected.[2]

Hertz used various methods to pursue his agenda. First, he was a public advocate, who spoke and wrote to support or oppose particular ideas and movements. Second, he used his official position in the United Synagogue to launch or prevent developments and initiatives, and to control the activities of ministers under his aegis. Finally, Hertz used the prestige of his person and office to influence events even where he lacked direct authority. Emancipation did not only restrict the power of rabbis; it also increased their responsibilities. If Jews were seen to be enjoying the rights of citizenship without fulfilling their responsibilities to the state, the general population would come to resent them. The Chief Rabbis saw it as part of their responsibility to exhort their co-religionists to work for the benefit of wider society, and show the non-Jewish community that Jews were making a valuable contribution, and Hertz fulfilled this function. After we have examined Hertz's religious and communal policies, we compare them to policies in similar communities outside the British Empire, particularly to the policies of rabbis in Germany and the United States, to place their response to modernity in the context of other Jewish religious responses. We begin our examination of Hertz by looking at the decisions he made about his own life, especially before he became Chief Rabbi, and the insights they give into his beliefs.

Hertz left full time education in 1894 with a double rabbinical ordination from the Jewish Theological Seminary, the bastion in America of the traditional wing of the acknowledgement school. The President of the Faculty, Morais, and the President of the Trustees, Joseph Blumenthal, signed one ordination; the other, the traditional *hattarat horaah*, was signed by six rabbis, including some seminary teachers, but also by figures we would place in the antipathy school. The fact that these rabbis co-operated with the seminary and ordained one of its graduates as a rabbi is further evidence that the antipathy school was willing to recognise the authenticity of the traditional wing of the acknowledgement school. Finally, Hertz was awarded a PhD in philosophy from Columbia University, on the ethical system of James Martineau.[3] The seminary also arranged Hertz's first pulpit, at Congregation Adath Jeshurun in Syracuse, where he took up office immediately after graduation.[4]

At Syracuse, Hertz expounded his belief in the Divine origin of *halakhah* and its absolute authority. He told his congregation, 'the Almighty gave these laws to purify man by their means; to teach him obedience'.[5] Hertz associated himself and his congregation with like-minded synagogues and became a founder member of the Orthodox Union, a mixture of highly acculturated and more traditional synagogues, but all with openness to modernity.[6] Hertz represented aspects of both groups: he was trained at a modern seminary but he had been born in Hungary and spoke Yiddish.[7] Only three or four years into his rabbinate, Hertz's principles were put to the test. The result was that when Hertz felt that his congregation was no longer subscribing to *halakhah*, he left. The issue which caused his departure was mixed pews.

According to Jewish law the sexes must sit separately during prayer. Freud Kandel has suggested that the Syracuse synagogue had mixed pews from the time that Hertz took the pulpit in 1894, and Hertz was prepared to tolerate them.[8] This would cast doubt on Hertz's commitment to *halakhah*. In fact it is clear from the papers from Hertz's time in Syracuse that mixed pews arrived only in late 1897 or early 1898.[9] By April 1898 Hertz had already applied to a new synagogue in South Africa and was collecting references, as he wrote in October 1898 'my exit from Syracuse was so sudden' – which suggests that it was prompted by a specific factor.[10] Hertz's refusal to serve a congregation with mixed pews prompted Marcus Jastrow to write in his reference 'with his conservatism there is little prospect for advancement under the conditions prevailing in this country'.[11] As Hertz was joining a congregation in the British Empire, he was entering the area of rabbinical authority of Hermann Adler. Adler wrote to Hertz to congratulate him on his appointment and noted, 'I was pleased to hear from the Rev. Dr. Pereira Mendes that you are a zealous and devoted adherent of orthodox Judaism'.[12] Hertz's decision to leave Syracuse clearly helped him gain a reputation, both amongst men like Jastrow who felt he was not of their outlook, and figures such as Adler who recognised a kindred spirit.

When Hertz joined the Witwatersrand Old Hebrew Congregation he continued to declare his belief in the binding character of *halakhah*. He told his new congregation in his induction sermon 'our motto shall be: The Torah and the whole Torah'.[13] The Witwatersrand community was diverse in origin with Yiddish as its common language, so Hertz's background served him well, and he called upon both the traditional and modern aspects of his education.[14] Hertz was able to make a connection with his new congregants by speaking their language, and to impress them with his traditional qualifications by giving a Talmudic discourse in Yiddish for an hour and a half.[15] However, he did not restrict himself to the *drasha*, the traditional form of rabbinic expression; he placed great emphasis on the sermon and the lecture, speaking on Jewish history, law, ethics and philosophy.[16] It was in South Africa that Hertz first made his name as a great preacher, eager to use the pulpit to propagate his message. Hertz's continuing commitment to the world outside the Jewish community is evident from his appointment as professor of philosophy at the University of the Transvaal, and his anti-Boer political activity, which led briefly to his expulsion from the country.[17]

In 1906 the pulpit of the New West End Synagogue in London became vacant following the death of Simeon Singer, and Hertz applied unsuccessfully; the post went to Joseph Hochman, to whom we shall return later.[18] Hertz's enthusiasm to come to London may have been based, in part at least, on an understanding that his theological position was ideally suited to Anglo-Jewry. Hertz's experience in Syracuse demonstrated that his brand of Judaism, based in the traditionalist acknowledgement school, was not popular in the United States. Congregations tended either to veer towards what Hertz regarded as unacceptable ritual practices, like mixed pews, or were wholly unmodernised, with no English sermon, poor decorum and a complete rejection of secular culture.[19] Hertz could talk to both groups but neither reflected his own approach. Congregations occupying the middle ground did exist, and were led by Hertz's role models such as Bernard Drachman and Pereira Mendes, but they were rare.

Ironically, as Freud Kandel has argued, his education at the JTS had made it nearly impossible for Hertz to find a suitable synagogue, which is why he had to travel all the way to South Africa to find an appropriate pulpit after he left Syracuse.[20] Anglo-Jewry, by contrast, was headed by leaders of the traditionalist wing of the acknowledgement school. Jews' College was led by traditionalists from the scientific branch of the acknowledgement school.[21] They were men of unquestioned personal piety who upheld the Divine origin of the Pentateuch, but who were also exponents of a modern, critical approach to Jewish study. It was in Anglo-Jewry, therefore, that Hertz could expect to find a home.

Hertz left Witwatersrand in 1911 to became rabbi of Congregation Orach Chayim in New York, one of the few communities in America we could place in the traditionalist wing of the acknowledgement school. Orach Chayim was a synagogue of German Jews based on Hirsch's community in Frankfurt. It was committed to *Torah im derekh erets*, combining halakhic observance with a positive approach to what was best in Western civilisation. This was no theoretical commitment; a requirement of membership was observance of the Sabbath.[22] Schechter warned Hertz that Orach Chayim's ideology might not suit his own. He stressed that 'their orthodoxy is of the Frankfurt brand, which is not the Seminary's'.[23] As we have noted, the seminary was a *Wissenschaft* institution, and Hirsch opposed *Wissenschaft*; in other words, the seminary belonged to the scientific branch of the acknowledgement school, while Orach Chayim belonged to the romantic branch. Hertz, however felt that Orach Chayim would suit his religious approach, which we have seen owed much to Hirsch.

Hertz used his inaugural sermon to celebrate both aspects of Orach Chayim's Hirschian legacy. He praised his new congregants as 'men and women with convictions and not merely opinions . . . brooking no disharmony between your religious profession and your religious practice'.[24] He also declared his support for their refusal to detach themselves from non-Jewish culture, declaring that 'the spiritual quarantine forced upon us throughout the middle ages can no longer be maintained' following the Enlightenment and Emancipation.[25] Hertz was able to combine work at the seminary and Orach Chayim without prompting objections from the congregation, providing further evidence that the hostility of Hirschians to *Wissenschaft* had significantly weakened by the beginning of the twentieth century.[26] It also suggests that we should be cautious about accepting Meirovich's argument that Hertz's continued association with Hertz's alma mater, the Jewish Theological Seminary, after its reorganisation under Schechter in 1902, through Schechter's leadership and that of his successors, Cyrus Adler and Louis Finkelstein, and in particular Hertz's close friendship with and admiration for Solomon Schechter himself, was a sure sign of untraditionalism.[27]

We can learn more about the implications of Hertz's decision to join

Orach Chayim for his theology from the career of his successor at the synagogue, Moses Hyamson.[28] When Hertz applied for the office of Chief Rabbi in 1912, other candidates included Hertz's teacher, Bernard Drachman, and Hyamson, who had been born in Russia but was educated at Jews' College, and had been a dayan of the London Beth Din since 1902.[29] When Hyamson lost the election to Hertz he took up the now vacant post at Orach Chayim. Hyamson combined his duties there with the lectureship in Codes at the JTS, which he held from 1915 until 1940.[30] Hyamson thus provides further support for the suggestion that there was no inherent tension between the two institutions, which explains why Hertz was happy to serve there.

Furthermore, Hyamson was that rarest of creatures, a rabbinical product of pre-First World War Anglo-Jewry. He was a dayan with a complete commitment to *halakhah*, but also an intellectual product of Jews' College where he was taught *Wissenschaft*.[31] That Hyamson felt at home at Orach Chayim demonstrates the similarity between Orach Chayim and the United Synagogue of London. We can understand this, as we would place both in the traditionalist wing of the acknowledgement school. Orach Chayim was in many ways a practical version of what the United Synagogue was in theory, a congregation with a positive disposition towards modernisation when that was compatible with *halakhah*. That may be why Orach Chayim looked to Hermann Adler for guidance.[32] This insight reinforces the argument that Hertz's theology was appropriate for few contexts outside Anglo-Jewry. Hertz was suitable for Orach Chayim precisely because of its similarity to the United Synagogue. Hertz's early rabbinical positions were therefore a reflection of his theology and they enabled him to practise the Judaism that he had learnt at the JTS. That was also true of his final office, Chief Rabbi of the British Empire.

The first area of Hertz's activity we examine is his use of the public statement, oral or written. Hertz said himself that 'my chief weapon is the word' – as it had to be in an age and place when a rabbi could not simply expect the obedience of his flock nor call upon the state to ensure obedience.[33] He had a natural rhetorical talent but this raw ability was continually developed and refined by hard work. The syllabus at the JTS included homiletics. Students would write sermons, which Morais would annotate with suggestions for improvement.[34] Even when he was a long-established writer and preacher, the effort he expended in crafting his words was immense. Ephraim Levine recorded that Hertz's sermons were the product of 'sustained preparation' because 'the burden of cares under which he laboured demanded verbal precision which can only be attained by long hours in the study'.[35] Cecil Roth, who also knew Hertz well, wrote of his letters to the press 'there would not be a word too much; there would not be a word too little; the phrasing was so perfect that it appeared easy and inevitable; only those who were nearest to him knew how much work and thought had gone into the preparation, and how many drafts had been discarded before the final form was reached'.[36] Levine and Roth's tributes, which formed part of what were essentially eulogies, may be overblown, but are unlikely to bear no relation to the truth.

Hertz regarded sermons and writings as tools to help him achieve his aims, which were particularly important in an age when the *herem* was useless. Contemporaries identified Hertz's communications to the community as a particular feature of his religious leadership. Alexander Altmann said Hertz 'interpreted the established results of solid scholarship to the man in the street. He gathered the harvest of Learning into vessels adapted for the understanding of the masses'.[37] S.M. Lehrman wrote that Hertz chose to direct his energies away from original scholarship and towards the popularisation of Judaism.[38] Roth thought that Hertz was elected as Chief Rabbi 'largely on the strength of his great oratorical powers' – an indication of the prime role of a Jewish religious leader after Emancipation.[39] In his induction sermon as Chief Rabbi, Hertz described his first function as 'teacher of the Book to the people of the Book' – that is, an educator more than a scholar.[40] We should therefore not be surprised that Hertz's sermons and addresses are filled with calls for fidelity to traditional Judaism, observance of the Sabbath and the dietary laws, attendance at the synagogue, correct observance of Passover, and so forth.[41]

Hertz did not just use his pulpit addresses to assert his own ideology but also to attack others, especially those of the adaptation and acceptance schools. In his graduation address he declared the mission of JTS graduates – 'we will follow the Elijah who is now calling us to be zealous for Israel's law' – and also attacked their opponents, warning that 'we shall be accused of stemming the wheels of progress' by opposing the acceptance school (Reform).[42] In an interview given to the *Jewish Chronicle* in 1911 while passing through London, Hertz asserted his total opposition to Reform Jewish theology and practice.[43] When he joined Orach Chayim as well as celebrating the synagogue's ideology he castigated its opponents, telling the congregation 'I shall look to you for your help in my conflict with illiberal liberalism'.[44] In 1914, just a year after Hertz came to London, he set about attacking the English leaders of the adaptation school.[45] This prompted a pained letter from the Reform leader, Stephen S. Wise, who had previously been a friend of

Hertz, who wrote, 'I am deeply grieved at some of the things you find it in your heart to say about the Liberal Jewish Movement'.[46] Hertz's most developed denunciation of Liberal Judaism came in the 1920s with his series of sermons entitled *The new paths*.[47] He followed these sermons with another set, later published as *Affirmations of Judaism*, which were ostensibly defence of traditional Judaism but contained many further criticisms of the Reform and Liberal movements.[48]

We have examined Hertz's critique of Liberal Judaism; we should now fill in the communal context. Robert Waley Cohen, an Honorary Officer of the United Synagogue, wrote to Hertz to protest against his attacks on the Liberals. He wrote 'many of us had felt that the destructive criticism of Liberal Judaism would not serve to strengthen genuine doubting waverers in their allegiance to Traditional Judaism . . . you have in your second series done little more than continue your criticism . . . This continuance of polemical criticism is very disappointing'.[49] Despite this opposition from his own lay leadership, Hertz continued to deliver the sermons and then published them. It followed from Hertz's attacks on non-traditional Judaism that he would not allow its representatives to preach in his synagogues, and despite pressure in 1919 he banned pulpit exchanges between ministers of the United Synagogue and the West London.[50] However, like Hermann Adler, Hertz attended a memorial service at West London.[51]

In 1934, there was further progress in Hertz's relationship with the congregation, when Hertz attended and spoke at the opening of the synagogue's Stern Hall. He said, 'I am the last person in the world to minimize the significance of religious difference in Jewry. If I have nevertheless decided to be with you this morning it is because of my conviction that far more calamitous than religious differences in Jewry is religious indifference in Jewry'.[52] Although Hertz was always, and somewhat inconsistently, less antagonistic toward English Reform than the Liberal movement it was still a significant step, which attracted criticism from the Union of Orthodox Hebrew Congregations.[53] Some might see it as hypocritical in the light of Hertz's noisy opposition to non-traditional Jewish movements. This suggestion is strengthened by the fact that, as we have noted, the West London Synagogue helped to fund Jews' College.

On the other hand, the visit could be attributed to Hertz's belief in the need for Jewish unity in the face of the rise of Hitler. Yet, even in those changed circumstances Hertz resisted active co-operation with non-traditional Jewish movements on religious issues. Thus, in 1942 he opposed as 'a real danger to Orthodox Judaism' the proposal for a United Synagogue for Great Britain bringing together Reform and Liberal with those which recognised the authority of the Chief Rabbinate.[54] Alderman and others have suggested that Hertz became much more traditional at the end of his life under the influence of Solomon Schonfeld. However, Hertz's opposition to the adaptation school throughout his career, in America and London, undermines this argument.

Hertz did not restrict his attacks to Jews he considered less traditional than himself, or even to Jews at all. As Freud Kandel observed, Hertz developed a critique of highly traditional Jewish groups.[55] In 1935 Hertz attended the consecration of the Golders Green Beth Hamidrash formed by Hirschian German-Jewish refugees. They implemented Hirsch's policy of *Austritt* – complete institutional separation from any other Jewish body, which prompted Hertz to decry those Jews who 'haven't sufficient Judaism to love their fellow Jews and to co-operate with them'.[56] This was an attack on a different stream within the acknowledgement school. Hertz also had criticisms of the antipathy school, for example of their neglect of the teaching of 'religion' (meaning theology, as opposed to texts and laws), and their failure to teach girls adequately, if at all.[57] These criticisms did not amount to Hertz denying that the antipathy school represented authentic Judaism, unlike his attacks on the acceptance school. As we have noted, within the alliance comprising the antipathy school and the traditionalist wing of the acknowledgement school, there could be disagreement without delegitimisation, which was reserved for the non-traditional wing of the acknowledgement school and the adaptation school.

Hertz took his advocacy to an international level, in what he called the 'Battle for the Sabbath at Geneva'.[58] In 1923 a League of Nations committee to investigate reform of the calendar proposed that every year being 364 days long the last day of an eight-day week at the end of each year should be a blank day. Thus, once a year, Monday would not follow Sunday immediately, but would be preceded by a blank day. This meant, of course, that the days of the old system would be thrown out of alignment with those of the new, so that the Sabbath would no longer be on a Saturday, but would wander around the week. This would cause massive inconvenience for observant Jews. Hertz led the Jewish campaign against the reform and mobilised Jewish protests around the world, including a petition with hundreds of thousands of signatures, which joined with those of other affected minorities, such as Seventh Day Adventists. After a seven-year campaign, Hertz and his allies defeated the proposed reform.[59]

Hertz also spoke out about matters that were not specifically religious, for example Zionism. Despite the anti-Zionist attitudes of much of the Anglo-Jewish lay leadership, Hertz declared his own support, and sometimes went further.[60] In 1917 the presidents of the Board of Deputies and the Anglo-Jewish Association wrote a joint letter to *The Times* condemning Zionism. This prompted Hertz to write his own letter: 'As Chief Rabbi of the British Empire, I cannot allow your readers to remain under the misconception that the said statement represents . . . the views held either by Anglo-Jewry as a whole or by the Jewries of the Overseas Dominions'.[61] This contradiction of the lay leaders of Anglo-Jewry required significant courage. By 1945 Zionism was much more accepted by the Anglo-Jewish public and lay leadership; Hertz had been Chief Rabbi for 32 years and was therefore a stronger figure, but his request to his ministers in that year to preach against British policy in Palestine, an instruction which Robert Waley Cohen counter-manded, was also brave.[62] The dispute here was essentially about how much support Jews should show towards the policies of the nation in which they lived, an issue which had confronted Hermann Adler.

Like his predecessor, Hertz was anxious to stress Jewish loyalty and in 1916 he wrote to the *Fortnightly Review* to rebut Claude Montefiore's suggestion that Zionism compromised loyalty to England. However, Hertz considered that loyalty could not be at any price and he did not require Anglo-Jewry to withdraw 'its longing for Zion'.[63] Waley Cohen disagreed and was willing to go further to maintain the appearance of Jewish loyalty to Britain. Hertz was no more cautious with foreign governments than with the British Government. Just a few months after arriving in England, he attended the International Congress for the Suppression of the White Slave Trade. There he condemned, Russia, a British ally, in the presence of the Russian ambassador, for its policy of forcing Jewish women who wished to enter certain towns and universities to register as prostitutes.[64] Cecil Roth's encomium that Hertz possessed 'a boundless courage and an inability to maintain a tactful silence in the face of wrongdoing' therefore does seem to have some truth to it.[65] However, Hertz was careful to avoid certain subjects. In 1919 a Unitarian minister wrote to him asking him to speak out against the doctrine of the Trinity. Hertz declined, replying that 'to attempt to do so would endanger the lives of . . . coreligionists in other countries'.[66]

The final type of public statement to consider is Hertz's literary works, to which he attached great importance, saying 'my greatest reward is the assurance given to me by Jews and non-Jews alike that the books I wrote . . . are rendering a real service'.[67] In addition to the collections of sermons, addresses and studies, Hertz issued *A book of Jewish thoughts*, his commentaries on the *Pentateuch and Haftorahs* and the *Authorised daily prayer book. A book of Jewish thoughts* was originally intended for Jewish soldiers in the First World War and comprised statements by Jews on Jews and Judaism, with one section dedicated to tributes to Judaism by non-Jews. It was phenomenally successful, went into 22 editions, was translated into at least seven languages and had sold a quarter of a million copies by 1953.[68] According to Hertz, the purpose of the book was to reveal to Jews and non-Jews the 'imperishable wealth of the Jewish heritage' and to increase respect for Judaism.[69] Hertz was carrying out the role he set for himself, to be a 'teacher of the Book to the people of the Book . . . interpreter of Israel . . . to the larger, often hostile world around him'.[70] This reflected the two sides of his role in the context of a modern community, maintaining allegiance to Judaism through persuasion and promoting Jews' good name before a non-Jewish audience, an aim which, we have seen, Hermann Adler also set himself.[71]

We have already examined the polemical intentions of the *Pentateuch and Haftorahs*, but we should restate them briefly. Hertz's idea for a popular, Jewish commentary shows a debt to Schechter, who called for such a work as early as 1899.[72] Hertz's dedication to the project of producing the *Pentateuch* was huge and demonstrates his own belief in its value. He launched the project in 1920 and set about recruiting his contributors and raising the money to finance production.[73] The first volume did not appear for almost a decade, coming out in 1929, and it was another seven years before the final volume emerged in 1936.[74]

Hertz's commentary had one overwhelming aim: to substantiate the view that the entire text of the Pentateuch was given directly by God. There were other, secondary, polemics within the *Pentateuch*, the most important of which was the attempt to show that Judaism was rational and there was no conflict between the Torah and science, for example regarding evolution. The work is shot through with attacks on classical and pagan civilisations and morality, detailing their deficiency and barbarity. Finally, Christianity is attacked as bastardised Judaism, bearing the ugly impress of paganism. These attacks highlight the judgements Hertz made about what was positive about the non-Jewish world and should be acknowledged, and what was not. These themes were laid out primarily in response to the work of Montefiore, the leading theologian of the English adaptation school, who denied the Mosaic authorship of the Pentateuch, and wanted to adapt Judaism to the intellectual and cultural currents of the non-Jewish world. In contrast to Hertz, Montefiore celebrated the ethical insights of the classical authors and the Gospel writers.

Hertz's commentary to the *Authorised daily prayer book* elaborated on his complex theology. He promoted 'the great fact of Revelation' and his conviction that 'the commandments of God are a bulwark against all animalism and godlessness', but also suggested that some psalms were post-Davidic and that the attribution to Moses of authorship of the first blessing in Grace After Meals was allegorical. These less traditional views represent Hertz's *Wissenschaft* alignment.[75]

Our discussion thus far has centred on Hertz as an advocate, but Hertz also wielded real power, as the religious authority for the United Synagogue and most provincial congregations, and as the custodian by law and the constitution of the Board of Deputies of the designation of congregations as Jewish for the purposes of solemnising marriages. We will turn now to how he used that power to achieve his objectives.

Hertz inherited the powers of his predecessors over the United Synagogue and its ministers, Jews' College, the London Beth Din, and for the certification of synagogues as made up of 'persons professing the Jewish religion' so they could conduct marriages valid in civil law. The most important ministerial incident that Hertz became involved in concerned the Rev. Dr Joseph Hochman, who in 1906 had been the successful candidate to succeed Singer at the New West End Synagogue. We have examined the clash between Hochman and Hermann Adler in 1910. After Adler's death, Hochman called for radical reform of the office of Chief Rabbi to give individual ministers considerable local autonomy and campaigned to reform the system of Torah readings at the New West End.[76]

Hochman clashed with Hertz from the start. He publicly opposed his appointment and, when Hertz sent a letter round to his ministers asking them to grow beards, Hochman shaved his off.[77] Hochman became increasingly extreme in his views and by 1915 he had moved across into the adaptation school. He advocated abolition of the dietary laws, mixed seating in the synagogue and riding to the synagogue on the Sabbath.[78] By some accounts he used to ride a horse to the synagogue himself and tie it up outside during the afternoon service.[79] Hertz made it clear that unless Hochman restrained himself he would revoke Hochman's licence.[80] In response Hochman resigned, asserting that he was 'unable to bring his views into harmony with the standpoint of the synagogue'.[81]

We have said that taking theology seriously will add to understanding. Here we see Hochman highlighting his views being as at the core of the difficulties he faced. As in the case of Morris Joseph, understanding theological differences and debates takes forward the analysis. After dragging the case through the secular press, including the *Christian Messenger*, Hochman joined the army. After the First World War he became a barrister, and eventually legal adviser to the King of Siam.[82] The Hochman affair shows that Hertz was not willing to tolerate the expression of unacceptable religious views by his ministers, to the extent that he was prepared to remove them from office. Any suggestion that Hertz was happy to turn a blind eye towards publicly expressed divergent views, as is implied by the contention that Louis Jacobs would have prospered under Hertz, is therefore inaccurate.

When Hertz became Chief Rabbi and President of Jews' College, the Principal of the College was Adolph Buchler. He was on the traditionalist wing of the acknowledgement school, a distinguished *Wissenschaft* scholar, meticulously observant and totally opposed to the teaching of anything other than traditional Jewish doctrines at Jews' College. Although their personal relationship was sometimes very tense, the two men were so close ideologically that Hertz invited Buchler to be co-editor of the *Pentateuch and Haftorahs*.[83] Other members of the college faculty fitted the same model, including Arthur Marmorstein and Samuel Daiches, whom we have discussed above.[84] Hertz's main contribution towards the staffing of the college was the appointment of Isidore Epstein, first as a lecturer in 1928 and then as Director of Studies and Acting Principal in 1945.[85] As a scholar Epstein was in the same mould as Buchler. His scholarship is evident from the Soncino translation of the Talmud, which he edited, and his work on Maimonides and the Responsa.[86] His mastery of theology, Jewish sources and non-Jewish scholarship is clear from his book *The faith of Judaism*, which also displays his opposition to Biblical Criticism.[87] Hertz and Epstein worked together to strengthen traditional Judaism. Epstein contributed to the commentary on the *Pentateuch and Haftorahs*, and Hertz wrote the preface to Epstein's 1931 collection of essays *Judaism of tradition*, Epstein's first published defence of the Mosaic authorship of the Pentateuch.[88]

Hertz's appointment of Epstein as Acting Principal was opposed by Samuel Daiches, who claimed that Epstein's traditional background did not equip him to lead a centre of modern scholarship.[89] Hertz's perseverance showed his desire to make Jews' College into an institution like the JTS of his youth, a traditionalist centre of the scientific branch of the acknowledgement school, where traditional and modern methods were taught, together with philosophy and theology, which Hertz wanted to include as part of the requirements for the rabbinical diploma.[90] The inclusion of these subjects was a departure from the Jews' College of Buchler, where the curriculum consisted almost entirely of text-based

Wissenschaft.[91] During his career as principal, Epstein traditionalised the curriculum and produced rabbis of greater learning, especially in Talmud and Codes, and more traditional practice.[92] Hertz arranged for the joint awarding of rabbinical ordination by the Chief Rabbinate, Jews' College and Yeshiva Etz Chayim, an institution of the antipathy school, whose students were far more expert in Talmud than those at Jews' College.[93] Hertz's keenness for United Synagogue ministers to combine 'learning old and new' can also be detected in the reading list he sent to new ministers. This included the great *Wissenschaft* works of Frankel and Graetz of the acknowledgement school, Geiger of the adaptation school and the traditionalist *Wissenschaft* writings of Hoffman. It also included examples of traditional scholarship produced by the antipathy school, for example the *Torah temimah* of Rabbi Barukh HaLevi Epstein.[94]

The greatest controversy to surround Jews' College in Hertz's time came from Waley Cohen's proposal in 1920, while Hertz was on his pastoral tour of the Empire, to split the college into two parts.[95] A 'Jewish Theological College' would teach traditional Judaism while a non-denominational 'Academy of Jewish Learning' would be open to all and not promote any particular branch of Judaism. The academy would involve close co-operation with the West London Synagogue.[96] Hertz opposed any non-traditional institution being connected to Jews' College or any educational co-operation with West London. According to Hertz, 'congregations are divided into two classes, Orthodox and other congregations' and there could be no co-operation between the two.[97] Hertz thus fiercely opposed the scheme and, as Meirovich has written, 'was prepared to resign' rather than accede to it.[98]

Later in his career, Hertz even tried to remove Reform and Liberal members of the educational bodies on which United Synagogue representatives also sat, in an attempted departure from long-standing Anglo-Jewish practice.[99] This contrasted with Hertz's attitude towards Yeshiva Etz Chayim, which he wanted to work with, although he did not agree with its narrow educational curriculum based on its antipathy to modernity. Buchler, who wanted any non-denominational 'Academy' to have nothing whatever to do with his college, supported Hertz, as did the *dayyanim* of the London Beth Din who produced a ruling that such an arrangement would be against Jewish law.[100] The proposal was defeated, but Hertz felt sufficiently strongly about the issue that he referred to it two decades later at his seventieth birthday celebrations, remarking that 'my reaction to the attempt . . . to establish an un-Orthodox wing to Jews' College, is still within the memory of many of you'.[101]

Alongside the United Synagogue ministry and Jews' College, the London Beth Din was the third institution whose membership was ultimately controlled by Hertz. When Hertz arrived as Chief Rabbi in 1913 he found the Beth Din staffed by the significant eastern European scholar Moses Avigdor Chaikin – whom we have described, using Heilman's term, as a 'tolerator' of modernity, falling between the antipathy and acknowledgement schools – and two English-trained, acknowledgement-school *dayyanim*, Asher Feldman and Moses Hyamson.[102] After Hyamson went to New York, Hertz was left with just two colleagues on the court. Hertz was eager to see the establishment of a prestigious Beth Din able to render authoritative decisions on *halakhah*, and swiftly appointed replacements. The major appointment was of Samuel Isaac Hillman, another tolerator who had previously served in Glasgow, with vast erudition in rabbinic texts. Protracted negotiations led to Hillman coming to London in 1914.[103] At the same time Hertz appointed two Anglicised *dayyanim*, H.M. Lazarus, who was the son-in-law of an earlier dayyan, Sussman Cohen, and Louis Mendelson, both educated at Jews' College and who fit well into the acknowledgement school.[104]

The Beth Din now had five *dayyanim* plus the Chief Rabbi as ex officio Av Beth Din (literally 'father of the court' or president). Of these, two (Hillman and Chaikin) were of international standing..[105] When Chaikin left for Tel Aviv in 1926, Hillman became the senior dayyan until he left for Palestine in 1934.[106] During that period, all technical halakhic questions addressed to Hertz were passed to Hillman.[107] For, although Hertz and Hillman may have disagreed on theological issues, such considerations were secondary to having a recognised authority who could command respect and uphold halakhic standards. Hertz did however retain the status of 'unquestioned and final authority' and disagreed with his *dayyanim* on occasion.[108] For example, in the First World War, Hertz supported the military service of *Cohanim* (members of the priestly tribe who must not come into contact with the dead), which the *dayyanim* opposed, as did Rabbi A.I. Kook, Chief Rabbi of Palestine, who was forced to spend the War in London, and who worked with Hertz on communal issues, and to whom Hertz turned for guidance. For example, Hertz asked Kook whether he should permit the eating of rice on Passover during the War.[109]

It is interesting to compare the way Hertz related to Rav Kook on the issue of *Cohanim* serving in the army, on the one hand, and in the case of whether rice could be eaten on Passover, on the other. Hertz asked for Kook's guidance over the consumption of rice, but took his own decision about *Cohanim* serving, even against Kook's opposition. On the surface this seems odd, as both involve halakhic judgements; more-over, if Hertz was prepared to acknowledge Kook's greater authority over eating rice, which would not even involve a rabbinic prohibition and at worst represented the contravention of a binding custom, why would he not submit to Kook's wishes over *Cohanim*, which involved a Biblical prohibition? We cannot even say that Hertz only asked Kook about rice because the issue was trivial, because if Hertz considered it to be of no importance he would simply have permitted rice to be eaten.

The answer may be that in the case of rice Hertz felt that the argu-ments were evenly balanced and sought Kook's ruling precisely because a fine judgement was needed, for which Kook's enormous erudition was required. However, in the case of *Cohanim* serving the answer was clear to Hertz. Large-scale Jewish exemption from military service would harm Jewish interests and Hertz took the view that this reality needed to be factored into the halakhic decision-making process. He did not need Kook's expertise to tell him that; indeed, he felt that this was at least one issue where he understood the matter better than Kook, and therefore not only took the decision without him, but did so explicitly against Kook's wishes.

Hertz made another series of appointments following the depar-tures of Chaikin and Hillman. While Hillman was still in London, Hertz appointed Mark Gollop, Minister of the Hampstead Synagogue, as a part-time dayyan.[110] He entered into lengthy negotiations with the Union of Orthodox Hebrew Congregations (Adath Yisroel, made up of highly traditional members of the acknowledgement school) and offered a seat to its senior rabbi, Dr Victor Schonfeld, but discussions broke down.[111] When Hillman left in 1934, the Beth Din lost its leading scholar and the situation became urgent. Hertz began a two-year search for an appropriate replacement for, as a United Synagogue minute records, 'the Chief Rabbi feels that it is important that the man who is appointed should be an outstanding authority'.[112]

Hertz had a number of candidates in mind, all of whom were distinguished scholars aligned to the acknowledgement school. He considered the Hirschian Eli Munk, Rabbi of the Golders Green Beth Hamedrash.[113] He also suggested Rabbi Dr Isaac Herzog, Hillman's son-in-law and Chief Rabbi of Ireland, and Rabbi Isser Unterman, rabbi in Liverpool, both later Chief Rabbis of Israel.[114] However, from very early in the process Hertz had a clearly preferred candidate, Yeheskel Abramsky, who like Hillman came originally from the antipathy school; again halakhic expertise was for Hertz more important than theologi-cal alignment within what he considered to be authentic Judaism.[115]

Freud Kandel has argued that Abramsky was Waley Cohen's candidate, chosen to restrict Hertz, but in fact Hertz was very keen for Abramsky to be appointed. A United Synagogue minute from March 1935 described Hertz as 'very anxious to have Rabbi Abramsky'.

Abramsky was possibly the greatest Jewish scholar to reside in England in modern times. He had been imprisoned in his native Russia until his release was engineered in 1931 by Hertz, who arranged for him to become the rabbi of Machzike Hadath.[116] The United Synagogue offered Abramsky a seat on the Beth Din on 25 June 1934. Abramsky agreed in principle, but made a firm acceptance conditional on Hertz resolving irregularities concerning the sales of kosher meat.[117] The issue of porging that had caused unrest in the community for several decades was unresolved. Abramsky demanded that no hindquarter meat be sold in shops under the jurisdiction of the Beth Din. Hertz and the Beth Din justified this situation on the grounds that a *shomer* was always provided at shops licensed to sell hindquarter meat, and the failure to license new butchers to sell such meat led to its illicit sale, and that therefore the policy enabled more people to maintain the dietary laws. Hertz conceded however that this was becoming increasingly less true.[118] Hertz and the Beth Din probably did not clamp down on abuses earlier because of the financial power of the butchers, who supplied a significant proportion of communal funds through the Beth Din licences. The butchers probably opposed mandatory porging because it can turn a piece of meat into unattractive strips and would put people off buying the more expensive cuts.

At first Hertz gave a general undertaking to address the problem, which Abramsky did not find acceptable. Then Hertz offered to prohibit the sale of any unporged hindquarter meat and sent a letter to the Board of Shechita instructing that no unporged meat be sold as a condition of the licence. Abramsky, however, remained firm and refused to accept a post on the Beth Din until all hindquarter meat was banned. At this point Hertz began to look around for other candidates. Hertz wanted a dayyan who could maintain the authority of the Beth Din even after Abramsky's criticisms had become public. Hertz wrote to Waley Cohen on 7 October 1934 that the new dayyan must have 'a strong enough personality to stand up against the coalition of forces that would gather round Abramski'. He alighted upon J.J. Weinberg, Rector of the Hildesheimer Seminary in Berlin, a highly distinguished traditionalist of the acknowledgement school's scientific branch and a great international halakhic authority. Weinberg initially expressed interest in the position; Isidore Epstein, Dayan Feldman and Waley Cohen all went to see him and were impressed. However, the seminary brought pressure to bear on Weinberg and urged him that it would disintegrate if he left, and in early 1935 Weinberg withdrew his candidature.[119]

Hertz was forced to turn again to Abramsky. This time Abramsky dropped his demand that no hindquarter meat be sold and, following the passing of a resolution by the Shechita Board to end the selling of unporged meat at the end of May 1935, Abramsky accepted the post of dayyan and was appointed on 20 June 1935 under the same conditions he had turned down in October 1934. On 12 July 1935 the Beth Din issued a public statement signed by all the *dayyanim*, including Abramsky, announcing the end of unporged meat. By the end of the year Waley Cohen was receiving complaints that the ban was driving butchers out of business, but by then the matter was settled. During the Second World War a shortage of porgers enabled Abramsky to prohibit the sale of all hindquarter meat, and his aim, and the original aim of Machzike Hadath first stated in 1891, was achieved.[120]

The Beth Din once again had a rabbinic giant, assisted by three English *dayyanim*. Hertz was enabled by the exodus of Jews from Germany in the 1930s to engage the services of two more acknowledgement-school *dayyanim*, of greater learning than their English counterparts. Isidore Grunfeld – a German lawyer, Jewish scholar and Hirschian – was appointed Registrar of the Beth Din in 1937 and was promoted to full dayyan when he received his rabbinic ordination. Julius Jakobovits, a graduate of the Hildesheimer Seminary and distinguished communal rabbi from the group of traditionalist German rabbis who opposed *Austritt*, was appointed to the Beth Din in 1943.[121] Morris Swift, English-born and educated not at Jews' College but at the *yeshivot* of Gateshead and the great European centres of Ponevitz, Radin and Mir, was appointed a part-time dayyan during the Second World War. Hertz also tried to appoint Israel Brodie to the Beth Din on his return to England from Australia in 1939, but Brodie first took a job with the Board of Deputies and then became a chaplain to the forces.[122]

By the end of his life, then, Hertz had significantly altered the composition of the Beth Din. When he arrived, he found the English Feldman and the eastern European Chaikin. By 1946 the Beth Din was significantly larger and stronger, more traditional and less Anglo-Jewish in orientation. There was still the Anglicised, acknowledgement-school Lazarus who sat part-time, but there was also Abramsky (and before him Hillman) and Swift, tolerators who originated in the antipathy school, and Grunfeld and Jakobovits who came from the most traditional and learned part of the acknowledgement school. This significant embedding of traditionalist elements in the Beth Din was the result of

Hertz's conscious policy to ensure that the Beth Din contained traditional scholars of international standing. These scholars had no training
or interest in *Wissenschaft*, but Hertz, like Hoffman and Buchler, did
not regard *Wissenschaft* as relevant to the process which determined
halakhah. The former was an academic and historical exercise, the
latter was based on authority and precedent where what mattered was
not how or why the process developed, but the conclusions that had
been reached.

There is no evidence that the Beth Din that Hertz created behaved in
any way other than he expected. Endelman has written that Abramsky
'moved the bet din in a conservative direction'; indeed, but that is what
Hertz appointed him to do.[123] But the strictness of Abramsky and his
colleagues can be exaggerated. Abramsky allowed the Beth Din to
supervise functions where non-kosher wine was served, although it
was stated that drinks were not under supervision. It is also significant
that Abramsky made it clear that he was happy to serve on the Beth
Din alongside a minister (Gollop) of a synagogue (Hampstead) with a
mixed choir, a halakhically dubious practice.[124] This serves to highlight
that responses to modernity did not necessarily determine halakhic
strictness. The tolerators Chaikin and Hillman from the antipathy
school had allowed the problems connected with *shehita* to continue
and even to grow; the ideologically similarly inclined Abramsky put a
stop to such practices, but was prepared to join the London Beth Din
even though that involved employing certain leniencies on other issues.
Victor Schonfeld by contrast, from the acknowledgement school, was
much more halakhically rigid and refused to join the Beth Din as that
would involve him in what he regarded as unacceptable concessions.

We have seen how Hertz enlisted the support of the Beth Din in his
campaign against the reforms to Jews' College in the 1920s; this was just
one of a number of examples of the Beth Din bolstering the authority
of the Chief Rabbi and vice versa. Moreover, the only group that Hertz,
who was famously combative, would defer to, were his colleagues on
the Beth Din. In 1943 Hertz permitted a couple to marry when the Beth
Din had told them to wait for 90 days. That prompted a written protest
from Abramsky, Lazarus and Grunfeld. Hertz sent a conciliatory reply
to his 'dear friends' in which he explained that he was not aware of
the Beth Din's ruling and had tried to contact Abramsky but had been
unable to do so.[125] This letter contrasts sharply with the stinging letters
Hertz exchanged with individuals who complained about his actions.[126]

Evidence of Hertz's support for the Beth Din comes from 1945, when
the honorary officers of the Finchley Synagogue refused to answer
a summons from the Beth Din and were supported by the Honorary

Officers of the United Synagogue. Hertz took the side of the Beth Din. A six-month dispute involving extremely harsh letters between Hertz and Waley Cohen climaxed in a meeting of the United Synagogue Council. In the end, the honorary officers of Finchley conceded and agreed to attend the Beth Din.[127] For his part, Dayan Abramsky was very careful to consult the Chief Rabbi on halakhic matters, even though both Hertz and Abramsky recognised that the latter was the greater authority.[128] Abramsky even wrote to contacts in Palestine ahead of a visit there by Hertz to ensure he received appropriate respect during his stay.[129]

Although Hertz passed many halakhic decisions to the Beth Din, in a number of cases he made his own rulings, especially regarding the conduct of United Synagogue services. These halakhic decisions, and their rationale, will give us an increased understanding of his practical approach to *halakhah*. We have seen his commitment in theory, and the value he placed on *halakhah* demonstrated by his desire to see an authoritative Beth Din. Hertz's own decisions add a final dimension. The United Synagogue had a history of requests to the Chief Rabbi for reforms to the ritual. Major conferences were called in 1880 and 1892 to petition the Chief Rabbi for specific reforms.[130] Hertz did not face a fully-fledged conference, but he did receive a large number of requests for individual modifications to the synagogue service.

In 1919 the Western Synagogue, which was not a member of the United Synagogue but accepted the authority of the Chief Rabbi, met with Hertz to ask for a number of changes. One request was for permission to have a non-Jew play the organ in Sabbath and Festival services, following the practice in Paris. Hertz replied, 'no orthodox synagogue in England has ever thus separated itself from the body of Traditional Judaism'. He dismissed the argument that it was the practice in Paris by saying that the actions of 'a few assimilationist Jews in France or Belgium who do not act in accordance with our Din' were irrelevant. Hertz however did permit the synagogue to recite the prayer for the congregation in English as well as Hebrew. So Hertz was not opposed to all change on principle, simply against changes which he regarded as violating *halakhah*.[131]

In 1920 a number of United Synagogue ministers asked Hertz to sanction replacing the annual cycle of Torah readings with the Triennial Cycle. They included the highly respected Hermann Gollancz of Bayswater, Michael Adler of the wealthy Central Synagogue and A.A. Green of the prestigious Hampstead Synagogue. Hertz took the view that the annual cycle had become a binding custom, and refused to allow its alteration.[132]

Another request to come to Hertz in 1920 concerned mixed choirs and came from the Bayswater Synagogue. We have seen how the issue of mixed choirs arose in the United Synagogue in the 1880s and 1890s. Bayswater did not adopt a mixed choir during Hermann Adler's lifetime because he was known to disapprove. Hertz had removed the women from the choir he had found at the Witwatersrand synagogue when he arrived in South Africa, but here he was more cautious.[133] He wrote 'I do not approve of a mixed choir' but seeing as other congregations already had them 'I cannot now veto'.[134] By the end of his Chief Rabbinate Hertz was able to be firmer, and did refuse to permit a synagogue to found a mixed choir.[135]

The text of *Kol nidre* had been of concern to some Jews since the Enlightenment and the quest for full Emancipation, since its cancellation of vows suggested that Jews could not be trusted. This concern had prompted Hirsch to remove *Kol nidre* from the service in 1839.[136] In 1932 Hertz granted the Great Synagogue of Sydney, Australia, permission to use the Sefardi text of *Kol nidre* instead of the Ashkenazi version, which they found less problematic. It was a deviation from custom and as such to be avoided, but it resolved the problem while retaining *Kol nidre* and Hertz could hardly deny the validity of the Sefardi text; moreover, it was in response to a request that reflected a genuine anxiety.[137]

Like Adler, Hertz faced the issue of prayers for the restitution of sacrifices. Adler had dealt with it by allowing the Hampstead Synagogue to read the Sabbath additional service according to the abbreviated Sefardi custom, to avoid having to pray aloud for the restitution of sacrifices, which many members found repugnant.[138] Hertz decided to make his own comment and effectively issued a ruling in his commentary to the *Authorised daily prayer book*. We have considered his statement from a theological perspective already, but there is also a policy perspective. Hertz was faced with dissent by an influential section of his community. His ruling reflects these considerations. While praising those who do pray for the return of the sacrificial service, he refrained from insisting that everyone must join them in their prayers. Rather he wrote 'let him whose heart is not with his fellow worshippers in any of their supplications, silently substitute his own prayers for them; but let him not interfere with the devotions of those . . .' who do pray for the restitution of sacrifices. He based this ruling on the halakhic reasoning that the additional service was late in origin and long considered to be voluntary. It did not endorse omitting the prayer, but it did recognise the feelings towards it and, in light of the room for halakhic flexibility, found a compromise.[139]

A case which reveals Hertz's respect for rabbinical authority, and his willingness to defer to other leaders was the request at the end of the First World War to place the banner of the Jewish Regiment inside the Great Synagogue. Hertz would only give his consent if the Jerusalem rabbinate allowed a standard to be placed in their main synagogue, the Hurvah.[140] This decision reflects a broader idea of Hertz's, to transfer all halakhic authority to Jerusalem.[141] This was despite the fact that, as we have noted, Hertz disagreed with the leading authority in Palestine and Jerusalem, A.I. Kook on some halakhic issues. In 1928 Hertz proposed an international rabbinical conference to deal with difficulties in Jewish divorce, although it never took place.[142] Another issue where Hertz was very conscious of the views of other authorities, and in particular his Beth Din, was the demand for votes for women seatholders in synagogue elections. For some time Jewish women had been playing a greater role in communal organisations, and outside the community women over the age of 30 became eligible to vote in British elections in 1918. These factors probably prompted the women's suffrage campaign in the United Synagogue in the mid-1920s. The Beth Din issued a carefully worded statement, which, while expressing disapproval of the idea, refrained from declaring it to be against Jewish law. Hertz gave permission for women to vote in elections, but stressed that it was the absence of a prohibition from the Beth Din that enabled him to issue a permissive response.[143]

Hertz had to respond to the special demands the World Wars placed upon the Jewish community, particularly those members actually fighting.[144] Hertz was determined that Jews should contribute fully to the war effort and made alterations to practice that he felt war required. In 1914 and 1939 he instructed his ministers that there were no religious grounds for conscientious objection, including, as we have seen, for *Cohanim*, and he refused to seek exceptions for yeshivah students once conscription was introduced. Both of these stances brought him into conflict with Kook.[145] Hertz ruled that 'Jewish law explicitly permits' combat on the Sabbath.[146] From 1915 to 1916 Hertz even permitted soldiers to undertake otherwise prohibited activities when they were only in training.[147] Hertz recognised that it would be impossible to provide soldiers with kosher food, but held that 'a great deal of . . . observance would be possible' for a man in uniform.[148] Hertz sought to maximise the level of possible observance by negotiating with the government about general policy, and seeking concessions in individual cases, for example regarding leave for festivals.[149] Requests for such concessions became more intense after 1916, when Jews holding Russian nationality were allowed to enlist and the number of observant Jews in the forces thereby increased.[150]

On the home front, Hertz was eager to comply with war regulations, such as the blackout. As such, he ruled that there should be no *Kol nidre* service on Yom Kippur 1939 and that the closing service (*neilah*) should be held early to finish before the blackout. As it would end before the close of the fast, Hertz pointed out that the shofar, which cannot be blown on Yom Kippur itself, should not be sounded at the end of the service.[151] On some of these questions it is clear that Hertz pushed the boundaries close to the edge of halakhic acceptability to enable Jews to contribute to the war effort. Of course, there is a world of difference between operating on the edge of the acceptable, and venturing beyond that, into sanctioning the unacceptable.

It is also important to note the motivation for Hertz's accommodating attitude. If Jews were seen not to be contributing to the war effort the resentment felt towards them by the general community would have been immense, promoting anti-Semitism and endangering the position of Jews in Britain. There is evidence that such feeling existed among the general population. After Hertz visited Flanders in 1914 Sir John French felt the need to issue a dispatch saying 'anyone who now chooses to question Jewish loyalty and military ardour does so in defiance of the declaration of the Commander-in-Chief of the British Army', yet in 1915 *The Times* accused the Jewish community's response to the call for recruits of being 'patchy'.[152] More significantly in terms of Hertz's ruling on *Cohanim*, when the Leeds Beth Din supported their town's *Cohanim*'s objections to military service, which was expressed at a protest meetings, anti-Semitic agitation was sparked off.[153]

These incidents could be understood as Hertz suspending *halakhah* in order to safeguard the position of British Jews, and therefore demonstrating that his halakhic loyalty only went so far, and that for all his vocal defence of Jewish law there were cases when he was willing to push it to one side. However, we can suggest a more complex interpretation. In each of these wartime cases it should be noted that Hertz did not perceive that he was dispensing with the *halakhah*, but rather interpreting it to take account of the circumstances, as all halakhic rulings must do. It is possible to dispute whether the decisions were halakhically correct, but importantly they were taken within the context of Jewish law. Hertz did not think that circumstances required breaking *halakhah*; rather, he thought the *halakhah* permitted otherwise unacceptable behaviour. The World Wars were therefore a microcosm of Hertz's whole rabbinate. He was balancing external pressure for change from his community and the demands of *halakhah*, which he was committed to upholding.

Even though Hertz's authority was ultimately based on consent, he still said 'no' when he believed he had to. This is what set him apart from the adaptation school. At the same time, Hertz tried to find a way to say 'yes' if he felt that was possible with integrity, for he knew that if his followers were dissatisfied there was nothing to prevent them leaving his congregations, or even Judaism entirely. This expansive attitude separated Hertz from some of his fellow traditionalists in the acknowledgement and antipathy schools, who adopted a vanguard approach, and for whom little or no change was acceptable. On the other hand, Hertz did find allies from the antipathy school, primarily Hillman and Abramsky, who, although they rejected modernity on principle, accepted it as a reality and were willing to tolerate it and made halakhic calculations about what leniencies to employ to maintain allegiance to traditional observance. For while all traditionalists were committed to *halakhah* there was disagreement among them about the strategies to adopt in its implementation.

Hertz's powers came not only from the United Synagogue but also from the Board of Deputies of British Jews. The Board was responsible under the terms of the 1836 Marriage Registration Act for certifying congregations as Jewish for the purposes of conducting marriages, and they left the decision to the Haham for Sefardim and the Chief Rabbi for Ashkenazim. This power involved Hertz in two major controversies regarding synagogues at either end of the Jewish religious spectrum: the Liberal Jewish Synagogue in London and the Gateshead Hebrew Congregation.

In 1934 the Liberal Jewish Synagogue, which Hertz had attacked in *The new paths* less than a decade earlier began to press for his recognition so that they could solemnise marriages valid in English law.[154] Chief Rabbi Hermann Adler had said in 1902 that their 'service cannot, I maintain, be considered a Jewish service' and had not granted them recognition.[155] Neither Nathan Adler nor Solomon Hirschell recognised West London, and in order to conduct marriages the synagogue had to pass a private act of parliament in 1856.[156] Hertz agonised over the decision, writing that he did not want to be seen as bestowing a *'hechsher* [a certificate of ritual fitness, most often used for food] on the Liberal Synagogue'.[157]

Ultimately, Hertz did grant recognition in a carefully worded statement. He wrote 'although I strongly disapprove of the religious practices and principles of the Liberal Synagogue, I am not justified in declaring that they have left the ranks of Jewry . . . If that had been the case, they would not have been given representation on the Board of Deputies, if the recognition . . . is now denied then they will, as Berkeley

Street have done years ago, seek relief by Act of Parliament. Such a course would . . . bring with it a discussion in Parliament of minor religious difference. I feel that such a discussion would be especially undesirable at the present moment . . . the Chief Rabbinate can take no responsibility for the legality or otherwise in Jewish law of any ritual act performed by the ministers of that Congregation'.[158] It seems, therefore, that Hertz recognised the Liberal Jewish Synagogue for the same reason he attended the opening of the Stern Hall of the West London: to foster Jewish unity in a difficult time and prevent the community looking bad in front of the non-Jewish population.[159]

One repercussion from the agitation of the Liberals was that Gateshead also received its marriage secretary. Hertz was disinclined to recognise Gateshead because they refused to accept his authority.[160] This was a continuation of the Adlers' policy of religious centralisation, but once Hertz recognised the Liberals it became untenable to deny the same to the highly observant Jews of Gateshead.[161] Their certification was approved on the very day that the Liberals received theirs, in January 1935.[162] These two examples show Hertz attempting to preserve his religious authority, in the case of the Liberals to suppress heresy. In the case of Gateshead, Hertz was worried about insubordination, and (if we wish to be charitable) a general concern not to encourage new congregations, lest they sap the strength of existing congregations.[163] However, in both cases Hertz gave way, forced by the pressure of circumstances.

The final area of Hertz's activity concerns matters where he possessed influence rather than power. In 1929 Hertz tried to prevent the BBC from broadcasting a service from the Liberal Jewish Synagogue.[164] Further afield, Hertz used his influence as President of the Institute of Jewish Studies of the Hebrew University of Jerusalem to stop ZP Chajes, who accepted Biblical Criticism, from delivering an inaugural lectureship at the university.[165] Chajes upheld *halakhah*, and as such belongs in the acknowledgement school, but his views on the Pentateuch made him a non-traditional member. For Hertz that made him unacceptable, hence his efforts to prevent him lecturing at the Hebrew University. On the other hand, Hertz was willing to co-operate with the adaptation school and others of lesser traditionalism on non-theological matters, when unity would strengthen the message he wanted to convey. For example, in 1927 the wall of the Bancroft Road cemetery was in a state of collapse and was due to be demolished, raising the prospect of desecration of graves. Hertz wrote a letter to the *Jewish Chronicle* to appeal for money to rebuild the wall. The letter was also signed by, among others,

Morris Joseph, Minister Emeritus of the West London Synagogue, and an ideological opponent of Hertz.[166] Despite their theological differences there is evidence that Hertz got on well, on a personal level, with the Liberal leaders Israel Abrahams and Montefiore – and, at first, the American Reform leader, Stephen S. Wise.[167] That supports the impression given by Hertz's written statements that theological differences did not necessitate any diminution in love among Jews.

Hertz also attempted to contain the Union of Orthodox Hebrew Congregations, formed around the highly traditional Adath Yisroel Synagogue in 1924.[168] Hertz resented the name of the organisation, which he felt implied that they were orthodox while he and the United Synagogue were not. He protested in private that their name was 'pure fake' and that 'for twenty years I have been fighting all power in the community[,] in favour of orthodoxy'.[169] This antagonism towards the Adath diminished after 1940, when Hertz's daughter married its spiritual leader, Solomon Schonfeld. Indeed in 1944 Hertz supported Schonfeld's attempt to sue Waley Cohen for slander for suggesting that he was trying to set himself up as Deputy Chief Rabbi. That confrontation caused a complete breakdown in the already difficult relationship between Hertz and Waley Cohen, and the United Synagogue Honorary Officers even discussed removing Hertz from office.[170]

Provincial communities outside the United Synagogue were difficult for Hertz to control, as we have seen in the case of Gateshead. One congregation fiercely protective of its independence was Oxford, which tended to look to Jewish scholars from its own ranks for religious guidance. Before the Second World War, Herbert Loewe, who taught rabbinics at Oxford University, filled this role. Hertz's relationship with Loewe began very well. As a soldier Loewe had written to Hertz in 1915 to ask what he could do on the Sabbath.[171] Hertz quoted Loewe approvingly and at length in his *Affirmations of Judaism* in 1927.[172] However, Hertz subsequently came to feel that Loewe was undermining traditional Judaism. Like Chajes, this was because Loewe was a non-traditionalist of the acknowledgement school – he upheld *halakhah*, but accepted the findings of Biblical Criticism on the Pentateuch.[173] Loewe suspected that Hertz was attempting to use financial pressure to force him to accept the Chief Rabbi's authority.[174]

Hertz was an ardent Zionist from his earliest years. In 1917 he used his influence to further the fulfilment of Zionism. Before the British Government issued the Balfour Declaration, it decided to ask leading British Jews whether they supported the founding of a Jewish homeland in Palestine.[175] They had seen there was significant Jewish opposition to Zionism, and if they were going to issue a statement to attract

Jewish support they wanted to be sure it would have that effect.[176] The government consulted eight leading Jews. Three were against the idea, one was neutral. The other four, including Hertz, were in favour. There was thus a narrow majority in support and, as Landman has written 'a negative or even a hesitant reply from Dr Hertz would have severely, if not fatally, prejudiced the chances of the Declaration'.[177] Stuart Cohen described Hertz's reply as a 'crucially favourable response'.[178]

Hertz had to employ tact in his relations with other faiths. In 1933 a Mr M. Collins attempted to stop the Golders Green parish church ringing its bells on Sunday as he found it a disturbance. He attempted to enlist Hertz in his campaign. Hertz firmly refused to assist Collins and expressed strong opposition to Collins's efforts, writing, 'unless he is to be grossly disloyal to his people there is one disability which every Jew is bound to place upon himself in this country; and that is to refrain from associating himself in any way, directly or indirectly, in any interference with the religious exercises of our fellow citizens of other faiths'.[179] Hertz's concern was therefore as much for the well-being of Jews as the religious freedom of Christians, who would take a dim view of Jews trying to restrict their religious freedom. Jewish well-being was also the reason that Hertz became involved in some interfaith activity, especially during the Second World War, although that never included theological discussion. He attended the World Congress of Faiths in 1943 and used it as a platform to defend Judaism and call attention to Nazi persecution, as he had been doing for some time.[180] When Hertz joined the Council of Christians and Jews he did so, according to H.M. Lazarus, on the condition that 'the fundamental principle of each religious denomination shall, in no way, by this co-operation suffer the slightest attenuation' testifying to his willingness to work with other faiths, but only on issues other than theology.[181] A final example of Hertz attempting to exert influence beyond his authority was his attempt in 1923 to influence elections to the Board of Deputies.[182]

We have surveyed the most important features of Hertz's practical religious policy, which he modelled to suit a time when a rabbi's word was no longer simply accepted by an acquiescent community. He invested huge efforts in persuading people of his views through sermons, speeches and writings. He employed an expansive approach and tried to find leniencies within *halakhah* in order to satisfy as many demands for change as possible and keep as many within the fold of traditional Judaism as he could, but he refused to permit anything which he thought violated *halakhah*. He used his powers as Chief Rabbi to enforce discipline amongst those who were obliged to accept his authority, such as his ministers, and he used the prestige of his office and his person to influence those over whom he exercised no direct authority. This helped to sustain Hertz's and the Chief Rabbinate's hegemony as the acknowledged central authority for the vast majority of Anglo-Jewry, which he inherited from Adler and passed on to Israel Brodie.

To be sure there were other factors, which Endelman and others have identified – British conservatism rubbing off on Anglo-Jews, the inconvenience of moving congregations, and tolerance towards Jews in British society which meant they felt little pressure to play down their Jewishness to name but three – but we should also acknowledge the role played by Hertz and the effect of his policies in maintaining in the United Synagogue a traditional body where the non-traditional felt comfortable, and the power of his advocacy in engendering support for his variety of Judaism. Hertz's activities were a result and a reflection of his theology. He was a traditionalist within the scientific branch of the acknowledgement school. He preached the *Wissenschaft*-influenced but traditional Judaism of his teachers at the JTS, and he practised and promoted it. He led Anglo-Jewry and he promoted its well-being in the general community. This helped to secure the dominance of the United Synagogue during Hertz's time, and after it. To take just one statistic, between 1912 and 1945 no fewer than 34 new congregations joined the United Synagogue.[183] We should now place Hertz's policies in context. In particular, examples from Germany, France and America of rabbis attempting to balance demands for change or the circumstances of the time with *halakhah*, and their reliance on new methods of persuasion and influence in place of the old rabbinic fiat, will deepen our understanding of Hertz's policy.

Hertz's theological position was shared by a group of Jewish leaders, for example Morais in America, and Hoffman and Weinberg in Berlin. In 1913 the JTS organised the congregations associated with it into the United Synagogue of America (USA) and Hertz delivered the invocation at the founding meeting.[184] The USA represented, in theory, the ideals that Hertz believed in, but it did not implement them. We have already seen one example of that, the introduction of mixed pews at Hertz's synagogue at Syracuse. In the following years, USA congregations permitted changes that Hertz never allowed in England. For example, in 1927 the United Synagogue of America published a Festival prayer book, which replaced the prayer for the restitution of the Temple service with a prayer recalling that the Temple service once took place, whereas Hertz left the text untouched, despite the difficulties some of his congregants found with it.[185]

There were some who hoped USA congregations would be traditional but acculturated, with English sermons and decorum but maintaining the traditional ritual, rather like London's Great or Bayswater synagogues.[186] However, most members of the United Synagogue of America deviated from this traditionalist vision, and less than half of the 21 founding synagogues of the USA held services which would have been acceptable in London's United Synagogue. The others featured mixed pews, organs on the Sabbath and heavily revised prayer books.[187] These changes were not prompted by a rejection of tradition; indeed membership of the USA was a statement of attachment to tradition. But this attachment was in many cases merely nostalgic, and insufficient to withstand a desire to be more American.

For example, the Temple of Aaron in St Paul was described as a place where 'conservatism was absolutely necessary to promote Modern American Judaism [and where] the old traditional form of the Jewish Ritual should be followed, omitting such portions of it that would not interest the younger folks'. Similarly, Shaare Zion of Sioux City sought 'a modern form of Jewish worship that would appeal to the growing generation of American Jews and at the same time safeguard the best Jewish traditions'. Shaarey Tefila of Far Rockaway was committed to 'retaining the authority of Israel's past, yet expressing that authority in the accents of America's present'.[188] A similar sentiment existed in Britain, which is why synagogues such as Hampstead sought to find a way to associate themselves with the Chief Rabbinate. The Chief Rabbis were able to exploit this nostalgia to protect *halakhah* and keep communities within the boundaries of tradition.

Mordechai M. Kaplan highlighted this division within the United Synagogue of America in his *Judaism as civilisation*. He divided the American Conservative movement into 'Left wing of Neo-orthodoxy' and 'Right wing of reformism'.[189] Both groups were more traditional than the adaptation school's Union of American Hebrew Congregations, and should therefore be classed as part of the acknowledgement school. However, as Kaplan showed, while the first group shared Hertz's theological stance and *halakhic* requirements, the second group did not. Kaplan highlighted the textbook by Julius Greenstone, an early graduate of the JTS, as an example of the first group's approach. Greenstone affirmed the revelation at Sinai, the binding nature of *halakhah*, the belief in the coming of the Messiah and the rebuilding of the Temple in Jerusalem.[190] Kaplan described the other group, which we have called the non-traditional wing of the acknowledgement school, as 'Conservative Reformism'. He argued that notwithstanding their insistence on *halakhah*, their rejection of the revelation at Sinai made their theology effectively 'identical with that of unqualified reform-ism' (adaptation school). They simply refused to 'accept the logical consequences of that philosophy'.[191] This analysis, which could equally be applied to Z.P. Chajes, is further evidence of the fundamental split within the acknowledgement school, which in terms of mutual acceptance and recognition was more profound than the split between the antipathy school and the traditionalists of the acknowledgement school. The presence of non-traditionalist members within the United Synagogue of America caused anguish to members of the JTS faculty, for example Moses Hyamson, who felt he could not accept the presi-dency of the seminary because that would associate him too closely with synagogues with unacceptable practices.[192]

There were three reasons why the JTS faculty could not prevent synagogues associated with it from deviating from what they believed was appropriate behaviour. First, in an attempt to provide a counter-weight to Reform among English- (as opposed to Yiddish-) speaking congregations, the United Synagogue of America opened its doors to a wide range of congregations, and once a synagogue with untradi-tional practices had been accepted it was difficult to enforce greater stringency.[193] This promoted an organisation which was a confederacy rather than a union, in which it was difficult to impose central control. Secondly, there was little attempt to impose control and an absence of firm leadership. The seminary faculty sought to promote a more tradi-tional form of worship through influence rather than instruction. Hertz, by contrast, was not reluctant to lay down the law to the congregations under his authority. However, there was no rabbinical leader in the United Synagogue of America with comparable powers to Hertz's in London, who could do so.[194]

However, it is not certain that the seminary leaders would have asserted their authority even if they had enjoyed it. The JTS devel-oped into a rather more open institution than any Hertz presided over. For example, Mordecai M. Kaplan denied the existence of God, but remained on the JTS faculty.[195] The confederate structure of the USA thus led to (and was reinforced by) a situation where power was pulled centrifugally, away from the centre towards individual congre-gations. Thus the USA did not publish a statement of appropriate ritual behaviour until the 1950s, and even then it was not binding on its congregations.[196] However the centrifugal context meant that even the Orthodox Union, an institution with a less open attitude, a highly traditional leadership and which disapproved of the JTS and the USA, tolerated synagogues with mixed pews. This suggests that the over-whelming factor in America was the social context, not the inclination

of the religious leadership.[197] Another community with religious practices which did not conform to Hertz's standards was the French
Consistoire. We have already noted Hertz's scathing reference to
the French practice of a non-Jew playing a synagogue organ on the
Sabbath as the activity of 'a few assimilationist Jews . . . who do not act
in accordance with our Din'.[198] French rabbis were faced with similar,
if more intense pressures than Hertz, but they conceded ground where
Hertz held firm. It was a difference of degree, but for Hertz, as for Adler,
the difference was decisive.

These, then, are two examples of leaderships which officially shared
Hertz's theology but were less traditional in practice, whether because
of greater tolerance, a lack of authority or a different interpretation of
halakhah. Hertz was closer in practice, as well as in theory, to his Berlin
contemporary, J.J. Weinberg, just as Adler was closer to Weinberg's
predecessors, Hildesheimer and Hoffman. Although traditional Jews
in Germany were a small minority, Weinberg was determined to maintain the allegiance of as many as possible. Weinberg therefore adopted
an expansive approach, although circumstances prevented him from
establishing hegemony. Like Hertz, he strove to find ways within *halakhah* to satisfy demands for change. He conceded where he thought
it was possible and desirable to do so, but was firm when he felt he
had to be. In 1933 the Nazis banned the slaughter of animals without
pre-stunning. The halakhic consensus was that pre-stunning made the
animal non-kosher. Weinberg, then the leading halakhist in Germany,
found ways to permit the stunning to take place without rendering the
animal non-kosher, which were not acted upon because of the opposition of leading eastern European scholars.[199] Nevertheless, this episode
demonstrates Weinberg's willingness to look for a halakhic solution to
a contemporary problem, a willingness not shared by many rabbis of
eastern Europe, who opposed concessions to the times as a matter of
principle.

After the Second World War Weinberg was asked by *Jechurun*,
a Jewish youth movement in France, whether boys and girls could
sing hymns together. A majority of authorities hold that listening to a
woman's voice is a sexual distraction to a man and is therefore forbidden, but Weinberg gave permission. He made a halakhic argument but
he also ruled that even if the prohibition did apply there were reasons
for suspending it. Weinberg argued that the prohibition was not so
much a law as a 'righteous custom and practice of modesty' and could
be over-ridden if circumstances demanded it and that as alienation from
Judaism was a real possibility if *Jechurun* was not allowed to continue,
concerns about women singing could be set aside.[200] Weinberg, like his

Berlin predecessors and like Hertz and Adler in London, balanced *halakhah* with the demands of the time to find a compromise.

Berlin therefore provides the best comparison with Hertz in both theology and practice. The common alignment to the scientific branch of the acknowledgement school of Hertz and the leaders of the Hildesheimer Seminary was combined with a willingness to concede on the points where they believed there was room for manoeuvre, to give traditional Judaism as wide an appeal as possible. This attitude separated Hertz and Berlin from America, where power was dispersed centrifugally and traditionalist leaders found themselves unable or unwilling to prevent practices of which they disapproved, and Paris, where the religious leadership enjoyed authority in theory, but were severely constrained in practice and in an effort to be expansive made rulings which Hertz found unacceptable.

Now we have analysed Hertz in theory and in practice, and placed his response to modernity in context, we can see that the evidence does not support many current historiographical conclusions. The evidence does not suggest either that Hertz's theology was untraditional or that his halakhic standards were low.[201] We have seen where Hertz should be placed in a general typology of the Jewish response to modernity and the power and organisational factors which affected his behaviour and made his approach similar to those of other Jewish leaders, especially JJ Weinberg and his predecessor in London, Hermann Adler.

Notes

1 J.H. Hertz, *Pentateuch and Haftorahs* (London 1960), 402.
2 D. Englander, 'Anglicized not Anglican: Jews and Judaism in Victorian Britain' in Parsons (ed), *Religion in Victorian Britain, I:Traditions* (Manchester 1988), 236.
3 Hertz Papers, Southampton University Library (HP SUL) 175/70/3; E. Levine, 'Memoir' in Epstein (ed), *Joseph Herman Hertz, 1871–1946: In Memoriam* (London 1947), 2.
4 R.E. Fierstein, *A different spirit: the Jewish Theological Seminary of America, 1886–1902* (New York 1990), 95–96.
5 HP SUL MS 175 44/3.
6 M. Davis, *The emergence of Conservative Judaism: the historical school in 19th-century America* (Philadelphia 1963), 315; M.L. Raphael, *Profiles in American Judaism* (San Francisco 1984), 137.
7 HP SUL MS 175 70/3.
8 M. Freud Kandel, 'The theological background of Dr Joseph H. Hertz' *Le'eyla* 48 (2000), 28.
9 HP SUL MS 175 37/2.

10 HP SUL MS 175 37/2.

11 HP SUL MS 175 25/4.

12 HP SUL MS 175 30/10.

13 HP SUL MS 175 25/2.

14 Levine, 'Memoir', 3.

15 HP SUL MS 175 37/2.

16 Levine, 'Memoir', 3.

17 I. Epstein (ed), *Joseph Herman Hertz, 1871–1946: In Memoriam* (London 1947), 74.

18 HP SUL MS 175 37/2.

19 Raphael, *Profiles in American Judaism*, 92–3, 96.

20 M. Freud Kandel, *Orthodox Judaism in Britain since 1913* (London 2006), 28, 50.

21 A.M. Hyamson, *Jews' College, London, 1855–1955* (London 1955),. 84; I. Epstein, 'Adolph Buchler' in Brodie and Rabbinowitz (ed), *Studies in Jewish History* (Oxford 1956), xiv–xxi; E. Marmorstein 'My father, a memoir' in Rabbinowitz and Lew (ed) *Studies in Jewish Theology* (London 1950), xxiii.

22 Levine, 'Memoir', 4.

23 HP SUL MS 175 44/6.

24 J.H. Hertz, *Early and late* (Hindhead, Surrey 1943), 126–127.

25 Ibid., 132.

26 Levine, 'Memoir', 4.

27 H. Meirovich, *A vindication of Judaism* (New York 1998), 14–18.

28 M. Scult, 'Schechter's Seminary' in Wertheimer (ed), *Tradition renewed* (New York 1997), I 63.

29 *Jewish Chronicle* (7 March 1902), 13.

30 J.S. Gurock, 'Yeshiva students at the Jewish Theological Seminary' in Wertheimer (ed) *Tradition renewed* (New York 1997) I 491.

31 See M. Hyamson, *The Oral Law* (London 1910), 1–10.

32 Chief Rabbinate Papers, London Metropolitan Archive (CRP LMA) ACC 2805/3/1/33.

33 Hertz, *Early and late*, 143.

34 HP SUL MS 175 22/1.

35 Levine, 'Memoir', 26.

36 C. Roth, 'Britain's three Chief Rabbis' in Jung (ed), *Jewish Leaders* (Jerusalem 1953), 490.

37 A. Altman, 'Memorial Address' in Gottleib (ed), *Essays and addresses in memory of JH Hertz* (London 1948), 5.

38 S.M. Lehrman in Gottleib (ed) *Essays and addresses in memory of J.H. Hertz* (London 1948), 34–35.

39 Roth, 'Chief Rabbis', 485.

40 J.H. Hertz, *Sermons, addresses and studies* (London 1938) [hereafter *SAS*], I:12.

41 See, for example, Hertz, *Early and late*, 153–159.

42 Hertz, *Early and late*, 122, 124.
43 M. Persoff, *Faith against reason: religious reform and the British Chief Rabbinate, 1840–1990* (London 2008), 156.
44 Ibid., 132–133.
45 Hertz, *SAS*, I 305–311.
46 HP SUL MS 175 30/2.
47 J.H. Hertz, *Affirmations of Judaism* (Oxford 1927), 149–185.
48 Ibid., 11–145.
49 A. Newman, *Chief Rabbi Dr. Joseph H. Hertz, C.H.* (London 1973), 16.
50 CRP LMA ACC 2805/4/5/44.
51 Persoff, *Faith against reason*, 113.
52 Newman, *Hertz*, 16.
53 M. Persoff, *Faith against reason*, 231.
54 Hertz, *Early and late*, 142.
55 M. Freud Kandel, *Orthodox Judaism in Britain* (London 2006), 80.
56 CRP LMA ACC 2805/2/6/35.
57 Hertz, *Affirmations*, 103, 114.
58 Hertz, *SAS*, 265–292.
59 Roth, 'Chief Rabbis', 488–489.
60 See, for example, Hertz, *Early and late*, 194–196.
61 Newman, *Hertz*, 10–11.
62 Ibid., 11.
63 J.H. Hertz, 'Zionism – a reply by the Chief Rabbi' *Fortnightly Review* (1916), 1032–1035.
64 Hertz, *SAS*, II 233–234; Roth, 'Chief Rabbis', 486–7.
65 Roth, 'Chief Rabbis', 486.
66 United Synagogue Papers, London Metropolitan Archive (USP LMA) ACC 3400/2/1/79.
67 Hertz, *Early and late*, 142.
68 Newman, *Hertz*, 12; Roth, 'Chief Rabbis', 489.
69 J.H. Hertz (ed) *A book of Jewish thoughts* (New York 1926), vii–viii.
70 Hertz, *SAS*, I:12.
71 H. Adler, *Anglo-Jewish memories* (London 1909), 84–86.
72 Meirovich, *Vindication*, 27.
73 Ibid., 29–30.
74 Ibid., 167.
75 J.H. Hertz, *The authorised daily prayer book* (New York 1948) [hereafter *ADPB*], 14, 19, 589, 967.
76 I. Finestein, *Anglo-Jewry in changing times* (London 1999), 237; *Jewish Chronicle* (24 May 1912); *Report on the Sabbath reading of the Scriptures in a triennial cycle* (London 1913).
77 Newman, *Hertz*, 15.
78 Meirovich, *Vindication*, 23.
79 L. Jacobs, *Helping with inquiries* (London 1989), 106.
80 Meirovich, *Vindication*, 23.

81 *Jewish Chronicle* (13 sAugust 1915), 6.
82 Jacobs, *Helping with inquiries*, 106.
83 Meirovich, *Vindication*, 29; HP SUL MS 175 61/6.
84 Marmorstein, 'My father', xxiii; S. Daiches, *Essays and addresses* (London 1955), 59, 82–83.
85 Hyamson, *Jews' College*, 115.
86 Jacobs, *Helping with inquiries*, 120; Meirovich, *Vindication*, 45.
87 I. Epstein, *The faith of Judaism* (London 1954), for example, 119–120.
88 Meirovich, *Vindication*, 40, 25; I. Epstein, *Judaism of tradition* (London 1931), 20–25.
89 CRP LMA ACC 2805/30/5/28.
90 HP SUL MS 175 61/6.
91 Interview with Isaac Levy, 21 May 2004.
92 Hyamson, *Jews' College*, 116, 120.
93 *Jewish Chronicle* (17 February 1950), 15.
94 HP SUL MS 175 50/4.
95 Meirovich, *Vindication*, 25.
96 CRP LMA ACC 2805 4/1/47.
97 Ibid.
98 Meirovich, *Vindication*, 26.
99 Persoff, *Faith against reason*, 245.
100 Meirovich, *Vindication*, 26; CRP LMA ACC 2805 4/1/47.
101 Hertz, *Early and late*, 142.
102 See J. Jung, *Champions of orthodoxy* (London 1974), 71–100 for a detailed description of Chaikin and his career.
103 Hillman Papers, Jewish and National Library, Jerusalem 401515/0285.
104 Hertz, *SAS*, I:325.
105 See A. Feldman, *The parables and similes of the rabbis* (Cambridge 1924).
106 Jung *Champions*, 100; London Beth Din Papers, London Metropolitan Archive (LBDP LMA) ACC 2712/15/1161.
107 USP LMA ACC 2712/15/1161.
108 HP SUL MS 175 30/12.
109 USP LMA ACC 2712/15/1161; B. Homa, *A fortress in Anglo-Jewry* (London 1953), 86.
110 R. Apple, *The Hampstead Synagogue* (London 1967), 85.
111 B. Homa, *Orthodoxy in Anglo-Jewry* (London 1969), 30.
112 USP LMA ACC 2712/15/1161.
113 CRP LMA ACC/2805/4/1/22; ACC/2805/14/9/33.
114 USP LMAACC 2712/15/1161.
115 USP ACC 2172/15/1161B.
116 Homa, *Orthodoxy in Anglo-Jewry*, 26.
117 USP LMA ACC 2712/15/1161.
118 Ibid.
119 Ibid.

120 Ibid.
121 Ch. Bermant, *Lord Jakobovits* (London 1990), 103, 28.
122 USP LMA ACC 2712/15/1554; J.M. Shaftesley, 'A biographical sketch' in Zimmels, Rabbinowitz and Finestein (ed), *Essays presented to Chief Rabbi Israel Brodie on the occasion of his seventieth birthday* (London 1967), xxiv.
123 T. Endelman, *The Jews of Britain, 1656 to 2000* (Berkeley 2002), 250.
124 USP LMA ACC 2712/15/1161.
125 HP SUL MS 175 49/7.
126 For example, Adolph Buchler: HP SUL MS 175 61/6; and Robert Waley Cohen: USP LMA ACC 2712/6/34/1.
127 HP SUL MS 175 35/11.
128 LBDP LMA ACC 3400/4/1/1/2; Interview, Chimen Abramsky, 25 October 2004.
129 Interview, Chimen Abramsky, 25 October 2004.
130 Endelman, *Jews of Britain*, 167.
131 CRP LMA ACC/2805/4/5/44.
132 HP SUL MS 175 35/7 and see *Report on the triennial cycle*. This is an interesting example of the place Hertz assigned to *Wissenschaft* and traditional methods of halakhic decision making. Evidence suggests (some of it unearthed by Buchler) that the triennial cycle was practised by Palestinian Jewry in the early period after the destruction of the Second Temple. Yet, both Buchler and Hertz rejected the call for the triennial cycle's reintroduction because what mattered for them was not what took place 1800 years earlier, but the rabbinical consensus on what was to be done in their own day, and that was to use the annual cycle.
133 R. Apple, *Mixed choirs in Jewish worship* (unpublished 2001), 12.
134 HP SUL MS 175 35/7.
135 CRP LMA ACC/3400/2/2/69.
136 M. Breuer, trans. E. Petuchowski, *Modernity within tradition* (New York 1992), 32.
137 HP SUL MS 175 49/7.
138 R. Apple, *The Hampstead Synagogue* (London 1967), 16.
139 Hertz, *ADPB* (New York 1948), 532–533.
140 HP SUL MS 175 49/7.
141 Hertz, *Pentateuch*, 933.
142 HP SUL MS 175 53/2.
143 HP SUL MS 175 49/7.
144 Important works on Jews and the First World War include D. Cesarani, 'An embattled minority: the Jews in Britain during the First World War' in *Immigrants and Minorities* 8/1 (1989), 61–81; M. Levene, *War, Jews and the new Europe: the diplomacy of Lucien Wolf, 1914–1919* (Oxford 1992); and E. Levy, 'Anti-Semitism in England at war, 1914–1916' in *Patterns of Prejudice* 4/5 (1970), 27–30.
145 J. Hyman, *Jews in Britain during the Great War* (Working Papers in

Economic and Social History No. 51, University of Manchester Department of History, 2001), 30, 33; J.H. Hertz, letter to ministers, 19 May 1939.

146 CRP LMA ACC/2805/4/4/6.

147 Hyman, *Jews during the Great War*, 19, 28.

148 J.H. Hertz, letter to ministers, 19 May 1939.

149 Hyman, *Jews during the Great War*, 29.

150 Ibid., 29.

151 HP SUL MS 175 66/5; J.H. Hertz, letter to ministers, 21 August 1940.

152 Hyman, *Jews during the Great War*, 16, 21–22 .

153 Ibid., 30–31.

154 Homa, *Orthodoxy in Anglo-Jewry*, 34.

155 H. Adler, *The old paths* (London 1902).

156 Homa, *Orthodoxy in Anglo-Jewry*, 35.

157 CRP LMA ACC/2805/4/1/22.

158 Homa, *Orthodoxy in Anglo-Jewry*, 34–35. Hertz was right; when the Liberals' certificate was revoked after Hertz's death by Dayan Lazarus, acting as Deputy for the Chief Rabbi, the Liberals did pass their own Act of Parliament (B. Homa, *Footprints in the sands of time* [Charfield, Gloucester, 1990], 150–151).

159 Persoff argues that Hertz issued his ruling against the opposition of Abramsky; if this is the case, it undermines the argument, put forward by Persoff amongst others, that Abramsky exerted profound influence over Hertz. Persoff, *Faith against reason*, 236, 252.

160 Ibid., 33.

161 CRP LMA ACC/2805/4/2/43.

162 Homa, *Orthodoxy in Anglo-Jewry*, 35.

163 LBDP LMA ACC 3400/2/1/78.

164 CRP LMA ACC/2805/4/1/13.

165 Meirovich, *Vindication*, 9.

166 A. Barnett, *The Western Synagogue through two centuries* (London 1961), 101.

167 HP SUL MS 175 54/8; CRP LMA ACC/2805/4/43; HP SUL MS 175 30/2.

168 USP LMA ACC 2712/15/1161; Homa, *Footprints*, 77.

169 USP LMA ACC 2712/15/1161.

170 USP LMA ACC 2712/15/1/43, 2712/7/4/43.

171 Hyman, *Jews during the Great War*, 19.

172 Hertz, *Affirmations*, 61.

173 C.G. Montefiore and H. Lowe (ed), *A rabbinic anthology* (London 1938), lxiv–lxv.

174 HP LMA MS 175 30/1.

175 S. Landman, 'Origins of the Balfour Declaration: Dr Hertz's contribution' in Epstein, Levine and Roth (ed), *Essays in honour of the Very Rev. J.H. Hertz* (London 1942), 261.

176 Ibid., 266–267.

177 Ibid., 269.

178 S.A. Cohen, *English Zionists and British Jews* (Princeton 1982), 190. Cohen argues, however, that after 1917 Hertz kept his Zionism more discreet for a few years, and was not as supportive as Weizmann would have liked (190–191). Mayir Verete has argued that the Balfour Declaration was not issued because of Zionist lobbying but was based on hard-headed British imperial calculations, principally to keep France out of Palestine, but also to enlist the support of Russian and American Jews: M. Verete, 'The Balfour Declaration and its makers' *Middle Eastern Studies* 6:1 (January 1970). Tom Segev is of the view that the Declaration was the result of Lloyd George's fantasy that the Jews controlled the world, and that Britain would benefit by aligning herself to their cause: T. Segev, *One Palestine, complete: Jews and Arabs under the British Mandate* (London 2000) 33, 43, 45. These views are not incompatible, however, with the notion that Hertz's attitude played a part in procuring the Declaration, because if the aim of the British Government was to curry favour with Jews, as both Verete and Segev suggest to a greater or lesser extent, they would want to make sure that expressing support for Zionism would have such an effect, and the opposition of the Jewish cabinet minister Edwin Montagu to Zionism might make them doubt that. The government certainly felt impelled to conduct its survey of opinion, which implies it cared about the answers it received.
179 LBDP LMA ACC 3400/2/1/79. The phrase 'grossly disloyal' was suggested by Robert Waley Cohen, which suggests that the two were capable of closer co-operation than is sometimes supposed.
180 Hertz, *Early and late*, 197–199, 51.
181 H.M. Lazarus, 'Hesped', in Gottlieb (ed), *Essays and addresses in memory of J.H. Hertz* (London 1948), 30.
182 LBDP LMA ACC 3400/2/1/79.
183 W.D. Rubinstein, *A history of the Jews in the English-speaking world: Great Britain* (London 1996), 234–235.
184 Meirovich, *Vindication*, 14.
185 D. Ellenson, *After Emancipation* (Cincinnati 2004), 482.
186 Raphael, *Profiles in American Judaism*, 96.
187 J. Waxman, 'Mi vaMi HaHolkhim' in Ginor (ed) *Yakar Le'Mordecai* (New York 1998), 283–326.
188 Raphael, *Profiles in American Judaism*, 92.
189 M.M. Kaplan, *Judaism as a civilisation* (New York 1934), 126, 160.
190 Ibid., 166.
191 Ibid., 127.
192 I. Robinson, 'Cyrus Adler: President of the Jewish Theological Seminary 1915–40' in Wertheimer (ed), *Tradition renewed* (New York 1997), I:125; see also J.S. Gurock, 'Yeshiva students at the Jewish Theological Seminary' in Wertheimer (ed), *Tradition renewed* (New York 1997), I:509.
193 Waxman, 'Mi vaMi HaHolkhim', 283.
194 J. Wertheimer, 'JTS and the Conservative Movement' in Wertheimer (ed), *Tradition renewed* (New York 1997), II:414–415.

195 J.S. Gurock and J.J. Schachter, *A modern heretic and a traditional community: Mordecai M. Kaplan, orthodoxy and American Judaism* (New York 1997), 110–111.

196 Raphael, *Profiles in American Judaism*, 119–121.

197 J.S. Gurock, 'Twentieth-century American orthodoxy's era of non-observance, 1900–1960' *Torah u-Madda Journal* 4 (2000), 92.

198 CRP LMA ACC/2805/4/5/44.

199 M. Shapiro, *Between the yeshiva world and modern orthodoxy: the life and times of Rabbi Jehiel Jacob Weinberg* (Oxford 1999), 117–129.

200 S. Berman, 'Kol Isha' in Landman (ed), *Rabbi Joseph H. Lookstein memorial volume* (New York 1980), 63.

201 G. Alderman, *Modern British Jewry* (Oxford 1992), 355, 359; Endelman, *The Jews of Britain*, 221. (For example Endelman refers to Hertz's 'live and let live attitude towards Liberal and Reform congregations', which is not a traditional position, nor was it Hertz's, as his sermons *The new paths* demonstrate.) See also 251, where Endelman refers to 'the latitudinarianism that was characteristic of Anglo-Jewry during much of its history' and 'the tolerance of the past' and 253 where he described the pre-war United Synagogue as advocating 'moderate traditionalism' as opposed to the 'fundamentalism' of the 1960s and later; Meirovich, *Vindication*, 13–18; M. Freud Kandel, *Ideology forsaken* (PhD thesis, University of Cambridge 2000).

Part III

Post–War developments

Chapter 9

From the Second World War to the Jacobs Affair

THE ANALYSIS PRESENTED in this book of the Chief Rabbis' thought and policies from 1880 until 1945 enables us now to consider developments after that date in their proper context. Scholars have argued that there was a significant shift in the religious character of Anglo-Jewry between 1945 and about 1970, and we can examine whether that was indeed the case. The most significant event in Anglo-Jewish religious history in that period was the Jacobs Affair. It is around that controversy that most discussion is based, and I therefore propose to address it directly and immediately.

Louis Jacobs was born in Manchester in 1920 into a semi-traditional Jewish home, but soon developed a passion for Jewish learning.[1] He attended the Manchester Yeshivah and the Gateshead Kollel, where he gained a reputation as an enormously promising Talmudist.[2] At this point his theological beliefs were entirely conventional, so much so that he attacked Jews' College for its neglect of traditional learning and its inclination towards *Wissenschaft*.[3] After the Second World War, Jacobs became assistant rabbi at the Golders Green Beth Hamedrash.[4] This synagogue's ideology fits within the romantic wing of the acknowledgement school. Its rabbi, E. Munk, had a doctorate in English literature and he and his members scrupulously observed *halakhah*.[5] It was during this time that Jacobs' views changed radically. While serving as Munk's assistant, Jacobs studied for a degree in Semitics at University College London, where he was taught by Siegfried Stein, whom we would place in the non-traditional wing of the acknowledgement school, as one who combined halakhic observance with an acceptance of Biblical criticism on the Pentateuch.[6] Jacobs became convinced that the Documentary Hypothesis was essentially accurate and the Pentateuch was a composite and human work, but that Jewish practice need not be affected.[7]

Jacobs kept his views private. He became rabbi of the Central Synagogue in Manchester in 1948. There he became close to Dr

Alexander Altmann, the Communal Rabbi of Manchester, whose view-point was similar to Stein's, and who cemented Jacobs in his new theological position.[8] In 1954 Jacobs left Manchester and became Minister-Preacher of the New West End Synagogue in London. His induction sermon reflected the approach of traditionalists of the acknowledgement school.[9] He denounced 'fanaticism, intolerance or narrowmindedness' but declared that 'the Torah requires the dedica-tion of the whole of our being to its service'.[10] Most significantly he quoted Hertz, asserting that he would uphold 'the teachings and prac-tices which have come down to the House of Israel through the ages; the positive Jewish beliefs concerning God, the Torah and Israel'.[11] As Jacobs wrote elsewhere, the view that 'God dictated the whole of the five books to Moses, word for word and letter for letter' was 'one held virtually without exception throughout the Talmudic and medieval periods'.[12] In 1954, then, Jacobs was keeping any untraditional views on the Pentateuch to himself.

However, in 1957 Jacobs published *We have reason to believe* in which he argued that Higher Criticism should be accepted, but that the 'respect, reverence and obedience *vis-à-vis* Jewish observance is not radically affected by an "untraditional" outlook on questions of Biblical authorship' because *mitsvot* 'have provided Jews with "ladders to heaven" and still have the power of sanctifying Jewish life . . . because of this we recognise that it was God who gave them and it is His will that we obey when we submit to the Torah discipline'.[13] This approach echoes that of other non-traditionalists from the acknowledgement school, for example Joseph Hochman, who called for a 'faith which seeks God's voice rather in the purpose than in the origins of His commandments'.[14]

It was, however, hotly disputed by traditionalists, such as Isidore Epstein, who saw the Sinaiatic source of *halakhah* as its justification. Epstein wrote, 'the fatal and inherent weakness of those who deny the Divine origin of the Bible, even if their personal religious behaviour conforms to the highest standard, lies in the lack of any valid objec-tive authority for what they teach or affirm'. Epstein argued that the non-traditional wing of the acknowledgement school fell just as short in this regard as the adaptation school, when he said 'thus we come to the real divergence, which, for want of any other name we may call the Orthodox Halacha from any other kind of Halacha such as that emanat-ing from the Conservative no less than Reform schools'.[15] This is why for traditionalists the origin of the Pentateuch was so important; for them the whole of *halakhah* stood on the question, and it was what separated them so completely from both the adaptation school and the non-traditional wing of the acknowledgement school.

We have reason to believe did not receive much attention at the time and in 1959 Jacobs was appointed Moral Tutor at Jews' College, with a view to his succeeding Isidore Epstein as Principal.[16] In the light of later events, this was very odd. Jacobs has hinted that Brodie was not completely happy with his appointment, and Norman Cohen argued that Brodie was bullied into accepting Jacobs by the lay leaders of the college, Alan Mocatta and Lawrence Jacobs.[17] Stefan Reif, a student at the college at the time, has suggested that Brodie, whose relationship with Epstein was not good, initially supported Mocatta's championing of Jacobs as a way of removing Epstein, before he realised the full implications of Jacobs as principal.[18] In any case, Brodie did not exercise his veto in 1959, although he did not permit Jacobs to teach Bible, and later claimed that he thought that Jacobs might moderate his views.[19] Jacobs, however, continued to court controversy once at the college, discussing his untraditional views with students, discarding the traditional head covering for much of the time and attending functions without rabbinical supervision.[20] There were threats of a boycott of Jacobs' lectures and a petition was assembled asking for Epstein's tenure as principal to be extended.[21]

When Epstein retired in 1961, Brodie would not appoint Jacobs as principal and in response Jacobs resigned as Moral Tutor.[22] The controversy spilled out into the wider community, and especially into the *Jewish Chronicle*. It thundered in December 1961 'in this, as in other issues, the Chief Rabbi allows himself to be guided by the extremists of the right . . . [whose] opinions are neither in theory nor practice acceptable to the majority of thinking Jews. They are . . . at variance with the benevolent Anglo-Jewish traditions of tolerance and reasonableness'. In January 1962 the Beth Din announced that Jacobs' views were 'in conflict with authentic Jewish belief and render him unacceptable' as Principal of Jews' College. In May, Brodie declared that his reason for blocking the appointment was Jacobs' 'published views' while Jacobs defended himself at a public meeting in June.[23] Positions were thus clearly established and a conclusion had been reached on the principalship of Jews' College. Jacobs' supporters founded the Society for the Study of Jewish Theology and appointed him Director.[24]

At this point the controversy could have died down, but in 1964 Jacobs' successor at the New West End resigned and the synagogue offered Jacobs his old pulpit. The Chief Rabbi's certificate was needed for the appointed to be made, but Brodie refused to grant it unless Jacobs renounced his views on the Pentateuch, which Jacobs refused to do.[25] Despite pressure from many quarters, including the London Beth Din (a significant point to which we shall return), Brodie refused to relent.[26] The New West End remained adamant that they wanted Jacobs. The result was that the United Synagogue replaced the honorary officers of the New West End.[27] By this time the affair was causing comment in the non-Jewish community, with articles in *The Observer*, *The Times*, *Church Times* and other publications.[28] Jewish figures from around the world became involved, including the future Chief Rabbi Immanuel Jakobovits, who stood firmly behind Brodie.[29] In May 1964, Brodie laid out his position to a meeting of rabbis and ministers. He told them 'an attitude to the Torah . . . which denies its Divine source and unity is directly opposed to orthodox Jewish teaching, and no person holding such views can expect to obtain the approval of the orthodox ecclesiastical authority'.[30] Faced with this impasse, Jacobs' supporters founded the New London Synagogue and installed him as rabbi.[31]

The dominant thesis concerning the Jacobs Affair can be swiftly summarised. Alderman argues that Jacobs' New London Synagogue is, in form at least, identical to pre-war United Synagogues, but that the United Synagogue's 'relentless move to the right' meant that Jacobs' brand of Judaism was out of place by the 1960s.[32] Endelman has written that Jacobs' 'Masorti movement . . . embodied the moderate traditionalism of the prewar United Synagogue' and Rubinstein concurs.[33] Cohen wrote of the Jacobs Affair: 'the old easy going tolerance was being relentlessly edged out. Freedom of opinion was diminishing and to qualify for respectability, a doctrine had to meet the most stringent requirements of rigidity' and that 'five years earlier rabbinical promotion would have been found' for Jacobs.[34] The reasons for these changes are ascribed to Brodie's weakness, which resulted in him being pulled away from the moderation of Adler and Hertz towards greater traditionalism by forces led by the Beth Din, which had become increasingly ascendant.[35] This contention was summed up in the New London Synagogue publication *Quest* in 1967, which argued that 'the growing intolerance manifested by the Chief Rabbinate and the Beth Din was gradually destroying what Hertz called "the Anglo-Jewish position in theology" which he defined as "Progressive Conservatism" . . . the new climate was mainly due to . . . the Dayanim'.[36]

Freud Kandel has constructed the most developed analysis of the Jacobs Affair. She argues that Brodie did not possess a theology of his own; he was essentially non-intellectual and his thought was dominated by a 'pervading fear and bewilderment of the 1950s and 1960s'.[37] He therefore lacked the tools necessary to defend the centrist ideology established by Hertz from a newly resurgent right wing, strengthened by the turn against modernity engendered by the Holocaust.[38] The result was that Brodie abandoned Hertz's model of synthesis and began to propound a theology that advocated compartmentalisation, engagement in the modern world for the sake of a living but for no higher purpose. In Heilman's terms, Brodie shifted from a syncretist to a tolerating position. As Freud Kandel writes, Brodie 'exhibited no trust in modernity's potential to contribute useful values'.[39] Brodie's weakness contrasted with an increasingly strict and powerful Beth Din, to whom Brodie had conceded halakhic authority and whom he was too weak to resist.[40] Thus, when the Beth Din mobilised against Jacobs, Brodie was carried along with them. When they relented, and supported the return of Jacobs to the New West End, Brodie had to prove his personal strength by taking a more extreme position.[41] Freud Kandel also highlights the shift in the lay leadership as an important factor, their increased traditionalism allowing a more rigid policy to be adopted.[42]

Crucially, according to Freud Kandel, the Chief Rabbinate and United Synagogue adopted a new theological position, which placed Jacobs' thought beyond the bounds of acceptability in a departure from what had come before.[43] Freud Kandel accepts that Hertz and Jacobs would have disagreed about the origin of the Pentateuch, but she suggests that as a fellow Jewish thinker engaged in synthesis, Hertz would have sympathised with Jacobs' predicament.[44]

The standard interpretation of the Jacobs Affair is therefore that Jacobs would have prospered under the theologically relaxed regimes of Adler and Hertz, and possibly even of Brodie, had not the latter, a weak character, been dragged towards greater stringency by a militant traditionalist group led by the Beth Din. This movement left Jacobs exposed as an exponent of suddenly unacceptable views, led to his expulsion from the United Synagogue, and the foundation of the New London Synagogue, which represented what the United Synagogue used to be.

Perhaps the best evidence that Brodie was not personally inclined to oppose Jacobs, but was pressured to do so by others, is the fact that he appointed Jacobs to the Jews' College faculty two years after the publication of *We have reason to believe*. We have seen some possible reasons for this, such as Brodie's claim that he thought Jacobs might change his mind, or Reif's suggestion that Brodie was preoccupied with ways to remove Epstein and therefore distracted from Jacobs himself. Neither of these explanations is wholly satisfactory, although the question as to why objection was not raised in 1957 or 1959 applies as much to the *dayyanim* as it does to Brodie. Why did they not protest when *We have reason to believe* first appeared, or when Jacobs joined Jews' College? This issue therefore remains a problem for all analyses of the Jacobs Affair, including mine.

As I mentioned at the beginning, my aim is to get to the roots of the problems I examine in Anglo-Jewish religious history by a serious analysis of theology. To test the existing understanding of the Jacobs Affair, we need to return to the theologies of Adler and Hertz, to Brodie's personal theological inclinations without pressure from outside, the theological position of the Beth Din and its influence over Brodie. We can then reflect on whether the understanding of the acknowledgement school we have built up in the course of this book can help us to formulate a better analysis of the Jacobs Affair.

The theologies of Hermann Adler and J.H. Hertz were very different to that of Louis Jacobs. In terms of our typology, they should be classed as traditionalist members of the acknowledgement school because they upheld the traditional account of origin of the Pentateuch. Jacobs, on the other hand, should be understood as a non-traditionalist member of the acknowledgement school, because although he regarded *halakhah* as binding he disputed the Mosaic authorship of the Pentateuch. Adler and Hertz regarded the division between the traditionalist and non-traditionalists of the acknowledgement school as fundamental: not merely an abstract theological issue of no significance as long as Jewish law was upheld, but of the greatest practical importance. We have seen how Adler and Hertz dealt with individuals with views like Jacobs', men like Morris Joseph, Joseph Hochman, Z.P. Chajes and Herbert Loewe. They excluded them from the United Synagogue and sought to deprive them of platforms outside it.

The *Jewish Chronicle*'s golden age of 'benevolent Anglo-Jewish traditions of tolerance and reasonableness' – or, as Cesarani has written, the *Jewish Chronicle*'s idea of the 'formerly latitudinarian' position of the United Synagogue – is, to a great extent, a myth created by Jacobs and his supporters to create a contrast between a supposedly liberal past and an intolerant present. [45] Louis Jacobs himself hinted at the importance of the *Jewish Chronicle* in setting out a particular view of the development of Anglo-Jewry when he wrote 'It was the *Jewish Chronicle* that first brought into the open the influence of the right'. The *Jewish Chronicle*, and those who echoed its analysis, propounded a false interpretation of both their own time and of Adler and Hertz. As Taylor argues, and as we have seen, Brodie's attitude to the Jacobs Affair followed exactly the pattern set by his predecessors.[46] Jacobs' contention that Hertz would not have barred him from the principalship of Jews' College because of the latter's commitment to 'Progressive Conservatism' (which, of course meant something very different to Jacobs' theology) therefore cannot stand.[47]

That is my argument, but there are a number of objections that could be raised to this interpretation. One could argue that Adler and Hertz did not take action against ministers like A.A. Green and J.F. Stern who were suspected of holding untraditional views. However, as we noted above, none of the Chief Rabbis from Adler to Jakobovits sought conflict. Brodie and Jakobovits tolerated Isaac Levy and Isaac Livingstone as ministers, although they were also thought to hold non-traditional views and were suspected of religious laxity. Brodie took on Jacobs for the same reasons that Adler took on Joseph, because he made his views public. Private views might be regrettable, but only once they became public did the Chief Rabbis find it necessary to take a stand.

I have argued that the idea of a move away from a period of tolerance and civility in Anglo-Jewish religious affairs was an invention of the *Jewish Chronicle* in the context of the Jacobs Affair. Endelman's work specifically challenges this view. He argues that this tolerance and civility was indeed abandoned as 'the religious atmosphere shifted rightwards' because 'Anglo-Jewry's leaders were increasingly self-made businessmen of East European background'.[48] Endelman has analysed a meeting of the Jewish Historical Society of England in 1953, when Redcliffe Salaman gave an account of 'the decline of moderate traditionalism in Anglo-Jewish practice and the ascendance of right-wing views and standards . . . counter to [earlier] easy going religious latitudinarianism'.[49] Chief Rabbi Brodie was in the audience, and heckled Salaman, attacked him in the vote of thanks and then, with the support of the new generation of communal leaders, sought to prevent the lecture being published.[50] Brodie took particular offence at Salaman's protest against the exclusion of children not considered Jewish by the Chief Rabbinate from United Synagogue religious classes, and the concern Salaman expressed about the humanity of *shehitah*.[51]

Endelman attributes Brodie's reaction to 'strict orthodoxy's new assertiveness'.[52] He argues that, as we have mentioned above, between the end of the Adlerian period and 1953 'the religious atmosphere in Anglo-Jewry shifted rightwards' and that the new generation of Anglo-Jewish leaders were more personally observant than their predecessors and 'more willing to defer to the chief rabbi and his *bet din* in religious matters.[53] Another piece of evidence Endelman brings is the 'Great Turbot Affair' of 1954 when turbot was served at a communal dinner under Beth Din supervision, which caused some consternation at the Chief Rabbi's table, because he was under the impression the fish was not kosher.[54] Others at the dinner continued to munch away at the meal, unconcerned with the niceties of *kashrut* which were exercising the Chief Rabbi, but with which they had never been overly preoccupied.[55]

This contrast, between the new elite's support for Brodie when he sought to suppress the Salaman lecture and the old elite happily eating their turbot, is interesting evidence for the change in the composition of the communal leadership which made it much easier for Brodie to have his way than it had been for Adler or Hertz. That, in fact, is my central argument. I contend that that the Chief Rabbinate maintained ideological consistency, and it was the changes in the lay leadership which allowed Brodie greater freedom than his predecessors to enforce his will. To this extent, therefore, I agree with Endelman's analysis. However, there are other aspects of it I would question.

First, we should not assume that although Salaman invoked the tolerance of an earlier age his specific remarks would have been acceptable even then. Salaman's lecture touched on the very delicate issue of *shehitah*, Earlier discussions of the issue by Salaman had been strongly opposed by the ultimate incarnation of the pre-War Anglo-Jewish leader, Robert Waley Cohen, who was, as Endelman points out, 'tolerant of heterodoxy'.[56] To protest at statements which queried *shehitah*, as Brodie did in 1953, was therefore not a departure from past practice. Secondly, the meal at which turbot was served was supervised by the Beth Din, which, according to Salaman and others, was adopting new and higher standards.[57] If so, why were they allowing turbot to be served? The two individuals to object most to the turbot were Brodie and the Haham, Solomon Gaon. They were both products not of post-War but of pre-War Anglo-Jewry, supposedly its period of *laissez faire*. Therefore, although the different reactions at the dinner itself are instructive, too much should not be read into the event itself. The fact turbot was served seems to have been more the result of accident than conspiracy, especially as the question of the *kashrut* of turbot is complex, and some varieties are, and have been, considered kosher, while others have not.

The behaviour of most people at the 1954 dinner gives cause to re-examine the other part of Endelman's analysis of changes in the laity. I argue that, though the laity did change, it was not in quite the way Endelman suggests. Endelman proposes that lay members of the community 'shifted rightwards' towards not just 'orthodoxy' but 'strict orthodoxy'. But can we, in fact, detect a 'swing to the right' among United Synagogue members by the time of the Jacobs Affair in the late 1950s and early 1960s?

The swing to the right has been the subject of much study. Ellenson argues that for nineteenth-century and early twentieth-century Jews the problem was how to be 'more modern'. For post-War Jews, who were perfectly comfortable with modernity, the question was how to be 'more Jewish'. The answer often led them to greater traditionalism.[58] Haym Soloveitchik has made a similar point. He has argued that this move to greater stringency is a function of greater acculturation. For past generations, being Jewish was automatic and unthinking. Observant Jews of earlier times felt completely comfortable with their tradition. They knew what it required of them and that was how they lived their lives. Their descendants, through their acculturation into Western society, lost that intimacy and in an attempt to fulfil the requirements of their faith investigated what their religious obligations were with an element of distance, which involved not just looking to what their parents has done, but by looking in the authoritative texts. Pleas for greater stringency that rabbis had been making for generations were heeded for the first time.[59] In this context, should we identify as an important factor in the Jacobs Affair the fact that it took place during the early stages of this phenomenon, and that Brodie benefited from it in terms of the freedom it gave him to assert his will?

Although the 'swing to the right' is a real phenomenon, its influence in England at the time of the Jacobs Affair was, as yet, minor. The fact that most diners at the turbot dinner continued to eat suggests that the laity had not shifted towards greater stringency. Indeed, the scholars who have examined this trend have identified the period when the dinner took place as predating the 'swing to the right'. Haym Soloveitchik sees the movement as beginning in earnest in about 1970 and then only amongst the already highly committed.[60] Isaac Chavel dates it as even later in Minnesota, well away from the epicentres that Soloveitchik described. Indeed, Chavel describes the 1960s as a time of centrist Modern Orthodoxy's greatest strength.[61] Danzger emphasises the role of the Six Day War in fuelling the return to greater traditionalism, which took place in 1967, and dates the first appearance of the term '*baal teshuva*' to describe the newly and intensely religious to 1972.[62] As late as 1978 Samuel Heilman wrote an article which portrayed centrism as in a commanding position. He detected stirrings of what became the 'swing to the right', writing 'there are also signs of a move towards stricter Orthodoxy', but he was very cautious and added 'it is too early to tell exactly what will occur' – in other words, although the trend was beginning to emerge, it was only at its very earliest stages.[63] All this suggests that the 1950s and early 1960s, the period of the Salaman lecture, the Turbot Affair and the Jacobs Affair, were too early for the 'swing to the right' to have got going, certainly in England. Changes in the general religious atmosphere in the community in general therefore cannot be considered responsible for those events.

There was a change in the nature of the lay leadership. As Cesarani and Shimoni have noted, by the Second World War eastern Europeans had taken the place of the old English elite in the leadership of the Board of Deputies, symbolised by Selig Brodetsky succeeding Osmond d'Avigdor Goldsmid as president in 1939.[64] In the United Synagogue, leadership passed from the Waley Cohen type to the Wolfson type, and this change and its effects are explored below. However, it was not an expression of the 'swing to the right' that Soloveitchik, Heilman and others have analysed. As we will see, what occurred was not the coming to power of leaders who advocated new-style stringency, the 'strict orthodoxy' that Endelman describes, but actually the traditional, moderate observance of pious Jews who had always existed in Anglo-Jewry, such as Samuel Montagu.

So much for the laity, but Endelman takes his analysis one step further, from the lay to the religious leadership. He argues that the outlook of the Chief Rabbinate itself had changed, and contrasts Brodie's intolerance with the pre-War position when, he argues, 'the outlook of the Chief Rabbinate and the United Synagogue was latitudinarian, undemanding, concerned more with unity, respectability and civility'.[65] Here Endelman is positing a change not just in the lay leadership but amongst the Chief Rabbis themselves, and here we have more cause to doubt his analysis. Morris Joseph and Joseph Hochman would have been surprised to be told that they lived in an age of latitudinarianism and tolerance, or – as Salaman called them – 'kindly make believe and gentlemanly behaviour'; we saw the protests about their treatment from correspondents to the *Jewish Chronicle* at the time.[66] We have seen that Hertz was concerned with unity and civility. He went to the opening of the West London Synagogue's Stern Hall and he jointly opened the Cambridge Synagogue with the Liberal Synagogue minister, Leslie Edgar; but we have also noted how Robert Waley Cohen protested to Hertz about his attacks on the Liberal Jewish Synagogue in the 1920s, and that Hertz was publicly called a 'bigot'.[67] The old elite may have been worried that in the 1950s Anglo-Jewry was being dragged 'back to the Middle Ages' in Leon Simon's words, but members of the elite had been worried about that since the 1840s, when some congregations did not support Solomon Hirschell and Nathan Adler's attacks on the West London Synagogue. These concerns continued under Hermann Adler and Hertz, and under Brodie too. The same complaints made about Brodie are a recurring theme amongst lay leaders who opposed the religious policy of the Chief Rabbis, and made an appearance again at the time of the Jacobs Affair.

If, as has been suggested, Brodie acted against Jacobs only because of pressure applied by the Beth Din, and not because Brodie himself rejected Jacobs' views, then we should find that Brodie's religious position was not antagonistic to Jacobs'. However, Brodie did dispute Jacobs' theology very profoundly. Brodie's views were those of the traditional but scientific branch of the acknowledgement school. This is apparent from his career and from his statements made before, during and after the Jacobs Affair. Brodie was Buchler's student at Jews' College and took from him both a traditional attitude to the Pentateuch and a commitment to *Wissenschaft* .[68] Like his predecessors Brodie was convinced that true scholarship would confirm the claims of tradition, or – as Jeffrey Cohen wrote at the time – 'the Orthodox Jew need have no fear of acquainting himself with the "modern scholarship." The time is nigh when . . . that which we accept as an act of Faith . . . will be axiomatically proved in the text-books of students'.[69] It was that attitude which took Brodie to undertake academic Jewish study at Balliol College, Oxford.[70]

In common with others whom we would place in the scientific branch of the acknowledgement school, such as Hertz and Hoffman, Brodie held that *halakhah* was dynamic and so it developed. Jewish law, he said 'is not static . . . it is always on the march' and 'its vitality is felt in the control and encouragement of versatile forms which new and complex human situations impose. And thus the new generation adds its quota to the continuity and enrichment of tradition'.[71] Indications of Brodie's scientific leanings include his hint that Psalm 26 dates from a post-Davidic period.[72] He was resounding in his praise for Buchler and other *Wissenschaft* scholars, whom he called 'scholars of great stature' whose 'contributions were immense and varied'.[73] Perhaps the most striking evidence for Brodie's continuing support for *Wissenschaft* is his appointment of H.J. Zimmels as principal in place of Jacobs.[74] Before he came to England, Zimmels had taught at Breslau, the great centre of traditionalist *Wissenschaft*.

Brodie also admired the romantic wing of the acknowledgement school. He praised 'Jewish education combined with what they called Derech Eretz' and the product of such an education, Isaac Herzog, whom Hertz considered appointing to the Beth Din in the 1930s.[75] Brodie described Herzog's 'remarkable intellect, endowed with Torah and enriched by comprehensive knowledge of the liberal arts and sciences'.[76] In no sense then could Brodie be described as hostile to Western culture or modern scholarship. Freud Kandel argues that Brodie compartmentalised his Judaism and separated scholarship from faith, so that one did not affect the other. However, Brodie did not need to compartmentalise in this way, because he did not believe that scholarship and faith were in contradiction. Brodie, like his predecessors, achieved a synthesis founded on a conviction that sound scholarship upheld the belief in Pentateuch and the nucleus of an Oral Law given at Sinai, and that therefore the *halakhah* which flowed from that event was binding.

We should therefore not entirely dismiss Rabbi Myer Berman's somewhat extravagant praise of Brodie: 'Dr Brodie was not a fanatical obscurantist but a modern, cultured, broadminded and tolerant traditional Jew of deep and sincere religious feeling . . . The Chief Rabbi required no prompting from "foreign scholars". He was motivated by the principles of religious convictions and he had the support of the whole of traditional Jewry'.[77] Contrary to Freud Kandel, it was not the case, therefore, that Jacobs advocated synthesis while Brodie favoured compartmentalisation. They both supported a synthesis, they merely disagreed on the content of that synthesis; Furthermore, the way they differed was the same as the way Adler and Hertz had differed with some of their opponents, such as Joseph and Hochman.

That Brodie received the support of traditionalists from both the acknowledgement and antipathy schools should not surprise us. We have seen how these two groups united on fundamental issues, especially the Pentateuch. Brodie's traditionalist credentials on this matter were impeccable. In 1952, five years before the publication of *We have reason to believe*, Brodie referred to 'the Law which He delivered by the hand of Moses and in 1957 to 'the Torah which was revealed on Mount Sinai."[78] He spoke of the 'authority, the validity, the relevance of the Torah, Written and Oral'.[79] Brodie shared Epstein's view that the authority for *halakhah* came from Sinai and he referred to 'the Din which is laid down in authoritative codes which have their source and sanction in the Torah from Sinai'.[80] Brodie was committed to establishing a Beth Din which upheld Jewish law, though that might be challenging to the community and might court unpopularity. As he said, 'the Rabbi dare not decide [Jewish law] . . . because he wishes to be described as a tolerant and easy going . . . who contrasts his humanitarianism . . . with the "barbarism" or bondage of the laws enacted in days gone by and which ought to be discarded' – similar sentiments to those which we have seen animated Adler and Hertz.[81]

Brodie however continued the expansive policy of his predecessors and although, just like Adler and Hertz, he encouraged synagogues to abandon mixed choirs he did not instruct them to do so; indeed, one can argue that Brodie was more timid towards the issue than Hertz was in his last years. Hertz issued a ruling against mixed choirs, whereas

Brodie never did, even though more were disbanded under Brodie.[82] We discuss the reasons for Brodie's greater success below, but we should note here that if the New London was similar in form to many pre-War United Synagogues, under Brodie, so were many still within the United Synagogue, such as Hampstead and the New West End.

In all these respects, Brodie was a true theological successor to Adler and Hertz. His Chief Rabbinate did not represent a departure from precedent which left Jacobs exposed to new and chilly ideological winds. Adler and Hertz were from the traditionalist scientific branch of the acknowledgement school and so was Brodie; they excluded ministers on theological grounds, and so did Brodie. As Berman pointed out, there was therefore no need for an extremist Beth Din to pressurise Brodie, but as that claim is made so often we should investigate it.

In 1967 *Quest* quoted approvingly from an article by James Parkes in *The Observer* where he described the members of the Beth Din as 'fearful of the dangers inherent in any concession to the modern spirit . . . they fear the very appeal to reason inherent in the teachings of Rabbi Jacobs'.[83] Parkes thus asserted that the *dayyanim* of the London Beth Din held views associated with the antipathy school, and were therefore bound to oppose Jacobs. The Beth Din in question consisted of Leb Grossnass, Abraham Rapoport, Moshe Swift, Meir Steinberg and Myer Lew. The leading halakhists, Grossnass and Rapoport were appointed by Brodie, and were from an antipathy school background, although not more so than Jacobs himself; Grossnass and Jacobs had studied together at Gateshead.[84] Brodie appointed them to be doughty defenders of Jewish law, and they took some uncompromising stands. For example, they refused to attend a celebration of the tercentenary of the readmission of the Jews to England at which Reform ministers participated.[85] Freud Kandel has argued that their supremacy in halakhic matters was new; but we have seen that, since the time of Jacob Reinowitz, the Beth Din (rather than the Chief Rabbi) handled halakhic decisions. Crucially, Grossnass and Rapoport were not interested in abstract theology and did not play a leading role in the affair.[86] Of the other *dayyanim*, Lew was a graduate of Jews' College, had a PhD and was committed to modern scholarship. Steinberg was uninterested in conflict and argument. Swift was outspoken and sometimes insensitive, but, as it happens, he was not responsible for bringing Jacobs' views to Brodie's attention.[87]

In fact it was Isidor Grunfeld, appointed by Hertz in 1937 (and, by the time of the affair, already in retirement), who gave Brodie a copy of *We have reason to believe* with the heretical passages underlined in red.[88]

Grunfeld had shown as early as 1949 the importance he attached to belief in the divine origin of the Pentateuch, when he said (regarding the Liberal Jewish Synagogue) 'between those who deny the divine origin of the Torah and those for whom Torah Min Hashamayim is a reality, there is obviously no common basis for a discussion on Judaism'.[89] Of all the *dayyanim*, Grunfeld was the one most rooted in the acknowledgement school. He possessed secular learning, and had trained as a lawyer. He was an exponent of *Torah im derekh eretz*, and translated Hirsch's writings. He was not an obscurantist or unworldly eastern European, but enjoyed a full appreciation of non-Jewish wisdom and significant exposure to the secular world. In short, he was a true representative of the traditionalist wing of the acknowledgement school.[90]

Reif has suggested that the faculty of Jews' College, all from the scientific branch of the acknowledgement school, were also instrumental in the anti-Jacobs campaign.[91] The exclusion of Jacobs was therefore not a coup by a militant antipathy school, which one could argue if it was the result of the efforts of Grossnass or Swift; rather, it was an effort by the traditionalist wing of the acknowledgement school to remove a figure from the acknowledgement school's non-traditional wing, effected by a dayan appointed under Hertz's supposedly tolerant regime. Indeed, the antipathy school *dayyanim* might not have pressed the matter. They did not support Jacobs' exclusion from the pulpit of the New West End in 1964, considering that he could do little damage in such an anglicised community, but Brodie held firm. We have seen how the traditionalist wing of the acknowledgement school, which differed subtly, but fundamentally, from the non-traditionalist wing, was always careful to maintain the theological integrity of their communities; the Jacobs Affair was another example of that.

Another example of Brodie acting as a result of his own convictions and not as a result of pressure from extreme traditionalists, comes from the very start of his Chief Rabbinate. After much agonising Hertz recognised the Liberal Jewish Synagogue in 1935 as a Jewish congregation for the purposes of marriages, to avoid the prospect of them passing their own act of parliament, which would have demonstrated Jewish divisions at a time when Jewish unity was essential. After Hertz's death, Dayan H.M. Lazarus was appointed Deputy for the Chief Rabbi until a successor was found, and, under the rather different circumstances of 1946, rescinded the recognition that Hertz had granted. When Brodie became Chief Rabbi in 1948 he confirmed Lazarus' decision.[92] Lazarus could not be considered as a figure from the antipathy school. He was a product of Jews' College, trained in the scientific branch of the acknowledgement school, just as Brodie was.

When Brodie took his decision in 1948, Grossnass and Rappoport had not yet been appointed, while Dayan Abramsky had been on the Beth Din in 1935 when recognition was originally granted. Brodie received wide support from the ministers of the United Synagogue – for example Isaac Levy, who delivered a blistering sermon in May 1949 in which he said "'Jewry . . . was united at Sinai" when the law was received and honoured . . . Jewry was disunited when the schismatic group of Korah attempted to undermine the stability of the community by rebellion against religious authority . . . tolerance is a virtue which can be overdone. To be tolerant of an evil is to condone it'.[93] Levy later became a leading supporter of Jacobs but his words in 1949 could have been applied to the Jacobs Affair. The fact that Levy and others took a different view in 1949 than in 1959–64 was perhaps owing to the fact that, unlike the Liberals, Jacobs affirmed *halakhah*. The Liberals were from the acceptance school, whereas Jacobs was from a different wing of the acknowledgement school. Levy and others did not appreciate the difference between the traditional and non-traditional wings of the acknowledgement school, whereas Brodie, like Adler and Hertz, did.

The Jacobs Affair has been identified as a turning point in Anglo-Jewish history away from moderation and tolerance, towards extremism and polarisation. If that interpretation is problematic, and my analysis would suggest that it is, then the general trend that has been adduced should also be reappraised.[94] What does the Jacobs Affair tell us, and not tell us, therefore, about a 'swing to the right' in Anglo-Jewry?

Brodie was certainly fortunate in having as President of the United Synagogue Sir Isaac Wolfson, who upheld the authority of the Chief Rabbinate and supported Brodie throughout his confrontation with Jacobs. Wolfson was probably the most observant President of the United Synagogue in its history. He was certainly more observant than his recent predecessors, although his piety should not be overstated: for example, he did not cover his head all the time, kept his shops open on the Sabbath, was not particularly learned and did not take on the stringencies that have often been identified as a symptom of the 'swing to the right'.[95] What Wolfson did believe was that the authority of the rabbi, and especially of the Chief Rabbi, ought to be upheld, although privately he did argue for Brodie to relent over Jacobs.[96] Wolfson's support enabled Brodie to act with far fewer constraints than Adler and Hertz, who had to contend with the Rothschilds and Waley Cohen.

The important dynamic in the history of Anglo-Jewry in the period under examination was therefore not in the attitudes of the Chief Rabbis, or of the rank-and-file membership, but of the lay leadership, and the fact that the latter became traditional and observant, not in the new stringent manner of the 1970s, but in the way that the most committed section of Anglo-Jewry had always been observant, the way that the Adlers and Hertz urged their community to be. Obviously Wolfson had a constituency of more pious United Synagogue members to support him, but, again, these individuals were pious in the 'old' rather than the 'new' sense. Yet, despite having greater traditionalist support, in his religious policy Brodie acted cautiously and did not reverse the concessions made by his predecessors, for example on the issue of mixed choirs. He even made more concessions in an attempt to operate an expansive policy, for example allowing women to sit on synagogue boards.[97]

Brodie having Wolfson as his United Synagogue president was the equivalent of Adler having Samuel Montagu. What differences there were in the behaviour of the two Chief Rabbis has more to do with that than with their own views. Although counterfactual, it is instructive to speculate what a United Synagogue led by Adler and Montagu might have looked like. Some clues may be drawn from the Federation of Synagogues, the synagogue body that they did jointly lead. There one would find Adler's ideal in action: the services of the synagogues were wholly in accordance with tradition, with little or no deviation from inherited practice, but the sermons were in English, the buildings were dignified and clean, and the atmosphere was decorous. The federation catered for the less acculturated section of the community; for an idea of the sort of synagogue where Adler wanted to see the affluent worship, one might turn to his own synagogue, Bayswater, where the service was conducted to high aesthetic standards in noble surroundings but which resisted demands for liturgical change and even provided a ritual bath.

Further evidence of continuity – from before 1945, to the Jacobs Affair and after – comes from the appointment of Brodie's successor. Every one of the candidates seriously considered by Wolfson held views common to the acknowledgement school, and represented a link with the theological paths of previous Chief Rabbis. These included J.B. Solovietchik, a distinguished philosopher, with a degree from Berlin University and a PhD, Louis Rabinowitz, who had a BA and PhD from London University, and two products of Yeshiva University, which combined secular and religious studies in its curriculum, Norman Lamm and Emmanuel Rackman.[98] At one point the post was offered to Jacob Herzog, son of Isaac Herzog, a rabbi with a PhD, a lawyer and at the time the most senior civil servant in Israel.[99] When Herzog was diagnosed with leukaemia and had to withdraw, Wolfson chose Immanuel Jakobovits.[100]

Freud Kandel has argued that Jakobovits was another advocate of compartmentalisation, who rejected Hertz's model of synthesis between Jewish and non-Jewish wisdom and who thought, rather, that only Judaism had values to teach.[101] In fact, however, Jakobovits' background was profoundly connected to the acknowledgement school which stood for such a synthesis. His father, Julius Jakobovits, attended the Hildesheimer Seminary (under David Hoffman) and Berlin University.[102] When Julius' first son was born, he named him after Immanuel Kant.[103] Julius had a distinguished rabbinical career in Germany, as a rabbi of the traditional section of the general community, which rejected *Austritt*.[104] After Hitler came to power, the family moved to London where Hertz appointed Julius to his Beth Din. Immanuel attended both the antipathy school Yeshiva Etz Hayim and Jews' College, where he was taught *Wissenschaft* and received his BA in Semitics and the ministerial diploma.[105] He later received a PhD on Jewish medical ethics.[106] He was thus connected to the scientific branch of the acknowledgement school through his and his father's education, and developed a close attachment to Hirsch's writings, thereby coming under the influence of the romantic branch.[107]

Jakobovits even showed sympathy with the aesthetic branch. In 1963 he described the theological significance of aesthetics in worship, and said 'the widely acclaimed beauty of our cherished synagogue must be matched by the beauty of our services and the attractiveness of all our activities, that it in truth be said of us . . . "How goodly are thy tents O Jacob!" Only by turning out prayers and religious exercises into a model of charm, sincerity and dignity can we recapture an enthusiastic appreciation of our faith in those who have strayed from the ways of the Torah which are the "paths of pleasantness"'. As Freud Kandel points out, Jakobovits did not welcome all non-Jewish culture into Judaism, and regarded much of it as unwholesome, but then, as we have seen, so did Adler and Hertz.

When the Jacobs Affair erupted, Jakobovits intervened on Brodie's side, and made a point which is typical of the traditionalist scientific branch of the acknowledgement school. Jacobs had claimed that 'no reputable scholar in the world has an approach that is basically different to mine' on the Pentateuch. Jakobovits retorted that such a claim was 'as patently absurd as it is immodest'.[108] Jakobovits named individuals who disagreed with Jacobs, such as Isidore Epstein and Dr Belkin, the President of Yeshiva University, who upheld that objective scholarship supported the claims of tradition.

The lay leadership may therefore have become more observant, but their appointment of Jakobovits did not signal a theological departure. Neither did Jakobovits' early policies. Although he said at his installation that 'I am not prepared to replace the Torah by an umbrella, either open or closed . . . I cannot bend or compromise Jewish Law which is not mine to make or unmake' he swiftly recognised the New London Synagogue for the purposes of conducting marriages, which Brodie had refused to do, on the pragmatic basis that keeping the wounds of the Jacobs Affair open did no one in the community any good.[109] It certainly does not indicate that Jakobovits established a new religious extremism, and neither does his permission for women to conduct their own prayer services, a new concession within *halakhah* in the expansive tradition of his predecessors, or his appearance on platforms with Reform rabbis.[110] It is true that Jakobovits forestalled a joint Israeli Independence Day service with the Reform and Liberal movements in 1968 and banned a member of the Conservative World Council of Synagogues, Bent Melchior, from preaching in a United Synagogue in 1972, but this was balanced by continual efforts to find a detente with Reform and Liberal synagogues and those who followed Louis Jacobs, efforts which did not meet with success.[111]

The Jacobs Affair did not represent a break with the past. Brodie shared his theology with his predecessors and adopted their policies in dealing with a non-traditionalist from the acknowledgement school who wished to serve in a synagogue under his authority. The Jacobs Affair was another example of a confrontation between the two wings of the acknowledgement school, and followed the precedents of Adler and Joseph in the 1890s and Hertz and Hochman in the 1910s. The Joseph and Hochman affairs caused as much disturbance in the community at the time as the Jacobs Affair, but had much less long-term resonance, probably because Joseph joined the West London Synagogue, and Hochman left the ministry entirely. The fact that the two sides in the Jacobs Affair, both of which should be classed within the acknowledgement school, had so much in common theologically – an openness to the modern world combined with respect for *halakhah* – served to confuse the issue just as it had done fifty and seventy years earlier.

Jacobs reports that 'time and again I was told "But everyone believes as you do. Surely the Chief Rabbi does not believe *that?*"'.[112] Just as the correspondent wrote to the *Jewish Chronicle* about Morris Joseph in 1892 'how many of our so-called "orthodox" ecclesiastics in the inner temples of their hearts worship the same image of Progressive Judaism as Mr. Joseph?'[113] But there was no confusion in the mind of Brodie, just as there had been none in that of Hertz and Adler. Grunfeld too, as a product of German Jewry where theological questions were considered of the highest importance, was well trained to detect subtle but vital differences, which others, such as Mordechai Kaplan, also identified. The Jacobs Affair is therefore significant not as a harbinger of a sharp break with Anglo-Jewish tradition, or of a turn towards extremism, but rather as another demonstration of the complexity of the acknowledgement school.

Notes

1 L. Jacobs, *Helping with inquiries* (London 1989), 1, 23. This analysis of the Jacobs Affair relies heavily on Jacobs' own account, which is the fullest available, but should be treated with caution. Therefore, for contentious points, other sources have been consulted. The most important analysis of Louis Jacobs' intellectual development is E.J. Cosgrove, *Teyku: the insoluble contradictions in the life and thought of Louis Jacobs* (PhD thesis, University of Chicago 2008).

2 Jacobs, *Helping with inquiries*, 20, 42.

3 Ibid., 68.

4 Ibid.

5 Ibid., 70. Freud Kandel argues that the Golders Green Beth Hamedrash was another source of an ideology which advocated the compartmentalisation of the secular and the religious spheres (M. Freud Kandel, *Orthodox Judaism in Britain since 1913* [London 2006], 125). This is doubtful, especially when we consider that Rabbi Munk's PhD was on Wordsworth's *religious development.* .

6 Ibid., 76.

7 Ibid., 77, 79. Cosgrove, *Teyku*, 55–65.

8 Cosgrove, Teyku, 55–65, 84–93.

9 Jacobs, *Helping with inquiries*, 86, 103.

10 L. Jacobs, *Sermon by Rabbi Dr. Louis Jacobs on the occasion of his induction as minister to the New West End Synagogue* (London 1954), 5.

11 Ibid., 3.

12 L. Jacobs, 'Reflections on a controversy' in *Quest* (London 1965), 4.

13 L. Jacobs, *We have reason to believe* (London 1957), 70, 73. There are flaws in this reasoning. The fact that Jews reached out to God does not mean that He reached back, and endorsed Jewish practice. Furthermore Jacobs does acknowledge that there is a human element to the *halakhah*, which presumably means that there are aspects of Jewish law which are not divine, and that therefore can be dispensed with without religious loss. See quotation from Jacobs' lecture 'The sanction of the mitzvoth' in I. Brodie, *The strength of my heart* (London 1969), 349.

14 Jacobs, *We have reason to believe*, 1.
15 *Addresses given at the Conference of European Rabbis* (London 1963), 25.
16 Jacobs, *Helping with inquiries*, 121.
17 Ibid; N. Cohen, 'The religious crisis in Anglo-Jewry' *Tradition* 8:2 (Summer 1966), 49. Lawrence Jacobs was no relation to Louis Jacobs.
18 S. Reif, personal communication, 23 September 2005.
19 Brodie, *Strength of my heart*, 345–346.
20 Jacobs, *Helping with inquiries*, 126; Cohen, 'Religious crisis', 50.
21 Jacobs, *Helping with inquiries*, 126.
22 Ibid., 129.
23 Ibid., 137–140.
24 Ibid., 144.
25 Ibid., 161. See also Brodie, *Strength of my heart*, 346–347.
26 Jacobs, *Helping with inquiries*, 162.
27 A. Newman, *The United Synagogue, 1870–1970* (London 1976) , 184–86.
28 Jacobs, *Helping with inquiries*, 169–178.
29 Ibid., 131.
30 Brodie, *Strength of my heart*, 350.
31 Jacobs, *Helping with inquiries*, 179–186.
32 G. Alderman, *Modern British Jewry* (Oxford 1992), 364.
33 T. Endelman, *The Jews of Britain, 1656 to 2000* (Berkeley 2002), 253; W.D. Rubinstein, *A history of the Jews in the English-speaking world: Great Britain* (London 1996), 414.
34 Cohen, 'Religious crisis', 46, 48.
35 See, for example, Alderman, *Modern British Jewry*, 364; and Endelman, *Jews of Britain*, 253 .
36 *Quest 2* (London 1967), 11.
37 M. Freud Kandel, *Orthodox Judaism in Britain since 1913* (London 2006), 106, 108.
38 Ibid., 109, 120, 122, 140.
39 Ibid., 158.
40 Ibid., 98, 100, 104, 111, 137, 153.
41 Ibid., 139.
42 Ibid., 145.
43 Ibid., 159.
44 Ibid., 151.
45 D. Cesarani, *The Jewish Chronicle and Anglo-Jewry, 1841–1991* (Cambridge 1994), 221. See pp. 217–222 for an account of the *Jewish Chronicle*'s involvement in the affair, including efforts by the editor, William Frankel, to muster support for Jacobs from American Conservative rabbis and British Jewish academics.
46 D. Taylor, *British Chief Rabbis, 1664–2006* (London 2007), 390.
47 Jacobs, *Helping with inquiries*, 138. Cosgrove arrives at the same conclusion: Cosgrove, *Teyku*, 347.

48 T. Endelman, 'Practices of a low anthropological level: a *shehitah* controversy of the 1950s' in Kershen (ed), *Food in the migrant experience* (Aldershot 2002), 89.

49 Ibid., 79.

50 Ibid., 78–79.

51 Ibid., 79.

52 Ibid., 88.

53 Ibid., 89.

54 Ibid., 90.

55 Ibid., 90–91.

56 Ibid., 86.

57 J.H. Hertz, *Affirmations of Judaism* (Oxford 1927), 183; Endelman, 'A *shehitah* controversy of the 1950s', 92.

58 D. Ellenson, 'A reaction to Samuel Heilman's analysis of orthodoxy' *Contemporary Jewry* 25 (2005), 282.

59 H. Soloveitchik, 'Clarifications and reply' *Torah u-Madda Journal* (5/1997), 137–149.

60 Ibid., 142.

61 I. Chavel, 'On Haym Soloveitchik's "Rupture and reconstruction: The transformation of contemporary orthodoxy society": a response' *Torah u-Madda Journal* (5/1997), 122–136.

62 M.H. Danzger, *Returning to tradition – the contemporary revival of orthodox Judaism* (New Haven, Connecticut 1989), 71. The term *baal teshuva* is older; it was its use for this particular sociological phenomenon that began in the early 1970s.

63 S. Heilman, 'Constructing orthodoxy' in Robbins and Anthony (ed) *In gods we trust* (New Brunswick, 1981), 157.

64 D. Cesarani, *Zionism in England, 1917–39* (D.Phil, Oxford University 1986), 209; G. Shimoni, *Jews and Zionism: the South African experience, 1910–1967* (Oxford 1980), 154. See also G. Shimoni, 'From anti-Zionism to non-Zionism in Anglo Jewry 1917–1937', *Jewish Journal of Sociology* 28 (1986), 19–48, and G. Shimoni, 'The non-Zionists in Anglo-Jewry, 1937–1948' *Jewish Journal of Sociology* 28 (1986), 89–115.

65 Endelman, 'A *shehitah* controversy of the 1950s', 88.

66 R.N. Salaman, *Whither Lucian Wolf's Anglo-Jewish community?* (London 1954), 7. Salaman also protested at the refusal to allow the Liberal Jewish Synagogue to conduct marriages (p. 13) a decision taken by Adler and upheld, initially at least, by Hertz. He also stated that Brodie had forgotten that the 'fundamental basis of Judaism' was ethical monotheism (p. 14). This was a teaching of Claude Montefiore, against which both Adler and Hertz had campaigned forcefully.

67 Hertz, *Affirmations*, 181.

68 J.M. Shaftesley, 'A biographical sketch' in Zimmels, Rabbinowitz and Finestein (ed), *Essays presented to Chief Rabbi Israel Brodie on the occasion of his seventieth birthday* (London 1967), xix.

69 J. Cohen, *In defence of tradition* (London undated), 16.

70 Shaftesley, 'Biographical sketch', xx, xxiv.

71 Brodie, *Strength of my heart*, 3, 183.

72 Ibid., 25.

73 I. Brodie, 'Foreword' in Brodie and Rabbinowitz (ed), *Studies in Jewish history* (Oxford 1956), vi; Brodie, *Strength of my heart*, 412.

74 Shaftesley, 'Biographical sketch', xxxviii.

75 Brodie, *Strength of my heart*, 101.

76 Ibid., 105.

77 Jacobs, *Helping with inquiries*, 135.

78 I. Brodie, *A word in season* (London 1959), 43; Brodie, *Strength of my heart*, 444.

79 Brodie, *Strength of my heart*, 54.

80 Ibid., 51.

81 Ibid., 51–52.

82 Interview with Dudley Cohen, 19 August 2001.

83 *Quest 2* (London 1967), 11.

84 Jacobs, *Helping with inquiries*, 141.

85 Cohen, 'Religious crisis', 41.

86 Jacobs, *Helping with inquiries*, 140.

87 Ibid., 141.

88 Ch. Bermant, *Lord Jakobovits* (London 1990), 69.

89 M. Persoff, *Faith against reason: religious reform and the British Chief Rabbinate, 1840–1990* (London 2008), 266.

90 Ibid., 136.

91 S. Reif, personal communication, 23 September 2005.

92 B. Homa, *Footprints in the sands of time* (Gateshead 1990), 150.

93 I. Levy, *Historic Judaism versus Liberal Judaism* (London 1949), 6–7.

94 Freud Kandel, *Orthodox Judaism in Britain since 1913*, 158.

95 Bermant, *Jakobovits*, 72–73; see H. Soloveitchik, 'Rupture and reconstruction' *Tradition* 28:4 (1994), 64–130.

96 Bermant, *Jakobovits*, 72–73; Freud Kandel, *Orthodox Judaism in Britain since 1913*, 140.

97 J. Guttentag, *Shul: a unique institution* (unpublished 2001), 2.

98 *Quest 2*, 13; Bermant, *Jakobovits*, 73–74.

99 Bermant, *Jakobovits*, 73–74.

100 Ibid., 77.

101 Freud Kandel, *Orthodox Judaism in Britain since 1913*, 167–168, 171.

102 Bermant, *Jakobovits*, 12.

103 Ibid., 11.

104 Ibid., 5, 8.

105 Ibid., 12–13.

106 Ibid., 41.

107 M. Persoff, *Immanuel Jakobovits: a prophet in Israel* (London 2002), 9.

108 Jacobs, *Helping with inquiries*, 131.

109 Ibid., 185; Bermant, *Jakobovits*, 87.
110 J. Cohen (ed), *Dear Chief Rabbi* (New Jersey 1995), 90; Bermant, *Jakobovits*, 186.
111 Persoff, *Faith against reason*, 339, 344, 346.
112 Jacobs, *Helping with inquiries*, 139.
113 *Jewish Chronicle* (1 July 1892), 9.

Chapter 10

The religious character of the Chief Rabbis and of Anglo-Jewry

O UR ANALYSIS OF the Chief Rabbis' theologies and religious policies advances the understanding of the religious history of traditional Jewry in the modern period in two ways. First, we can make specific revisions to the current historiography on the Chief Rabbis, and on some other Jewish communities and their religious leaders. More importantly, our study allows us to help in the construction of a general typology of the Jewish religious response to modernity, which a number of scholars have been developing. This study's particular contribution concerns the types of response adopted by what we have called the acknowledgement school.

I will turn first to my revisions to the historiography on the Chief Rabbis and others. We have considered the thesis of Alderman, Endelman and others that Hermann Adler and J.H. Hertz were neither substantial scholars nor theologians, and that they espoused a Judaism that was lukewarm and lax (Alderman), took a tolerant and latitudinarian attitude to diversity in theology and practice, were much concerned with unity and civility, and were perceived to be so by the more traditional (Endelman). Overwhelmed by a concern for communal unity and personal hegemony, they set religious standards for their community which could for the most part 'just about be reconciled to orthodoxy in the loosest sense'.[1] These attitudes rendered them unacceptable to traditionalist eastern European leaders and their followers in Britain, who held Hermann Adler in low esteem, and made the Chief Rabbis' aggressively centralising policy unwise and inappropriate.[2] This centralising tendency was asphyxiating and led to scholarly and theological stagnation.[3]

Scholars, for example Meirovich, have understood J.H. Hertz's platform of 'progressive conservatism' as not being a traditional theological position. Meirorich and he and Freud Kandel have both argued that this 'middle-of-the-road' ideology came under attack from European refugees led by Yehezkel Abramsky, the most powerful engine moving the Chief Rabbinate away from its earlier, more tolerant and liberal position.[4] Meirovich's *Vindication of Judaism* argues that Hertz deviated from Jewish tradition on issues concerning Biblical and rabbinic texts, and Jewish Law.[5] He places Hertz in the *Wissenschaft des Judentums* school, which he defines as untraditional because of its critical study of Jewish texts.[6] On this basis, and as a result of Hertz's association with the Jewish Theological Seminary in New York, Meirovich identifies Hertz as a follower of Zachariah Frankel, who (Meirovich argues) opposed the traditional leaders S.R. Hirsch and Esriel Hildesheimer.[7]

There is a consensus that Brodie's lack of scholarship and personal weakness, and the new assertiveness of the right wing, led him to defer to the Beth Din who imposed traditionalism unknown in Anglo-Jewry, leading (according to Freud Kandel) to the abandonment of a Hertzian synthesis of Jewish and non-Jewish wisdom in favour of a compartmentalising approach, in which faith and the outside world were kept strictly separate.[8] This is the basis of their approach to the Jacobs Affair.[9] They argue that Jacobs occupies the theological position of the pre-war Chief Rabbis, or at least a position which they regarded as within the bounds of acceptability, a position from which Brodie departed as he moved towards greater traditionalism.[10] Evidence for this interpretation includes what are identified as new and intemperate attacks on Reform and Liberal Jewish leaders by Brodie and Jakobovits, resulting in increased polarisation.[11] They argue that the hostility towards non-traditional views, culminating in Brodie's exclusion of Jacobs on theological grounds, was unprecedented.[12] Others concur with this view of a move towards increased traditionalism. Norman Cohen talked of the new 'ascendancy of the right wing' in the United Synagogue and the end of 'the old easy going tolerance'.[13] In the 1970s Jakobovits highlighted the narrowing gap between the United Synagogue and groups such as the Adath.[14]

I have questioned that consensus. I argue that there was a high degree of continuity among the Chief Rabbis, from Nathan Adler to Brodie and Jakobovits, both in theology and in practice. I have made the case that the suggestions that between 1880 and 1970 the Chief Rabbis became more traditional, and that Louis Jacobs would have flourished under Adler or Hertz, are untenable. I have sought to demonstrate that the Chief Rabbis' theological positions combined a belief in the Divine origin of the Pentateuch (and the conviction that such a belief was of the highest importance), in the origin on Sinai of the core of the Oral Law and in the sanctity and authority of Jewish law, with other, more modern attitudes, such as on the development of the Oral Law and the value of non-Jewish wisdom. This attitude ensured that, although the leaders of more traditional Jewry disagreed with the Chief Rabbis, they nevertheless regarded them as authentic representatives of Judaism. Neither they nor the Chief Rabbis themselves extended this attitude to others who were untraditional in theology, even if they were traditional in practice. Similarly, although there were tensions between the Chief Rabbis and recent immigrants, there was also co-operation, mutual regard and respect.

Nevertheless, the differences between the Judaism of the Chief Rabbis and that of highly traditional Jewry were significant. All of the Chief Rabbis, from Adler to Jakobovits, rejected aspects of the non-Jewish world but were open to what they considered the best of modernity. They favoured the use of critical techniques to investigate those texts that tradition acknowledged had a human component (non-Pentateuchal Biblical books and the Talmud). They had a sophisticated understanding of the development of *halakhah*. They respected non-Jewish wisdom and recognised that non-Jews could possess authentic personal spirituality, whatever the flaws in their religious creeds. This view was intellectually honest and consistent because the Chief Rabbis believed that the essentials of tradition, as they understood them, were supported by the findings of scholarship. It is historically inaccurate to suggest that *Wissenschaft* and traditionalism were incompatible. The Chief Rabbis were part of that group led by Hildesheimer, Hoffman, Weinberg and others, who were both traditional and inclined to *Wissenschaft*, who took broadly the same view of what was essential and what was not in Jewish tradition. Unlike those who wished, for well-considered reasons, to maintain tradition unmodified, they contributed to the evolution of tradition, for tradition does change as new ideas enter, are embraced by some and then recognised by a growing proportion of the traditional community as acceptable. The Chief Rabbis were remoulders as well as transmitters of tradition.

The Chief Rabbis' theologies were reflected in their communal policies. They fought against those in the Jewish community who adopted different religious approaches. They excluded them from the United Synagogue (Morris Joseph, Joseph Hochman and Louis Jacobs are the leading examples) or wrote and spoke against them, as both Adler and Hertz did in their confrontation with the Liberal Jewish Synagogue. They built up communal institutions to reflect their attitudes. They constructed a Beth Din which had the expertise and the will to uphold *halakhah*. It was the Chief Rabbis who determined the stance of the

Beth Din and not the other way around, as has often been argued. They sought to create at Jews' College an institution that would teach the traditional dogmas of Judaism alongside the modern scholarly methods they regarded as essential for the flourishing of Jewish life and learning. As a result both the Beth Din and Jews' College were staffed by halakhists and scholars of international stature.

The Chief Rabbis were committed above all to keeping as many individuals as possible loyal to tradition. This effort had two major aspects. First they looked for ways to accommodate requests for change within *halakhah* so as not to exclude people dissatisfied with the status quo from the traditional community. They therefore made concessions within *halakhah* for the sake of inclusivity, although such concessions were a departure from their ideal position. This was as much the case with Brodie and Jakobovits (neither banned mixed choirs, for example) as it was with Adler and Hertz. Second, they centralised authority to keep control of the fine judgements that such a policy required, so that the line between acceptable change and contraventions of the *halakhah* was not crossed. Some specific policies did change over the period, but this was the result of changes in the community, not the Chief Rabbinate. In particular, the changing nature of the lay leadership (specifically, its increased traditionalism) gave Brodie greater freedom to implement his beliefs. Endelman and others have noted the importance of this shift, although this study would attach more importance to that dynamic than Endelman, and less to changes in the Chief Rabbinate itself. There was a constant dialogue over the period between the position occupied by the Chief Rabbi and that occupied by his community. As its position moved closer to his, his policies were able to reflect more accurately his ideal position.

The Chief Rabbis made judgements on which battles to fight and which to avoid with considerable skill and success, helping to maintain a level of institutional affiliation to traditional Judaism of over 80% until the late twentieth century, an achievement unparalleled in modern Jewry.[15]

To be sure other factors were at play: as Endelman has written, 'convenience, habit, family tradition and indifference', as well as concerns over burial rights, were all important in preventing people who did not share the official philosophy of the United Synagogue from leaving it.[16] Sacks has highlighted the role played by the inherent traditionalism of the British-influenced Anglo-Jews.[17] Englander has pointed to the association of the United Synagogue with the Anglican Church as an 'official' form of religion, and therefore with respectability.[18] However, all these factors (apart from the last) applied also to the United States, where, as Gurock has shown, before the Second World War the Orthodox Union was the largest synagogue body, but was largely composed of individuals who did not share its theology or halakhic standards. Yet by 1970 the proportion identifying as 'orthodox' had fallen to 11%.[19] This rapid falling away did not happen in Britain and, as Taylor has argued, since a major difference between the two communities was the Chief Rabbinate, the policies of the Chief Rabbis must be recognised as a – perhaps the – major factor.[20]

We have made an attempt to refine the typology of the Jewish response to modernity and see where the Chief Rabbis fit into this framework. We divided that response into four categories: antipathy (propounded by the followers of the Rabbi Moses Sofer, called resistors by Berger and rejectionists by Heilman), acknowledgement (called accommodators by Berger and syncretists by Heilman), adaptation (Reform Judaism) and acceptance (those who favoured abandoning Judaism altogether).

The Chief Rabbis all held views common to the acknowledgement school, which wished to acknowledge the best aspects of modernity without sacrificing the essentials of Judaism, as they understood those categories. They opposed the antipathy school, which rejected the notion that there was anything of value in modernity, the adaptation school, which wanted to amend Judaism (dispensing with much *hala-khah* and adopting universalistic attitudes) in the light of modernity, and the acceptance school, which advocated dispensing with Judaism altogether. The Chief Rabbis' inclination towards *Wissenschaft* associated them most strongly with the scientific branch of the acknowledgment school, but unlike some others from this branch, like Chajes, the Chief Rabbis' belief in the Divine authorship of the Pentateuch placed them in its traditional wing. The Chief Rabbis were also influenced by Hirsch's romantic branch, which wanted to embrace the best of non-Jewish culture, and by the aesthetic school, which was strongest in France and which sought to bring Jewish life, particularly worship, up to the standards of Western beauty. The Chief Rabbis also took advantage of a strain within the acknowledgement school which was a major feature of its American variety: nostalgia. British Jews did not generally wish to cut themselves off from tradition; they merely wished to remove what they regarded as offensive, but isolated, aspects. The Chief Rabbis capitalised on this disinclination towards radicalism, and their success was partly due to their taking advantage of circumstances which had the potential to aid their cause.

Although the influence of each group within the acknowledgement school can be detected in the approaches of the Chief Rabbis, there were major disagreements between them. The romantic school condemned *Wissenschaft* and its proponents, such as Hildesheimer. Hildesheimer, for his part, was unconvinced of the spiritual content of non-Jewish culture and sceptical about the enthusiasm with which Hirsch embraced it. Nevertheless all theological disagreements within the acknowledgement school, and between the antipathy and the acknowledgement were of secondary importance compared to the issue of the origin of the Pentateuch. The crucial division did not concern the differences between the scientific, romantic and aesthetic branches but between the traditionalists (either within the acknowledgement school or in the antipathy school) and the non-traditionalists (again, either within the acknowledgement school or in either the adaptation or acceptance schools).

Whatever views a rabbi might hold, if he accepted the origin on Sinai of the Pentateuch he was recognised as legitimate by the general traditionalist community. That is why Israel Salanter condemned aspects of Hildesheimer's educational policy but said he envied Hildesheimer's place in the next world. That is also why, for all their halakhic controversiality the French rabbinate was never placed entirely beyond the pale, because it remained firm in matters of dogma; when it regularised its halakhic positions, it was accepted fully back into the fold. In the mid-twentieth century in the United States, both the Orthodox Union and the United Synagogue of America contained mixed seating synagogues, yet the Orthodox Union was granted legitimacy by traditionalist Jewry whereas the United Synagogue of America was not. The reason for this distinction was not their positions on practice, but on dogma, especially the question of the Pentateuch.

The great similarity in the positions of, say, Hertz and Brodie on the one hand, and Jacobs on the other, is therefore deceptive. All could be considered as from the scientific branch of the acknowledgement school as they claimed to uphold the binding nature of *halakhah*. The difference between them on the origin of the Pentateuch might seem academic; but it was crucial. Hertz and Brodie were traditional and Jacobs was not. By isolating different strands of thought within the acknowledgement school, our typology enables us to see that this difference in attitude towards the Pentateuch was the decisive issue that divided the two men, just as it had divided others before, such as Adler and Joseph and Hertz and Chajes; indeed, there is good evidence that it divided all Jewish theologians in the modern period.

Different groups within the acknowledgement school had different institutional approaches. In America, power was pulled centrifugally

towards individual congregation so only loose synagogue confederations could be formed. Hirsch and his supporters were convinced that
only small and committed groups could survive and favoured a vanguard approach leading to small and intense, or nuclear, communities.
Others favoured some co-operation and led traditional groups within a
wider community. In France the traditional leadership enjoyed official
hegemony, but were constrained by a powerful lay leadership.

The British case was different from these models. The Chief Rabbis
adopted an expansive ideology, to bring as many as possible into the
fold by leniency where possible within *halakhah*. This strategy was
vital to the establishment of their freely accepted religious hegemony in
Anglo-Jewry, with the result that schools other than the acknowledgement school remained comparatively small. There were representatives
of the acknowledgement school in Britain who took a different organisational approach, including the leaders of the Machzike Hadath and
Adath Yisroel. They imported the uncompromising vanguard approach
of Hirsch and set out to create nuclear communities. They conflicted
with the Chief Rabbis not over major theological issues, but over the
best way to organise communities that could endure. The Chief Rabbis
favoured the expansive approach; Werner, Jung and Lerner were each
exponents of vanguard who, for example, rejected liturgical changes
that would make the synagogue service more attractive to those falling
away. Lerner and Hermann Adler may both have been 'Rabbi Dr' and
this was symbolic of agreement on many issues, but disagreements on
how to implement their shared theology created a huge gulf between
them.

This distinction is another example of how our typology helps us to
identify subtle, but crucial, differences. This enables us to understand
why individuals who seem so similar, disagreed so strongly on issues
such as these. The typology we have developed here therefore goes
further than clarifying our perceptions of the Chief Rabbis; it enables
us to understand the Jewish religious response to modernity better as
a whole.

The fineness of the distinctions in our typology is one reason why the
conclusions reached here have not been drawn before. As we have
noted, one 'Rabbi Dr' can look much like another, and it is only in
detailed examination that the differences emerge; and only within a
framework which makes ideological distinctions can the implications
of those distinctions be fully understood. It is because he did not properly appreciate the complexities within the acknowledgement school,
for example the differences between Hirsch and Hildesheimer, that

Meirovich was able to place them both in an opposite camp to Hertz; and similarly, it was because he did not see how much united Lerner and Adler ideologically, that Julius Jung did not precisely identify what did divide them, and why.[21]

The most significant example of this phenomenon in the historiography concerns Louis Jacobs and the Chief Rabbis. Jacobs, Adler, Hertz and Brodie had so much in common, including a commitment to *halakhah*, a sympathetic attitude to modern scholarship and an openness to non-Jewish culture, that it was easy to overlook what did divide them, which was not a practical but a theological question: who wrote the Pentateuch? They were all synthesists, to use Freud Kandel's term, but they disagreed about the correct approach to synthesis. One does not need to suggest that Brodie moved from a position of synthesis to compartmentalisation to explain the Jacobs Affair, as Freud Kandel does. It was a result of the type of synthesis Brodie and his predecessors had been advocating for over a century. By tracing how this question was used as a benchmark of acceptability by traditionalists in the modern period, our typology has helped to clarify the nature of the intellectual relationships between figures who appear, on the surface, to have either more or less in common than they actually did.

This problem that has so afflicted the study of the Chief Rabbis stems from the widespread belief, flowing from claims attributed to Moses Mendelssohn in the eighteenth century, that Judaism is not concerned with faith but is rather a religion of practice.[22] It is frequently stated that while Christianity places emphasis on creed Judaism is about action.[23] It was this emphasis on the importance of practice rather than belief that led scholars to underemphasise the question of the origin of the Pentateuch as one of decisive importance for the individuals they analysed. We have seen that in the modern period traditional Jewish leaders put enormous emphasis on belief.[24] However the idea that belief was secondary led scholars away from an examination of the crucial issues in some of the major controversies in which the Chief Rabbis were involved, such as the Joseph, Hochman and Jacobs affairs. Just as at the time many onlookers could not see the difference between one man who observed the Sabbath and the dietary laws and another, so historians downplayed the importance of the divisions between them, because they concerned issues of belief and not of practice.

The discussion of the Chief Rabbis has been clouded because it has been dominated by the interpretations of Louis Jacobs, his supporters and sympathisers such as the *Jewish Chronicle* of the 1950s and 1960s, and Meirovich. The founding myth of Jacobs' Masorti organisation is that Jacobs would have abided happily under the broad-minded benevolence, tolerance and civility of Adler and Hertz. Historians such as Alderman and Endelman have accepted this view and – because they considered the Chief Rabbis to be uninteresting theologically – they have not scrutinised the dominant account. Freud Kandel took Hertz's theology much more seriously, but still reproduced the established argument that Brodie moved away from his predecessors' position. In fact, there is ample evidence in the secondary literature, let alone the primary sources, which undermines this interpretation.

Immanuel Jakobovits wrote fifty years ago that 'not a single scholar, as far as I know, has tried to assess the place of Anglo-Jewry in the development of Judaism itself.'[25] This neglect, which Meirovich, Freud Kandel and others are now putting right, ensured that the history of how the British Chief Rabbis dealt with the Jewish encounter with modernity has remained obscure. Their approach, which was to acknowledge modernity, to encourage adherence to tradition but also to remould that tradition, has therefore been ignored. The study of the same Jewish response to modernity in Germany, the United States and France was also overlooked until the work of Ellenson, Shapiro, Berkovitz, Fierstein and others made amends. Much work remains to be done to bring our insight into the British case up to the level of our understanding of these other communities.

Notes

1 G. Alderman, *Modern British Jewry* (Oxford 1992), 106–109, 146–148; T. Endelman, *The Jews of Britain, 1656 to 2000* (Berkeley 2002), 250–253 V.D. Lipman, *A history of the Jews in Britain since 1858* (Leicester 1990), 92; I. Finestein, *Anglo-Jewry in changing times* (London 1999), 247.

2 Alderman, *Modern British Jewry*, 108–109, 146–147; B. Homa *A fortress in Anglo-Jewry* (London 1953), J. Jung, *Champions of orthodoxy* (London 1974); A. Newman *Chief Rabbi Dr. Joseph H. Hertz, C.H.* (London 1973), 20.

3 Endelman, *Jews of Britain*, 120; Alderman, *Modern British Jewry*, 355, 359.

4 Endelman, *Jews of Britain*, 250.

5 H. Meirovich, *A Vindication of Judaism* (New York 1998), 13.

6 Ibid., 8.

7 Ibid., 15.

8 M. Freud Kandel, *Orthodox Judaism in Britain since 1913* (London 2006), 159.

9 Meirovich, *Vindication*, 361; Endelman, *Jews of Britain*, 253.

10 Alderman, *Modern British Jewry*, 364; Endelman, *Jews of Britain*, 252.

11 Endelman, *Jews of Britain*, 252.

12 Ibid.

13 N. Cohen, 'The religious crisis in Anglo-Jewry' *Tradition* 8:2 (Summer 1966), 46.

14 I. Jakobovits, 'An analysis of secular versus religious trends in Anglo-Jewry' in Lipman and Lipman (ed), *Jewish life in Britain* (London 1977),.

15 In 1972 81% of Jewish marriages in Britain were performed under the auspices of synagogues defined as 'orthodox'. In the same year 82% of members of the United Synagogue claimed they kept a kosher home, whereas only 19% of members of the Reform and Liberal Jews made that claim. Belonging to the United Synagogue kept people more observant. S. Sharot, *Judaism: a sociology* (Newton Abbot 1976), 160, 162.

16 Endelman, *Jews of Britain*, 254.

17 J. Sacks, *Community of faith* (London 1995), 88.

18 D. Englander, 'Anglicized not Anglican: Jews and Judaism in Victorian Britain' in Parsons (ed), *Religion in Victorian Britain* (Manchester 1988), 260.

19 J.S. Gurock, 'Twentieth-century American orthodoxy's era of non-observance, 1900–1960' *Torah u-Madda Journal* 4 (2000) 87, 93, 99.

20 Sacks also argues that the factors other than the policies of the Chief Rabbis cannot account entirely for the success of the United Synagogue. Sacks, *Community of faith*, 88; D. Taylor, *British Chief Rabbis, 1664–2006* (London 2007), 258, 331, 368.

21 Although, as we have mentioned above, Jung was a pro-Federation of Synagogues polemicist that does not mean that his analysis of Adler and Lerner's positions was not genuinely held.

22 S. Schechter, *Studies in Judaism, first series* (Philadelphia 1919), 148–149.

23 See, for example, M. Kellner, *Must a Jew believe anything?* (London 2005) or L. Jacobs, *Helping with inquiries* (London 1989), 151.

24 Mendelssohn himself has been misinterpreted: he did not discount the credal aspect of Judaism entirely. As Altmann argues, Mendelssohn did uphold 'a few fundamental tenets on which all our teachers are agreed, and without which the Jewish religion simply could not exist': the existence of God, Divine Providence and (crucially for our purposes) the giving of the Law. A. Altmann, *Moses Mendelssohn, a biographical study* (London 1998), 544.

25 I. Jakobovits, *Journal of a rabbi* (London 1967), 49.

Bibliography

Unpublished sources: individual

Apple, R., 'Mixed choirs in Jewish worship' (unpublished 1987)
Apple, R., 'Mixed choirs in Jewish worship' (unpublished 2001)
Guttentag, J., Shul a unique institution (unpublished 2001)
Interview with Chimen Abramsky, 25 October 2004
Interview with Dudley Cohen, 19 August 2001
Interview with Alan Greenbat, 22 August 2005
Interview with Isaac Levy, 21 May 2004
Interview with Graeme Morris, 5 February 2006
Olsberg, M., undergraduate dissertation (Cambridge University 2005)
Personal communication: James Kennard, 10 October 2001
Personal communication, Stefan Reif, 23 September 2005

Unpublished sources: archive

E.N. Adler Papers, Jewish Theological Seminary, New York
Chief Rabbinate Papers, London Metropolitan Archive
J.H. Hertz Papers, Hartley Library, Southampton University
J.H. Hertz, letters to ministers, (19 May 1939, 21 August 1940), Hartley Library,
    Southampton University.
I. Hillman Papers, Jewish and National Library Archives Jerusalem
H.M. Lazarus Papers, Southampton University Library
London Beth Din Papers, London Metropolitan Archive
United Synagogue Papers, London Metropolitan Archive

Periodicals

British Weekly (5, 12, 19, 26 November 1886)
Jewish Chronicle (2 January 1863, 4 August 1865, 11 August 1865, 5 April
    1878, 5 March 1880, 12 March 1880, 9 April 1880, 26 March 1886, 3 June 1892,
    10 June 1892, 1 July 1892, 26 May 1893, 22 September 1893, 15 May 1896,
    8 September 1896, 18 May 1900, 3 January 1902, 7 March 1902, 28 March

1902, 4 September 1908, 26 January 1912, 24 May 1912, 13 August 1915, 17 February 1950, 14 February 1969)
Jewish Quarterly Review, (1893,1894)
Jewish Review (July 1910, September 1911)
Nineteenth Century (1878, 1881)
Quest (London 1965), *Quest 2* (London 1967) [annual]

Biblical and rabbinic texts

Babylonian Talmud, tractate *Bava Batra*
Bahya ibn Pakuda, *Hovot HaLevavot*
J. Karo, *Shulhan Arukh*
M. Maimonides, commentary to the Mishna
Mishna, Orla
Torat Elokim (Vilna 1875)

Other books and published contribution

Addresses given at the Conference of European Rabbis (London 1963)
Addresses given at the eighteenth conference of Anglo-Jewish preachers (London 1973)
Adler, A., *The discipline of sorrow* (London 1911)
Adler, C. et al. (ed), *Jewish encyclopaedia* (New York 1906)
Adler, H., *Niftulei Elohim* (London 1869)
Adler, H., 'Elisha ben Abuya' *Jewish Chronicle* (22 March 1878)
Adler, H., 'Jews and Judaism: a rejoinder' *Nineteenth Century* (1878) 133–150
Adler, H., 'Some recent phases of Judeophobia' *Nineteenth Century* (1881) 813–829
Adler, H., *Hebrew, the language of our prayers* (London 1885)
Adler, H., in *Immortality: a clerical symposium* (New York 1885), 87–109
Adler, H., *The Sabbath and the synagogue* (London 1889)
Adler, H., *This book of the Law* (London 1891)
Adler, H., *The functions of the Jewish pulpit* (London 1892)
Adler, H., *Is it well with thee?* (Birmingham 1893)
Adler, H., *A good heart* (London 1893)
Adler, H., *The loss of HMS Victoria* (London 1893)
Adler, H., *Sanitation as taught by the Mosaic law* (London 1893)
Adler, H., *Home worship* (London 1894)
Adler, H., 'The Sabbath and the organ' *Jewish Chronicle* (4 January 1895), 7
Adler, H., *Religious versus political Zionism* (London 1898)
Adler, H., *The old paths* (London 1902)
Adler, H., 'The sons of the prophets' in Harris (ed) *Jews' College Jubilee Volume* (London 1906), 1–20
Adler, H., *Anglo-Jewish memories* (London 1909)

Adler, M. and Barnett, A., *The history of the Hammersmith Synagogue* (London 1950)

Adler, N.M., *Laws and regulations for all the synagogues in the British Empire* (London 1847)

Adler, N.M., *The Jewish faith* (London 1848)

Adler, N.M., *Solomon's judgement* (London 1854)

Alderman, G., *The Federation of Synagogues, 1887–1987* (London 1987)

Alderman, G., *Modern British Jewry* (Oxford 1992)

Alderman, G., 'Power, authority and status in British Jewry: the Chief Rabbinate and shechita' in Alderman and Holmes (ed) *Outsiders and outcasts: essays in honour of William J. Fishman* (London 1993), 12–31

Alderman, G. and Holmes, C. (ed), *Outsiders and outcasts: essays in honour of William J. Fishman* (London 1993)

Altmann, A., 'Memorial address' in Gottleib (ed) *Essays and addresses in Memory of JH Hertz* (London 1948), 1–6

Altmann, A., *Essays in Jewish intellectual history* (Hanover, New Hampshire 1981)

A. Altmann, *Moses Mendelssohn, a biographical study* (London 1998)

Apple, R., *The Hampstead Synagogue* (London 1967)

Arnold, M., *Culture and anarchy* (London 1869)

Bach, H.I., *The German Jew* (Oxford 1984)

Bader, G. and Jung, M. 'Meir Tsevi Jung' in Jung (ed) *Jewish leaders* (Jerusalem 1953), 297–316

Barnett, A., *The Western Synagogue through two centuries (1761–1961)* (London 1961)

Bayme, S., 'Claude Montefiore, Lily Montagu and the origins of the Jewish Religious Union' *Jewish Historical Studies* 27 (1982) 61–71

Bentwich, N., *Solomon Schechter* (London 1959)

Berger, P., 'A sociological view of the secularization of theology' *Journal for the Scientific Study of Religion* 6:1 (1967), 3–16

Berkovitz, J.M., *Rites and passages* (Philadelphia 2004)

Berman, S., 'Kol Isha' in Landman (ed) *Rabbi Joseph H. Lookstein Memorial Volume* (New York 1980) 45–66

Bermant, Ch., *Troubled Eden* (London 1969)

Bermant, Ch., *Lord Jakobovits* (London 1990)

Black, E.C., *The social politics of Anglo-Jewry* (Oxford 1989)

Black, E.C., 'The Anglicization of orthodoxy: the Adlers, father and son' in Malino and Sorkin (ed) *From east and west* (Oxford 1990), 295–325

Black, G., *Living up west* (London 1994)

Blank, J.E., *Minutes of the Federation of Synagogues* (London 1912)

Breuer, E., '(Re)creating traditions of language and texts: the haskalah and cultural continuity' *Modern Judaism* 16:1 (1996), 161–183

Breuer, E., Review of *Vindication of Judaism* by H. Meirovich. *Jewish Quarterly Review* 91 (January–April 2001), 447–449

Breuer, M., trans. Petuchowski, E., *Modernity within tradition* (New York 1992)

Brodie, I., 'Foreword' in I. Brodie and J. Rabbinowitz (ed) *Studies in Jewish history: the Adolph Bücher memorial volume* (Oxford 1956), v–vi

Brodie, I., *A word in season* (London 1959)

Brodie, I., *The strength of my heart* (London 1969)

Buchler, A., 'The reading of the Law and the Prophets in a triennial cycle' *Jewish Quarterly Review* (1893), 420–468; (1894), 1–73

Carmilly-Weinberger, M., 'The similarities and relationship between the *Judisch-Theologisches Seminar* (Breslau) and the Rabbinical Seminary (Budapest)' *Leo Baeck Institute Year Book* XLIV (1999) 3–22

Carr, E.H., *What is history?* (London 1961, 2nd edn 1987)

Cesarani, D., *Zionism in England, 1917–1939* (D.Phil, Oxford University 1986)

Cesarani, D., 'An embattled minority: the Jews in Britain during the First World War' in *Immigrants and minorities* 8/1 (1989), 61–81

Cesarani, D. (ed), *The making of modern Anglo-Jewry* (Oxford 1990)

Cesarani, D., *The Jewish Chronicle and Anglo-Jewry, 1841–1991* (Cambridge 1994)

Chavel, I., 'On Haym Soloveitchik's "Rupture and reconstruction: the transformation of contemporary orthodoxy society": a response' *Torah u-Madda Journal* 5 (1997), 122–136

Cohen, F.L. and Davis, D.M. (ed) *The voice of prayer and praise* (London 1933)

Cohen, I., *A Jewish pilgrimage* (London 1956)

Cohen, J., *In defence of tradition* (London [c.1962] undated)

Cohen, J. (ed), *Dear Chief Rabbi* (Hoboken, New Jersey 1995)

Cohen, N., 'Trends in Anglo-Jewish religious life' in Gould and Esh (ed) *Trends in Jewish life* (London 1964) 41–66

Cohen, N.W., 'Diaspora plus Palestine, religion plus nationalism: the seminary and Zionism, 1902–1948' in Wertheimer, *Tradition renewed*, 115–176

Cohen, S.A., *English Zionists and British Jews* (Princeton, New Jersey 1982)

Cohen Albert, P. *The modernization of French Jewry* (Hanover, New Hampshire 1977)

Cosgrove, E.J. *Teyku: the insoluble contradictions in the life and thought of Louis Jacobs* (PhD thesis, University of Chicago 2008)

Daiches, S., *Essays and addresses* (London 1955)

Danzger, M.H., *Returning to tradition – the contemporary revival of orthodox Judaism* (New Haven, Connecticut 1989)

Davidman, L., 'Accomodation and resistance to modernity' *Sociological Analysis* 51/1 (Spring 1990), 35–51

Davies, A. (ed), *Antisemitism in Canada* (Waterloo, Ontario 1992)

Davis, A., and Adler H.M. (ed), *Service of the synagogue, Pentecost* (London 1909)

Davis, M., *The emergence of conservative Judaism: the historical school in 19th-Century America* (Philadelphia 1963)

De Lange, N., *An introduction to Judaism* (Cambridge 2000)

Drachman, B., *The unfailing light* (New York 1948)

Eisen, A., 'Theology, sociology and ideology: Jewish thought in America, 1925–1955' *Modern Judaism* 2:1 (February 1982), 91–103

Eisen, A., 'Constructing the usable past: the idea of tradition in twentieth century American Judaism' in Wertheimer (ed) *The uses of tradition* (New York 1992), 429–461

Ellenson, D. and Jacobs, R., 'Scholarship and faith: David Hoffman and his relationship to *Wissenschaft des Judentums*' *Modern Judaism* 8 (1988) 27–40

Ellenson, D., *Rabbi Esriel Hildesheimer and the creation of a modern Jewish orthodoxy* (Tuscaloosa, Alabama 1990)

Ellenson, D., '*A vindication of Judaism: the polemics of the Hertz Pentateuch*: a review essay' *Modern Judaism* 21 (2001), 67–77

Ellenson, D., *After emancipation* (Cincinnati 2004)

Ellenson, D., *Wissenschaft des Judentums, historical consciousness and Jewish faith*, Leo Baeck Memorial Lecture 48 (New York 2004)

Ellenson, D., 'A reaction to Samuel Heilman's analysis of orthodoxy' *Contemporary Jewry* (2005), 279–283

Ellison, R.H., *The Victorian pulpit* (Susquehanna, Texas 1998)

Elman, Y. and Gurock, J.S. (ed), *Hazon Nahum* (New York 1997)

Elton, B.J., 'Did the Chief Rabbinate move to the right? A case study: the mixed choir controversies, 1880–1986' *Jewish Historical Studies* 39 (2004), 121–151

Elton, G.R., *The practice of history* (Sydney 1967)

Endelman, T., *The Jews of Georgian England* (Philadelphia 1979)

Endelman, T., *Radical assimilation in English Jewish history, 1656–1945* (Bloomington, Indiana 1990)

Endelman, T., 'English Jewish history' *Modern Judaism* 11 (1991), 91–109

Endelman, T., *The Jews of Britain, 1656 to 2000* (Berkeley, California 2000)

Endelman, T., 'Practices of a low anthropological level, a *shehitah* controversy of the 1950s' in Kershen (ed) *Food in the migrant experience* (Aldershot, Hamshire 2002), 77–97

Englander, D., 'Anglicized not Anglican: Jews and Judaism in Victorian Britain' in Parsons (ed) *Religion in Victorian Britain* (Manchester 1988), 235–273

Englander, D., (ed) *A documentary history of Jewish immigrants in Britain, 1840–1920* (London 1994)

Epstein, I., *Judaism of tradition* (London 1931)

Epstein, I., Levine, E., and Roth, C. (ed), *Essays in honour of the Very Rev. J.H. Hertz* (London 1942)

Epstein, I. (ed), *Joseph Herman Hertz, 1871–1946: In Memoriam* (London 1947)

Epstein, I., *The faith of Judaism* (London 1954)

Epstein, I., 'Adolph Buchler' in Brodie and Rabbinowitz (ed.) *Studies in Jewish history* (Oxford 1956), xiii–xxii

Evans, R., *In defence of history* (London 2001)

Feldman, A., *Parables and similes of the rabbis* (Cambridge 1924)

Feldman, A., *Sabbath spice and festival fare* (London 1927)

Feldman, A., *The London Beth Din* (London 1929)

Feldman, D., *Englishmen and Jews* (New Haven, Connecticut 1994)

Fierstein, R.E., *A different spirit: the Jewish Theological Seminary of America, 1886–1902* (New York 1990)

Fierstein, R.E. and Waxman, J. (ed), *Solomon Schechter in America: A centennial tribute* (New York 2002)

Finestein, I., *Jewish society in Victorian England* (London 1993)

Finestein, I., *Anglo-Jewry in changing times* (London 1999)

Finestein, I., *Scenes and personalities in Anglo-Jewry* (London 2002)

Fishman, W.J., *East End Jewish radicals, 1875–1914* (London 1975)

Frankel, J. and Zipperstein, S.J. (ed), *Assimilation and community* (Cambridge 1992)

Frankel, Z., *On changes in Judaism*, www.ucalgary.ca/~elsegal/363_Transp/ZFrankel.html

Freud Kandel, M., *Ideology forsaken* (PhD thesis, University of Cambridge 2000)

Freud Kandel, M., 'The theological background of Dr Joseph H. Hertz' *Le'eyla* 48 (2000), 25–33

Freud Kandel, M., *Orthodox Judaism in Britain since 1913* (London 2006)

Friedlander, M., *The Jewish religion* (London 1922)

Furst, R., *Hakirah or Mehkar: the religious implications of an historical approach to* Limmudei Kodesh (ATID, Jerusalem 2001)

Gartner, L.P., *The Jewish immigrant in England, 1870–1914* (London 1973)

Gartner, L.P., 'A quarter century of Anglo-Jewish historiography' *Jewish Social Studies* 48 (1986), 105–126

Ginor, Z. (ed), *Yakar Le'Mordecai* (New York 1998)

Ginsburg, E.P., *Jewish faith in action: selected writings of Rabbi Dr. I. Epstein* (London 1995)

Ginzberg, L., *Students, scholars and saints* (Philadelphia 1928)

Gollancz, H., *Sermons* (London 1910)

Gollancz, H., *The masters* (Oxford 1929)

Goodman, M., 'Vice versa: Samuel Montagu, the first Lord Swaythling' *Jewish Historical Studies* 40 (2005), 75–103

Gopin, M., 'An orthodox embrace of gentiles? Interfaith tolerance in the thought of S.D. Luzzatto and E. Benamozegh' *Modern Judaism* 18 (1998) 173–196

Gordis, D.H., 'David Zevi Hoffman and civil marriage: evidence of a traditional community under siege' *Modern Judaism* 10 (1990) 85–103

Gottlieb, W. (ed), *Essays and addresses in memory of J.H. Hertz* (London 1948)

Gould, J. and Esh, S. (ed), *Trends in Jewish life* (London 1964)

Graetz, H., *History of the Jews* (Philadelphia 1956)

Graupe, H.M., *The rise of modern Judaism* (Huntington, New York 1979)

Green, A., *A social history of the Jewish East End in London, 1914–1939* (Lampeter, Wales 1991)

Green, A.A., *Sermons* (London 1935)

Green, K.H., 'Moses Mendelssohn's opposition to the *herem*: the first step toward denominationalism?' *Modern Judaism* 12 (1992), 39–60

Grunfeld, I., *Judaism eternal* (London 1956)

Gurock, J.S., 'Resisters and accomodators' in Rader Marcus and Peck (ed) *The American rabbinate* (Hoboken, New Jersey 1985), 10–97

Gurock, J.S., *American Jewish orthodoxy in historical perspective* (Hoboken, New Jersey 1996)

Gurock, J.S., 'Yeshiva students at the Jewish Theological Seminary' in Wertheimer (ed) *Tradition renewed* (New York 1997), 471–514

Gurock, J.S., 'Another look at the proposed merger: lay perspectives on Yeshiva–JTS relations in the 1920s' in Elman and Gurock (ed), *Hazon Nahum* (New York 1997), 729–742

Gurock, J.S. and Schachter, J.J., *A modern heretic and a traditional community: Mordecai M. Kaplan, Orthodoxy and American Judaism* (New York 1997)

Gurock, J.S., 'Twentieth-century American orthodoxy's era of non-observance, 1900–1960' *Torah u-Madda Journal* 4 2000), 87–107

Gutwein, D., *The divided elite* (Leiden 1992)

Harris, I., 'History of Jews' College' in I. Harris (ed) *Jews' College Jubilee Volume* (London 1906), iii–cci

Heilman, S.C., 'Constructing orthodoxy' in Robbins and Anthony (ed) *In gods we trust* (New Brunswick, 1981), 141–157

Heilman, S.C., 'The many faces of orthodoxy, part 1' *Modern Judaism* 2:1 (February 1982), 23–52

Heilman, S.C., 'The many faces of orthodoxy, part 2' *Modern Judaism* 2:2 (May 1982), 171–198

Heilman, S.C., *Portrait of American Jews* (Seattle 1995)

Heilman, S.C., 'How did fundamentalism manage to infiltrate contemporary orthodoxy?' *Contemporary Jewry* 25 (2005), 258–272

Hertz, J.H., 'Zionism – a reply by the Chief Rabbi' *Fortnightly Review* (1916), 1032–1035

Hertz, J.H. (ed), *A book of Jewish thoughts* (New York 1926)

Hertz, J.H., *Affirmations of Judaism* (Oxford 1927)

Hertz, J.H., *Pentateuch and Haftorahs, Genesis* (London 1929)

Hertz, J.H., *Sermons, addresses and studies* (London 1938)

Hertz, J.H., *Early and late* (Hindhead, Surrey 1943)

Hertz, J.H., *The Authorised Daily Prayer Book* (New York 1948)

Hertz, J.H., *Pentateuch and Haftorahs* (London 1960)

Hertz, J.H., *Affirmations of Judaism* (London 1975)

Heschel, S., *Abraham Geiger and the Jewish Jesus* (Chicago 1998)

Hirsch, S.R., trans. B. Drachman, *The nineteen letters* (New York 1899)

Hirsch, S.R., trans. I. Levy, *Pentateuch* (London 1959)

Hirsch, S.R., trans. Grunfeld, *Judaism eternal* (London 1959)

Hirsch, S.R., *Collected writings* (New York 1988)

Hochman, J., *Jerusalem Temple festivities* (London 1908)

Hochman, J., *Jewish separation and human progress* (London 1910)

Hochman, J., *Orthodoxy and religious observance* (London 1910)

Homa, B., *A fortress in Anglo-Jewry* (London 1953)

Homa, B., *Orthodoxy in Anglo-Jewry* (London 1969)

Homa, B., *Footprints in the sands of time* (Charfield, Gloucester, 1990)

Houghton, W.R., (ed) *Neely's history of the parliament of religions and religious congresses at the World's Columbian Exposition* (Chicago 1893)

Hyamson, A.M., *The London Board for Shechita, 1804–1954* (London 1954)

Hyamson, A.M., *Jews' College London, 1855–1955* (London 1955)

Hyamson, M., *The Oral Law* (London 1910)

Hyamson, M., *Sabbath and festival addresses* (New York 1936)

Hyman, J., *Jews in Britain during the Great War* (Working Papers in Economic and Social History No. 51, University of Manchester Department of History, 2001)

Immortality: a clerical symposium (New York 1885)

Jacobs, L., *Sermon by Rabbi Dr. Louis Jacobs on the occasion of his induction as minister to the New West End Synagogue* (London 1954)

Jacobs, L., *We have reason to believe* (London 1957)

Jacobs, L., *Helping with inquiries* (London 1989)

Jakobovits, I., *Journal of a rabbi* (London 1967)

Jakobovits, I., 'An analysis of secular versus religious trends in Anglo-Jewry' in Lipman and Lipman (ed) *Jewish life in Britain* (London 1977) 33–48

Jakobovits, I., *If only my people* (London 1984)

Joseph, M., *The ideal in Judaism* (London 1893)

Joseph, M., *Judaism as life and creed* (London 1903)

Joseph, M., 'The jubilee of political emancipation' in *Transactions of the Jewish Historical Society of England* 6 (1912), 88–111

Jung, J., *Champions of orthodoxy* (London 1974)

Jung, L., (ed), *Jewish leaders* (Jerusalem 1953)

Jung, L. (ed), *Guardians of our heritage* (New York 1958)

Kaplan, M.M., *Judaism as civilisation* (New York 1935)

Katz, J., 'Religion as a uniting and dividing force' in Katz (ed) *The role of religion in modern Jewish history* (Cambridge, Massachusetts, 1975), 1–17

Katz, J., 'Sources of orthodox trends' in Katz (ed) *The role of religion in modern Jewish history* (Cambridge, Massachusetts, 1975), 29–68

Katz, J. (ed), *The role of religion in modern Jewish history* (Cambridge, Massachusetts, 1975)

Katz, J. 'Orthodoxy in historical perspective' in Medding (ed) *Studies in contemporary Jewry* (Bloomington, Indiana 1986)

Katz, J. (trans. Brody, Z.), *A house divided: orthodoxy and schism in nineteenth-century European Jewry* (Hanover, New Hampshire, 1998)

Katz, J., 'The changing position and outlook of halakhists in early modernity' in Landman (ed) *Scholars and scholarship in Jewish history* (New York 1990), 93–106

Katz, J., *Divine law in human hands* (Jerusalem 1998)

Kellner, M., *Must a Jew believe anything?* (London 2005)

Kershen, A.J. (ed), *Food in the migrant experience* (Aldershot 2002)

Kohut, A., 'Secular and theological studies' *The Menorah* (13 July 1892), 49

Landman, L. (ed), *Rabbi Joseph H. Lookstein memorial volume* (New York 1980)

Landman, L. (ed), *Scholars and scholarship in Jewish history* (New York 1990)

Landman, S., 'Origins of the Balfour Declaration: Dr Hertz's contribution' in Epstein, Levine and Roth (ed) *Essays in honour of the Very Rev. JH Hertz* (London 1942) 261–270

Lazarus, H.M., 'Hesped' in Gottlieb (ed) *Essays and addresses in memory of J.H. Hertz* (London 1948), 25–30

Lehmann, R., 'Hermann Adler – a bibliography of his published works' in Noy and Ben-Ami (ed), *Studies in the cultural life of the Jews in England* (Jerusalem 1975), 101–150

Lehrman, S.M., *Jewish customs and folklore* (London 1949)

Lehrman, S.M., 'Joseph Herman Hertz' in Gottlieb (ed) *Essays and addresses in memory of J.H. Hertz* (London 1948), 31–35

Leiman, Sh.Z., 'Rabbinic openness to general culture in the early modern period' in Schachter (ed), *Judaism's encounter with other cultures: rejection or integration?* (New York 1997), 143–216

Lederhendler, E., *Jewish responses to modernity* (New York 1994)

Levene, M., *War, Jews and the new Europe: the diplomacy of Lucien Wolf, 1914–1919* (Oxford 1992)

Levine, E., 'Memoir' in Epstein (ed) *Joseph Herman Hertz, 1871–1946: In Memoriam* (London 1947), 1–32

Levy, A., *History of the Sunderland Jewish community* (London 1956)

Levy, E., 'Anti-Semitism in England at war, 1914–1916' in *Patterns of Prejudice* 4/5 (1970), 27–30

Levy, I., *Historic Judaism versus Liberal Judaism* (London 1949)

Liberles, R., *Religious conflict in social context* (Westport, Connecticut 1985)

Lipman, V.D., *A century of social service* (London 1959)

Lipman, V.D. and Lipman, S.L. (ed) *Jewish life in Britain* (London 1977)

Lipman, V.D., *A history of the Jews of Britain since 1858* (Leicester 1990)

Malino, F. and Sorkin, D. (ed), *From east and west* (Oxford 1990)

Marks, D.W., *Sermons* (London 1855)

Marmorstein, A., 'My father, a memoir' in J. Rabbinowitz and M.S. Lew (ed) *Studies in Jewish theology* (London 1950)

Marmorstein, J., 'David Hoffman, defender of the faith' *Tradition* 9:4 (1966), 91–101

Marx, A., *Essays in Jewish biography* (Philadelphia 1904)

Medding P.Y. (ed), *Studies in contemporary Jewry* (Bloomington, Indiana 1986)

Meirovich, H., *Vindication of Judaism* (New York 1998)

Meyer, M.A., 'Modernity as a crisis for the Jews' *Modern Judaism* 9:2 (May 1989), 151–164

Meyer, M.A., *Jewish identity in the modern world* (Seattle 1990)

Meyer, M.A., 'Tradition and modernity reconsidered' in Wertheimer (ed) *The uses of tradition* (New York 1992), 465–470

Meyer, M.A. and Plaut, W.G. (ed), *The Reform Judaism reader* (New York 2001)

Meyer, M.A., *Judaism within modernity* (Detroit 2001)

Meyer, M.A., 'Two persistent tensions within *Wissenschaft des Judentums*' *Modern Judaism* 24:2 (May 2004), 105–119

Miller, S.H., 'Religious practice and Jewish identity in a sample of London Jews' in Webber (ed) *Jewish identities in the new Europe* (London 1994), 193–204

Montagu, L.H., *Samuel Montagu, Baron Swaythling* (London [1913] undated)

Montefiore, C.G., 'Is Judaism a tribal religion?' *Contemporary Review* 9 (1882), 9–16

Montefiore, C.G., *The Hibbert lectures 1892* (London 1897)

Montefiore, C.G., *Liberal Judaism and Hellenism* (London 1918)

Montefiore, C.G. and Lowe, H. (ed), *A rabbinic anthology* (London 1938)

Morais, S., 'The Talmud' *The Occident* (26 July 1868), 165–166

Namier, L.B., *The structure of politics at the accession of George III* (London 1927)

Newman, A., *Chief Rabbi Dr Joseph H. Hertz, C.H.* (London 1973)

Newman, A. (ed), *Provincial Jewry in Victorian Britain* (London 1975)

Newman, A., *The United Synagogue, 1870–1970* (London 1977)

Newman, A. (ed), *The Jewish East End, 1840–1939* (London 1981)

Newman, E., 'The responsa of Dayan Jacob Reinowitz, 1813–1898' *Jewish Historical Studies* 23 (1969–1970 (23) 22–33

Noy, D. and Ben-Ami, I (ed), *Studies in the cultural life of the Jews in England* (Jerusalem 1975)

Orenstein, P., *Historical sketch of the Beth Hamedrash* (London 1905)

Paneth, P., *Guardian of the Law* (London [1940–1945] undated)

Parsons, G. (ed), *Religion in Victorian Britain* (Manchester 1988)

Parsons, G., 'Reform, revival and realignment: the experience of Victorian Anglicanism' in Parsons (ed) *Religion in Victorian Britain* (Manchester 1988), 14–66

Persoff, M., *Immanuel Jakobovits: a prophet in Israel* (London 2002)

Persoff, M., *Faith against reason: religious reform and the British Chief Rabbinate, 1840–1990* (London 2008)

Phillips, O.S. and Simons, H.A., *The history of the Bayswater Synagogue, 1863–1963* (London 1963)

Plaut, W.G., *The rise of Reform Judaism* (New York 1963)

Rader Marcus, J. and Peck, A.J. (ed), *The American rabbinate* (Hoboken, New Jersey 1985)

Raphael, M., *Profiles in American Judaism* (San Francisco 1984)

Reif, S.C., *Judaism and Hebrew prayer* (Cambridge 1993)

Report on the Sabbath reading of the Scriptures in a triennial cycle (London 1913)

Robbins, T. and Anthony, D. (ed), *In gods we trust* (New Brunswick, New Jersey 1981)

Robinson, I., 'Cyrus Adler: President of the Jewish Theological Seminary 1915–1940' in Wertheimer (ed) *Tradition renewed* (New York 1997), 103–160

Roth, C., 'Britain's three Chief Rabbis' in Jung (ed) *Jewish leaders* (Jerusalem 1953), 477–490

Roth, C., *A history of Jews in England* (Oxford 1964)

Royal Commission on Divorce and Matrimonial Causes, *Evidence* (1912–1913)

Rubinstein, W.D., *A history of the Jews in the English-speaking world: Great Britain* (London 1996)

Ruderman, D.B., *Jewish Enlightenment in an English key* (Princeton, New Jersey 2000)

Sacks, J., *Community of faith* (London 1995)

Salaman, R.N., *Whither Lucian Wolf's Anglo-Jewish community?* (London 1954)

Schachter, J.J. (ed), *Judaism's encounter with other cultures: rejection or integration?* (New York 1997)

Schechter, S., *Studies in Judaism* (London 1896; new edn, New York 1958)

Schechter, S., *Studies in Judaism*, 2nd series (Philadelphia 1908)

Schechter, S., *Seminary addresses and other papers* (New York 1969)

Schischa, S., 'Hermann Adler, yeshiva bahur, Prague 1860–1862' in J.M. Shaftesley (ed) *Remember the days* (London 1966) 241–277

Schonfeld, V., *Judaism as life's purpose* (London 1930)

Schreiber, A.M., 'The Hatam Sofer's nuanced attitude towards secular learning, *maskilim* and reformers' *Torah u-Madda Journal* 11 (2002–2003) 123–173

Scult, M, 'Schechter's seminary' in Wertheimer (ed) *Tradition renewed* (New York 1997), 43–102

Segev, T., *One Palestine, complete: Jews and Arabs under the British Mandate* (London 2000)

Shaftesley, J.M., 'A biographical sketch' in H.J. Zimmels, J. Rabbinowitz and I. Finestein (ed) *Essays presented to Chief Rabbi Israel Brodie on the occasion of his seventieth birthday* (London 1967), xi–xxxix

Shaftesley, J.M., 'Religious controversies' in S.S. Levin (ed) *A century of Anglo-Jewish life* (London 1970), 93–113

Shapiro, M. B., 'Review essay: sociology and *halakha*' *Tradition* 27:1 (1992), 75–85

Shapiro, M. B., 'Rabbi David Zevi Hoffman on Torah and *Wissenschaft*' *Torah u-Madda Journal* 6 (1995–1996), 129–137

Shapiro, M.B., *Between the yeshiva world and modern orthodoxy: the life and times of Rabbi Yehiel Yaakov Weinberg* (Oxford 1999)

Shapiro, M.B., 'A response to Samuel C. Heilman's "How did fundamentalism manage to infiltrate contemporary orthodoxy?"' *Contemporary Jewry* 25 (2005), 273–278

Sharot, S., *Judaism: a sociology* (Newton Abbot 1976)

Shatzkes, P., *Holocaust and rescue* (London 2004)

Shimoni, G., *Jews and Zionism: the South African experience, 1910–1967* (Oxford 1980)

Shimoni, G., 'From anti-Zionism to non-Zionism in Anglo Jewry, 1917–1937', *Jewish Journal of Sociology* 28 (1986), 19–48

Shimoni, G., 'The non-Zionists in Anglo-Jewry, 1937–1948' *Jewish Journal of Sociology* 28 (1986), 89–115

Shuchat, R., 'Attitudes towards cosmogony and evolution among rabbinic thinkers in the nineteenth and early twentieth centuries' *Torah u-Madda Journal* 13 (2005), 15–49

Silber, M.K., 'The emergence of Ultra-Orthodoxy' in Wertheimer (ed) *The uses of tradition* (New York 1992), 23–84

Silverstein, A., *Alternatives to assimilation* (Hanover, New Hampshire 1994)

Simons, H.A., *Forty years a Chief Rabbi: the life and times of Solomon Hirschell* (London 1980)

Singer, S., *The authorised daily prayer book* (London 1891)

Singer, S., *Orthodox Judaism in early Victorian London* (PhD dissertation, Yeshiva University 1981)

Smith, R.M., 'The London Jews' Society and patterns of Jewish conversion in England, 1801–1859' *Jewish Social Studies* 43 (1981), 275–290

Sorkin, D., 'The impact of emancipation on German Jewry' in Frankel and Zipperstein (ed) *Assimilation and community: the Jews in nineteenth-century Europe* (Cambridge 1992) 177–198

Sorkin, D., 'The case for comparison: Moses Mendelssohn and the religious Enlightenment' *Modern Judaism* 14:2 (May 1994), 121–138

Sorkin, D., *Moses Mendelssohn and the religious Enlightenment* (Berkeley, California 1996)

Soloveitchik, H., 'Rupture and reconstruction' *Tradition* 28:4 (1994), 64–130

Soloveitchik, H., 'Clarifications and reply' *Torah u-Madda Journal* 5 (1997), 137–149

Spiers, D.B. (ed), *Hagadah for Passover* (London 1954)

Strumpf, D., 'Hirsch Hildesheimer' in Jung (ed) *Guardians of our heritage* (New York 1958) 423–445

Taylor, D., *British Chief Rabbis, 1664–2006* (London 2007)

Temkin, S., 'Orthodoxy with moderation: a sketch of J.H. Hertz' *Judaism* (Summer 1975), 278–295

Tosh, J., *The pursuit of history* (London 1991), 278–295

Tulchinsky, G., 'Goldwin Smith, Victorian Canadian antisemite' in Davies (ed), *Antisemitism in Canada* (Waterloo, Ontario 1992)

Umansky, E., 'Lily Montagu: religious leader, organiser, prophet' *Conservative Judaism* 34:6 (1981), 17–27

Verete, M.,'The Balfour Declaration and its makers' *Middle Eastern Studies* 6:1 (January 1970), 48–67

Wasserzug, D., *Why I am orthodox* (London 1913)

Waxman, C.I., 'Dilemmas of modern Orthodoxy: sociological and philosophical' *Judaism* 42:1 (Winter 1993), 59–70

Waxman, J., 'Mi vaMi HaHolkhim' in Ginor (ed) *Yakar Le'Mordecai* (New York 1998) 283–326

Webber, J. (ed), *Jewish identities in the new Europe* (London 1994)

Wertheimer, J. (ed), *The uses of tradition* (New York 1992)

Wertheimer, J., *A people divided* (New York 1993)

Wertheimer, J., 'JTS and the conservative movement' in Wertheimer (ed) *Tradition renewed* (New York 1997), 403–442

Wertheimer, J., *Tradition renewed* (New York 1997)

Williams, B., *The making of Manchester Jewry* (Manchester 1976)

Williams B., 'East and west in Manchester Jewry' in Cesarani (ed), *The making of modern Anglo-Jewry* (Oxford 1990)

Zivotofsky, A.Z. and Amar, A., 'The halakhic tale of three American birds, turkey, prairie chicken and muscovy duck' *Journal of Halakha and Contemporary Society* 46 (Fall 2003), 81–104

Index

Abramsky, Yehezkel, 10, 214–218
Adath Yisroel (London) 86, 224
Adler, Hermann 6, 8, 30–32, 57,
    Chapters 5 and 6 *passim*
Adler, Nathan Marcus 27, 29–30, 73,
    80, 84, 121, 142
    Laws and regulations 28–29
Aesthetics of Jewish worship 88–89,
    116, 144, 183, 257
Aggadah 170
Agudat harabbanim (USA) 152–154
Alderman, Geoffrey 5–7, 71, 264
Altmann, Alexander 43, 242
Anti-Semitism 113
Army service 214, 220
Association for Furthering
    Traditional Judaism in Great
    Britain 141
Auerbach, Tsevi Benjamin 55
Austritt 47, 67, 207
Authorised daily prayer book
    121–122, 210

Balfour Declaration 224–225, 236
Bamberger, Seligman 101
Barth, Jacob 57
Bayswater Synagogue 115
Bible
    Authorship 62–64, 78–79, 99, 167,
    178
    See also Pentateuch
Brodie, Israel 7–11, 33, Chapter 9
    passim, 265, 269

Buchler, Adolf 33, 58, 129,
    211

Calendar reform 207
Chaikin, Moshe Avigdor 134–135,
    213
Chajes, Z.P. 6, 223
Choirs, synagogue 124–125, 219,
    252–253
Chosenness of Israel 92
Christianity 83, 90–91, 113, 182
Christian missionary activity 90, 110,
    155
Classical culture 89, 181–183
Cohen, Sussman 133–134
Colenso, J.W. 76
Communism 93
Conservative Judaism 15, 123
Contemporisation 92–93

Daiches, Samuel 130, 211
Dietary laws *see Kashrut*
Drachman, Bernard 59, 66

East End Scheme 139
East London Synagogue 124
Emancipation 21, 24, 30, 54, 90, 94
Endelman, Todd M. 5, 7–8, 244,
    247–248, 250, 264
Epstein, Isidore 129, 211–212,
    242
Etz Chayim, Yeshiva 212
Evolution 85–86, 179–180

Federation of Synagogues 31, 134, 138–139
Feldman, Asher 130, 134, 216
Finchley Synagogue 217
Frankel, Zachariah 12, 52, 54–56, 58
French Jewry 46, 87, 135, 143–145, 229
Freud Kandel, Miri J. 10–11, 190, 244–245, 251–252
Friedlander, Michael 17, 30, 119, 128

Gateshead Jewry 223
Gebetbuch der Israeliten 123
Geiger, Abraham 42–43, 54–55 123
German Jewry 145–152
Great Synagogue (London) 23–24
Grossgemeinde 47, 67
Grunfeld, Isidore 216, 253–254

Halakhah
  Authority 63, 80, 82–83, 99, 172–174, 201, 242, 252, 271
  Development 63, 99, 171–172, 174, 220, 266
  Philosophy of 80–81, 175, 242, 267
Halevy, Isaac 57
Hampstead Synagogue 31, 111, 114, 118, 124, 126
Hebrew prayer 111
Hertz, Joseph Herman 6–8, 10–11, 32–33, 59–60, Chapters 7 and 8 *passim*, 264–265, 269
  Book of Jewish thoughts 208–209
  Conservative Judaism 4, 12
  Hattarat horaah 38
  Pentateuch and Haftorahs 165, 209
  Progressive conservatism 12, 173, 246
Hevrot 139
Hildesheimer, Esriel 15, 52, 54, 57–58, 61–62, 67, 85, 87, 133, 145–151
Hildesheimer Seminary *see* Rabbinerseminar Berlin

Hillman, Samuel Isaac 140–141, 213
Hirsch, Samson Raphael 27, 46, 47, 52, 54–55, 58, 61–62, 87, 97, 133, 151–152
  See also Austritt; Torah im derekh erets
Hirschell, Solomon 24
Historical School, 12, 50, 56
Hochman, Joseph 128, 210–211
Hoffman, David Z. 27, 57, 63–64, 80, 85, 87
Hyamson, Moses 130, 134, 204

Immigrants, Jewish 111–112, 138–139
Immortality 98, 177

Jacobs, Louis 4, 7, 9–10, 33, 45, Chapter 9 *passim*, 265, 269, 271
  We have reason to believe 242
Jakobovits, Immanuel 3, 8, 13, 34, 257–258
Jakobovits, Julius 34, 216
Jewish Chronicle 246–247
Jewish religious labels 17, 40, 60
Jewish Religious Union 31, 88, 111, 142
  See also Liberal Jewish Synagogue, Liberal Judaism
Jewish Theological Seminary (New York) 12, 15, 59–60, 66, 123, 164–165, 200–201, 228
Jews' College 58, 77, 128–132, 211–212, 243, 254
Joel, Manuel 97, 123
Joseph, Morris 100, 102–103, 126–127, 224

Kaplan, Mordecai M. 44, 127, 227
Kashrut 135–136, 247
Kohut, Alexander 59–60
Kook, Abraham Isaac 61, 213–214

Labels, Jewish religious *see* Jewish religious labels
Lazarus, Harris M. 32, 254

Lerner, Mayer 86, 119, 140
Liberal Jewish Synagogue 31, 176, 222–223, 235
 See also Jewish Religious Union, Liberal Judaism
Liberal Judaism 77, 167, 186–188, 206, 254
 See also Jewish Religious Union, Liberal Jewish Synagogue
London Beth Din 8, 132–135, 138, 213–218, 245, 253

Maccoby, Hayim Zundel 106, 110, 140
Machzike Hadath 31, 136–138
Marks, David Wolf 25, 78
Masorti movement 271
Meirovich, Harvey 11, 12, 52, 60, 96, 264–265
Mendelssohn, Moses 43, 93, 273
Messiah 100, 176
Mission of Israel 93–94
Missionaries *see* Christian missionary activity
Modernity 22
 Jewish response to Chapter 3 *passim*, 268
Montagu, Samuel 31
Montefiore, Claude Goldsmid 51, 76–77, 89, 91, 100, 131
Morais, Sabato 59–60, 165
Mysticism 97, 175–176

Nationhood, Jewish 94
New London Synagogue 244
New West End Synagogue 114, 202, 242–244
Non-Jewish learning and culture 85–86, 179–182, 266
 See also Torah im derekh erets

Orach Chayim, Congregation (New York) 75, 203–204
Oral Law 55, 63, 67, 78–79, 129, 168–170, 266
 See also Talmud

Organ in the synagogue 111, 121–122
Orthodox Union (USA) 48, 152–154

Particularism, Jewish 93
Patriotism 90, 95, 98, 100, 112
Pentateuch
 Authorship 64, 75–77, 99, 127–129, 165–167, 252, 265, 269, 271
 See also Bible
Positive Historical Judaism *see* Historical School
Progressive conservatism *see* Hertz, Joseph Herman: progressive conservatism

Rabbinic ordination 130–131, 141
Rapoport, Solomon Judah 31, 57, 74, 84, 97
Rationalism 98
Reconstructionism 51
Reform Judaism 42, 51, 61, 62, 93
 Pittsburgh Platform 59
Refugees, Jewish 111
Reinowitz, Jacob 74, 119, 132
Religious labels *see* Jewish religious labels
Religious pluralism 185–186
Religious tolerance 183–184, 225
Resettlement community in London 23
Ritual reform, synagogue 114–121, 142, 218–219
Ritual slaughter *see* Shehita
Romanticism 54
Royal Commission on divorce and matrimonial causes 140–141

Sacrifices 97, 177, 219
Salaman, Redcliffe 247–248
Salanter, Israel 62
Schechter, Solomon 167
 Catholic Israel 174
Schonfeld, Victor 86, 180–181, 214
Sermon, the 109, 199, 204–205

Shearith Israel, Congregation (New York) 75
Shehitah 31, 136–138, 215–216, 247
Singer, Simeon 127, 131
Smith, Goldwin 91, 113
Sofer, Hatam *see* Moses Sofer
Sofer, Moses 23, 41–42, 50
Spiers, Bernard 72, 86, 132
Stern, J.F. 127
Swaythling, Samuel, Lord *see* Montagu, Samuel
'Swing to the Right' 45, Chapter 9 *passim*

Talmud
    Composition and development 62–63, 78
    See also Oral Law
Torah im derekh erets 46, 60, 99, 180–181, 203, 251, 257
    See also Non-Jewish learning and culture
Traditioning 122
Triennial Cycle 129, 218, 234

United Synagogue of America 46, 48, 226–227

United Synagogue (London) 13, 30, 245, 255
Universalism 91, 100

Vilna Gaon *see* Elijah, Gaon of Vilna

Waley-Cohen, Robert 208
Weinberg, Jehiel Jacob 17, 59, 63, 229
West London Synagogue of British Jews 25–26, 28, 76, 78, 111, 124, 127, 206
Western Synagogue 126, 218
Wissenschaft des Judentums 12, 46, 52–54, 61, 64, 72, 77, 84, 87, 99–100, 128–129, 170, 177–179, 251, 266, 268
Witwatersrand Old Hebrew Congregation 202
Wolfson, Isaac 255–256
Women's voting rights 220

Zangwill, Israel 79
Zionism 32, 90, 96, 100, 188–189, 207–208, 224
Zimmels, Hirsch J. 251
Zunz, Leopold 52–54